ISLAM AND CHRISTIANITY

MUTUAL PERCEPTIONS
SINCE THE MID-20TH CENTURY

edited by

Jacques WAARDENBURG

PEETERS
1998

PREFACE

The present book contains a selection of the contributions, both in English and French, which were read and discussed at an international Symposium which was held at Crêt Bérard, near Lausanne, from 18 to 21 April 1995. Its subject was "Changes in mutual perceptions of the three monotheistic religions since the mid-19th century". The Symposium was organized by the Interfaculty Department of History and Sciences of Religion at the University of Lausanne, under the auspices of the Swiss Society for Science of Religion*.

The papers published here concern mutual perceptions of Christianity and Islam. They describe on the one hand some important changes which have taken place in Roman Catholic, Protestant and Orthodox views and appreciations of Islam. On the other hand they discuss a variety of recent Muslim views and appreciations of Christianity. The book ends with two contributions of a highly symbolic character. The first was sent as a message to our meeting by a Muslim colleague caught in the siege of Serajevo who had been invited but was unable to come. The second was presented by an American participant who has been calling for interfaith dialogue throughout his lifetime.

Throughout our discussions the participants of the Symposium were well aware that there is a growing openness on the part of a number of adherents of Islam and Christianity to understand better each other's faith and religion. In view of the world-wide problems which impose themselves at the present time, we were also looking for more practical cooperation, for instance in the fields of education and of the media, ensuring a better information about each other's religion and ways of life.

Thanks are due to the Swiss National Science Foundation and the Swiss Academy for the Humanities and Social Sciences for having made the Symposium and the present publication possible. Waheed Hassab Alla assisted in making the Indexes of the book. Besides the short *Contents* on p. VII, a more detailed *Table des Matières* is to be found on p. 317.

Lausanne, 15 June 1997   Jacques WAARDENBURG

---

* A first Symposium of this kind, on Muslim perceptions of other religions, had been held at Crêt Bérard in December 1991; its contributions will be published in 1999. A third Symposium, on the situation of Muslim-Christian dialogue, is to take place at Crêt Bérard in December 1997; its contributions will also be published.

CONTENTS

INTRODUCTION

How people see and judge each other, in particular when they come from different cultures or even religions, is a fascinating question. It becomes even more fascinating when manifest changes in perception occur, as age-old models and paradigms of representing the other are replaced by direct interaction. These models and paradigms can then be shown to be largely the result of factual ignorance and prejudices that are untenable in the present state of affairs and hinder the discovery of other people.

The authors of the papers presented here were asked to examine where and to what extent significant new orientations can be discerned in the views that Muslims and Christians have of each other. We began with three hypotheses. First, the images which both groups of believers had of the other had remained rather static for centuries. Secondly, these images had started to change, here and there, during this century, for a number of reasons such as a better knowledge of each other's religion and more direct contacts on an equal footing. Thirdly, significant changes in image-formation have indeed occurred in the second half of this century, that is to say in the post-colonial period. If these three hypotheses are true, and supposing these changes turn out to be durable, one might in fact speak of the beginning of a new era in Muslim-Christian relations. It was clear to all of us that something important was at stake in this workshop and we assigned the following three tasks to ourselves.

First of all, we had to verify whether significant new orientations have indeed occurred in the vision which both communities have of each other, in what circles they have developed and why.

Second, we wanted to see if, and to what extent, reorientations in the view of the other religion have also entailed a certain reinterpretation or relativization of the viewer's own religion. And, the other way round, to what extent has a new view of one's own religion brought about a significant new view of the other religion.

Third, we wondered what part certain activities undertaken by adherents of the two religions together have played in bringing about such changes of perception. We were particularly interested in the effects of common action for the sake of justice, peace and other basic norms and values.

It is up to the reader to judge how far this program has been fulfilled.

Abdelmajid Charfi's paper on Islam and Christianity since the mid-20th century, with its realistic approach to the present situation in Muslim-Christian relations, is significant. Right from the start he denied that one could speak of *one* particular Muslim vision of Christianity; in fact there is a variety of Muslim views. He chose to concentrate on those problems with which both religions are confronted so as to compare their responses to them. He focussed particularly on the effects of the contextual changes of modernity and their impact on religious thought. Charfi here used what he called a social definition of a religion as offering to its adherents specific interpretations of reality. Each community in fact needs a stock of interpretations from which to choose in given circumstances. Any study of the mutual perceptions of Islam and Christianity should take into account the many factors involved in using particular interpretations at any given moment and the kinds of spokesmen formulating such interpretations. A major point of his exposé was that the theologies of the two religions still give too little attention to theological thought as developed in the other one, which they need to take account of and assimilate in some way.

A lively discussion followed the presentation of this paper and one of the central themes was that of secularization. The speaker distinguished between a factual secularization, which implies that in social and cultural life explicit references to religion are disappearing, and what may be called a "rhetorical" secularization. Here certain social and political facts or decisions which are not intended or motivated religiously in themselves subsequently receive a religious justification. Secularization has taken place both in Western and Muslim societies, though there are different degrees and structures of secularization and though the situation may vary on different social levels and in different domains of life.

In fact, one should speak on both sides of a crisis of man's religious consciousness. Whereas in former times religion was studied for its truth, which was something to be known, nowadays it is studied as an object to be interpreted. The believers, for their part, are afraid of this and want to defend their religion; this tendency is quite clear in contemporary fundamentalist currents. They may arrive, however, at what may be called sectarian positions with regard to the mainstream of their religions. In any case, religious thinking, both Muslim and Christian, is in crisis at the present time.

The first part of the book is devoted to changes which have occurred in Christian perceptions of Islam, in particular on the level of the churches.

Christian Troll reports in his paper on the changes which occurred in the official view of the Roman Catholic Church before, during and after the Second Vatican Council. One can speak of a breakthrough in the rather inflexible position of the Catholic Church, which goes back to the medieval period. The changes concern the view of Islam itself, the place assigned to Islam within the Catholic Church's overall vision of the other religions, and the positioning of Islam as a partner of the Church in a pluralistic world. For Roman Catholics the official teachings of the Church have absolute authority and should be followed, and this gives the new Catholic view of Islam a worldwide impact and also influences Orthodox and Protestant positions.

Besides the official Church doctrine, however, there are the views of individual Church members who have a wide variety of orientations with regard to Islam. Such views had earlier helped to modify the attitudes of individual Catholics to Muslims and Islam. During Vatican II these individuals contributed decisively to changing the official view of Islam, once the official attitude to Judaism had been altered, for obvious reasons. Troll's paper gives an idea of these voices insofar as they led to a more positive attitude than before; he leaves opposing views out of consideration. The practical effects of the changed Church view of Islam can be found in the *Guidelines for Dialogue with Muslims* published by the Secretariat for non-Christian Believers, renamed the Pontifical Council for Dialogue between Religions. The successive editions of the *Guidelines* also reflect the development of attitudes.

In the discussion on this richly documented paper it was pointed out that the generation of the breakthrough is nowadays sixty or over. The openness of its members has apparently given way to a certain movement of retreat after the investment of much energy in Christian-Muslim dialogues. Especially since the rise of Islamicist movements and the Gulf War of 1990-91, the openness to dialogue which one remembers from the sixties and seventies has decreased markedly. One question that was asked but could not be answered was to what extent the changes of attitude in favor of dialogue are in fact of a political nature and to what extent they should be seen as reflecting a new orientation of Church doctrine. Another question is how these changes in attitude have been perceived and judged by Muslims, insofar as they have been aware of them at all. This has probably depended on the experience they have had of Catholic Christians in daily life.

All of this hints at the gigantic task facing the Catholic Church, once it had taken a new official position towards Islam on the level of a

Church Council, to bring the contents of the relevant texts into practice on the level of ordinary life and Church people in general, and not only in the relatively peaceful West. Yet the Vatican declaration shows a positive dynamics in the Catholic faith at the time and a Church that is not there to rule but to serve. At present, however, these progressive Catholic voices in favor of Christian-Muslim dialogue can no longer be considered as representative of the Catholic view that has developed in practice in the eighties and nineties.

Speaking in his paper about changes in Protestant views of Islam, Jean-Claude Basset stresses the fact that Protestantism for a long time was rather isolated from Islam. Fundamentally it was an internal opposition movement within Christianity against the claims of the Roman Catholic Church of having definitive authority on the level of doctrine, practice and organization. It was only after some three centuries, through the start of the Protestant missions in the 19th century, that Protestants came in direct contact with Muslims. This led to better knowledge and gradually also to a more respectful approach.

It was through the World Council of Churches that the larger Protestant Churches arrived at a new and more unified attitude to Islam. In 1969 the World Council of Churches developed direct contact with Muslims and in 1971 its Sub-unit for Dialogue with People of Living Faiths and Ideologies was established. It lasted until 1992. Notwithstanding the great differences between the various Protestant traditions, they have all undergone considerable changes as compared with the period before the mid-20th century. The idea of Christian responsibility in the world, transcending political conflicts and in favor of the underprivileged, whether Christian or non-Christian, has had a powerful impact on a basic willingness to cooperate and engage in dialogue with Muslims. As in the Catholic Church, in Protestant Churches certain voices have been raised claiming that relations with Muslims, now that they are better known, could be more promising and enriching than the general opinion in Protestantism has been aware of. In the Anglo-Saxon world theological orientations advocating a revision of traditional Protestant thought on matters of the salvation of non-Christians have developed. On the whole, Protestantism has also revised its attitudes to Judaism and this has brought some people to think about Islam as well.

In the discussion which followed the presentation of this paper several burning questions were raised. Is there not an inherent tension between dialogue and mission, understood as a task imposed on Christians to bring others to the Christian faith? Is there not need for an intra-religious dialogue among Protestants who produce contradictory statements about Israel as a people and as a state in their dialogues with Jews and with Muslims? Whereas several Protestant Churches have made pronouncements on their attitude to Jews, similar pronouncements on the Christian attitude to Muslims have been lacking. An important point turned out to be the delimitation of Protestantism. Can the Anglican Church, which has sometimes taken a very open attitude to Islam, be considered as Protestant? And what about the Evangelicals, who do not always want to be considered as Protestants and are known to be rather uncompromising towards Islam — not to speak of the many more or less sectarian groups who carry on their missions to Muslims at any price and by any means? For many Protestants, Muslims represent a completely foreign world for which they cannot have much sympathy. Moreover, in many countries Protestants are minorities for whom Islam is not an immediately relevant issue. It is probably through the World Council of Churches, as formerly through the missions, that Protestant Churches have become aware of the planetary dimensions of Islam and the encounter of Christianity with Islam. The initiative to interreligious dialogue in the World Council of Churches came from Protestants, who have also played a responsible part in it. On the other hand, the Sub-unit for Dialogue would not have been established without the decisive voice of the Near Eastern Orthodox Churches.

During the discussion it became quite clear that Protestants share hardly anything in the attitudes they take to Islam. The sole authority they all accepted, the Bible, of course has no reference whatsoever to Islam. Both the missionary work of so many Protestant communities and the efforts for dialogue made by a number of Protestant Churches carry their own styles and often seem to be mutually exclusive. The idea of dialogue itself would seem to go against Protestant principles!

On a practical level, most Protestants would certainly like to meet Muslims as individuals and speak with them on a level of faith and personal commitment. But they react instinctively to the close links between religion and politics in Islam, what they see as the lack of free religious expression, which gives Muslims communities their more collective character and exposes them in Protestant eyes to manipulation. Other Protestants seem to recognize in Islam certain "Protestant" features, for instance in so-called "fundamentalism". On the level of faith, what set out to be a Christian-Muslim dialogue risks becoming a self-imposed monologue.

Of the many different Churches, the Orthodox ones, including here the Syrian, Coptic and Armenian Orthodox Churches, but leaving aside the Nestorians, have had the most immediate and longest experience of living with Muslims. This has been the case in the Middle East since the mid-7th century, in the Balkans since the 15th century, and since the mid-16th century under Russian rule in Russia. Whereas in the Balkans the Muslims constituted the minority, in the Middle East the Christians have for long been in the minority. In both regions, however, perhaps with the exception of the Maronites, Muslims and Christians have generally belonged to the same ethnic groups, mainly Slavic and Arab.

As Professor Argyriou points out in his paper, there are certain striking parallels between Orthodox Christianity and Islam in their responses to modernity and the West. Neither of them has participated actively in the construction of modernity with its rationality and individualism. In both cases there has been a remarkable tension between the desire to imitate the West's external achievements and the refusal to sacrifice what are felt to be fundamental values transmitted from the past. In both cases there has been a striking interiorization when people have gone back to the sources of their religion. In both cases too there are similar currents of national revival and movements of resistance against the West. In quite a few cases Orthodox Christians and Muslims have made common cause against enemies coming from the West, Catholics and Protestants, political imperialists and economic exploiters. However, they have also fought each other in bloody campaigns of conquest and wars of liberation. In any case there is a dense common history between Orthodox Christians and Muslims of various ethnic backgrounds.

Initiatives for a constructive dialogue between the two groups have been taken during the last decades in particular in Lebanon and by and around Bishop Georges Khodr. Recently dialogues have been organized between Greek Orthodox and Iranian Shī'īs and the Orthodox Center in Chambésy has organized meetings with delegations from the Royal Academy in Amman. At present, Islamic studies have started at some universities in Greece and the Orthodox University of Balamand in Lebanon has established a Center for the study of Christian-Muslim relations. Even the Russian Orthodox Church has shown some openness to contacts with Islam, notwithstanding a Russian tradition of a domination of Muslims and contempt of Islam which was religiously legitimated.

Future historians will look for explanations for these changes in Christian perceptions of Islam. They have occurred not only on the level of individuals familiar with both Islamic thought and Christian theology, often with some missionary experience, but also and particularly on the level of the major Churches. One significant aspect of these changes of perception was the preparedness of the Roman Catholic Church first, and the major Protestant Churches somewhat later, to enter into dialogue with Islam.

The international context of decolonization and the Cold War should not be forgotten. The Churches, in order to pursue their task in a world which had become different, had to learn to enter in dialogue with that world and its people. And shortly before, most Christian Churches had made a fundamental *volte face* in their attitude to the Jews. This made it possible at Vatican II to raise the question of the Church's attitude to Muslims and Islam; for once, even — or at least — in the highest quarters of a Church, established theological thought and judgments with regard to another religion could change. A rigid and rather closed theology could be affected by solid knowledge of another religion and by fruitful experiences of dialogue with its adherents.

Perhaps I may add a personal observation here. After World War II, there was a movement among Christians in Europe toward ecumenism, and in 1948 the World Council of Churches was established. Christians clearly desired to escape from established institutional and theological structures and to set out into rather unknown territory. The fixed boundaries between different kinds of Christians were somehow restrictions of freedom.

I have always tended to ascribe this intense desire for freedom to the wartime experience, but in fact there was more going on which may help to explain such profound changes in the perception of Islam.

During the fifties, the post-war generation revolted against the strictures of European societies in several West European countries and looked for what may be called a humanization of life. This took various ideological forms and later led to the student revolts of 1967 and 1968. At the same time interest in the newly independent countries was awakened and in some quarters there was an intense desire to communicate with people from them and know more about their cultures and ways of life which had been played down by the Euro-centrism of the colonial period. In both movements, directed at internal and external situations, Europe lost its absoluteness and self-centeredness. Instead, Europeans wanted to communicate and discover other people as they are.

A similar movement, self-critical and looking for communication, seems to have taken place in the leadership of the larger churches. If the

Christian truth remained absolute, its human expressions at least were relativized; if necessary, they could be subjected to self-criticism and, if need be, de-Europeanized. Probably only the best minds could see Christianity in such a global perspective, in which Europe no longer occupied the central place, but they were able to communicate their vision to the leaders of at least the larger churches. The new perception led to these churches accepting the formula of dialogue, whatever the ambiguities of the term. Just as the churches had accepted the work of the missionary societies, which had mostly worked privately, as their own responsibility, so they accepted the task of dialogue with other religions and did not leave it simply to private initiatives.

Consequently, on the one hand churches gave their adherents the possibility of meeting people of other faiths. On the other hand they could establish contacts with non-Christians, whom they would otherwise hardly have reached. In any case, the spiritual search into other religions and the interaction with believers in them remained under church guidance. The wave of enthusiasm for cultural encounter and spiritual emulation could be channeled through the churches' official program of dialogue. Dialogue as the venture of persons from different cultural and religious backgrounds freely discovering and communicating with each other, with a measure of discovery and free negociation, had to defend itself now from control by church or political institutions.

According to this view, it is the search for a breakthrough which offers a plausible explanation for the change in perception of Islam and other religions in Europe in the 1950s and 1960s. Such a breakthrough was sought for not only on a cultural but also on a social and ideological level. After the colonial period it also took the form of a quest for communication with the world outside Europe, culturally, intellectually, and socially. On the whole it put an end to the absolutization of Europe and the Eurocentric worldview, and created awareness of aspects of Islam which colonial or ecclesiastical eyes had not been able to see.

The second part of the book deals with the opposite problem, changes in Muslim perceptions of Christianity during the same period, the second half of the 20th century.

Hugh Goddard's paper gives a useful survey of what may be called striking changes towards greater openness and readiness to dialogue. There is a difference between those Muslim thinkers who were educated during the colonial period and those who were educated after it. Those authors treated who were born before 1914 had still been educated in the whole range of Islamic tradition and had received a Western education besides or after that. Some of them studied for some time in Europe, working under European scholars and making friends with Christians.

The authors who went to school after World War II mostly grew up in newly independent countries. They went through far more political turmoil than the previous generation. Even if they could study in Europe, they were as much conditioned by the circumstances of their own new country as the previous generation had been by colonial conditions.

Goddard traces the biographies of the Muslim authors he treats, paying special attention to their education and participation in Muslim-Christian encounters or their position on the broader question of relationships between the Muslim and the Western world. All of those he treats participated in Muslim-Christian dialogues.

In the discussion the question was raised of the representativity of the authors analyzed. With their Western education and their relatively positive views of the West and Christianity, they constitute a minority even of the large number of Muslims with some Western experience. Did they write their books for Western readers or for Muslims, or for both? Did Muslims in fact read their books? Were they really intermediaries or just persons who were profoundly influenced by the West and sympathized with Christianity? To what extent did they identify themselves consciously as religious Muslims, as those people did who took a definite stand while working in the West, such as Fazlur Rahman or Isma'il Raji al-Faruqi in the United States?

It was also questioned to what extent the authors treated were really interested in Christianity. None of them wrote a book on Christianity. They rather seem to have developed their own broader thinking in which Christianity had its place. In that case one could better speak in their case of a new, modern kind of Muslim thought which took Christianity, among other subjects, into account. It would be important to know how Christians read and appreciated these open-minded Muslims and if they responded to them.

In any case, the simple fact of the existence and activity of these liberal minded Muslims was recognized as significant. A century ago such people would have been difficult to imagine. And on a philosophical level their presence perhaps indicates a deeper shift in Muslim thinking about Christianity and religion in general. There may even be question of a fundamental epistemological change.

During the last twenty-five years in particular a number of Islamic movements have arisen which seek to go back to the sources of religion and insist on the need for social action to put Islamic norms and values into practice. These movements are usually given the misleading label "fundamentalists". They put forward more political perceptions of Christians and Christianity. They differ significantly, however, and so do their perceptions, judgments and actions, which are little known in Europe. In his paper Professor Ahmad Moussalli makes a sharp distinction between radical and moderate forms of fundamentalism.

Radical fundamentalists in the line of Sayyid Qutb see an essential conflict between true, that is to say Quranic, Islam and Christianity. Whereas the first follows Muhammad's teaching of monotheism, the latter has deviated from the — in their eyes equally monotheistic — teachings of Jesus, become permeated with pagan features and been institutionalized with an authoritarian hierarchical church structure. In this perspective, all conflicts between Muslims and Christians have been basically religious conflicts between those who are religiously right and wrong. Likewise, there is a fundamental conflict between Quranic Islam and Muslim regimes that offend justice and maintain ignorance (jâhilîya) about the basic tenets of Islam. This conflict is even worse, since it takes place within the Muslim community itself. Only Quranic Islam, of divine origin, knows what the true laws for society are; all other religious and secular societies have made their own laws. Sayyed Qutb ascribes a number of the West's, and in particular North America's specific problems to the fact that they have had to live with a form of Christianity which developed after Jesus. In its Enlightenment revolt against the Church and its authoritative teachings it has tended to make an idol of reason. In its unbridled lust for power it has tried to dominate Islam. In the face of all these corruptions around Christianity and these attacks on Islam a militant attitude is required, that of jihâd.

The moderate fundamentalists, in the line of Hasan al-Bannâ, have a different approach. They do not keep themselves aloof from society but involve themselves in it; they do not disdain politics but participate in it. If there is a conflict, it is not between Muslims on the one hand and other religions or ignorance on the other hand, but between believers, including Christians, on the one hand and materialism on the other. Moderate fundamentalists believe in a dialogue with other religions in terms of civilizations. Muslims and Christians in particular have common roots in the past and they also have their holy books. Western constitutional rule as such is not contrary to Islam. Muslims, for their part, should not try to dominate others.

Both types of fundamentalism seek to return to the roots of Islam, which they identify as the Quran. The result is a scriptural religion. They deny the relevance of history in favor of a direct understanding of Scripture, unlike traditionalists, for whom history and religious tradition have a certain sacred character. For the radical fundamentalists the Sharî'a *is* a given text, namely the Quran supplemented by the Sunna, to be obeyed. The moderate fundamentalists, by contrast, hold that the Sharî'a is a human interpretation and practical application of the text. All "fundamentalists" are agreed that there is no authority of interpretation in their reading of Scripture. All interpretations are equal in so far as they do not contradict the text, which enjoys absolute authority.

Many questions were raised in the following discussion, since the subject was rather new and highly informative. As Professor Moussalli indicated, his proposed typology should be refined and enriched with examples from a variety of "fundamentalist" authors.

On looking back one may regret that there was not a separate paper on Protestant fundamentalist perceptions of Islam, laying the same stress on Scripture as the sole source of religious truth. Here, too, a distinction between radical and moderate fundamentalists can be made. Would the moderates on both sides be able to speak to each other and develop similar solutions to common ethical or other problems? These would be different both from radical fundamentalists' and from traditionalists' solutions.

For liberals and secularists, in both the Western and the Muslim world, the whole fundamentalists' approach appears as regressive and anti-modern and they oppose it. As a result, they see the fundamentalists as an enemy and depict them as a more or less homogeneous group. One of the many virtues of this paper is that it pays attention to important differences among fundamentalists and develops a typology of them. It makes clear that Muslim fundamentalists can perceive Christianity and Christians in different ways.

The next paper concentrates on the views expounded by two Muslim authors about the position of Christians in a Muslim society. The first is the Lebanese Muhammad Husayn Fadlallâh, a prominent leader of the Shî'î Hizbollah who has been directly involved in Lebanese politics and the civil war. The second is Fahmî Huwaydî in Egypt, a Sunnî journalist attached to the influential newspaper al-Ahrâm. Whereas in Lebanon the number of Christians is estimated to be slightly less than that of the Muslims and the state is composed of numerous religious communities with a large degree of autonomy, in Egypt the number of Copts is considerably less than that of the Muslims and the country is ruled by a strongly centralized government. Such facts of course influence the views which the two authors develop in their respective countries, views which can be read just as much politically as religiously.

It should be noticed that the Christian communities in both countries — as in Palestine, Syria, Jordan and Iraq — have been living there since ancient times, preceding the Arab conquest in the seventh century A.D. The Christians speak Arabic and consider themselves, like the Muslims, mostly as Arabs. North Africa and the Arabian Peninsula have no such ancient Christian communities.

It is important to notice that both authors make a sharp distinction between Arab and European Christians, linking the latter to the West which they judge rather negatively. A number of the features of European Christians which they hold to be "Christian" are in fact "Western".

Muslim discussions about the place of Christians in a Muslim society are linked to discussions about the relationship between Islam and the state, where many different positions exist. In classical Islamic doctrine, the position of Christian as well as Jewish minorities in an "Islamic" state based on the Sharî'a, is that of *dhimmîs*, "protected people" who, professing another though recognized religion, are not equal with Muslims. In modern 20th century thought as prevails in the West and among jurists in a number of Muslim countries, all the citizens of a country should enjoy equal status and no difference should be made between them because of their religious adherence, although certain religious institutions may have more political influence than others. Most Muslims who write about the subject take a position in between these two. The debate about the introduction of *dhimmî* status for Christians in "Islamic" states is connected with the authors' views about the application of the Sharî'a in them and their wishes as to the nature of the ideal Islamic state. Saudi Arabia and Iran, Pakistan and Sudan, Morocco and Mauretania, for instance, provide very different models.

Waheed Hasab Alla's paper compares the ideas of Fadlallâh and Huwaydî and their legal argumentation. Besides continuously referring to the Quran and Sunna, these authors draw on medieval jurists who wrote on the subject and on some contemporary Muslim thinkers. They pay little attention to empirical data or to theories about minorities developed by non-Muslim thinkers in the West or elsewhere. The Islamic legal way of dealing with the problem of Christian minorities is little known in the West and is very different from the way in which

Europeans discuss, for instance, the position of Muslim minorities in their countries. In the first case we have to do with a legal starting-point which is substantive and religious, in the second case with one which is formal and neutral. The first one has difficulty in accepting the situation of religious pluralism and the concomitant equality of all religious communities; the second one can accept religious law only as the internal rules of a community, and cannot give it sanction by the state.

Several points were raised in the discussion. First of all, it was suggested that in order for such texts to be properly understood, they should be presented in their context. Fadlallâh was writing in Lebanon at the time of the civil war and foreign interventions, while Huwaydî developed his ideas in Egypt, in the post-Sadat period when the tide of Islamic opposition movements was rising. Also, both authors made their proposals within a wider discussion about Islam and society.

Second, it is clear that neither author is an academic scholar. They have insufficient knowledge either of the history of Islamic thought or of that of Christianity to do justice to the intricate problems involved. It is questionable whether they would be able to conduct a dialogue at all; they rather express "neo-dogmatic" positions and in fact constitute a danger for any true dialogue. On the other hand, these two authors represent obvious tendencies in present-day Arab society and thought. They are interesting precisely because their opinions differ from the official political or academic discourse. Thus, authors like these are most relevant if one wants to understand current Muslim perceptions of Christian minorities and their place in society. It may be doubted, however, whether such Muslim thinkers want to perceive the minorities as they present themselves: rather, they pursue a discourse *about* them from which the minorities themselves are excluded.

Third, the need for a critical analysis of contemporary Muslim Arab writing on the subject of non-Muslim minorities was recognized. Merely describing the positions of the authors and their ideas as they present them is not sufficient. A critical approach should be adopted, bringing out internal contradictions where they exist, taking into account the data which the authors do not mention for whatever reason, and paying attention to those points which are particularly stressed.

The discussion ended with a methodological question. If one wants to form an idea of changing Muslim perceptions of Christianity from texts, what should be the criteria for choosing those texts? Should one concentrate on their intellectual solidity? On their social influence? On their relative newness? Or should one look for the extent to which they create a discourse on dialogue and start playing a vital part in the dialogical process itself? The issue — how indigenous Christians are seen in Muslim societies — is highly relevant. New ideas and practices in this area, recognizing Christians as citizens equal with Muslims in theory and practice, law and social life, would imply a real change of perception.

As a comment on this discussion, it goes without saying that one perceives others with whom one lives together as neighbors in a different way from foreigners, who live elsewhere and appear as traders, men of culture, technicians or tourists. The distinction becomes more complex, however, when these foreigners exercise power of any kind in or over Muslim communities. Especially when the dominating foreigners share the religion of a minority in a Muslim society, there are risks on all sides. Especially if the minorities themselves are viewed as potential enemies because they are linked to dangers coming from outside, the perception of them, even when they are protected, deteriorates sharply or may even become a "non-perception" altogether through different forms of psychological blindness. The same holds true, of course, for Muslim minorities in Europe and the way in which they are perceived by Europeans.

Since Adnan Silajdžič had not been able to attend, we accepted his paper without further discussion.

The final chapter in this volume is Leonard Swidler's ardent plea for recognition of the signs of the time, that is to say the rise of a global consciousness and the need to arrive at a corresponding global dialogue. In his view, after centuries of monological discourses we are coming now to relations of dialogue, forced as we are to relativize our absolutist positions of the past and to discover our own assumptions and presuppositions. We shall be able to perceive reality better by using perspectives other than our own on it. For Swidler, knowingly to refuse dialogue in Muslim-Christian relations is becoming a sin; if the necessity of dialogue is denied, self-destruction will inevitably be the result. But there is good reason for hope. Consciousness itself is changing in the direction of dialogue beyond the frontiers of civilizations; this will make us discover more and more the common human basis of our experiences.

This position evidently evoked various responses in the discussion. Besides the rise of a global consciousness may there not be processes of disintegration of consciousness at work and even destructive forces of various kinds, of which we should be aware? Have there not always been dialogues between Muslims and Christians, since the very beginning of Islam; so what is new to them nowadays? The speaker's answer was that nowadays we are consciously willing to learn from each other and each other's truth, instead of teaching each other our own truth as was the case in former times. In support of his contention, Swidler submitted that on many levels (media, telecommunication, information, science, etc.) there *is* already question of a global consciousness and increasing interdependence. The process is now starting to happen on a religious level too; this is particularly visible in the United States, where it is facilitated by established pluralism. Intellectuals too have to go ahead with this global consciousness.

In a next round, questions were pushed further. What about a deeper concern about truth or search for truth, leading to a religious commitment or even conversion? In interreligious dialogue, what is one discussing about; does one believe one possesses the truth or only an interpretation of the truth? Is the ultimate aim to reach agreement with each other and to arrive at a global consensus through dialogue? But is not dialogue a means rather than an end in itself? Why should global dialogue, after all, be linked with religious feelings and beliefs?

Finally, the observation was made that what seems at first sight to be an exchange and dialogue between different civilizations is in fact a one-way traffic from the West and in particular the United States. One participant remarked that behind the search for a global consciousness a certain power game is at work and that one should be aware of the political dimension of bringing about a global consciousness. It is not only the political power of particular nations but also the economic power of international corporations and the psychological power of news agencies which want to work globally and eliminate resistance. Swidler answered that we should set those forces on a different course from their own blind self-fulfillment and self-absolutization. But are there not radical differences in the world, such as the opposition between the few rich and the many poor, which are not brought into the open in this paper? Is it not too easily assumed that the rules of a global dialogue can be set in North America? Certain conflicts such as Nazism cannot be solved by dialogue but only by opposition. The author agrees that dialogue may not be a panacea for everything but it opens new ways to the future and it should be used as a means to overcome tensions and to avoid conflicts. For Swidler, in Muslim-Christian relations dialogue is mandatory. The two dialogue partners are all over the world and much of the future of humankind will depend on their dialogue.

It should be recognized, however, that there have been at various places other changes of mutual perceptions of Islam and Christianity as well, in the sense of a denigration of the other religion or its practice. But these negative perceptions seem to have been largely due to circumstances which have made normal communication impossible. In this way, in the Lebanese civil war and in the war in Bosnia, for instance, certain Christians could consider their Muslim opponents with contempt and hatred, turning on them a lust for destruction. The other way round, in the wake of independence Muslims could see Christianity and Christian missionaries from a political point of view only, ascribing to them sordid plots and devices which even agents of intelligence bureaux would have had difficulty in concocting. All of this must be interpreted as signs of despair and the reasons should be looked for, first and foremost, in the situations in which people became entangled.

A particularly striking example of the degradation in perceptions of the other's religion in periods of political tension and war is that of mutual Jewish-Muslim perceptions since the rise of Zionism and the establishment of the state of Israel. Whereas Islam has always respected Moses as a prophet, the Torah as a revelation and Judaism as a heavenly religion, the political view has now taken the upper hand. A close analysis of Arab Muslim publications on Judaism* shows that this religion has been perceived during the last decades as a tool of political schemes ascribed to Zionism. This runs parallel to perceptions of Christianity as a tool of political schemes ascribed to imperialism. The other way round, Israeli scholars when dealing with Islam in the contemporary Middle East have been interested foremost in its political aspects. Muslims seem to be seen by Jews hardly as people with a religion that is very similar to Judaism. On each side, perceiving the "religious" aspects of the other party's religion has been made nearly impossible through increasingly tense relationships.

Our workshop was an academic enterprise, and at the end, the student participants in particular put the relevant question, how to translate our discussions into adequate action. This is of course a problem for any workshop of intellectuals, but it is particularly true in the case of the mutual perceptions of religious communities. Without pushing our discussions into the domain of politics, time and time again, on both the Christian and the Muslim side we came across powerful worldly forces which, nowadays as in the past, seem to condition the ways in which religious communities perceive, think and act. Even if the people concerned base themselves on their religion as their supreme value in their

* M.Y.S. Haddad, *Arab Perspectives of Judaism. A study of image formation in the writings of Muslim Arab authors 1948-1978*. Doctoral dissertation, University of Utrecht, 1984, 564 p.

thought and action, the way in which they do so seems to be guided by interests of various natures. Repeatedly we asked ourselves what political and economic interests and forces have been at work in the background during the current changes of perception. This is a legitimate question not only for political scientists but also for students of religion.

The limitations of the workshop are evident. Obviously the materials studied have been selected: official and unofficial statements of churches and church members, writings of certain chosen authors who crossed the deserts and seas between Muslim and Western countries, writings of a politician and a journalist. The area of study was practically confined to the Middle East and then only the Arab part, leaving out other important regions and peoples.

The relations between Muslims and Christians are a new field of research; the nature of these relations in given contexts is difficult to grasp. Political scientists tend to stress the conflicts and speak of clashes between civilizations, whereas students of religion tend to look at common norms and mutual influences and speak of interaction between religious communities.

If we are realistic, as researchers should be, we cannot be over-optimistic about the practical influence of the positive changes which have occurred in mutual perceptions between some Muslims and some Christians on the overall relationships between Muslims and Christians in the world. What strikes the attentive observer is the limited freedom in which these relationships develop, if they have the chance to develop at all. In wide areas "dialogue" is still limited or hardly possible, for reasons beyond the people concerned.

Yet, on both sides positive reorientations are taking place. They may yet be decisive, fuelling the will to see each other better than was possible under the shadow of ancient stereotypes. Islam and Christianity as religions may be different but Muslims and Christians do not need to see each other necessarily as antagonists. As a matter of fact, they are not.

Jacques WAARDENBURG

CHANGING CATHOLIC VIEWS OF ISLAM

Christian W. TROLL s.j.

1. Introduction

1.1. Scope and clarifications

This inquiry into changing Catholic views of Islam — not of Catholic-Muslim dialogue — will begin by examining the views of the *magisterium*, the teaching office of the Catholic Church, as it articulates itself in the official teaching of the Bishop of Rome and the Pontifical Council for Interreligious Dialogue. It also will take into account magisterial statements of some regions of the Church such as the relevant letters of the Catholic Patriarchs of the Orient and of the Regional Bishops' Conference of the Maghreb.

The second part will present the views of Islam of a small number of Catholic scholars who have been selected here because they have expressed their views of Islam **as** Catholics and have made a palpable impact on ongoing Catholic thinking in this area. Naturally, with the growth of Christian ecumenical awareness it has become difficult, if not at times impossible, to draw clear demarcation lines between Catholic and non-Catholic Christian thought. The selection of a small number out of the many individuals whose views of Islam could justifiedly be presented here, to some extent is arbitrary.

We shall ask how in statements of these bodies and individuals Islam is viewed and portrayed, and which aspects are emphasized, omitted or hardly mentioned. We shall inquire, further, what 'place' Islam is given within a given Catholic spiritual and theological vision of things, how the chief elements of the teaching of Islam are evaluated, for instance: monotheism, prophethood and revelation, Muhammad and the Qur'an, theological anthropology, law and ethics. Finally, we are interested to know how Islam is perceived as a 'fellow' religion in the increasingly plural, as well as unified, contemporary world and in which ways the 'conversation' with Muslims and with Islam may have modified the Catholic's perception of her own faith.

By Islam here we mean the community of Muslim believers (*umma*) in its widest sense, as the totality of all those persons who profess the *shahâda* and refer to the Qur'an as the final expression of God's will. We take Islam here also to signify the body of divine injunctions and teachings normatively proposed in the past and present by the community of Muslim believers, in the infinitely varied, concrete social forms which constitute that community.

1.2. Three views of Islam and Catholic-Muslim relations typical of the period immediately before the Second Vatican Council

My decision to begin with special studies of Islam goes back to the year 1959. I was working then on a Master's thesis in the field of historical theology on the topic: 'The China Missions of the Middle Ages'[1]. In the Missiological Library of the Jesuit Residence in Bonn I came across the essay: 'The Need for Islamic Studies', by the Dutch Jesuit J.J. Houben, then professor of Islamology at Nijmegen and Beirut. (Houben. 1953)

Houben describes the Muslim World as passing through the most momentous crisis in its history. Aware of the fact that it is the political side of the crisis that has been catching the attention of the educated public, Houben is anxious to underline that this crisis in fact 'is deeply religious…, is the necessary result of the nature of Islam itself.' (ibid., p. 180) Given the theocratic nature of Islam, the crisis concerns the traditional system of religio-political Islamic thought. For Houben, theocracy, religious and political despotism and 'the unity of state and church' are mutually linked hallmarks of Islam as it has developed since the earliest centuries of its history.

Hence, if Muslim society is ever to become democratic, the traditional theological doctrine of Islam will have to be broken or at least modified. Houben considers it the task of Catholic intellectuals in contact with Islam to inject 'Christian ideals' into the kind of 'renascent Islam' that some Muslims recently have been struggling to bring about in their effort to break the hold which the traditional, 'orthodox' theological schools have on Islam.

> Not only all the missionaries working in Muslim countries but every Catholic throughout the world must realize that the fate of hundreds of millions of Muslims hangs in the balance and that in order to help them to solve the difficulties along religious lines, a deeper knowledge of their mentality and of Islam in general as a religion and as a polity is certainly one of the most pressing needs for the Catholics of our times. (ibid., p. 191)

---

[1] 'Die Chinamission im Mittelalter', *Franziskanische Studien* 48 (1966), p.111-150; 49 (1967), p.22-79.

Not much later I became interested in the thought of the Benedictine scholar of missions, Thomas Ohm. In 1961 he published the booklet: *Mohammedaner und Katholiken* (Ohm. 1961) with the aim of countering the widespread 'sense of hopelessness' among Catholics regarding the mission to Islam. This 'hopelessness' arises above all from the almost total failure in converting Muslims to the Christian faith. The booklet aimed at generating new thought among Catholics and forming new attitudes to Muslims.

Ohm does not hesitate to state that 'from the seventh until the twentieth century most Catholics have seen in Islam the enemy and the adversary, even the mortal enemy and the most dangerous adversary, and have been thinking of battles and "crusades" against the Muslims.'(ibid., p. 24) 'Even now' [i.e. around 1960], Ohm remarks, 'many [Catholics] consider Christianity and Islam religions that exclude one another as light and darkness, good and evil.' (ibid., p. 28)

In contrast, Ohm continues, from the beginning of the twentieth century onwards there have been a number of eminent personalities, groups and initiatives that have striven — against the mainstream of Catholic outlook and practice — for a new approach to Islam.

In the final part, Ohm makes a threefold summary statement in response to the questions: 'How are Catholics to think about Muslims and their religion, what position and attitude are they to adopt?'

(1) **'The** way to God is Jesus Christ. "I am **the** way, **the** truth and **the** life" (John 14:6). **The** religion, the absolute, the exclusively true religion is the religion of our Lord Jesus Christ...Islam is not **the** and not even **one** religion that is offered by **God**, taught, created, revealed and ordered by Him.' (ibid., pp. 61-62) [the emphases are Ohm's]

(2) Hence 'Christians **are bound in duty** to the Muslims and are sent to them... God does not want "crusades" against Islam but he commands the proclamation [to Muslims] of the Good News. Christ has given a universal command to mission. All non-disciples are to be made disciples and followers of Jesus. The Muslims too must not remain without the integral Good News of Christ, "the unfathomable treasure of Christ" (Eph. 3:8).' (ibid., p. 62)

(3) But with all this, Ohm does not believe 'that the Muslims are excluded from salvation and will be condemned'. He rejects the idea that 'the sum total of doctrines, rules for life, laws, forms of worship, ordinances and customs' found in Islam, 'would be in every respect erroneous and evil.' (ibid., p. 64)

Ohm's theological embarrassment and helplessness becomes evident when, towards the end of his essay, he states that Catholics cannot accept Islam's claim 'to be **the** or even **a** true religion' and yet, at the same time, he qualifies Islam as '**genuine religion** and not only substitute religion or religion in disguise' ['wenn auch nicht **die** oder eine wahre Religion, so doch **echte Religion**, nicht bloss Ersatzreligion oder verkappte Religion']. (ibid,. p. 69)

Ohm recognizes the continuing serious challenge of Islam to Christian faith and theological reflection: 'Christians cannot struggle enough to arrive at a knowledge of the meaning Islam has for them on the part of God, in the history of salvation. They cannot ask themselves too often what task has been assigned to Islam with regard to the Christians.' (ibid., p. 68)

His own answer reads: 'Islam is a call to the Christians to do penance for the evil that they have done to Muslims, it is a spur for Christian self-examination. Islam will not leave the Christians in peace until they bring out in their lives visibly and effectively the essence of Christian faith (*das wesentlich Christliche*), a call to worship God in spirit and truth.' (ibid.) Hence, 'the spirit that the Christians need in their mission to Islam is not the spirit of enmity and antipathy but rather the spirit of friendship, brotherhood, sympathy, understanding — the Holy Spirit of agape.' (ibid., p. 85)

It is instructive to read Ohm's booklet in conjunction with the essay: 'Chrétiens en face de l'Islam', published in 1956 in the influential French monthly *Études*. The essay — apparently unknown to Ohm — was written by the French Jesuit missionary André d'Alverny who, as the long-standing Director of the Centre Religieux d'Études Arabes (CREA) at Bikfaya in Lebanon and, as professor of Arabic literature at the 'Institut Oriental de l'Université St. Joseph', trained hundreds of missionaries and scholars concerned with the world of Islam.

In the central part of his essay, D'Alverny addresses the specifically theological question: what place should the Muslim religion occupy within the Catholic vision of faith. D'Alverny states his premise without ambiguity or compromise:

> 'There can be no doubt for us Christians that there exists only one divine religion, as there is only one God and one sole truth: that is the religion prepared by Judaism, revealed by Christ, transmitted by the Catholic Church. It is impossible for us to admit that the other religions should be different participations in one and the same divine religion. We could accept that they are "natural" religions, fruits of man, objectivations of his innate tendency to recognize a superior force, given the fact that man, even before being a rational and laughing animal, is a religious one.' (D'Alverny. 1956, p. 167)

D'Alverny qualifies Islam as '*essai de religion naturelle*', denying its explicitly divine character. For D'Alverny, Islam 'presents itself' as a revelation, it 'pretends' to be a search for God and His reign and 'to satisfy the truly religious needs of the human person', but it is in fact only a human discovery, a human institution, as are the religion of the Greeks or Hinduism. (ibid., p. 167)

On the other hand, it is undeniable that by its 'rigid monotheism' Islam — which is neither a Jewish sect nor Christian heresy, as sometimes has been maintained, because it never professed, and therefore never deserted, either of these religions — 'met the Jewish and Christian doctrines and that, by osmosis, a certain number of truths, proper to these two religions have been able to penetrate into what Islam presented as revealed: future life, creation, angels... Equally, a number of "sacred stories" in quite disfigured shape have been able to enrich its preaching.' (ibid., p. 168)

And yet, with all this, Islam, for D'Alverny, is 'a purely human effort — which one may find admirable — towards monotheism in a Semitic climate, but nothing more.' (ibid., p. 169) Islam's denial of Incarnation, Redemption and Trinity, constitutes a limit imposed by reason to God's mystery. The unity of God as defined and proclaimed by Islam implies the refusal to accept what God reveals of Himself. Hence: 'The God of Islam is not the God of the Christian revelation.'(ibid., p. 170)

> 'Perhaps Islam has been a personal grace for Muhammad, an attraction towards the world of authentic revelation, via the so great figure of Abraham. But we have to affirm also that Islam constitutes a refusal, the refusal to profoundly submit to the mystery of Christ and of the Cross, not in explicit terms, certainly, but in fact. That being the case, Islam cannot be more for us than human institution.' (ibid.)

D'Alverny is aware of the Christians' 'unworthiness of professing this superiority of the religion [Christianity] to which God has called us'. (ibid.) Whilst our judgement about the religious doctrine of Islam must remain firm, the Christians must be 'witnesses of the God of Love to the Muslims'. (ibid., p. 173) They should collaborate with the Muslims, especially in serving the disadvantaged. Finally, inspired by the life of Charles de Foucauld (1858-1916), they are called to substitute themselves, in the love of Jesus, the Redeemer, for their Muslim brothers in what lacks in the latters' unfinished offering. (cf. ibid., 175)

2. The Second Vatican Council's view of Islam and Christian-Muslim Relations

2.1. The relevant texts analyzed

The views of Islam expressed by the three authors presented in the introduction are typical of mainstream Catholic thought during the

decade immediately preceding the Second Vatican Council (Oct.1962 —
Dec. 1965). When, during the second session of that Council, the project
of a text about Judaism was presented, the Catholic Oriental patriarchs
and bishops living in Muslim countries asked for 'balance', in other
words, that justice should be done not only to the reality of Judaism but
also to Islam. This demand issued in two relatively short but important
and decisive texts. Although they are primarily concerned with the
Catholics' practical attitude towards Muslims, they imply elements of a
fresh Catholic theological view of Islam. Number 16 of the 'Dogmatic
constitution on the Church' *Lumen Gentium* declares:

> 'But the plan of salvation also embraces those who acknowledge the Cre-
> ator, and among these the Muslims are first; they profess to hold the faith
> of Abraham and along with us they worship the one merciful God who will
> judge humanity on the last day.' (Tanner. 1990, vol 2, p. 861)

The study of the proceedings of the Council makes it clear that it did
not want to state an objective link between Islam, Ishmael and the biblical revelation. The reference to Abraham is put on the subjective level:
'they profess...'. Islam is situated first among the non-Biblical,
monotheistic religions and it is audaciously affirmed that the Muslims
adore the same God as the Christians.

The second text of the Council is longer and more substantial. It constitutes paragraph three of the 'Declaration of the Church's relation to
the non-Christian religions' *Nostra Aetate* in which were put together
the schemata about Judaism, Islam and the other religions. After stating
in paragraph two the principles of the Christian vision of the religions in
general: to accept all that they contain of the true and good as coming
from God, without however falling into syncretism, the Council states:

> 'The Church also looks upon Muslims with respect. They worship the one
> God living and subsistent, merciful and almighty, creator of heaven and
> earth, who has spoken to humanity and to whose decrees, even the hidden
> ones, they seek to submit themselves whole-heartedly, just as Abraham, to
> whom the Islamic faith readily relates itself, submitted to God. They ven-
> erate Jesus as a prophet, even though they do not acknowledge him as God,
> and they honour his virgin mother Mary and even sometimes devoutly call
> upon her. Furthermore they await the day of judgement when God will
> requite all people brought back to life. Hence they have regard for the
> moral life and worship God especially in prayer, almsgiving and fasting.

> Although considerable dissensions and enmities between Christians and
> Muslims may have arisen in the course of the centuries, this synod urges all
> parties that, forgetting past things, they train themselves towards sincere
> mutual understanding and together maintain and promote social justice and
> moral values as well as peace and freedom for all people.'(Tanner. 1990,
> vol. 2, pp. 969-970)

Two characteristics of this text are immediately evident: first, it high-lights the common or related points between Islam and Christianity, not-ing at the same time the essential difference: the Christian profession of the divinity of Jesus. Second, it opens up the possibility of a collabora-tion between the two religions, at the service of the most pressing needs of contemporary humanity. (Cf. Caspar. 1987, pp. 83-87 whom I follow here closely.)

The opening sentence of the paragraph, apparently a trite formula, in fact constitutes a unique statement and an absolutely new beginning insofar as it is an official declaration about Islam issued by the highest teaching authority of the Church. The faith in God as One and His ado-ration are the centre and heart of Islam. This is also the first article of the Christian faith: 'Credo in unum Deum' even if, for Christians, the divine Oneness opens itself to the trinity of the persons. Muslims and Chris-tians adore together the one God, but they do not always give him the same 'names', nor do they give the same meaning to apparently similar 'names'. Therefore the Council mentions explicitly some of these 'names', those specially important to Islam (mentioned repeatedly in the Qur'an) and common to both religions. An annotation to the text of the Council refers to the letter of Pope Gregory VII to Al-Nasir, the eleventh-century amir of Mauretania, where the Pope greets the amir as his 'brother in Abraham' and as a believer in God, One and Creator[2].

Although the Council refused to add 'through the prophets' to the phrase 'who has spoken to humanity', because of the ambiguity of the reference to the prophets (who are not always the same, do not always have the same 'face' nor play the same role, in Islam and Christianity), this phrase is of the greatest importance as to Christian qualification of the Muslim faith: the Muslim faith does not relate to a God invented by human reason. Mus-lim faith relates to the transcendent God who has made himself known by his Word entrusted to humanity, to the prophets — even if this is not the same Word nor are they the same prophets as for the Christian faith.

The Muslim faith is essentially *islâm*, active submission to the Will of God, to 'whose decrees, even the hidden ones, they seek to submit them-selves whole-heartedly'. Thus is noted the 'mysterious' aspect which this faith comprises: reasonable without being rational, in line with the Qur'an which demands of the believer the acceptance of the will of God, even if it appears paradoxical to the eyes of reason. It is as type and model of this faith of submission that Abraham finds his true role in the Muslim faith.

---

[2] The letter was written in AD 1076. See C. Courtois, "Grégoire VII et l'Afrique du Nord", in *Revue Historique*, T. CXCV (1945), p.97-122; 193-226.

Jesus and Mary are among the most venerated persons in the Qur'an. The text indicates the refusal to see in Jesus more than a great prophet. This will be taken positively by Muslims who glory in this refusal which is born from the desire to respect the transcendence of God. Mary is also respected as the virgin mother of Jesus according to Islam, which has never hesitated on this point.

Muslim eschatology is briefly indicated. The resurrection of the body and the judgement which follows it are one of the essential points of the Muslim and the Christian faith. The modalities and the criteria of this judgement can differ from one theology to the other. It remains that, according to the Qur'an as well as according to the Gospel, everyone will be judged by their actions (*remunerabit*) and that, for the Christian as well as for the Muslim, 'the world which comes from God, returns to God', to find there its fulfilment.

'They have regard for the moral life' is the phrase that remained, after the Council had discussed a proposed, fuller text: 'for the moral life, individual as well as familial and social'. The Council refused to refer explicitly to family and social morality because of the Qur'an's passages on polygamy and repudiation and because of mainstream Islam's teaching on the essential link between the spiritual and the temporal and between religion and state.

The Muslim cult is described by its three foremost manifestations: ritual prayer, the alms-tax and fasting. Of the profession of faith only its first part, the faith in the One God, was mentioned at the beginning of the text. The pilgrimage could have been mentioned but it is far from being practised by all Muslims, and the Council did not intend in any way to present a complete exposition of Islam.

> 'The second part of the text concerns the present and future perspectives of understanding and collaboration between Christians and Muslims. The past of hatreds and wars must be "forgotten", i.e., not ignored but overcome. Mutual understanding — objective and respectful — will require much effort and progress on both sides. But the "dialogue" itself must be surpassed in order to arrive at collaboration between believers towards one objective: to confront together the challenges of modern thought and civilization, not only in order to save faith in God, especially among the young, but in order to make a sincere and committed faith contribute to saving our civilization from the dangers accruing to it from neo-paganism and in order to construct [together] a better world.' (Caspar. 1987, p. 87)

There can be no doubt that the Council's statements regarding Islam, in the light of history represent a radical novelty. However, soon after the closure of the Council, the Dominican scholar of Islam and Christian-Muslim

Relations, Georges Anawati (1905-1994), in a critical analysis of these statements pointed out their remarkable silence regarding the figure of Abraham and Islam's [possible historical as well as] spiritual link with him through Ishmael and, above all, concerning Muhammad, and hence the prophetic character of Islam. In his 'Exkurs zum Konzilstext über die Muslim' in the semi-official edition of the German version of the texts of the Council in 1967, Anawati stated: 'One can say that the Declaration summarizes with a minimum of words Muslim *theodicy* but not what is essential to the Muslim *faith* of which the belief in the mission of Muhammad is one of the most important elements'. (Anawati. 1967, p. 486)

The silence of the Council concerning the second part of the Muslim profession of faith (*shahâda*) doubtless represents the most sensitive point for the Muslims. The Council chose to deal with it by — silence. However, Anawati added the confident, prophetic note: 'Once dialogue has gained momentum, one will be obliged to deal with this capital element in detail.'(ibid. p. 487)

2.2. Louis Massignon and the Second Vatican Council

During the decades preceding the Council no scholar had so intensely and persistently tried to transform Catholic views of Islam as Professor Louis Massignon (1883-1962). Having discovered his Catholic faith through the study of the great Muslim mystic al-Hallaj[3], Massignon became convinced that Christians had to accomplish what amounted to a Copernican re-centring in order to understand Islam. In other words, Christians had to place themselves at the very axis of Muslim doctrine 'par un renversement à la Copernic, au centre même de l'islam, là ou vit cette étincelle de vérité dont se sustient invisiblement et mystérieusement tout le reste.' (Prière sur Ismaël (1935)[4]) Massignon was open to the Muslim notion that the three religions issued from the same source. He accepted the connection of Muslims to Abraham via Ishmael: they were the heirs of his blessing, and of his vocation of being specially chosen. He viewed Muhammad as *prophète négatif* in the sense that he denies God being more than what he affirms him to be. Muhammad is the herald of intransigent monotheism.

For Massignon Muhammad is no longer the 'Antichrist' as a certain section of the Church had presented him in the past. He rather is the one

---

[3] The full English trsl. of the new edition of the French original by Herbert Mason, *The Passion of al-Hallaj*. Mystic and Martyr of Islam. 4 vols. Princeton, N.J.: Princeton Univ. Press, 1982. Cf. also Y. Moubarac, *Pentalogie Islamo-Chrétienne*. Tome I: L'Oeuvre de Louis Massignon. Beyrouth. Éditions du Cénacle Libanais, 1972-73.

[4] Quoted in Caspar. 1987, p.80. Cf. also ibid., p.108, note 15.

who expects Christians and Jews to put themselves in the place of the Muslims in order to join in the one salvation proposed by God ('celui qui attend que des chrétiens et des Juifs se substituent aux musulmans pour se réunir en un seul salut proposé par Dieu'). This substitution implies that Christians take on themselves the sins, the insufficiencies, the sufferings, the limitations of its doctrines and its legal prescriptions. It implies that Christians live dependant upon Islam in order to save it in the same way in which Christ depends on those whom he saves. Massignon was deeply convinced that all Muslims, those already judged and saved as well as all those alive today, 'sont là pour être intériorisés par nous-mêmes, en nous substituant à eux.'[5] For Massignon, Islam is an Abrahamic schism, as it were, preceding the Decalogue which founds Judaism, and Pentecost which founds Christianity.

Whereas, on the one hand, Vatican II's positive description of central aspects of the Muslims' faith and practice and its new outlook on Islam would be unthinkable without Massignon's insight and commitment, on the other hand, the Council, as has been shown, refrained from adopting key elements of Massignon's idiosyncratic theologico-prophetic vision of Islam and its prophet. It was careful not to let the privileged position that Islam occupies among the other great religions in the history of salvation, overshadow the originality of the Judeo-Christian revelation with its culmination, in the eyes of the Christian faith, in the divine-human person of Jesus Christ. The Council also was convinced that the historical descent of the Muslims from Ishmael, as claimed by the Muslims, is far from having been proven from the available evidence[6].

3. The Post-Vatican II Magisterium on Islam and Christian-Muslim Relations

3.1 Papal gestures and allocutions

The years immediately after the Council witnessed countless initiatives that began to transform the Catholic vision of Islam and of Christian-Muslim relations. Of special importance in this context was the creation in 1964 of the Vatican Secretariat for Non-Christians, in 1989

---

[5] Harpigny. 1975, p.314; Massignon lived these ideas in the Badaliyya movement. For the origin and meaning of this movement see Basetti-Sani. 1972, p.23, note. See also text above 1.2, referring to D'Alverny. 1956, p.175.

[6] For further theological comment on this matter see Dupuis. 1989, p.151-160, esp. p. 158ff.

renamed Pontifical Council for Dialogue between Religions (PCID). It sponsored many meetings between Christians and Muslims and promoted Christian-Muslim relations systematically in various ways. Its attitude, initiatives and offices were implemented on regional and national levels. Influential *Guidelines for a Dialogue between Muslims and Christians* were first published around 1970 and an entirely reworked edition appeared in 1981. (Secretariatus. 1969, and Pontifical Council. 1990) The popes began the practice of world-wide pastoral visits and made it a point during these travels to encounter and address representatives of Muslim communities sharing national life with local churches (and with other religious communities). These local churches in turn exhorted their members to strive for discrete and fraternal service of their Muslim neighbours.

Thus we have a continuous flow of statements of the *magisterium* referring to interreligious dialogue in general and to Christian-Muslim relations more specifically. (Cf. Gioia. 1994) Looking at the popes' encyclicals, speeches to special groups during papal journeys, speeches at private audiences, addresses marking recurring occasions (such asWorld Peace Day), the accreditation of ambassadors, we discover certain statements that develop the Catholic vision of Islam beyond the conciliar statements.

One dominant theme is the conviction that the submission to the same unique, personal Creator God (cf. S. 29:45 and *Lumen Gentium*, no. 16: 'nobiscum Deum adorant') on the part of Muslims and Christians constitutes a link of 'fraternity' on which is based a comparable vision of the human person. This in turn provides a foundation of ethics and a common mission, for the service of humanity for the glory of God, which is at least partly shared with Christians.

Common to all these post-conciliar statements is the intention to underline what is common, without forgetting the differences, even deep and glaring ones. These however are never held to render meaningless an open and fraternal encounter between Muslims and Christians as human beings and as believers in the one God.

The statements seem to be marked by a pedagogic intention, highlighting in the Islamic tradition those aspects and values which resemble most the Christian tradition. In contact with Islamic realities, the Christian tradition is challenged to let itself be purified and enriched in its historical being. Thus, the *magisterium* proclaims its respect and even sincere 'admiration' for the believing and practising Muslim, insisting at the same time on the dignity of every human being as God's creature, a

dignity that calls for the effort to realize fraternity, equality and freedom
and to recognize effectively the fundamental right of individuals and of
communities to profess their faith without hindrance.

The *magisterium* appreciates the Muslims' concern for the effective
translation of the religious message into the realities of society and
polity but underlines at the same time the Christian distinction between
the religious-spiritual and the strictly political-social order. It empha-
sizes the love of God and neighbour as the key element of Christian doctrine. (Cf. Rossano. 1982)

One conspicuously new element in the teaching of Pope Paul VI is the
express respect not merely for Muslims as individuals, but for the faith
they profess. In Kampala, the capital of Uganda, during his visit in 1969
Paul VI explicitly associated the memory of the Muslim 'confessors of
the Muslim faith' with that of the Catholic and Protestant martyrs.
(Goia. 1994, p. 172) On the same occasion he begged for God's bless-
ings upon the Muslim community in the avowed awareness that Muslims and Christians are united in their prayer to God and together
responsible for furthering prosperity and peace in Africa.

Pope John Paul II has devoted more attention to the relations between
Christians and Muslims than any of his predecessors. His overriding attitude is one of respect for the valid religious experiences of Muslims. He
wants Catholics to approach Muslims, not merely eager to speak and
give but also to be open to learn, being aware that they can be challenged and enriched by them.

It is clear from the encyclical *Redemptor Hominis* (1979) that John Paul
II teaches that 'by his Incarnation, he, the son of God, in a certain way
united himself with each human being' and that the Holy Spirit is operative in the lives of non-Christians, not in spite of their religious adherence
but rather as its essence and foundation. (ibid., para. 8-10) During the
same year, in his address to the Secretariat for Non-Christians, quoting Mt
8:10: 'Not even in Israel have I found such faith', the Pope stresses the
importance for Catholics to observe genuinely religious non-Christians, in
order 'to read and listen to the testimonies of their wisdom and thus to
have direct proof of their faith... Respect and esteem for the other, and
what he has in the depths of his heart, is essential to dialogue.' (Goia,
1994, nos. 332 and 335) In other words: a Christian who has no love for
Muslims (or members of other faiths) and for their beliefs, which lie at the
heart of their religious self-understanding, is not able to speak with much
depth or even validity about their religion. He must undergo a 'change of
heart' before he is ready to undertake dialogue with them.

John Paul's teaching about the faith of Muslims explicates what had remained ambiguous in *Nostra Aetate* and in *Lumen Gentium*. The conciliar decrees had cautiously declared that 'Islamic faith readily relates itself to Abraham' (NA, Tanner. 1990, p. 969) and that the Muslims 'profess to hold the faith of Abraham.' (LG, Tanner. 1990, p. 861) Both phrases leave open the possibility for a 'restrictive' interpretation which would hold that although Muslims consider themselves to be in the line of faith of Abraham, in fact Christians do not consider them as such. In contrast, John Paul II on several occasions has drawn a parallel between the Islamic self-identification as descendants of Abraham and that of Christians.

Thomas Michel draws attention to 'the soteriological implications of this position in the light of the Pauline theology that "Abraham was saved through his faith":

'One might ask whether Muslims are not saved in a manner analogous to the Jews, as children in faith of Abraham who are inheritors of the promises made to the patriarch. In any theological evaluation of Islam made by Roman Catholics, the relevance of such papal teachings is apparent and must be taken into consideration.'(Michel. 1985, p. 13)

John Paul II seemed to point in this direction when he declared to the Catholic community in Ankara in 1979:

'Faith in God, professed by the spiritual descendants of Abraham — Christians, Muslims and Jews — when it is lived sincerely, when it penetrates life, is a certain foundation of the dignity, brotherhood, and freedom of men and a principle of uprightness for moral conduct and life in society.' (quoted in Michel. 1985, p. 13)

'In affirming the societal and moral effects of this faith, Michel comments, the Pope seems to be presuming that such faith is genuine and not a relationship to God which Muslims merely impute to themselves.' (ibid.) Because of this shared faith which is the foundation of dialogue and cooperation the Pope urges Catholics

'to consider every day the deep roots of faith in God in whom also your Muslim fellow citizens believe, in order to draw from this the principle of a collaboration with a view to the progress of man, emulation in good, to the extension of peace and brotherhood in the profession of the faith peculiar to each one.' (Ankara, 1979, quot. in Michel. 1985, p. 13)

In this statement, John Paul II goes beyond advocating dialogue on the part of theologians and religious leaders. He views Islam as practised by ordinary, devout Muslims stimulating the Catholics' appreciation of the sovereign presence of God who, they know by faith, calls them continually to be followers of Christ, open to the daily action of his Spirit.

John Paul II views the Muslim faith — which is unconditional submission, on the model of Abraham, to the Will of God — as a basic
'meeting place' between Christians and Muslims. Referring to Titus 3:8
he reflects on the common vocation of Christians and Muslims as they
live together in a modern plural setting that guarantees freedom of worship and of education. This vocation is a call to get to know one another
better, to coexist peacefully, accepting mutual differences and overcom-
ing mutual prejudices, and thus to enrich one another by moral and spiritual emulation in the work for reconciliation and for the service of the
disadvantaged. (Cf. Gioia. 1994, no. 444 (Belgium) and John Paul. 1985
(Casablanca)).

3.2. The Vatican Guidelines

The Vatican Guidelines (Secretariatus. 1969; Pontifical Council.
1981/90) on the whole refrain from stating theological views of Islam.
Explaining the principles and conditions for a true dialogue, they aim at
making Catholics aware of distorted images of Islam in past and present.
They encourage them to open themselves to a genuine encounter with
the diverse groups and classes of Muslim believers that make up the
umma. The most striking feature of the view of Islam underlying the
Guidelines is their emphasis on Islam 'as a faith, as progress towards
God and final realization of all man's potentialities.' (Secretariatus.
1969, p. 143) 'Esteem' and 'respect' for Muslims can develop properly
only when and if Islam is considered 'first of all as a faith' (ibid., p. 144)
In the spirit of dialogue, the Guidelines exhort the Catholic to 'take
account first of all of the conceptions they themselves [i.e., the Muslims]
put forward' instead of 'imposing his own ideas on the Muslims of
today'. (ibid., p. 91) It may well be that out of the deep commitment to
overcome past distorted attitudes and views, the Guidelines fall here and
there into the trap, especially effective with Christian students of Islam,
of undervaluing, within the normative ideal that Islam presents of itself,
the socio-political dimension and also, of not sufficiently distinguishing
the ideal from the actual, past and present, realizations of it. Have the
socio-political concerns, methods and means — so much emphasized in
various influential segments of the Muslim world, past and present, as
forming an integral part of the Islamic design — been given the full
attention they deserve?
The totally reworked second edition of the Guidelines strikes one as
being optimistic when it contrasts the 'political, cultural and religious

confrontations of the past' with today, when 'relations between Christians and Muslims seem now to have entered a time of respect and understanding in which Christians, for their part, try to appreciate Muslims on the basis of the best in the latter's religious experience'. (Pontifical Council. 1990, p. 15) Does the text here refer to the Church's normative teaching or to the really existing prevailing attitudes of Catholics to Muslims and Islam? The prevailing attitudes of Catholics in many parts of the world in fact continue to be marked by ignorance and prejudice as well as by real but uncomfortable experiences.

At the sole point where the text speaks of a 'theological evaluation of Islam in the light of the Gospel', it qualifies Islam 'as a monotheistic and prophetic religion having ties — not yet well defined — with the Judeo-Christian tradition, and as a faith in which the Abrahamic model of faith and submission to God is upheld in all of its implications.' (ibid. p. 113) However, it refrains from any further elaboration.

The *Guidelines* clearly break new ground when, years after the closure of the Council, they address the question of Christians' views of the Prophet of Islam, asking Catholics to 'renounce firmly...negative judgements which came out of former concern for polemics and apologetics'.

> 'Christians should assess in an objective way, and in consonance with their faith, exactly what was the inspiration, the sincerity and the faithfulness of the Prophet Muhammad, making their judgement within the framework, first, of his personal response to the commands of God, and then, on a wider scale, that of the working of providence in world history.' (Pontifical Council. 1990, p. 57)

Here, for the first time, an official Vatican text explicitly states the problem about which the Council maintained an awkward silence. However, the position taken by the *Guidelines* is not without problems. First it concedes, that whilst Christians find in the Prophet of Islam 'evidence of certain mistakes and important misapprehensions', they perceive 'that Muhammad was a great literary, political and religious genius, and that he possessed particular qualities which enabled him to lead multitudes to the worship of the true God.'(ibid., p. 58) This view of Muhammad as 'a great literary, political and religious genius' reminds us of Thomas Carlyle's (1795-1881) presentation of Muhammad in the famous Lecture II: 'The Hero as Prophet'. It presents Muhammad as an outstanding exemplar of the great number of exceptionally gifted, original people. This contrasts sharply with the orthodox Muslim perception of Muhammad as an ordinary, even an 'unlettered' person whose greatness consists 'solely' in that God called him and entrusted to him the final, perfect revelation, i.e., the Qur'an and in that Muhammad transmitted this message faithfully.

Certainly, the Guidelines add the remark that Christians, recognizing Muhammad's constant witness in word and deed to faith in the One God and his call for justice and human dignity, 'also discern in him marks of prophethood' (ibid., p. 58). Furthermore, the Guidelines qualify the phrase of Patriarch Timothy of Baghdad (780-823): 'Muhammad followed the way of the prophets' as 'appropriate', 'for he surely conformed to their example, without however, corresponding fully to the One whom they foretold.' (ibid.)

And yet, we agree with Hans Zirker's perspicacious remark in this context that such a perception of Muhammad 'neither does justice to the historical figure of Muhammad in the sense of the phenomenology of religions nor to the message of the prophets of the Old Testament (which did not "foretell" Jesus so unambiguously that one would have simply to follow them centuries later so as to "correspond fully" in the Christian sense to Jesus).' (Zirker. 1993, p. 160)

However, it remains the merit of the revised *Guidelines* to have at least stated this crucial question, unavoidable in the process of further Christian-Muslim theological reflection[7].

Nowhere do the *Guidelines* deal with the striking contrast in the prophetic career of the two respective foundational figures: Jesus' choice of non-violent suffering, and the Prophet of Islam's decision on political assertion and military action with the purpose of securing a guaranteed political space for the implementation, spread and dominance of Islam's message of faith. Nor does it raise the question whether what we describe here as choice and decision on the part of Jesus and Muhammad, can justifiably be seen as two vocations.

3.3. The Regional Bishops' Conference of North Africa

Among magisterial statements concerning Islam and Christian-Muslim relations made by regional Catholic Bishops' Conferences, the Letter of the Bishops of the Maghreb: 'Chrétiens du Maghreb: le sens de nos rencontres' published in 1979, merits special mention here. The Letter gives expression to a distinct vision of coexistence and collaboration with Muslims: a deliberate, almost total, abstraction is made of the specific, Islamic allegiance of the near totality of North Africans, of the fact that it is the Islamic tradition that informs the religious and cultural life of the

---

[7] In this critical assessment of the Guidelines we closely follow Zirker's analysis. See Zirker. 1993, p.158-160.

people of the Maghreb. On its thirty pages or so, the letter refers only five times to Islam or Muslims. Underlying this option are contextual factors: the Christian communities of the Maghreb already at the time of the writing of the letter, and even more so today, constitute a tiny minority. They are made up of small groups of persons, mostly foreigners, living in the Maghreb for professional reasons. A tiny nucleus of lay persons, priests and religious, assume the responsibility of a more continuous presence.

The central piece of the letter is a theological reflexion about the situation of the human person before God. The bishops invite the Christians to look beyond the sociological frontiers of the Church and to reflect about the saving action of God towards every human person, in terms of the theological notion of the 'kingdom of God'. They emphasize that all men and women are created in Christ and called to put on, in him, the divine image.

> 'The kingdom of God does not come to be only where people accept baptism. It also comes wherever human beings are engaged in their true vocation, wherever they are loved, wherever they create communities in which one learns to love: family, associations, nations. It comes wherever the poor are treated as human beings, wherever adversaries are reconciled, wherever justice is promoted, where peace is established, where whatever is true, beautiful and good makes human beings grow....To recognize that these tasks are common to all men and women, means to situate the Christian vocation at the heart of any struggle for a truly human existence..' (Conférence, 1979, p. 1038).

Nowhere does the letter point out where the Christians can find **in Muslim faith and practice** such values proclaimed and realized, nor does it assist them to develop within their Christian faith, in openness and critical respect, a place for such values. The bishops speak of the Muslim as such only tangentially, only in so far as she deserves to be respected in her choice and liberty as the believer in a different tradition.

Thus, this document gives expression to a Christian theology that, on the one hand, is eager to develop eloquently the universal dimensions of the Christian mystery in past and present but, on the other, shows itself either uninterested or unwilling to reflect upon, and to evaluate, the specific nature of Islamic faith and practice and their place within a Christian vision of the universal history of religion and salvation.

Very shortly before his violent death the late Bishop of Oran, Pierre Claverie (1938-1996)[8] in collaboration with, and in the name of, the

---

[8] The collection *Lettres et messages d'Algérie* (Claverie, 1996) contains two remarkable, recent critical essays (1986; 1995) on the present state of Christian-Muslim relations and dialogue. They perspicaciously discuss the necessary conditions, the limits and equiv-

Conférence Épiscopale du Nord de l'Afrique published *Le livre de la foi* (Claverie & Conférence, 1996), a 'working document' for those who sense the need to reflect about their Christian experience in the North-African context.

This succinct text only rarely presents elements of the Muslim faith explicitly in comparative perspective (cf. ibid. p. 13: Qur'an; pp. 34ff.: Creator-creature relationship; pp. 70ff.: Prophethood; pp. 118f.: *umma*) stressing that 'we have made every effort to make these [comparisons] with a scrupulous respect'. The text significantly keeps silent on how Catholic faith assesses such central issues of Muslim faith as those just mentioned. And yet, an analysis of the text would show that its emphases and choices (not least the centering of the whole of Catholic faith around the notion of 'Word of God') must be read as responding to the challenges of the Muslim faith which, however, in this booklet, remain largely unmentioned.

However, when discussing the faith of Abraham, our text does present the Jewish, Christian and Islamic vision of Abraham and after pointing out convergences and divergences in these visions, it concludes:

> 'Can one unite the children of Abraham, his posterity, who since the time of their origin live in tumult and divergence? The common factor is the vision of the human person, creature, in a privileged relationship with a Creator God, a relationship marked by confidence and total trust. Yet the nature of the relationship differs among the three. For Islam it refers to that which is considered the nature of the human being as such ('every human being is born a *muslim*'). For Judaism it consists in listening to a Word, it is response to a vocation. For Christianity it consists in following a person. So, where the three traditions most converge they most separate from one another. Certainly, Abraham is the father of the believers: all invoke him as their common ancestor. Yet, the interpretations of what the original story has bequeathed on each of them differ. All the same, the three refer to a common foundation, and, relying on the convergences, it should be possible to make the effort to deepen the elements each one of them holds, by confronting what is confessed by one with that of the others. Because it

ocations of Christian-Muslim dialogue, especially of organized public dialogue meetings. On the need for reciprocity see pp. 194,197; the need of having **true** questions see pp. 200f; and on the crucial importance of the wider political power constellations which in many instances condemn organized dialogue to failure see p. 192. Some pages of Bruno Chenu (prés.), *Sept vies pour Dieu et l'Algérie* (Paris:Bayard Éditions/Centurion, 1996) give a glimpse of the prior of the Cisterican community of monks of Tibhirine (Algeria). Christian de Chergé (d. 1996), perceived Islam's spiritual message and resources and the meaning of a dialogue of contemplatives: cf. e.g. his essay 'Priants parmi d'autres priants', pp. 30-48; also pp. 79-108; 210-212. See also 'In Memoriam du Cardinal Duval et des sept moines trappistes. Souffrances, amour et réconciliation', *Pro Dialogo*, Bulletin (P.C.I.D., Rome) 93: 1996/3, pp. 296-312.

would seem that the experience of faith, in its most spiritual dimension, in many ways is shared by all three. (Claverie & Conférence. 1996, p. 64)

As to the question of religion and state, the text speaks of 'one contemporary Muslim current...' which 'tries to impose Islamic states in the whole of the Muslim world, in the conviction that religion and power have to be linked'. (ibid., p. 130) However, referring to H. Djaït (*La Grande Discorde*. Gallimard, 1989) the text claims that the most fruitful periods of Islam, religion and civilization, were those when religion and power were distinct, and the darkest those when they were not.

3.4. The Letters of the Catholic Patriarchs of the East

The recent pastoral letters of the oriental Catholic patriarchs (Patriarches. 1992 and 1994) display a quite different attitude and outlook on Islam and Muslim society. True, they are concerned with 'the Christian presence in the Orient' (1992) and 'the coexistence of Muslims and Christians in the Arab world' (1994) and hence speak about Islam and Muslims only by implication as it were. However, the letter of 1992 already speaks of the Christian Arab cultural identity 'as an inseparable part of the cultural identity of the Muslims' and vice versa (Patriarches. 1992, p. 606). They describe the 'authentic spiritual and religious values' of both Christians and Muslims as an aid 'to overcome the problems that obstruct our living together.' (ibid., p. 607) We are far removed here from the option of the bishops of the Maghreb to leave on one side the fact of the specific cultural and religious Muslim identity of their North African co-citizens.

The Patriarchs' letter on coexistence states that the 'relations with Islam and the Muslims constitute a specific and fundamental aspect of the identity of our Churches, within the framework of the universal Church.' (Patriarches, 1994, p. 320) They show themselves convinced that during this phase of history in the world at large 'the religions without any doubt..., play a particular and efficient, if not determining, role with regard to the incessant increase in these relations between the diverse groups of humanity.' (ibid., p. 321) So, they 'invite all religious and spiritual forces to join their efforts in order to assume their responsibilities in the contemporary world vis-à-vis its various problems.' (ibid, p. 321)

The third part of the letter, 'Together for an egalitarian society', considers positively the Muslim concern with the political role of Islam.

> 'No one can remove religion from public life or limit it to the liturgies and devotions; because religion is dogma and life that has to do with the whole of human existence, private and public, individual and social ....To link

citizenship to religious values is not an evil. On the contrary, religious
values give a soul to citizenship. But in this case it is necessary that religion should orient the person totally to God, to the perfect respect of the
creature of God and of every religious conviction, especially when we have
to do with the religion of a minority in a given society or nation. The laws
of the state must guarantee the rights of the minority religion with the same
rigour as it guarantees those of the majority or of the religion of the State.'
(ibid., 330;331)

The patriarchs exhort the Catholics to develop on their part 'spiritual
solidarity and responsibility before God.' (ibid., p. 334) They advocate
in fact — without mentioning the term explicitly — the attitude of
badaliyya: the Catholics of the Orient are asked to include in their
prayers the sentiments and concerns of their Muslim neighbours and to
assume together with Muslims the same responsibility before God:
'Each one must put himself in the place of the other; with him, in the
presence of God, in an attitude of submission and conversion, he lives
the same difficulties, the same challenges and the same hopes and aspirations.' (ibid., p. 335; see also fn.5)

The immediate aim of the patriarchs' letter quite clearly is to shape an
attitude and a spiritual practice among Christians. However, by implication they do express the hope that a majority of Muslims in the Arab
world may opt for forms of peaceful coexistence with the minorities on
the basis of respect for the equal rights of every human person, in the
spirit of genuine spiritual reciprocity and emulation.

4. Individual Catholic views of Islam and of its place within a Chris-
tian vision of faith

4.1. Jean-Muhammad Abd-el-Jalil (1904-1979)

Among the persons who, inspired by Louis Massignon and also Dom
Miguel Asín Palacios (1871-1944), contributed substantially to trans-
forming Catholic views and attitudes towards Islam during the decades
previous to Vatican II, Paul Mulla (1881-1959) and Jean-Muhammad
Abd-el-Jalil (1904-1979) occupy pride of place. Mehmet Ali Mulla-Zadé
was born in Iraklion (Candia) on the island of Crete, then still part of the
Ottoman empire. His father was a Turk, his mother Egyptian-Albanian.
As a student at the university of Aix-en-Provence he met the philosopher
Maurice Blondel (1861-1949) who was to mark his religious and intellectual outlook deeply. Blondel became Mulla's godfather when he was
baptized in 1905, and chose the name Paul. In 1911 Mulla was ordained

priest. Pope Pius XI in 1924 charged him personally with teaching 'Institutiones Islamicae' at the Pontificio Istituto Orientale in Rome. (Cf. Molette, Charles. 1988)

Jean-Muhammad Abd-el-Jalil OFM (1904-1979) hailed from a Moroccan family of Andalusian origin. In 1928, as a student at the Sorbonne in Paris, he joined the Catholic Church and soon afterwards the Franciscan order. In 1935 he was ordained priest and from 1936-1964 he held the chair of Islamic Studies at the Institut Catholique de Paris. Paul Mulla guided Abd-el-Jalil in a 'decisive manner towards baptism' (cf. Abd-el-Jalil. 1980b, p. 4) and Louis Massignon was his godfather.

Mulla's and Abd-el-Jalil's attitude towards the Muslims and Islam and Christian-Muslim relations were not far apart and may be best indicated here by a quotation from a text Abd-el-Jalil wrote for the Fathers of the Second Vatican Council in 1964. Beginning with the words of Pope Paul VI, spoken earlier during the same year with regard to Christian ecumenism:

> 'Not to be a frontier, but to open a door, not to put an end to dialogue, not to blame for the errors committed in the past, not to wait for what has not happened during the past four centuries to happen but rather to go and search fraternally — that is what the present Council wants to do.'

Abd-el-Jalil continues:

> '*Mutatis mutandis* these words can be applied even to the Muslims. It is our duty to understand them, to love them 'pour deux', until the point when this humble and burning perseverance — accompanying them on their ways (sense of the Presence of God; sense of His Transcendence; sense of His continuing creative action; sense of the power of His Word), just as Christ, discreetly but firmly, accompanied the disciples of Emmaus — will finally kindle their heart and open their eyes to the Christian "realities"...' (Abd-el-Jalil. 1980a, p. 113-114).

Not long afterwards Abd-el-Jalil wrote in more detail his conception of a genuine dialogue between Muslims and Christians. (See: 'Liminaire pour un dialogue vrai entre Musulmans and Chrétiens', Abd-el-Jalil. 1980b, pp. 17-20)

Abd-el-Jalil's basic view of Islam, first stated in an essay in 1938 (Abd-el-Jalil. 1947) contrasts markedly with that of his contemporary, Louis Massignon. Abd-el-Jalil puts what he calls 'official Islam' and its affirmation — 'avec une fermeté qui a quelque chose de farouche' — of the dogma of God's Unity, at the centre of our attention:

> '... official Islam excludes any possibility — even by grace — of intimate knowledge and communion with God. There is no real analogy between Creator and creature, and there cannot be friendship in the strict meaning

of the term between the human person and God...Islam throws us back into
a preparatory phase of the Old Testament, hardening its spirit and exag-
gerating the accent which the Old Testament put on the divine Transcendence.' True, the Muslim faith is a witness, superior in value to philosophical monotheism or syncretistic theodicies, 'but the divine fatherhood which
Israel affirmed vaguely, is rejected [by Islam] as tainted by anthropo-
morphism.' (Abd-el-Jalil. 1947, pp. 14;15;16)

Referring to Islam's teaching on *niyya* (the right intention), Abd-el-
Jalil recognizes an element of interiority in Islamic cultic practice, 'but
Islam gives too much importance to external acts, to rites, to the manifest fulfilment of the law. It studies with a desperate meticulousness the
extrinsic qualities and defects, looking only 'for the social mark of sin',
leaving each one in front of God who remains inaccessible in His
absolute transcendence... Religious life thus becomes mechanical,
scrupulous and formalist, whilst retaining much dignity and solem-
nity.'(ibid., p. 33)

An admiring student of Massignon and his classic study of al-Hallaj,
Abd-el-Jalil acknowledges the existence of the ascetical-mystical movement in Islam, known as Sufism. It has 'attempted a liberation... from
the legalistic grip of official teaching imposed as total expression of
orthodoxy'. But, he stresses, 'the hostility of the "doctors of the Law"
as also the absence of a doctrinal authority that could guide and protect
this movement of interiorization of Islam, have considerably hampered
it.'(ibid., pp. 34-35)

Abd-el-Jalil puts great emphasis on the link, in Islamic doctrine and
psychology, between strict monotheism and 'holy war' (his rendering of
the term *jihâd*). 'Although this offensive war (*cette guerre offensive*) is
not obligatory for all the Muslims taken individually, every "believer"
carries at the bottom of his soul something of the aggressive character of
Muslim monotheism which has the ambition to impose itself on all the
earth, establishing on it the recognition of the "*précellence* (preeminent
position) *de la parole de Dieu*".' (ibid., p. 37)

Abd-el-Jalil died during the year of the Iranian revolution. We do not
find in his writings terms such as Islamic integralism, Islamicist movement or fundamentalism. However, as early as 1938 he analysed perceptively the nature and significance of what he then termed '*jeune
Islam*'(ibid., 54) 'which adopts the posture of religious as well as political and economic defense' (ibid., pp. 54-55) against a materialist, de-
christianized and de-spiritualized Europe.

'The kingdom of Saudi Arabia [Abd-el-Jalil writes in 1938] is at the flank
of this young Islam like a burning wound (*cautère brûlant*), a purifying and

galvanizing fire, a totalitarian and theocratic force, equipped, without apparent compromise, with modern means. From there stretches over the remainder of the Muslim world the powerful breath of pure Islam; that Islam which the Qur'an names "the best of communities", "just mean" (*juste milieu*) and arbiter between Judaism and Christianity, witness and upholder of justice of the Sole Allah throughout the history of all the peoples of the earth.' (ibid., p. 55)

But the fact of this powerful trend in contemporary Islam must not, Abd-el-Jalil insists, 'immobilize our understanding of Islam and the charity of our faith, conjuring up a kind of "apocalyptic" vision of the future. We would be unjust if we were to consider the Muslim solely as "warrior of Allah", as a person animated by an admittedly ardent but simplistic faith, attracted altogether by the appetite for domination, the allurements of booty and the appeal of a heaven of sensual delights. Thus we would ignore, perhaps even despise, the nobility and the chivalrous character which the very idea of "Holy War", properly understood, can develop in the Muslims.' (ibid., p. 55)

Instead Catholics should try to discover the germs of authentic religious wealth hidden behind a rigid crust of official legalism, and appreciate the real, healthy and constructive aspirations towards a deeper spiritual life, a less simplistic understanding of unity and a life in solidarity and friendship with the 'others'. (ibid., pp. 55-56)

4.2 Youakim Moubarac (1924-1994)

The Maronite priest Youakim Moubarac — for years a close collaborator of L. Massignon — must be considered the most enthusiastic and insistent of his disciples. We can here point to only a few aspects of his complex and weighty contribution to our theme. Moubarac's ever evolving views of Islam await to be presented and evaluated by way of a thorough monographic study.

In his remarkable, controversial doctoral thesis at the Sorbonne, *Abraham dans le Coran*, Moubarac tried to prove that the message of the Qur'an right from its inception centred on the figure of Abraham[9].

A chief concern of Moubarac has been to evolve, in the spirit of Massignon, the Catholic vision of Islam[10]. Acknowledging the merit of a good number of objective presentations of Islam by Christian scholars in the recent past, and praising Abd-el-Jalil's 'vision of Islam from within'

---

[9] For Anawati's critical review see Anawati. 1964, p.608-618.

[10] Cf. 'Y a-t-il une nouvelle vision chrétienne de l'Islam?' [written in about 1967], in Moubarac. 1972-3, p.81ff.

(Cf. Abd-el-Jalil. 1949), Moubarac felt the need for a properly theological reflection about Islam 'situant ce phénomène sur le plan de l'histoire prophétique.'

In a substantial essay, written about 1967, dealing with 'the questions that Catholicism puts to itself concerning Islam' (Moubarac. 1972-3, pp. 93-145), Moubarac classified the prevalent, past and present, Catholic views about Islam in the divine design and the economy of salvation as 'polemical', 'descriptive and scientific', 'concordist and syncretistic' and 'dialogical', the latter being the position of Massignon. He presented his own vision of Islam, not long afterwards, in the context of his assessment of the acquisitions of past Christian Islamology, in an essay in *Concilium*: 'La pensée chrétienne et l'islam. Principales acquisitions et problématique nouvelle'. (Moubarac. 1976)

Moubarac traces the salient steps of progress in Catholic Islamology: the outlook of Massignon prevailed over that of Lammens (see below) in the work of Louis Gardet. Roger Arnaldez marked a further step forward in 1974 with his distinction between the subjective and objective sincerity of Muhammad. Since then it has been widely accepted that one and the same Qur'an can be 'read' differently — from the point of view and within the ideological vision, for instance, of agnostics, Marxists, Christians etc. — even if such 'readings' (*lectures*) are not acceptable to the faith vision of Muslims. Furthermore, after the seminal work of Massignon about al-Hallaj, Islamic mysticism remains for Christian thinkers a privileged ground of study from where classical Islamic positions can be questioned. Hence, from now onwards Catholic scholars take into consideration the variety within Islam and the permanent tension between its diverse aspects and realizations.

With all this, a new problematic (*problématique*) has emerged in Christian Islamology: the question of the legitimacy of the great religious movement that is Islam, in the design of God. Islam is seen not as an independent way of salvation but rather as starting and presupposing that unique way of salvation which is the one in Jesus Christ.

Moubarac analyses two ways in which Catholic scholars have presented 'Islam as Ismailism'. One is the Ismailite vision of Islam based on 'the great dissection of the Qur'an' by orientalists like Henri Lammens (1862-1937). According to Lammens, Muhammad in a first phase realizes the greatness of Christ whom he puts above Abraham and Moses, his preferred models, proclaiming him and him alone, Word, Spirit from God. However, at the moment of decision [for *hijra* to Medina], Lammens holds, Muhammad made a decisive mistake. He refused to draw the proper conclusions from his own premises. Thus, from then onwards Islam had found its own, distinctive character: a forgery of Biblical monotheism with Christian elements, disfigured by a Judaizing interpretation. Lammens views Islam as an 'Arab branch of the Ebionite trunk, in a thinner version, as it behoves the flora of the desert'. But this 'copy', conceived in the image of the twofold Scriptural original (Old Testament and New Testament) remaining incomplete, it had to be impressed with the Ismailite stamp. It provides the hitherto lacking national element: The great patriarch (i.e. Abraham) will have to accept Islam, the revised and considerably arabicized edition of talmudic Judaism. (Cf. ibid., p.49).

Lammens situates at Medina the moment at which Muhammad returns to a purely judaizing inspiration — which by the stamp of Ismailism was to give Islam a national Arab character. It is at Medina that the Meccan prophet would have learned what he did not know till then. The Qur'anic forgery of biblical monotheism is perfected when the Jews of Medina, wanting to humiliate and definitely discourage him, teach Muhammad what, being an uncivilized Arab, he ignored, i.e. that he was the miserable descendent of Abraham, by means of the slave woman that bore Abraham his son Ismail. It was then that Qur'anic Abrahamism became Ismailism. (cf. ibid., p.49)

The other version of 'Islam as Ismailism' is that of Charles Journet. Employing Thomistic terms he qualifies the religious condition of Islam as a 'natural' condition (*condition de nature*). This parallels Islam's claim to be *dîn al-fitra*, the original, natural religion of humanity. But considering the Islamic notion of itself as 'religion of nature' too primitive and vague (referring to Adam or Noah), some Christian theologians proposed to view Ismailism as giving expression to God's design for His people from Abraham onwards. Thus in the 1950s Charles Journet qualifies 'the message of Muhammad, supreme treasure of Islam' as *révélation surnaturelle* of the unique and transcendent God to Abraham.

'Le message de Mahomet, trésor suprême de l'Islam, c'est la *révélation surnaturelle* du Dieu unique et transcendant faite à Abraham. Ouverte chez lui au mystère de la Trinité et de l'Incarnation rédemptrice, mais bloquée, figée lors du faux pas d'Israel, elle est reçue par Mahomet, en vertu d'une méprise non coupable, comme anti-trinitaire et anti-chrétienne, d'où la terrible et durable ambiguité de ce message.'

('Whereas with Abraham this revelation was open to the mystery of the Trinity and the redemptive Incarnation but blocked or frozen, as it were, after the mistake of Israel, it is now received by Muhammad, in virtue of a non-guilty disrespect, as anti-trinitarian and anti-Christian — hence the terrible and lasting ambiguity of this message.') (Ch. Journet quoted in Moubarac, 1976, p.47)

For Journet then, the content of the Qur'anic message is the notion of
the unique and transcendent God, originally manifested to Abraham in
the prophetic light of Biblical revelation which however has become
anti-trinitarian and anti-Christian in the distorting mirror of a disrespect
(*méprise*) common to Israel and to Islam. The notion of God here is not
simply a philosophical one but an originally revealed one... (cf. ibid.,
p. 48)

Commenting on Lammens, Moubarac stresses that, obviously, Muslims cannot accept that Muhammad should have discovered only at
Medina — and according to a malevolent Jewish informer, at that —
what is to be the proper and distinctive hallmark of the Muslim faith as
Abrahamic heritage. Muslim consciousness cannot but reject the dissection of the Qur'an into what amounts to two opposing parts, that is, into
a Muhammad of Mecca who repeats past beliefs and a Muhammad of
Medina, transformed into an Arab prophet on the basis of Jewish information. Moubarac claims that his work *Abraham dans le Coran*
(Moubarac, 1958) has for ever disproved the theories of Lammens and
those following him.

But the kind of Ismailite vision of Islam proposed by Journet, according to Moubarac is equally unacceptable and inconceivable for Christian
consciousness, on Christian premises. It is clearly contradicted by
Qur'anic Abrahamism. The latter is a primordial attitude in the Qur'an.
The contacts of Muhammad with Jews and Christians at Medina did not
'melt' his message into an 'Arab' rendition. Rather they confirmed him
in his appeal to an 'ecumenical' encounter beyond the differences.

From a Christian point of view, the idea of justifying the choice of
Muhammad by the Biblical vocation of Ishmael is even less acceptable.
The New Testament refers to the relevant texts in the Old Testament
(Genesis 16; 21:8-21) only in Paul's allegory in the Letter to the Gala-
tians (4:21-31) which reverses the literal meaning of the Genesis texts.
Moubarac estimates that since the basic element of this theory is the idea
of exclusion and of the radicalization of the Promise and Election, it cannot but be rejected by any straight consciousness. (cf. Moubarac. 1976,
p. 50)

However, Moubarac goes beyond assessing critically past positions.
He offers positive elements towards an inter-religiously-responsible
Christian theological view of Islam. As historical criticism and contemporary Biblical hermeneutics have produced a fresh theological reading
of Genesis I-XI, the interpretation of Genesis XII ff. will have to free
itself from abusively historicistic overtones in order to highlight the true

reality of Promise and Election so that they 'manifest the divine generosity in the face of any privilege of clan or class.' In the light of this
generosity we must deem 'not only in accordance with the Gospel but
also according to the promise made to Abraham, that all are excluded by
sin, all redeemed by grace.' (ibid., p. 51)

Such considerations duly deflate Muslim Ismailism, Jewish exclusivism and Christian elitism alike. Aware of the fact that there exist
other exemplary instances, outside Biblical sacred history, there is a
need to delimit, if not relativize, the concept of sacred history and to
enlarge it towards world-wide dimensions[11]. In other words, Moubarac
insists on the need for Christian theology to correct the apparent nar-
rowness of a christological soteriology, limited to the history of Israel
and to the Church, by a mysteriology of the Logos and of the Spirit that
spans universal history. ('corriger l'étroitesse apparente d'une christolo-
gie sotériologique limitée à l'histoire d'Israel et de l'Église par une mys-
tériologie du Logos et de l'Ésprit étendue à l'histoire universelle.'
(Moubarac. 1976, p. 52)

In this context Moubarac reiterates Massignon's conviction that the
Qur'an's calling the virginity of Mary a 'sign' constitutes a summons to
Christianity. By this 'sign', Muhammad definitely breaks with 'Mo-
saism'. It points to a continuity in sacred history between the 'first
Adam' and the eschatological return of the 'second Adam', in other
words, it points to the third temple, not made of human hands.

Taking up an idea precious to Jules Monchanin (cf. Monchanin,
1938), Moubarac proposes to rethink the problem of time; distinguishing physical, chronological time from salvation-history time. Chronolog-
ically speaking, the 'time' of Islam succeeds that of Judaism and of
Christianity. But substantially, and as to its structure, Muslim civilization is close to Abrahamic 'time' and even closer, it would seem, to
Mosaic 'time'. 'Une audacieuse philosophie du temps devrait inverser,
par rapport au Christ, la position de l'Islam.' (Monchanin, 1938, p. 25)

Finally Moubarac pleads not to put Islam too easily and exclusively in
parallel with Judaism:

> 'Instead of appearing to privilege Islam by making it participate in the pre-
> rogatives of Israel of which the other religions would be deprived, we
> would say that this parallelism between the two 'discourses' (*discours*) in
> the Church, i.e. the Judeo-Christian and the Islamo-Christian, should rather
> privilege the totality of the religions on behalf of all of whom Islam raises

[11] Moubarac refers in this context to G. Khodr's famous communication at Addis
Abbeba, publ. in *Irenikon* (Chevetogne), 1971, p. 191-202.

a protest against a Christian prerogativism which it has inherited from Jewish prerogativism and which is based, in the last analysis, on the jealousies
between women.' (ibid., p. 53)

A truly Christian universalism 'must be transposed definitively from the
quantitative to the qualitative and be stripped of any missiological propen-
sity for statistics.' The Christian Church must rather live 'deeply buried in
the Muslim world — according to the vocation of the grain that dies.'(ibid.)

4.3 Giulio Basetti-Sani (1912-)

Among the numerous publications of Giulio Basetti-Sani the work
The Koran in the Light of Christ is the one that states for the first time
clearly his view of Islam, its Prophet and its basic message. (Basetti-
Sani. 1977)[12] In the first part, the author traces the remarkable transformation of his outlook on Islam, during the earlier part of his adult life.

Basetti-Sani tells us that reading in his youth the life of Anthony of
Padua and an account of the martyrdom of the first Franciscans in
Morocco, as well as of the history of the Crusades, inspired him to join the
Franciscan order. In 1936, he came into contact with Jean-Muhammad
Abd-el-Jalil and through him with Massignon, by then Professor at the
Collège de France. The advice Massignon then gave him in the course of
a personal conversation influenced Basetti-Sani permanently. Massignon
pointed out to the young friar the significance of his 'personal and particular Franciscan vocation for the Muslim world, within his own religious
order...It was he who helped me to realize the urgent necessity of a deep
love for the Muslims, following the example of Saint Francis; it was he
who taught me to suffer for them.' (Basetti-Sani, 1972, p. 12)

During two years of study at the Istituto Orientale in Rome, from
1937-1939, Basetti-Sani followed the lectures on Islamic institutions by
Msgr. Paul Mulla. During these years Basetti-Sani began to view 'the
problem of Islam' not only as 'one of the most urgent problems of the
Church' but also as a personal challenge. Mulla provided the stimulus to
find a theologically satisfying answer to the question: 'What does Islam
signify in the history of humanity which has been created to orient itself
and insert itself in the mystery of Christ?' (ibid., p. 15)

Basetti-Sani, with disarming honesty, recalls the answer he then gave
publicly to this question. Addressing a Christian audience in Egypt in
1941 he stated:

---

[12] I here translate from the Italian original (1972) since the English translation (1977)
does not render the original fully and exactly.

Muhammad is an instrument…a sad instrument of Satan for realizing in human history — a history created for being Christian and Catholic — a new aspect of the reign of Satan, in opposition to the Church of Christ. Satan tries to set his anti-Church against the true and sole Church. Islam fulfils the function of opponent to the kingdom of God and thus is the work of Satan. Allah, the 'god of the Qur'an' is the antithesis of the one and true God. The Qur'an negates the concept of the God-who-is-Love and replaces it with that of Allah, the capricious Judge. The 'Qur'anic god' is Satan. The Jesus of the Qur'an is the antithesis of the living and true Jesus of the Gospel. Thus the Qur'an bears also in its christological doctrine a diabolic stamp. The Qur'an is anti-Gospel. (Basetti-Sani, 1972, p.17, footnote)

The 'naturalism of Islam' means the absolute exclusion of any super-natural order. The Christian struggle between spirit and flesh is resolved by the Qur'an 'peacefully', 'in a compromise of sensual materialism.' (ibid., p. 19, footnote) The fruits of Islam once again confirm the lack of divine character and attest instead the presence of the activity of Satan. Thus Islam is one of the most serious, disastrous (*funesto*) and dangerous Satanic realities and is most destructive of the kingdom of God. (cf. ibid.)

However, not long afterwards, witnessing in Egypt the performance of the ritual prayer of Muslims, he begins to feel an inner urge to look within himself and to begin to judge himself, rather than judge Islam. Again he encounters Massignon who impresses upon him the principles of charity and scientific honesty and points out to him the hypocrisy of wanting to apply such methods and principles of exegesis to the Qur'an which one does not want to see applied to the Bible.

About that time, seeing one day a group of poor Muslims in a barque on the river Nile performing their ritual prayer, he suddenly realizes that he must love the Muslims. He received then, as he writes, 'una nuova visione dell'Islam', new eyes for viewing the Qur'an, Muhammad and Islam. (cf. Basetti-Sani. 1972, p. 25)

By 1950 it had become clear to Basetti-Sani that he must concentrate all his energy on a study of the Qur'an, 'il plasmatore essenziale della mentalità e della coscienza musulmana.'(ibid., p. 28) He clearly states his new vision of the Qur'an and its message. He has come to under-stand that for the evaluation of Islam in the light of the history of salva-tion, the study of the Qur'an is absolutely central. The Qur'an has to be accepted hypothetically as the true Word of God, the foundation of a para-Biblical revelation, given by God to some peoples in order to pre-pare them for the announcement of the Gospel.

Basetti-Sani, fully aware of the traditional 'reading' of the Qur'an by Muslims, feels authorized to take up, in an attitude of respect and reverence, the study of this book which he considers to be 'hypothetically revealed', in order to rethink it and interpret it anew, in the light of the second Vatican Council. Christians, 'in a sincere and fraternal effort', must help the Muslims discover 'the seeds of the Word', the fact that the Qur'an ultimately is oriented towards Christ. In fact, a veil has hindered the Muslims to this day from seeing, and becoming fully aware of, the whole true and authentic content of the Qur'an regarding Christ — just as a veil prevented the Jews from discovering Jesus Christ in the Scriptures of the Hebrew Bible. (cf. Basetti-Sani, 1992, pp. 24)

Christians have to find in the Qur'an the Christian symbolism and the christological typology it contains. The Biblical personalities of the Old Testament that we find in the Qur'an have not yet been given the importance they have as typological prefigurations of Jesus. 'For instance the presentation of Adam [in the Qur'an] to be adored by the angels, corresponds (*si traduce*) in the Christian tradition to the announcement to the angels of the Incarnation.' (Basetti-Sani, 1992, p. 37) In short: 'it must be permitted to a Christian to search for "the seeds of the Word" in the Qur'an and to demonstrate, in the spirit of Saint Paul, that all that is good and just in the Qur'an, finds its deepest and most perfect completion in Jesus Christ.' (ibid., pp. 38f.)

On these premises, Basetti-Sani arrives at the following assessment of Muhammad and, by implication, of Islam:

> 'Entrusted [by God] with a partial revelation, Muhammad has been a valid instrument for bringing about the reign of God. For fourteen centuries he has initiated a substantial portion of humanity into the mystery of God, as a genuine preparation for the fullness of revelation which exists in the truth of Christianity. Recognizing the authenticity of the prophetic mission of Muhammad and of the relative and objective, albeit not absolute, goodness of Islam, the Christian is asked to do his best so that the manifestation of Christ and Mary as proclaimed in the Qur'anic message, will be ever more recognized as a seed that must grow towards the full knowledge of the mystery of God.' (Basetti-Sani, 1992, p. 351)

4.4 Jacques Jomier (1914-)

Jacques Jomier, a French priest of the Order of Preachers, throughout his life has been striving to formulate a theologically informed Catholic appreciation and assessment of the faith and practice of Islam. He spent the greatest part of his adult life in Cairo and is the author of remarkable studies on central aspects of recent and contemporary Islamic thought, education and religious practice in Egypt. In his case, too, we can here only shortly indicate a few of his views of Islam.

In conclusion to his latest work *Dieu et l'homme dans le Coran* Jomier states 'the fundamental options which distinguish the Muslims and the Christians and which determine their whole religious attitude.' (Jomier. 1996, p. 219) Jomier reminds us of the intrinsic insufficiency of human language in expressing the truth of God as He is and he makes it clear that he speaks here on the normative level, by way of ideal types. Trying in this way to pinpoint the specific character of the Qur'an's teaching on God and the relationship between God and man Jomier says: For the Muslims God is above all the Master, the Lord of the universe and of all humans; however, a master and lord without any of the imperfections that we encounter in this world. For the Christian God is essentially Father, but in a sense that must be carefully specified...In both cases we have to do with a master and lord who has no need of possession or of created servants; and, if one speaks of father one does so in order to underline the perfection of God and the delicacy of his tenderness and the fact that he grants life in its fullness.

As to the frequently raised question of the love of God in Christian and Muslim faith teaching, Jomier judges that Muslims perceive God to love like a most merciful master, whereas the Christians compare his love to that of a father. And, whereas Islam understands itself as the reestablishment of the original patriarchal religion that continues to be valid, even exclusively so, and refuses any other type of monotheism...Christianity teaches that progress has taken place in revelation: the prophets, the psalms, the very history of the elect people are the motivating forces of a spiritual movement which will reach its summit with Christ, in whom it continues to expand. (cf. ibid., p. 220)

The other outstanding point of contrast between the Qur'an and the Christian Scriptures, for Jomier, concerns sin. According to the Qur'an human beings are weak; they can choose between good and evil but have need of being guided by God. The root sin is polytheism. The Bible insists on sin and its profound drama more than the Qur'an. Human beings find it difficult to consistently realize the good whereas evil, often against their deepest aspirations, overpowers them. Hence the insistence on humility, trust in God, the need to be forgiven, saved; the ideal of the Beatitudes (Matthew 5:1-12) and the appeal to love as Christ loved us. The only unforgivable sin is the sin against the Holy Spirit.

Jomier thinks that these two emphases go together with two types of model, on the normative level, 'because on the level of real life [of the two religious traditions] the situation is much more complex.' (ibid.)

'On the one hand, the model is that of justice backed by force should it prove necessary. When, with the increase of the Muslim forces in Medina, armed struggle finally had become possible, the Prophet of Islam had recourse to arms against the Meccans and against the last Jewish tribe offering resistance in the oasis [of Medina]. On the other hand, Jesus went to the bitter end of his mission; he could have withdrawn and prepared for an armed battle, whereas in fact he remained in his place in order to witness up to death. True, in real life both Christians and Muslims are confronted with similar problems, and society needs a certain organization. Yet, all the same, the difference of model, the fundamental option, does make a difference. On the Christian side, this option is like a seed, like an appeal to individuals to work in a mixed society; on the Muslim side one has to do with a code of life which ideally concerns this as well as the next world, nevertheless at times, in case of a conflict between the two, finds itself obliged to sacrifice this life for the next,' (ibid., p. 221)

The clear differences between the Christian and the Muslim vision of the human person — about their proximity there can be no doubt — have their origin above all in the fact 'that because of a different sense of the greatness of God, the Qur'an in no way admits God calling the human person beyond the level perceived by a natural theology... The respect for the transcendence of God forbids the human person to go beyond that level, and according to the Qur'an God absolutely will not intervene to modify that situation.' (ibid., p. 222)

In his earlier work *Pour connaître l'Islam* (1988) Jomier presents a chapter on 'The Problem of Muhammad' where with rare courage, honesty and clarity yet without any trace of polemics, he states his views on some of the essential differences between central Christian and Muslim faith perceptions. On the Christian reticence to qualify Muhammad theologically as a prophet in line with those of the Biblical Scriptures, he states:

'The Jesus of Islam is at the service both of Muhammad whom he announces and of the Qur'an. Muslims, too, have every interest in proclaiming him a prophet so as to give more weight to his support. By contrast, if Christians were to accept the prophecy of Muhammad in the strict sense, they would have to go against everything they are told by the weightiest religious documents in their possession. The situation is certainly not the same in the two cases.' (Jomier, 1989, p. 141)

'If the word prophet is given an absolute sense, and denotes someone all of whose words pronounced in the name of God are vested with divine authority so that all then have to obey them, Christians cannot concede this title to the founder of Islam. They cannot obey him without reserve, for that would be to become Muslims. To accept Muhammad as a Prophet in the strict sense, which includes showing faith and obedience, is impossible for Christians. Christians will always use the word prophet with qualifications;

in other words, they will not accept all that a 'prophet' says, but accept some things and reject others.' (ibid., pp. 146-147)

'...I think that in the present instance we have to avoid the word prophet. To use it would entail giving it a limited sense which Muslim faith would not accept. It is better to express ourselves in another way: to recognize the truths that the Muslim message contains, to respect the spiritual journey of sincere Muslims, and to see Muhammad as a religious and political genius. Or, alternatively, we should recognize that within Islam numerous believers are in a relationship with God that grace has brought about in them.' (ibid.)

Jomier, from the viewpoint of an unambiguously Catholic theological vision of faith, judges it 'necessary to invent a new theological category to denote those who are profoundly religious but are in radical opposition to existing official frameworks, and who are rebelling against forms of Christianity which have either become fossilized or are caught up in cultural or national questions...' And he adds in a questioning mood the following stimulating reflection: 'A saint could achieve genuine reform without betraying the essentials of the message. Rebels who are not saints re-read the message of the Bible in their own way, in their own cultural context. This new form may illuminate particular points (in Islam, for example, the Lordship of God), but reject other essential ones.... Might Islam not have been born in this way, in accordance with the will of God, given the circumstances and the situation of the time? God only knows.' (ibid., pp. 147-148) In the same chapter Jomier goes so far as to suggest the idea that God might have sent and inspired Muhammad (and hence the *umma*) in order to reform a fossilized church, to stimulate it to emulate them and drive Christians to reform themselves without abandoning the other truths which the explosion of the reform had failed to recognize. (cf. ibid., p. 148)

4.5 Robert Caspar (1923-)

For decades Robert Caspar has been one of the leading Catholic experts of Islam. As long-standing professor of Islamic studies in Tunisia and Rome, he collaborated as *peritus* (officially appointed, specialist advisor) of the Second Vatican Council in the formulation of its texts concerning Islam, and he worked for years as consultant of the Secretariat for non-Christian Believers. In 1977 he co-founded the 'Groupe de Recherches Islamo-Chrétien' (GRIC)[13].

---

[13] About the origin and nature of this remarkable initiative see Caspar. 1989, p. 1-13.

In the present context we hardly can do better than present the chief points Caspar makes in his autobiographical account 'Une rencontre avec l'Islam' published in 1991. (Caspar. 1991) Caspar describes how, during the past half-century the perception of the relationship of the Christian faith and the non-Christian world have evolved and diversified substantially, especially with regard to the question of the meaning of Christian mission and missionary witness. Basically we have to do with the passage from the consciousness of teaching the truth possessed by the Catholic Church to those who do not have it, to the consciousness of holding a portion of the truth among people who also have their portion of it. Conscious of living not in an age of unbelief but rather in the age of religious pluralism, it is the faith of the believer itself that is challenged, not just a certain structure of doctrines, a certain ecclesiology or christology.

Tracing his personal evolution in this perspective, Caspar recalls how during his student years in Tunis, in 1952, one of his Christian professors began his lectures on Islam thus: 'Islam is a diabolic religion. I should go further: it is an especially diabolic religion.' And he went on to explain:

> 'If it is undeniable that the Qur'an contains some truth and some good, then this is precisely the cunning of Satan who dons the appearance of good in order to lead astray the souls; what Sufis call *talbîs Iblîs*: the deception of Satan.' (Caspar. 1991, p. 16)

For Caspar, there can be no doubt that the Second Vatican Council marks 'an absolutely new beginning in the history of the Church and of its mission.' However, it left open the theologically crucial question: 'Can a Christian recognize in Muhammad a real prophetical charisma?' Within the wide spectre of a 'minimalist' (Islam: a temptation of Satan) and a 'maximalist' response (in the school of Massignon), until the end of the 1970s, Caspar adopted a 'middle-of-the-road' position. It concedes to Muhammad a partial prophetic charisma, for the portion of truth contained in the Qur'an and in Muslim tradition, in so far as this portion coincides with the Christian truth, and in spite of the fact that one may hold the Qur'an and Muslim tradition to be formal denials of the Christian mysteries: Trinity, Incarnation and Redemption.

However, soon Caspar was led to go further. He began to perceive the Qur'an as powerfully unified and informed by the faith in one God. At the same time he realized the importance in Christian theology of the distinction between the pre-Easter message of Jesus, the paschal faith of the Church and the doctrine of the councils. Caspar himself explains his theological evolution in more detail, emphasizing two factors that caused his theological thought about Islam to evolve.

Informed by the recently developed Christian theology of religions, especially in the line of Karl Rahner (1904-1984)[14], he comes to hold two points: one, the paschal faith in the Risen Christ, 'who has entered the glory of the Father', i.e. the belief in Christ as being present and alive at the heart of every human person and of any effort towards the true and good; second, the faith conviction that the non-Christian religions are part and parcel of the divine plan of salvation and hence, are legitimate and saving, in so far as they offer their followers the necessary elements of knowledge and help by the grace of God, in opening themselves to God and to their brothers.' (ibid., p. 19)

The other factor Caspar holds responsible for having moved him towards a new vision of Islam, is the encounter in depth he has been living with Muslim believers from all levels of society in Tunisia. This relationship with many Muslim believers went beyond friendship. They allowed him to touch with his own fingers, as he puts it, 'la densité, la compacité de la foi chez les plus simples, leur recours et leur confiance en Dieu dans la peine comme dans la joie.' (ibid., p. 20) It became absurd for him to ascribe such a rich religious life, totally impregnated with the Muslim tradition — even if its manifestations often are not considered orthodox by the minutiae-obsessed and haughty doctors of the Law — to illusion or even to the deception of Satan.

It took a good amount of time for Caspar to liberate himself from certain traditional, uncritically-held assumptions and apologetic justifications which prevented him from revising his outlook. He was greatly helped in this by his friendships and his collaboration with a number of contemporary Muslim researchers, especially in the context of the work of the already mentioned 'Groupe de Recherches Islamo-Chrétien' (GRIC). Concluding this part of his analysis he states: 'C'est l'islam et les musulmans qui m'ont fait découvrir le Christ vivant que je reduisais trop à des formules théologiques.' (ibid., p. 21)

Caspar's present vision of Islam, as well as of the Christian faith in the awareness of Islam, is best indicated by the summary of his four propositions:

(1) *Islam participates in the universal plan of salvation*

Together with Judaism and Christianity, Islam constitutes the group of 'prophetic' religions or revelations. These are to be distinguished from the 'mystical' religions which centre on a mystical experience, as for

---

[14] Cf. Dupuis. 1989, p.161-195 and ibid., Bibliographie générale, under Rahner.

instance the great Asian religions. Islam was born from the specific religious experience lived by Muhammad: the experience, basically, of the oneness of the transcendent God, expressed by elements hailing not so much directly from the authentic anterior Scriptures of the Jewish and Christian religions as from apocryphal traditions and materials marginal to those Scriptures. The diverse elements of the Qur'an are powerfully unified and brought to life by this basic experience of the one, transcendent God. It is this experience which lies at the heart of Islam and sums it up.

What holds true regarding the Scriptures of the Old and the New Testament is true of the Qur'an as well: it is not a Word of God or a revelation 'à l'état pure'. Only the Word in God Himself, the Word which the Christians recognize as Word of God in God (and which is more than an attribute of God) is revelation 'à l'état pur'.

The Word of God in God, according to the Christian faith, has revealed itself to humankind, by means of 'statements' in human language situated in space and time, in languages and cultures which it 'needed' to express itself and to be understood by human beings. These 'statements' in human language are the inevitable and necessary conditionings which 'limit' the range and reach of the Word of God as their universal and unique principle. Thus can be understood the 'contradictions' between the human expressions of the Word of God within and between the great religions. The 'contradictions' between the Bible and the Qur'an, between the Christian and the Muslim tradition, are not greater than those between the Old and the New Testament, between the Christian and the Jewish tradition. It is not God who contradicts himself; it is the people who speak in his name.

However, these human 'conditionings' do not entirely eclipse the light that is reflected in, and gives life to, every revelation, every religion.

In this sense one can affirm that the Qur'an in its entirety, as an indivisible whole, is the vehicle of a *Word of God* (une *Parole de Dieu*); that Muhammad has benefitted from a *prophetic charisma* (*charisme prophétique*); and that the Muslim religion, as a tradition that has issued from the Qur'an and been enriched by thirteen or fourteen centuries of life and reflection of the Muslim believers, including the mystics, enables [the believer] to *reach the one God* (*rejoindre le Dieu unique*), to imbue his/her life with Him and thus *to be way of salvation* (*d'être voie de salut*). [the emphases are Caspar's] (Caspar. 1991, p. 22)

(2) *The Word of God in Jesus Christ*

But the recognition of Islam — and of other religions — as legitimate and saving, i.e. as a vehicle of the word of God which is at the same time authentic and formally different from the Word of God in Jesus Christ, must in no way lead to a form of syncretism or 'indifferentism'. In the eyes of the Christian faith, the religions are not equivalent objectively — even if the best religion — personally and subjectively speaking — is the one that leads the human person here and now, to a genuine openness towards God and one's neighbour.

> 'I would cease to be a Christian if I did not believe that the Word in Jesus Christ is **the most profound (*la plus profonde*), the unsurpassable revelation concerning God and man that ever has been made** (author's emphasis), precisely because Jesus Christ is more for us Christians than a prophet; he is the incarnate Word of God.' (ibid., p. 23)

But if the Word of God in God is perfectly adequate and coextensive with God, its expression in the man Jesus — if one only takes his humanity seriously — cannot be coextensive with God. The man Jesus of necessity is marked by the contingencies and limitations of his humanity; he cannot exhaust the infinite riches of the Word.

> 'D'où la formule relative, "la plus profonde", car Dieu seul en Dieu est absolu. Ce qui ne doit pas ouvrir la porte au relativisme, pour lequel toutes les religions se valent, ni même à cette forme de syncrétisme qui voit dans chacune des révélations des expressions "complémentaires" de l'ineffable.' (ibid., 23)

(3) *Christ — risen for all*

Faith in Christ, who died and rose from the dead, implies that Christ, freed from the limits of time and space, regains his status as God. Coextensive with the Father and the Spirit, he is indivisibly but really present to each and every human being.

These affirmations of the Christian faith are likely to shock the non-Christian. He will view them as a last effort to qualify the faith and experience of Christianity as superior. They are however nothing but the logical and inevitable consequence of the faith in the resurrection of Jesus Christ.

In the light of his faith, the Christian, not least the Christian missionary, will nourish his faith and his respectful encounter with the believers of another religion, by 'seeing' Christ, the Risen Lord, living in each of them.

(4) *The Church — sacrament of salvation*

The Church does **not 'cover' the universality** of the presence of Christ, the Risen Lord, nor the Kingdom of God into which Christ has invited all human beings to enter. The Church is not the Kingdom of

God but rather its **sign**, its **sacrament**. Its function, its 'mission' is to render visible in the world his 'face' and the way towards the Kingdom as shown to us by the teaching of Jesus and especially by his life and death.

Every human being is called to enter the Kingdom of God, but not every human being is called **here and now** to enter the Church. One becomes a member of the Church of Jesus Christ not in order to find salvation — it can be found outside the Church — but rather in order to live in that relationship to the Kingdom which has been revealed by Jesus Christ: to go towards the Father through the Son and in the Spirit, to find in the life of the Church the community of faith of those who believe in Jesus Christ as the full and final revelation of God and in order to be nourished here and now by his teaching and his sacraments and, finally and essentially, in order to become oneself a witness of the evangelical way towards the Kingdom among one's Christian and non-Christian brothers and sisters.

The essential function of the Church is **mission**. Its basic preoccupation: **how to witness to the Kingdom in the way of Jesus Christ and his Gospel**. The form of this witness will vary according to the variety of concrete situations.

'Au-delà du dialogue, il s'agit de rencontrer aussi profondément que possible le non-chrétien, pour s'édifier mutuellement et chercher ensemble, dans la lumière de l'Esprit, la volonté de Dieu sur chacun de nous pour, avec le secours divin, se soumettre à cette volonté. C'est le sens coranique du mot *islam*.' (ibid., p. 25)

4.6 Hans Küng (1928-); Adolfo González Montes (1946-); Hans Zirker (1935-).

The views of these three scholars are presented together since their authors are Catholic professors of theology based in Europe. The Swiss Catholic **Hans Küng** (1928), professor emeritus of ecumenical theology and former director of the Institute of Ecumenical Research at the University of Tübingen, can be considered to be the first systematic theologian to have entered into a doctrinal dialogue with Islam at the university level. He has done so in the context of the larger project: 'Christianity and the World Religions'. This was also the title of the transcript of an actual dialogue that took place in the summer semester of 1982 at the University of Tübingen in the framework of its General Studies program. Küng organized a cycle of lectures and discussions together with three specialized academic representatives of Islamic,

Hindu and Buddhist studies and responded to the presentation of each of the four religions. (see: Küng. 1984; here: engl. trl. 1986)

Küng conceives of dialogue in the context of the 'wider ecumenism' which, to his mind, has become inevitable in an age of '*awakening of global ecumenical consciousness*' (ibid., p. xv) when the cultures and religions, conscious of their responsibility for promoting global peace, have to move to coexistence in community, if not to '*pro-existence*'. In this perspective Küng tries to make out what in Islamic faith is conducive to reaching this goal and hence positive, and what not.

The critical dialogue with Islam, like that with the other religions, forms an essential element of 'wider ecumenism'. It is methodologically conceived upon the pattern of intra-Christian ecumenism:

> 'Ecumenism should not be limited to the *community of the Christian churches*; it must include the *community of the great religions*, if ecumenism — in accordance with the original meaning of *oikumene* — is to refer to the whole "inhabited world."' (ibid.)

In his "Christian Responses" Küng wants to provide two things: (1.) Christian self-criticism in the light of the other religions; (2.) Christian criticism of the other religions in the light of the Gospel, which will naturally mean comparing like with like, not one random item with another. (ibid., pp. xviii-xix) The project will hopefully lead towards '*mutual critical enlightenment, stimulation, penetration, and enrichment* of the various religious traditions.'(ibid. p. xx)

A basically new outlook, along the lines of Vatican II, is needed. In theological terms this implies first of all to accept, in contrast to a secular teaching tradition to the contrary, that 'Islam, too, can be a way of salvation' (ibid., p. 24), a statement that for Küng clearly follows from *Lumen Gentium*, n° 16.

Furthermore, if the Church is sincere in its 'respect for the Muslim', unambiguously stated in *Nostra Aetate*, n° 3 [text cited above under 2.1.], then, for Küng

> 'that same Church — and in fact all the Churches — must also "look with great respect" upon the man whose name is omitted from the declaration out of embarassment, although he alone led the Muslims to the worship of the one God, who spoke *through* him: Muhammad the Prophet.' (ibid., p. 27)

Since for Küng *Nostra Aetate* implies the attribution of the title of prophet to Muhammad, it also implies the recognition of 'his message' as God's word:

> '...if we recognize Muhammad as a post-Christian prophet, then to be consistent we shall have to admit the point most important to Muslims: That

Muhammad didn't simply get his message from himself, that his message
is not simply Muhammad's word, but *God's word*.' (ibid., p. 31)

However, '*God's word*', and hence, revelation, in which sense? In the
sense that the text of the Qur'an would 'contain God's *ipsissima verba*',
that it would 'be a miraculous, absolutely perfect, holy book which must
be accepted down to the last letter'? (ibid., p. 31) 'That as every one
knows,' Küng replies, 'is how many Christian fundamentalists have
interpreted and still do interpret the *verbal inspiration of the Bible*.'
(ibid., p. 31) And assuming at this point a rather magisterial tone, basing
himself on a relatively small and marginal number of more or less contemporary, unrepresentative Muslim scholars, he demands: 'the *divine
word of the Qur'an* must be understood at the same time, from the standpoint of a reflective, educated Muslim, as the *human word of the
Prophet*.' (ibid., p. 35) Realizing the temerity of his demand, Küng had
stated a little earlier on:

> 'If Christians do not dispute the *transcendent religious character* of the
> Qur'an, yet "we may be allowed to pose the question of its *historically
> contingent qualities*, despite the fact that traditional Muslims feel threat-
> ened by this problem as traditional Christians feel threatened by parallel
> issues concerning the Bible.' (ibid., p. 32)

Proceeding, possibly too easily, by what we might call 'ecumenical
parallelisms' Küng asks: 'historical criticism of the Bible... has fa-
voured contemporary biblical faith..., why not also have historical *criticism of the Qur'an* (which would benefit a Muslim faith suited to our
times)'? (ibid., p. 35) Citing in his support a small number of Muslim
scholars who would belong to the category of 'reflective, educated Muslim', Küng, 'along with the majority of Christian exegetes' postulates
that

> 'the alternative, a) either purely God's word and therefore binding revela-
> tion or b) purely man's word and therefore non-binding human experience,
> is outdated. For the Qur'an, as for the Bible, *God's word* can be heard only
> in *human words*; divine revelation is imparted only through human experi-
> ence and interpretation.'(67f.)

Küng further shows himself convinced that an understanding of revelation as word for word dictated by God to the Prophet, a literalist understanding of revelation (which implies 'the fundamentalist approach to
scriptural law' (ibid., p. 62)), inevitably leads either to reislamization,
i.e. to legalism and politicization of Islam or, alternatively, to areligious
secularization. He suggests that as for Christianity so for Islam the con-

scious shift to 'a truly contemporary ecumenical paradigm' (ibid., p. 69) is a must. He is convinced that a basic theological solution to the dilemma: either politicized Islam or areligious secularization, can only be found by a truly historical understanding of the Qur'an with all its implications and consequences. The normal, and to this day normative, Muslim understanding of Qur'anic revelation Küng theologically simply disregards and qualifies as illegitimate and unrealistic in the context of today's world. His study and evaluation of Islam's teaching on the place of woman confirms him in this judgement.

Küng underlines emphatically that the two faiths share important features of the belief in the one God (one and only God; God of history; God, a partner the believer can speak to; gracious and merciful God) and thus, together with Judaism 'are the joint representatives before the world of faith in the one God; they share in a single grand world movement of monotheism'. (ibid., p. 87) Furthermore, they are also close in their theological teaching on predestination and immortality. What then divides the two faiths theologically?

Küng discerns the crux of the issue between the two faiths in the question of the 'radicality of love':

> 'The really challenging feature of love in Jesus' sense, as compared with Muhammad's, emerges only when that love, which aims to preserve everything human, is seen in all its radicalness.'(ibid., p. 92)

Jesus' love is radical, and uniquely radical because of (1) the *unbounded readiness to forgive*; (2) his 'crucial appeal for service'; and (3) his 'voluntary *renunciation without getting anything in return*' (cf. ibid., pp. 92f.)

In contrast, for Küng, stands Muhammad's way of linking faith and violence and his earthly success as prophet, general and statesman. In other words, with Muhammad,

> 'a theology of triumph was present from the very start, since God will not only liberate his chosen ones from all dishonour, but he has in fact already liberated them in the figure of Muhammad, the successful prophet, general and statesman (indeed, according to the Qur'an and against all historical evidence, God did not, in the end, let Jesus die on the cross).' (ibid., p. 94)

For Küng, it is beyond question that 'Islam faces a challenge raised by the man from Nazareth with regard to violence and nonviolence, hatred and love of one's enemies, success and failure.' (ibid., p. 111)

However, the crucial theological difficulty for Muslim-Christian understanding really is this: 'In the face of the coming Kingdom of God, how to overcome legalism by fulfilling God's will in love?' (ibid.,

p. 112) Jesus' claim went as a matter of fact beyond that of a prophet in that he assumed God's authority (especially with respect to the Law and the forgiveness of sins). Hence he is given the title Son, yet

> 'not [in the sense of] a physical divine sonship, as Islam always assumed and rightly rejected (because it awakened associations of intercourse between a god and a mortal woman), but [in the sense of] God's *choosing Jesus and granting him full authority*' (ibid., p. 118)

And Küng significantly adds that 'the primitive Christian community, made up entirely of Jews, would have no difficulty holding this view. Nor would Islam.'(ibid.)

But what is it then in the end that marks off Christians from Muslims? 'It is this trusting commitment to *Jesus* as the ultimate standard of the Christian concept of God and man. The part that the Qur'an plays for Muslims is played for Christians not by the Bible, but by Christ — God's word made manifest in human form.' (ibid.)

On the basis of his 'pre-chalcedonian' Christology, that is, his passionately-held conviction that the Council of Chalcedon (451 CE) by expressing the christological dogma in Hellenistic categories departed from the christology of the New Testament writers, and relying heavily on the far from prover hypotheses stated in Claus Schedl's (cf. Schedl. 1978) analysis of the christological texts of the Qur'an to the effect that Muhammad adopted "an early-Christian model" of a "Servant-of-God Christology" (ibid., p. 125), Küng comes to surmise that 'Muhammad's "Christology" may not have been all that different from the Christology of the Jewish Christian church.' (ibid.) Hence he thinks that — supposing the exegetical findings [especially those of Claus Schedl] are correct and can be further clarified — 'both sides' will be challenged

> 'to move beyond the old alternative, Jesus *or* Muhammad, and — assuming all the necessary distinctions and limitations — to think more forcefully of a synthesis between Jesus *and* Muhammad. 'The point here is that Muhammad himself can to a certain extent be viewed as a witness for Jesus — a Jesus who could have been understood not by Hellenistic Gentile Christians, but by Jesus' first disciples, who were Jews...' (ibid., p. 126)

Hence, for Küng 'Christianity and Islam cannot be set off against each other as totally separate religions. Rather, they are — like Judaism and Christianity —interwoven religious movements.' (ibid., p. 128)

Küng, quoting the Qur'anic phrase referring to Muhammad "I am only a 'clear warner'" (sura 46:9) wishes Muhammad to function for Christianity as a *'prophetic corrective'* admonishing Christians continuously that 'the one incomparable God has to stand in the absolute centre of faith; That associating with him any other gods or goddesses is out of the question; That faith and life, orthodoxy and orthopraxy, belong together everywhere, including politics.' (ibid., p. 129)

All this, however, does not gainsay the fact that 'in both Christianity and Islam we are dealing with a *faith decision* for which one must render a reasonable account to oneself and to others.' ibid.)

The Spanish theologian and ecumenist **Adolfo González Montes** (1946-) in an incisive essay published recently, in hardly veiled forms critiques Küng's central point. González Montes fully agrees with Küng's view of Islam being a 'prophetic corrective' for Christianity:

'...Islamic monotheism challenges Christianity by arousing in Christian sensibilities the same repugnance at a confusion between God and the world that could lead to replacing God by human beings and their own works and constructs' and it can help '...highlighting more starkly the limitations of a theology of the Trinity that assimilates the cross of Christ to the historical pain of the world, since the identification of God with the world cannot affect God's transcendence over the world.' (González Montes, 1994, p. 71)

In other words: Islam helps to spot the temptation of Christianity 'to a sort of theopathy incompatible with divine transcendence' — a theological idea 'which is not the same as eliminating from God the dynamism of the intra-Trinitarian love that goes out beyond itself and manifests itself in the love story of the "Son of God"'. (ibid.)

González Montes cautions: 'Attempts to formulate christology in language closer to Islamic thought cannot mean the abandonment of the Christian dogma of the Trinity, which is an example within the Godhead of a dialogue-based understanding of human existence free from all totalitarianism.' (ibid., p. 74)

At the same time González Montes detects in the Christian 'concern to put the necessary stress on the "difference" between the Father and the Son... **the risk of tipping Christian christology towards modern forms of adoptionism based on Islamic christology, supported by the rationalism of contemporary thought.**' (ibid., p. 72; emphasis mine)

Furthermore, he touches upon an, admittedly moot yet certainly relevant, point that is totally absent from Küng's discourse. In his view

'behind Islamic opposition to Christian christology is the desire to defend a totally comprehensive monotheism, which is theological, not cultural, in nature **but which also has clear political implications, which inspire some of the current forms of Islamic fundamentalism...** Being theological, Islam's "political principle" finds its best explication in opposition to Christian christology. Islam seeks the definitive overthrow of Christianity as an economy of revelation by incorporating Jesus into the history of prophetic revelation, because what Islam knows about Jesus is not in fact christology but theology. Jesus is the word of God (*kalimat Allâh*), and was given the Spirit, not to be a manifestation of God and his mystery, but to be at his service and declare his unalterable will, the object of which is the total submission of human beings to the divine will, the object of the prophecy that culminates in the Qur'an.' (ibid., p. 72-73, emphasis mine)

Although it is true that Christianity in the course of its history had this tendency,

'but the "evangelical principle" of Christianity has prevented it from being transposed into politics as a religious system...in Christianity it is precisely the theology of the incarnation and paschal mystery of Christ, because it is based on the divine state of the one who "abases" himself and takes on the human state (Phil. 2), that makes it possible to distinguish between the reign of God — which is hidden, and does not allow us to know, except by faith, where God's victory has been won — and the reign of this world, and also between the church and secular political organization.' (ibid., p. 72, 73)

Although it can be said that the universalism of Islam mirrors that of Christianity and therefore is in direct conflict with it, the essential difference consists in that Islamic theology localizes the victory of God in Islam's successful endeavour 'to unite all peoples under the sovereignty of Allah' whereas in consequence of the Christian teaching of God's *kenosis,* in Christian theology the reign of God, i.e. 'God's victory', and 'the reign of this world' are distinct.

Hence González Montes holds it to be an unfounded belief that 'Islam was reacting to a mistaken interpretation of Christian christology':

'Although in its beginnings the rejection of the divine Trinity was based on wrong information about it...Islam is nonetheless very clear that its own goal is to relativize Christian christology. Islamic monotheism regards divine sovereignty as safeguarded only by the ultimacy of Muhammad's mission, the seal of prophecy. This implies the incorporation of Christ into prophecy, and the removal of his divinity, with the consequent neutralization of the theological principle of Christian christology.' (ibid., p. 73)

Thus, for González Montes the issue Christian faith raises in its teaching on Incarnation and Trinity 'remains in its core and intention irreducible to the Islamic view'. (ibid.) The Church 'by using the resources of Hellenistic philosophy', did not alter the christological belief of its origins but rather preserved it. And, González Montes reminds us: these formulations in the garb of Hellenistic philosophy were 'perfectly comprehensible to the Islamic scholastic tradition.' (ibid., p. 74)

The German philosopher and theologian **Hans Zirker**'s (1935-) concern with Islam originated in the context of training teachers of ethics and religion in Germany in order to enable them to deal creatively with the new pluralist situation at schools and colleges there.

Zirker's chief concern in all his writing on Islam and on Christian-Muslim relations is to contribute to the development of a convincing hermeneutic of the Christian faith in a religiously plural world. He is convinced that the relationship between Christianity and Islam in the contemporary world can be adequately understood only as part of a trilateral relationship: any pertinent analysis will have **to take into account the secular and plural nature of the society where these two religions meet**.

Islam presents a special challenge to Christianity and hence to Christian theology in that it is a post-Christian religion of world-wide dimensions. Both Islam and Christianity claim to proclaim in faith the final, unsurpassable historical form of the relationship between God and the human person, and yet both also have experienced their — apparently unsurmountable — inability to gain the aimed-at universal allegiance of all humanity. Hence, none of the two religions can ascertain and communicate (*ermitteln und vermitteln*) its faith position adequately without taking on board from the beginning the challenges and claims of the other, the rival position. Dialogue has to be viewed as a primary task: to make explicit the meaning and credibility of one's own convictions — rather than only as a secondary task which follows from the need to relate, and to give an account, to the world outside.

Zirker views Islam, and wants it to be viewed thus by Catholics, as a respected, equal partner with whom — in the context of plural, 'secular' society — to develop shared normative standards in order to gain a basis of communication and action that transcends the limited area marked by the faith of just one particular religion.

Zirker stresses that the specific claims to truth on the part of either Christianity or Islam stand within the experiment of their history and thus are part of an ongoing 'experiment'. Religions are *Lerngemeinschaften*, cultures in the experiment of human history. If Christians wish to do justice to Islam within their theology, then it does not suffice to bracket Islam with all other religions and simply to enumerate, in the spirit of the Second Vatican Council, those elements that Islam has in common with the biblical tradition.

> 'Rather, one will have to reflect, above all, on whether and how the claim of the Christian faith to finality can be maintained together with the fact of the ongoing history of religions, in such a way that the latter does not have

to be simply qualified as illegitimate... Hence the Christian debate with
Islam demands above all a dealing with and response to (*Verarbeitung*) the
ongoing history of religion and also of the Church.' (Zirker, 1993, p. 27)

Thus Zirker wants Christian thought to take seriously into account
that 'Islam belongs to the history of Christianity; in spite of being for
Christanity "another religion", it is at the same time also an element of
Christianity's identity.'(ibid., p. 36) He pleads with his fellow theologians to understand Islam as a serious challenge, that the critical assessment of the history of dogma will have to deal with — as, analogously
speaking, it had to deal with the criticism of the Protestant reformation
and was modified in the process.

In all his writing on Islam, Zirker forcefully and convincingly has presented Islam as an important, theologically highly challenging, religious
factor in the plural contemporary world. (cf. ibid., p. 58)

4.7 Henri Sanson (1917-)

We conclude our survey with the views of the French-Algerian Jesuit
Henri Sanson, a noted sociologist, philosopher and spiritual director. In
a recent work, *Dialogue intérieur avec l'islam* (Sanson, 1990, taken up
succinctly in Sanson. 1995), he presents his spiritual-theological view of
Islam. He approaches Islam primarily not as a professional theologian
but as a spiritual guide. As such he has engaged over the years in an
interior dialogue with Islam or, more precisely, 'a Christian meditation
in Islam'. He describes the way he integrates 'Islam, as Presence, at the
very heart of the reflection the Christian makes about his own existence'
(ibid., p. 5), in his own case, an existence lived inside Algerian society
as it is shaped by the vision and way of life of Islam. Sanson's spiritual
approach would seem to command attention since it is both a result of,
and an inspiration for, present-day Catholic theological thought on Islam
and lived Christian-Muslim relations.

Sanson proceeds by three steps. After stating (1) what he means by
Islam, he tells us (2) how he sees God in Islam and Islam in God and,
finally, he asks himself (3) what it is that he 'sees' when he says that he
sees Islam through God and God through Islam.

In the first place Sanson is concerned to ascertain the value of Islam
as religion, as a system in which he and other Catholics live (for instance
in Algeria) and which, to some extent, lives in them. This system can be
defined as being 'structured in reference to a transcendent God; to a
Book of God; to a Messenger of God; to a Law of God; to a polity or

community of Muslims.' (ibid., p. 41) Sanson proposes to assess the value of Islam not by 'integrating' it into Christianity but rather by 'interiorizing' it. 'Integrating' would proceed by classifying people, taking account of their proximity to, or distance from the truths affirmed in the Islamic faith. 'Interiorizing' instead proceeds by considering people in themselves, not primarily with regard to the truths they affirm but rather considering their interior dispositions.

In this perspective, Sanson affirms the saving value of Islam 'for all the Muslims of good faith, of good will who seek God with the best of conscience and with freedom.' And he adds:

> 'The reflection about Islam as way of salvation has thrown me back unto myself, to discerning my own interior dispositions concerning the Christian ways of salvation, to my own *dépassements* (surpassings): "If your justice does not surpass that of the scribes and Pharisees…" (Mt 5:20)' (ibid., p. 45)

Sanson endeavours to see and become conscious of what he sees. Hence he asks: 'When I, within the Church which is in Algeria, see — try to see — Islam in God and God in Islam, what do I see?'

> 'I let Islam live before and in me as an entity which has an existence and a history, which is a culture and a civilization, which refers to a religious ideology and first of all: to the Qur'an and its God. I apprehend it as a reality in which I live and which lives in me: I am inside it as someone from outside… Islam lives in my meditation as a particular collective being within the universe and humankind… And whilst I meditate, I ask myself about what, of this Islam, I see in Christ and what, of Christ, I see in this Islam.' (ibid., p. 143)

Sanson insists that he is talking not about seeing 'by a practical, doctrinal or relational look (*regard pratique*)' but rather about seeing 'by a look of faith (*regard de foi*)'…'Je fais de l'Islam une lecture christique.' (ibid., p. 146f.)

In this way **Sanson sees 'of Islam in Christ'**

(a) **the Absolute of God**: although there exists a difference in Christian and Muslim teaching about God, one finds, at bottom, in both cases the same absolute reference to God as ultimate instance of all, including the political. (cf. ibid., p. 145)

(b) **the humility of the human person before the greatness of God**: Beyond all the differences that exist in the way humility, adoration and obedience are realized in the Christian and in the Islamic traditions, '…dans l'humilité en islam, j'entrevois, sinon la totalité, du moins, un aspect essentiel de l'humilité chrétienne.' (ibid., p. 145)

(c) **the nearness of God to the human person, and especially to his faithful: one of the key ideas of Islam**. This nearness is not the same as immanence. This 'transcendent nearness of God', however, 'even if it is perceived as outward (*extérieur*), is lived as an all-powerful presence', a presence 'that is lived also as a mercy and a tenderness...the most patent sign (*âyah*) of which is the Qur'an.' (ibid., p. 146)

Since the Spirit is active in everything and in everybody, how does the Christian see the Spirit guide Islam's and the Muslims' action (*faire agir*), and, correlatively, how does he see Islam and Muslims working for God — always, of course, taking into account the Muslims' freedom?

> 'It is no doubt easier to discern the action of God in persons than in doctrines... One must however affirm: God works in Islam and not only in Muslims: it is up to us to "see" how! Furthermore, one has to affirm, there happen things in Islam and not only in Muslims, which are of God (il se passent des choses dans l'islam, et non seulement dans les musulmans, qui sont de Dieu): it is up to us [the Christians] to try to discern them!' (ibid., p. 187) 'Christians and their Christianity and Muslims and their Islam are, both of them, called to salvation and fulfilment.'(ibid., 187)

In summary: Sanson (a) shares profoundly the witness of Islam: There is no God but God. It conforms to the dynamism of the Spirit which has no limit but the Absolute itself. He even can write: 'I love Islam when it proclaims that there is no authentic adoration but that of God and of God alone.' (ibid., p. 188)

Sanson also (b) experiences as profoundly spiritual the aspiration of Islam to unity — not only by its constant proclamation of the unity of God but also by its incessant effort to give effective expression to the unity of all humans within the *umma* of God. He looks at this will to unity in the light of the will of the Hebrews of the Old Testament to be one people, assembled under the guidance of God.

Sanson (c) admires the greatness of Islam in that it radically affirms the necessity to be obedient to God. Whereas he does not overlook the fact that there exist 'essential differences [between Christianity and Islam] with regard to the way in which the will of God that has to be obeyed is conceived', he holds it to remain true that Islam is a religion 'of the 'surpassing (*dépassement*) of egocentrism and of the egoisms that generally accompany the latter.' (ibid., p. 189) This 'surpassing' is the fruit of the Spirit alive in Islam.

Sanson (d) appreciates the prayer of Islam, including its ritual prayer. Muslim prayer — in certain ways distinctly different from Christian prayer — is primarily prayer of total submission.

Sanson equally (e) appreciates in Islam the consciousness of the presence of God: 'The Muslim lives, awaiting the Last Judgement, in the awareness of God's incessant *regard*. Islam is a religion of the presence of God to the human person.'

> 'Without being a Muslim I understand that because of (*grace à*) Islam human persons can live spiritually, since they live in reference to the Absolute, with the passion of unity, in submission to God, handing themselves over to God totally, under the constant glance (*regard*) of God. There they find points of support which inform their profound aspirations opening up paths to their interior (movement/progress) search (*cheminements*). Islam also has saints.' (ibid., p. 190)

Sanson considers the fresh efforts in contemporary Islam towards reviving the theological and juridical sciences proof of the vitality of the Spirit alive in Muslim society. Naturally these efforts move within the field of forces defined by the attraction/repulsion of radical Islam and secularism (*laïcité*). The Spirit incessantly likes to renew and revive what has grown old.

Correlatively, Islam is making a contribution to the faith in God in our world at large. Islam joins Christianity and Judaism in announcing to the world that God has testified to Himself in our world and history. Furthermore, Islam contributes by the radicalness of its practice of faith stressing integral, unconditional and total obedience. Admittedly, some Islamic movements succumb to the danger of fanaticism, providentialism (*providencialisme*) and predestinationalism (*prédestinationisme*). However, as far as Sanson is concerned, 'this does not gainsay the fact that in all this a magnificent witness is given to the unequalled sovereignty of God... a little too much, it is true, to the detriment of the human freedoms which are also inalienable.' (ibid., p. 192)

Henri Sanson believes that Islam in our day is engaged in an effort of religious thought that will enable it eventually to offer to the world a message which is both true to Islam's origins and renewed in its formulations and interpretations. 'Jésus a donné au judaisme de pouvoir se dépasser: pourquoi l'islam ne se dépasserait-il pas soi-même pour s'adapter et s'accomplir?' (ibid., p. 192)

5. Conclusion

In this essay we deliberately have adopted a roughly chronological and genetic approach. We have emphasized the views of a selected number of individuals, highlighting the development of their outlook on Islam. A good number of other, important individual voices had to be omitted in the present context (e.g. Miguel Asín Palacios, Georges Anawati OP, Louis Gardet, Roger Arnaldez, Adel-Théodore Khoury (1930-), Henri Teissier (1929-)

However, an account of **Catholic** views must not fail to take into account the central place the teaching office (*magisterium*) holds in Catholic faith and the crucial role it plays in the development of any Catholic outlook and theology worth the name. The views of Catholics, as we were able to witness in the present essay, contribute to and shape the evolving teachings of the *magisterium*. At the same time the official and semi-official statements of the *magisterium* guide and challenge the Catholic believers, individually and corporately.

Furthermore, the development of Catholic theological views of Islam is the fruit of the continuous interaction between, on the one hand, apostolic-missionary action and, on the other, vision of faith and theological reflection. And these in turn are influenced by increasing intra-Christian ecumenical dovetailing, and even interpenetration, in action and thought, as well as by the way the Muslim community develops and/or is perceived to develop at a given place and period of time.

The experience of a missionary presence in societies where conversion in the sense of change of institutional allegiance from Islam to Christianity is virtually excluded and where the public airing of Christian ideas by Christian believers is more than restricted, as for instance in the Maghreb, has palpably contributed to the evolution of a new conception of missionary work: missionary presence conceived on the pattern of Nazareth, a presence in contemplation and service abstaining from public proclamation of Christ and invitation to Church membership, and a presence by way of attentive listening and systematic efforts to understand the lived and the proclaimed reality of Islam, in dialogue with Muslims. Some Catholic missionaries have perceived their presence among Muslims in terms of a catalytic function rather than in terms of direct agency.

The life of the Church and its missionary reflection have been affected by the accelerating, substantially changing world political context: fifty years ago the 'classical' colonial order began to approach its demise. Since then there have emerged in the Muslim world countless independent nations and also new forms of Muslim international organization. Today we can speak of a renewed *umma*-consciousness among Muslims, linked with the growth of effective, modern structures of cohesion and growth enabling the Muslim community increasingly to play a decisive role in global affairs. Organizations like the Muslim World

League (*Rabitat al-'Alam al-Islami*) and the Organization of the Islamic Conference (OIC) make Islam a global competitor as well as potential partner of the Catholic Church.

The rapid revolution in the area of communication on various levels has led to the shrinking of distances and the globalization of consciousness. The question of worldwide coexistence in justice and peace between nations of different cultures and religions, nations that in themselves are being marked increasingly by culturally and religiously plural life, has become an overriding concern of the Catholic Church. Hence it has begun, officially with Vatican II, to see Islam as a major religious partner in this global constellation.

Although cases of conversion of individuals from Catholicism to Islam but also vice versa are more frequent than is generally known, it has become quite clear by now that Islam is not likely to absorb Christianity or vice versa. Hence the Catholic Church is more and more conscious of its religious responsibility, as part of its universal mission, to find ways of contributing effectively to global coexistence, if not proexistence, in justice and peace[15].

The pre-Vatican II views of Islam had in common that they perceived the study of the culture and religion of Islam basically as an obligatory and essential strategic part of the missionary apostolate. They believed Christianity to be the only divine religion, rightfully claiming to be supernaturally revealed, whereas they considered Islam a merely natural religion, having arisen 'from below'.

Hence, we find the consciousness that Catholics could learn from and be inspired by Islam at that period only among pioneers like Asín Palacios, Massignon and Abd-el-Jalil. Up to Vatican II Islam was seen primarily as a competitor in the effort to gain converts and to strengthen its influence among the populations in Africa and in parts of Asia. It was considered more a hindrance or threat to missionary expansion than a theological challenge and a source of spiritual enrichment. The pre-Vatican II views of Islam betray a certain embarrassment in that, whereas they cannot but concede to Islam certain moral and spiritual values, they are convinced that acknowledging Islam, even only as 'a genuine religion', would amount to a betrayal of the Catholic faith.

---

[15] In this context see the recent document: 'Christian/Muslim Reciprocity: Considerations for the European Churches' published by the Comité <Islam in Europe> of the Council of European Bishops' Conferences (CCEE) and the Conference of European Churches (KEK). (Geneva October 1994 and March 1995).

Right into the middle of this century there existed a palpable lack of a Catholic theology of religions that would realistically and honestly account for the values of Muslim life and hence of Islam. The latter was experienced more and more in situations of shared life and work together in co-citizenship. Also, Islam and the Muslims' life and thought became better known through the modern sciences of religion and education in general.

Vatican II — we have shown how much the ground for its teaching on Islam and on the other religions at large had been prepared by a number of pioneers — emerges as an event of crucial importance for the more recent Catholic approaches to Islam, marking irreversibly what has been termed the Copernican revolution in Christian-Muslim relations.

Although the texts directly dealing with Islam do not explicitly make new theological statements, they flow directly from the new theological vision of the Church. The statement of *Lumen Gentium* n°16 to the effect that Christians and Muslims submit to the same unique, personal Creator God, constitutes a link of 'fraternity' on which is based a comparable vision of the human person. The passage of the encyclical by John Paul II in *Redemptor Hominis* (n° 8-10) — much in line with Vatican II teaching — that the Holy Spirit is operative in the lives of non-Christians, not in spite of their religious adherence but rather as its essence and foundation — provided the theological foundation, for instance, to the historical address to the Christian community of Ankara during the following year where John Paul II views the Muslim faith — which is unconditional submission, on the model of Abraham, to the Will of God — as a basic 'meeting place' between Christians and Muslims.

In other words, Christians and Muslims are seen as being called to live together in a modern plural setting that guarantees freedom of worship and of education. They are called to spiritual emulation in the work for reconciliation and for the service of the disadvantaged. By implication it is claimed that such efforts at collaboration will strengthen rather then weaken each one's identity.

G. Anawati's critical remark shortly after the closure of the Council concerning its silence regarding the figure of Abraham and regarding the second part of the Muslim profession of faith (*shahâda*) — the belief in the mission of Muhammad — was perspicacious and prophetic. Practically all serious Catholic theological reflection has centred on aspects of Islam related to the prophethood of Muhammad and the revelatory character of the Qur'an.

The primary concern of the earlier Moubarac to establish 'Qur'anic Abrahamism' as a primordial attitude in the Qur'an had to do with his conviction that it was possible and desirable, on the theological as well as the practical level, to work out a special 'ecumenical' relationship between the three Abrahamic religions. The later Moubarac, taking up one of Massignon's intuitions, veered away from putting too much emphasis on the special relationship of the three religions. This excessive theological emphasis on the special relationship was, Moubarac suggested, based on a kind of unwarranted 'prerogativism' between Christians and Muslims. In his latest writings Moubarac moved decidedly away from this emphasis towards a truly Christian universalism lived out in selfless service and in substitution for all men and women called to be saved as brothers and sisters of Jesus Christ.

Basetti Sani's 'new vision of Islam' entails his accepting the Qur'an hypothetically as the true Word of God, as the foundation of a para-Biblical revelation vouchsafed in order to prepare some peoples for the announcement of the Gospels. He approaches the Qur'an in ways somewhat similar to the way the Church Fathers approached the scriptures of the Jewish Bible. The Qur'an, if and in so far as it is read in the light of the fullness of the Christian faith, turns out to be totally oriented towards Christ. Muhammad, as the bearer of a partial revelation, has initiated a substantial portion of humanity into the mystery of God as a genuine preparation for the fullness of revelation which exists in the truth of Christianity. However it would seem that neither Catholic nor, obviously, Muslim faith and theology, will recognize themselves in Basetti-Sani's generous but ultimately, theologically, restrictive approach.

It is my guess that from among the non-official, individual Catholic views of Islam those of Jacques Jomier would meet with broad assent among educated Catholics. Jomier combines a long experience of a life immersed in the Christian and Muslim milieu of Cairo with a profound knowledge of the traditions of Catholic as well as Islamic religious thought and practice. When he conceives of Muhammad on the pattern of a reformist leader and underlines the ongoing critical role of Islam vis-à-vis Christianity he is not just warming up the old idea of Islam as a heresy, already found e.g. in the writings of John of Damascus (c. 675 — c.749) (cf. Caspar. 1987, pp. 97f.). He rather views Islam as a clearly distinct and original religion that is convinced to have received from God via Muhammad a universal mission, including the claim to supersede the communities of the Jewish and Christian faith; a religion, furthermore, that was born on the margins of the world shaped for centuries by elements of the Biblical tradition and that bears clear marks to this effect.

This religion and its founder, Jomier surmises, whilst it remains true that it rejects essential elements of the Christian message, yet it may still have, right from its beginning, in accordance with God's will, a purifying and reforming function vis-à-vis the Christian Church.

Robert Caspar views the Qur'an as the vehicle of a Word of God, believes Muhammad to have benefitted from a prophetic charisma and the Muslim religion to be a way of salvation. These affirmations for him are not contradicted by his simultaneous affirmation that Jesus Christ is the most profound, the unsurpassable revelation concerning God and man that ever has been made. Missionary witness for Caspar, in the light of his theology of religions, is the effort to encounter the Muslim believer as profoundly as possible for mutual edification and in order to search together, in the light of the Spirit, the will of God for each one of us.

Within the setting of contemporary academic theology in Germany, Hans Küng has been the first to move decidedly from intra-Christian ecumenism to inter-religious ecumenism and to discuss in this context key theological issues between Christianity and Islam. Although Küng acknowledges in this context the importance of Vatican II and does in no way deny his moorings in the Catholic tradition of spirituality and religious thought, he would seem in at least some of his basic Christian positions to have left the specific, in his view outdated (i.e. belonging to a past paradigm) Catholic frame of reference, with its characteristic submission to the ongoing dogmatic and moral guidance of the apostolic teaching office (*magisterium*) in Roman Catholic understanding. Hence, one is entitled to surmise that his daring and somewhat summary statements concerning the prophethood of Muhammad and the revelatory character of the Qur'an do not represent mainstream Catholic theology.

González Montes' incisive essay on 'the challenge of Islamic monotheism' would seem to illustrate this point. He also puts clearly on the agenda the crucial question of a possible essential link between Islam's theological rejection of Christian christology and its theocratic vision and claim[16].

Hans Zirker first of all endeavours to show that Islam must be viewed as a respected, equal partner, with whom, in the context of

---

[16] On the question of the relationship between Islamic monotheism and power see the remarkable recent work by Bürgel. 1991.

plural, 'secular' society, shared normative standards will have to be developed for providing a shared basis of communication and action within wider, plural society. Whereas Küng insists in a somewhat prescriptive mood on the necessity for Islam to enter the 'ecumenical paradigm' as Küng defines it — entailing a re-reading of the Qur'an and the legal tradition — and whereas he also seems to hold possible a christological accord in the line of earliest Judeo-Christian christology, Zirker rather wants Christianity to take into account that Islam, in spite of being another religion, is also an element of Christianity's identity. In consequence, he demands, first of all, to deal with Islam as a serious challenge to traditional Catholic understanding of the history of dogma in general and to the traditional Catholic understanding of the doctrine of the finality of revelation in the person of Jesus Christ more specifically.

We have concluded our essay with Sanson's spiritual reflections on 'Islam in the mirror of Christian faith', because his writing forcefully displays the attitude of critical openness in the service of ongoing 'discernment in the Spirit', of Muslim reality. The attitude, methodology and vision displayed in his relevant writing would seem to merit wide attention as an inspiring and promising, specifically Catholic, resource on the way ahead.

SELECT BIBLIOGRAPHY

ABD-EL-JALIL, Jean-Mohammed. 1947. *L'Islam et nous*. Paris: Cerf. Enlarged and revised 1980a.

ABD-EL-JALIL, Jean-Mohammed. 1949. *Aspects intérieurs de l'Islam*. Paris: Seuil.

ABD-EL-JALIL, Jean-Mohammed. 1980a. *L'Islam et nous*. Paris: Cerf. (enlarged re-edition)

ABD-EL-JALIL, Jean-Mohammed. 1980b. 'Un Franciscain doublement fidèle: J.M. Abd-el-Jalil (1904-1979)'. (three of his articles of autobiographical character, introduced by M. Borrmans) *Se Comprendre*. 80/2 (février). 20p.

ANAWATI, Georges-C. 1964. 'Vers un dialogue Islamo-chrétien.' *Revue Thomiste*, 64, p. 280-326; 585-630.

ANAWATI, Georges-C. 1967. 'Exkurs zum Konzilstext über die Muslim.' *Lexikon für Theologie und Kirche. Das Zweite Vatikanische Konzil*. Teil II. Freiburg: Herder, p. 485-87.

ANAWATI, Georges-C. 1974. 'Foi chrétienne et foi musulmane d'aujourd'hui.' in *Cristianesimo e Islamismo. Roma, 17-18 Aprile 1972*. Roma: Accademia Nazionale dei Lincei. p. 191-210.

ANAWATI, Georges-C. 1987. 'An Assessment of the Christian-Islamic Dialogue.' Ch. II in *The Vatican, Islam and the Middle East*. ed. Kail C. Ellis.
Syracuse, New York: Syracuse University Press. p. 51-68.

ANAWATI, Georges-C. 1990. 'Promouvoir une fraternité vraie et féconde.' *La
Foi en Marche*. Les problèmes de fond du dialogue islamo-chrétien. Pre-
mier Congrès International à distance organisé par Crislam. Rome:
P.I.S.A.I.

ARNALDEZ, Roger. 1964. 'Conditions d'un dialogue avec l'islam'. *Les Missions
Catholiques*. 94-95: 19-38.

ASIN PALACIOS, Miguel. 1934-1941. *La espiritualidad de Algazel y su sentido
cristiano*, 4 vol., Madrid.

BABUT, J.-M. 1957. 'Ismael, fils d'Abraham. Essai de théologie biblique'. *Le
Monde non-chrétien*. 43-44: 274-95.

BASETTI-SANI, Giulio. 1969. *Per un dialogo cristiano-musulmano. Mohammed,
Damietta e La Verna*. Milano: Ed. Vita e Pensiero.

BASETTI-SANI, Giulio, 1972. *Il Corano Nella Luce di Cristo*. Bologna EMI.

BASETTI-SANI, Giulio. 1975a. *L'Islam e Francesco d'Assisi. La missione profe-
tica per il dialogo*. Firenze: La Nuova Italia.

BASETTI-SANI, Giulio, 1975b. *Muhammad, St. Francis of Assisi and Alverna*.
Fiesole: St. Franceso.

BASETTI-SANI, Giulio, 1977. *The Koran in the Light of Christ*. A Christian Interpretation of the Sacred Book of Islam. Chicago: Franciscan Herald Press.
(Original: *Il Corano Nella Luce di Christo*. Bologna: EMI, 1972).

BASETTI-SANI, Giulio. 1989. *Maria e Gesù figlio di Maria nel Corano*. Palermo:
Renzo e Rean Mazzone.

BASETTI-SANI, Giulio. 1992. *L'Islam nel piano della salvezza*. N.pl.: Edizioni
Cultura della Pace.

BÜRGEL, Johann Christoph. 1991. *Allmacht und Mächtigkeit: Religion und Welt
im Islam*. München: C.H.Beck.

CASPAR, Robert. 1966. 'Le Concile et l'Islam' *Etudes*, t. 324, p. 114-126.

CASPAR, Robert. 1968/1969. 'La foi musulmane selon le Coran'. *Proche-Orient
Chrétien*. t. XVIII, p. 17-28, p. 140-66; t. XIX, p. 162-93.

CASPAR, Robert. 1973. 'Abraham en Islam et en Christianisme.' *Comprendre*
(Paris) (série saumon 118).

CASPAR, Robert. 1980. 'Parole de Dieu et langage humain en Christianisme et
en Islam?' *Islamochristiana* (Rome), 6: 33-60.

CASPAR, Robert. 1985. 'La signification permanente du monothéisme de l'Islam'. *Concilium*, 197: 85-96.

CASPAR, Robert. 1987. *Traité de Théologie Musulmane*. Tome I: Histoire de la
Pensée Religieuse Musulmane. Rome: P.I.S.A.I.

CASPAR, Robert. 1989. *The Challenge of the Scriptures*. The Bible and the
Qur'an. Maryknoll: Orbis. (Translation of the French original (1987).)

CASPAR, Robert. 1990. *Pour un regard chrétien sur l'islam*. Paris: Centurion.

CASPAR, Robert. 1991. 'Une rencontre avec l'Islam. Evolution personelle et
vision actuelle.' *Spiritus*. 32 (no. 122), p. 15-25.

CASPAR, Robert & A group of Christians living in Tunisia. 1989. *Trying to
Answer Questions*. Rome: P.I.S.A.I.

CLAVERIE, Pierre. *Lettres et messages d'Algérie*. Paris: Karthala.

CLAVERIE, Pierre & LES ÉVEQUES DU MAGHREB. 1996. *Le livre de la foi*. Paris: Cerf.
CONFERENCE EPISCOPALE REGIONALE DE L'AFRIQUE DU NORD. 1979. 'Chrétiens au Maghreb — Le sens de nos rencontres.' *Documentation Catholique*. No. 1775, p. 1032-44.
CORBIN, Henri. 1959. 'De l'histoire des religions comme problème théologique'. *Le Monde non-chrétien*. 51-52: 135-51.
D'ALVERNY, André. 1956. 'Chrétiens en face de l'Islam'. *Etudes*. p. 161-75.
DE BEAURECUEIL, Serge. 1965. 'Prêtre des non-chrétiens'. *Parole et Mission*, vol. 33.
DE EPALZA, Miguel. 'Massignon et Asin Palacios, une longue amitié et deux approches différentes de l'Islam.' *Cahiers de l'Herne*, p. 157 ff.
DUPUIS, Jacques. 1989. *Jésus-Christ à la Rencontre des Religions*. Paris: Desclée.
FITZGERALD, Michael L. 1988. 'Mission and Dialogue: Reflections in the Light of Assisi 1986'. *Bulletin* (Secretariatus. Roma). XXIII/2, p. 113-20.
FITZGERALD, Michael L. 1994. 'Other Religions in the Catechism of the Catholic Church'. *Islamochristiana* 19: 29-41.
FITZMAURICE, Redmond. 1992. 'The Roman Catholic Church and Interreligious Dialogue: Implications for Christian-Muslim Relations.' *Islam and Christian-Muslim Relations*. 3: 83-107.
GARDET, Louis. 1970. *L'Islam. Religion et Communauté*. Paris: Desclée.
GASBARRI, Carlo. 1962. *Islam e cristianesimo. Lineamenti per una storia dei rapporti ideologico-umani fra i due mondi*. Milano: 'Bibbia e Oriente'.
GAUDEUL, Jean-Marie. 1991. *Appelés par le Christ ils viennent de l'Islam*. Paris: Cerf.
GEFFRÉ, Claude. 1992. 'La portée théologique du dialogue islamo-chrétien.' *Islamochristiana* 18: 1-23.
GEFFRÉ, Claude. 1983. 'Le Coran, une parole de Dieu différente.' *Lumière et Vie*. 163: 21-32.
GEFFRÉ, Claude. 1985. 'La théologie des religions non-chrétiennes vingt ans après Vatican II.' *Islamochristiana*, 11: 115-33.
GEFFRÉ, Claude. 1989. 'La foi à l'âge du pluralisme religieux.' *La Vie Spirituelle*, 143: 805-15.
GIOIA, Francesco (a cura di). 1994. *Il dialogo interreligioso nel magistero pontificio: Documenti 1963-1993*. Città del Vaticano: Libreria Editrice Vaticana.
GONZALES MONTES, Adolfo. 1994. 'The Challenge of Islamic Monotheism: A Christian View'. *Islam: A Challenge For Christianity* (*Concilium*,1994/3) ed. Hans Küng and Jürgen Moltmann.
HARPIGNY, Guy. 1975. 'Muhammad est-il Prophète?' *Revue théologique de Louvain*. 6: 311-23.
HAYEK, Michel. 1964. *Le Mystère d'Ismael*. Paris: Mame.
HOUBEN, J.J. 1953. 'The Need for Islamic Studies.' *Scientia Missionum Ancilla*.(Festschrift A.I.M. Mulders). Nijmegen: Dekker & van den Vegt.
John Paul II. 1979. *Redemptor Hominis*.
John Paul II. 1985. 'The Speech of the Holy Father John Paul II to young Muslims during his meeting with them at Casablanca (Morocco). *Islamochristiana*. 11: 201-8.

JOMIER, Jacques. 1961. 'Les idées de Hanna Zacharias'. *Études*, t. 308, p. 82-92.

JOMIER, Jacques. 1963. 'Une nouvelle vision de l'islam', *Parole et Mission*. 20: 113-27.

JOMIER, Jacques. 1971. 'The idea of the prophet in Islam'. *Bulletin* (Rome). 18:149-163.

JOMIER, Jacques. 1988. 'Le Professeur Louis Massignon (1883-1962) et le dialogue Islamo-Chrétien.' *Bulletin* (Rome). 68:161-68.

JOMIER, Jacques. 1989. *How to Understand Islam*. London: SCM. (Fr. original: *Pour connaître l'Islam*. Paris: Cerf, 1988.

JOMIER, Jacques. 1996. *Dieu et l'homme dans le Coran*: l'aspect religieux de la nature humaine joint à l'obéissance au Prophète de l'Islam. Paris: Cerf.

JOURNET, Charles. 1951. *L'Eglise du Verbe Incarné*. Vol.2. Paris: DDB.

JOURNET, Charles. 1961. 'Qui est membre de l'Eglise?' *Nova et Vetera*. p. 199-203.

KHODR, Georges. 1971. 'Christianisme dans un monde pluraliste. L'économie du Saint Esprit.' *Irenikon* (Chevetogne), 44: 191-202.

KÜNG, Hans. 1985. *Christianity and the World Religions. Paths of Dialogue with Islam, Hinduism and Buddhism*, with J. van Ess, H. von Stietencron and H. Bechert, Doubleday and Collins. Orig. *Christentum und Weltreligionen*. München: Piper, 1984.

KUSCHEL, Karl-Josef. 1995. *Abraham. A Symbol of Hope for Jews, Christians and Muslims*. London: SCM Press. (trsl. from German orig. 1994)

LEDIT, Charles. 1952. *Mahomet, Israel et le Christ*. Paris: Colombe.

LELONG, Michel. 1984. *L'Eglise nous parle de l'Islam: Du Concile à Jean-Paul II*. Paris: Chalet.

MASSIGNON, Louis. 1935. 'Les trois prières d'Abraham — Seconde prière.' Tours.

MASSIGNON, Louis. 1948. 'Le Signe Marial'. *Rhythmes du Monde*. 3: 12ff.

MASSIGNON, Louis. 1962. *Parole donnée*. Paris: Julliard.

MASSIGNON, Louis. 1963. *Opera Minora*, ed. Y. Moubarac, 3 vols., Beirut: Dar al-Maaref.

MASSIGNON, Louis. 1992. *Examen du "Present de l'Homme Lettré" par Abdallah ibn al-Torjoman*. (Suivant la traduction française parue dans la Revue de l'Histoire des Religions, 1886). Roma: P.I.S.A.I.

MICHEL, Thomas. 1985. 'Christianity and Islam. Reflections on Recent Teachings of the Church.' *Encounter* (Rome: P.I.S.A.I.) No 112.

MICHEL, Thomas. 1986. 'Pope John Paul II's Teaching about Islam in his Addresses to Muslims'. *Bulletin* (Secretariatus, Roma) XXI/2: 182-91.

MOLETTE, Charles. 1988. *'La Vérité ou je la trouve'*. Mulla: Une conscience d'homme dans la lumière de Maurice Blondel. (Préface du Card. Henri de Lubac) Paris VIe: TEQUI.

MONCHANIN, J. 1938. 'Islam et Christianisme'. *Le Bulletin des Missions*. (S. André les Bruges). Vol. XVII, p. 10-23.

MOUBARAC, Youakim. 1958. *Abraham dans le Coran*. Paris: Vrin.

MOUBARAC, Youakim. 1969. 'Fragen des Katholizismus an den Islam' in: H. Vorgrimler und R. Vander Gucht (eds.), *Bilanz der Theologie im 20. Jahrhundert*. Freiburg: Herder. Vol.1, pp. 422-456.

MOUBARAC, Youakim. 1971. *Les Musulmans. Consultation islamo-chrétienne*. Paris: Beauchesne.

MOUBARAC, Youakim. 1972-3. *Pentalogie Islamo-Chrétienne*. Tome III: L'Islam et le Dialogue Islamo-Chrétien. Beyrouth: Editions du Cenacle Libanais.

MOUBARAC, Youakim. 1976. 'La pensée chrétienne et l'Islam: principales acquisitions et problématique nouvelle.' *Concilium*. 116: 39-36.

MOUBARAC, Youakim. 1977. *Recherches sur la pensée chrétienne et l'Islam dans les temps modernes et à l'époque contemporaine*. [Publications de l'Université Libanaise, section des études historiques XXII]. Beyrouth.

OHM, Thomas. 1961. *Mohammedaner und Katholiken*. München: Kösel.

PATRIARCHES CATHOLIQUES D'ORIENT. 1992. 'La présence chrétienne en Orient: témoignage et mission.' *La Documentation Catholique*. No. 2052, p. 595-611.

PATRIARCHES CATHOLIQUES D'ORIENT. 1994. 'Ensemble devant Dieu: pour le bien de la personne et de la société' (La coexistence entre musulmans et chrétiens dans le monde arabe). *Documentation Catholique*. No 2113, p. 320-36.

PEYRIGUERE, A. 1960. 'Testament spirituel'. publ. par Y. Moubarac. *Mardis de Dar el-Salam*. Cahier Foucauld-Peyriguère. Le Caire — Paris.

PONTIFICAL COUNCIL FOR INTERRELIGIOUS DIALOGUE. 1990. *Guidelines for Dialogue between Muslims and Christians*. prepared by M. Borrmans. Trsl. from French original (publ. 1981) by R. Marston Speight. New York: Paulist Press.

PRUVOST, Lucie, 'From Tolerance to Spiritual Emulation: An analysis of official texts on Christian-Muslim dialogue.' *Islamochristiana* 6: 1-9.

ROSSANO, Pietro. 1982. 'Les grands documents de l'Eglise Catholique au sujet des Musulmans'. *Islamochristiana*. 8:13-23.

SANSON, Henri. 1990. *Dialogue intérieur avec l'Islam*. Paris: Centurion.

SANSON, Henri. 1993. *L'Islam*. [Que Penser de...? Dossiers sur des questions actuelles — Trimestriel, N°17], Namur.

SCHEDL, Claus. 1978. *Muhammad und Jesus*. Die christologisch relevanten Texte des Korans neu übersetzt und erklärt. Wien/Freiburg/Basel: Herder.

SECRETARIUS PRO NON-CHRISTIANIS. 1969. *Guidelines for a Dialogue between Muslims and Christians*. Roma: Ancora.

TANNER, Norman P. (ed.). 1990. *Decrees of the Ecumenical Councils*. Vol. 2 (Trent-Vatican II). London/Washington (DC): Sheed/Georgetown.

TROLL, Christian W. 1973. 'A New Spirit in Christian-Muslim Relations'. *The Month* (London), Vol. 134, p. 296ff.

TROLL, Christian W. 1984. 'Islam and Christianity Interacting in the Life of an Outstanding Christian Scholar of Islam: the case of Louis Massignon (1883-1962)' *Islam and the Modern Age* (New Delhi), 15: 157-66.

TROLL, Christian W. 1995. 'Christianity and Islam: Mutual Challenges. Hans Zirker's recent work on Islam' *Orientalia Christiana Periodica* 61: 571-580.

WAARDENBURG, Jean Jacques. 1962. *L'Islam dans le miroir de l'Occident*. Paris/La Haye: Mouton.

ZAEHNER, R.C. 1962. *At Sundry Times*. London.

ZACHARIAS, Hanna. 1960. *Vrai Mohammad et faux Coran*. Paris.

ZACHARIAS, Hanna. 1955. *De Moise à Mohammed*. 2 vols. Cahors. 2nd ed. 1964. Paris: Scorpion.

ZIRKER, Hans. 1992. *Christentum und Islam: Theologische Verwandtschaft und Konkurrenz*. 2nd. rev. ed. Düsseldorf: Patmos.

ZIRKER, Hans. 1993. *Islam: Theologische und Gesellschaftliche Herausforderungen*. Düsseldorf: Patmos.

NEW WINE IN OLD WINESKINS
CHANGING PROTESTANT VIEWS OF ISLAM

Jean-Claude BASSET

The present attempt to review Protestant attitudes towards Islam and Muslims since the 1950s is divided into three parts: first, a brief recapitulation of the situation which prevailed up to the Second World War; then a survey of the changes in orientation that have subsequently occurred in the area of dialogue; and lastly, the implications of these changed attitudes for pastoral care and theological reflection.

1. Protestantism and Islam prior to 1950

Historically speaking, Mohammed's sermons at Mecca predated Luther's at Wittenberg by 800 years. The Arab-Muslim expansion of the Umayyads affected Near Eastern Byzantine and Spanish Latin Christianity. At the time of the Crusades (1096-1291), Protestantism had still to be born and up to the Renaissance, conflicts and the exchange of goods or prisoners between Christians and Muslims were concentrated in and around the Mediterranean area.

Fundamentally, the Reformation was a reaction to the situation in the Catholic Church and papacy; it was therefore mainly confined to Western Christianity. In common with the Orthodox churches — apart from an attempted rapprochement with Constantinople — the Jews and Muslims were onlookers rather than partners.

Geographically speaking, Protestantism was born in Northern Europe, and its development in Scandinavia and the Anglo-Saxon countries only strengthened its isolation from the Islamic world. On the Muslim side, Ottoman Turks considered that Africa and Asia had more to offer than Europe and thus to be of greater interest.

Sociologically, Muslims, especially Arabs, have had until now many more contacts with Catholics or Orthodox than with Protestants who have only small and recent communities in the Middle East. Even in the West, Protestant-Muslim relations constitute a new venture among people who know very little about each other.

1.1 The Reformers and Islam

For Luther (1483-1546), just like Erasmus (1469-1536) and Nicholas of Cusa (1401-1464), the successful advance of the Turks, which brought them to the very gates of Vienna in 1529, was a punishment from God for the Christians' infidelity and an invitation to mend their ways. For obvious reasons, Luther rejected the idea of a Crusade under the banner of the Pope and left it to the worldly authorities, the "Holy Roman Empire of the German Nation" as it was called, to defend the life and property of its subjects.

Luther had some extremely harsh words for the Turks who, in his eyes, constituted, together with the Pope and the Devil, the three enemies of God[1]. If he was often abusive and contemptuous, it is true that his knowledge of Islam was almost non-existent. To his credit, however, it must be said that he personally encouraged the publication of an existing Latin translation of the Qur'ân by Theodore Bibliander. Accordingly, he wrote: "I would very much like to read the Qur'ân myself [...] Everyone is satisfied with the one single certainty that Muhammad has been an enemy of the Christian faith. But exactly where and how, point by point, has not yet been revealed and that it is necessary to do."[2] Unfortunately, reading the Qur'ân seems only to have reinforced his preconceived ideas.

Calvin (1509-1564) was no better informed or disposed towards the Muslims, despite François the First's alliance with Suleiman the Magnificent. He reiterated in his *Institutes of the Christian Religion* one of the persistent prejudices of the Middle Ages: "Even though they openly brag that the sovereign creator is their God, the Turks nevertheless substitute an idol in His place so much do they condemn Jesus Christ."[3] In contrast, Sebastian Castellio (1515-1563) was much more tolerant and better informed in his treatise on the impunity of the heretics published in 1555[4].

Thus, as V. Segesvary has pointed out in his thesis on Islam and the Reformation, the major event remains the publication in 1543 in Basel of

---

[1] See G. RUPP, "Luther against 'The Turk, the Pope and the Devil'", in *Seven-Headed Luther. Essays in Commemoration of a Quincentenary 1483-1983*, p. 256-273.

[2] "Verlegung des Alcoran Bruder Richardi" (1542) in *Luthers Werke*, W.A. Vol. 53, p. 272.

[3] J. CALVIN, *Institutes of the Christian Religion*, Book 2, ch. VI, §4. Philadelphia, 1966; see J. SLOMP, "Calvin and the Turks", in Y. Y. HADDAD / W. Z. HADDAD (ed.), *Christian-Muslim Encounters*, The University Press of Florida, Gainesville, 1995, p. 126-142.

[4] *De l'impunité des hérétiques*, bilingual edition, Latin — French, Geneva, 1971.

what is known as the Bibliander Collection[5], so named after the humanist and orientalist, Theodore Buchmann (1504-1564), who was Zwingli's disciple and successor in Zürich. We find in this *Collection* the Latin translation of the Qur'ân made in the 12th century by Robert Ketton from the Cluny Collection initiated by Peter the Venerable (1092-1156), and other works such as Ricoldo da Monte Croce's *Confutatio*, all preceded by the recommendations of Luther, Melanchton and Bibliander. If apologetic concern dominates this controversial publication, Bibliander maintains that it is as necessary to be interested in the Qur'ân as it is in the writings of Antiquity, the Jews and the "Papists" and to seek knowledge objectively: "I believed that it was interesting for theological study and beneficial for the Church to publish the doctrine of Muhammad and the exploits of his disciples at a time when the interests of Christianity and the Muslim Turks were closely entwined by wars, hostilities, prisoners and alliances."[6]

Whether in Wittenberg, Zürich, Strasbourg or Geneva, all the Reformers reproached Islam for its monotheistic rejection of the Trinity and the divinity of Christ; its belief that salvation depended more on the fulfilment of duties laid down in the Qur'ân than on divine grace; the moral laxity of polygamy and the recourse to violence as far as the very heart of Christian Europe.

1.2 The Missionary Approach

Once its existence had been established and recognized in a limited but very influential region of Europe, Protestant as well as Anglican Churches could no longer regard Islam in the same negative, unilateral and biased way that the founders had done. However, there was little change until the colonial expansion of such Protestant countries as Great Britain and the Netherlands and the development of missions in the 19th century in which the Lutherans and the Reformed Churches took an active part, together with the Anglican Church, established in 1534 in England by King Henry VIII as a sort of *via media* between Catholics and Protestants, as well as the Baptists, puritan heirs of the Reformation established in North America since 1639, and the Methodists from the English revival movement led by John Wesley (1706-1791).

---

[5] Th. BIBLIANDER (ed), *Machumetis Saracenorum principis, eiusque successorum vitae, ac doctrina, ipseque Alcoran*, Basel, Jean Oporin, 1543; see V. SEGESVARY, *L'Islam et la Réforme. Etudes sur l'attitude des réformateurs zurichois envers l'islam (1510-1550)*, Lausanne, L'Âge d'Homme, 1977.

[6] Th. BIBLIANDER, *Machumetis...*, Vol. 1, fol. a 5/r, quoted by V. SEGESVARY, *op. cit.* p. 195 (note)

Among the missionaries[7], an Englishman, Henry Martyn (1781-1812) was one of the first Protestants to devote all his energy to Islam in a spirit of apologetic controversy, first in India and then in Iran. He was followed in a more polemical way by a German, Karl Gottlieb Pfander (1803-1865), whose famous work in Persian, *Mizân al-Haqq* [The Balance of the Truth][8], published in 1835, has been widely translated, resulting in more than one Muslim response.

At the turn of the 20th century, there was a more respectful regard for Islam, in Egypt, in the writings of William Temple Gairdner (1873-1928), an Anglican who saw Islam as a *preparatio evangelica*, especially in its mystical dimension[9]. Similarly, a member of the Presbyterian Church in the USA, Samuel Marinus Zwemer (1867-1952), founder and Editor from 1911 to 1947 of the journal *The Moslem* (later *Muslim*) *World*, was a child of the conventional critical approach but showed a wider interest in events in the Muslim world. While steadfastly believing in the superiority of the Christian faith, Zwemer nevertheless recognized the religious genius of not only Muhammad but also Ghazali as Muslim seekers after God[10].

The change in Protestant thinking was also reflected in a series of missionary conferences, of which the first, held in Cairo in 1906, adopted a more open and respectful attitude towards Islamic belief and practice[11]. This same spirit was again present at the first international conference of Protestant missionaries in Edinburgh in 1910[12], which led to the creation of the International Missionary Council in 1921. Also to be mentioned are the Conferences of missions to Islam held in Lucknow (1911) and Jerusalem (1924)[13], and the second International Missionary

---

[7] For the history of Anglican and Reformed missions among Muslims from 1800 till 1938, see L. VAN DER WERF, *Christian Mission to Muslims: the Record*, Pasadena, Wiliam Carey Library, 1977; also D. A. KERR, "Christian Witness in Relation to Muslim Neighbours", *Islamchristiana*, 10, 1984, p. 1-30.

[8] K. PFANDER, *The Mizânu'l Haqq*, revised and enlarged by W. ST CLAIR TISDALL, London, The Religious Tract Society, 1910.

[9] Apart from a large literature written for Muslim lands, see W. H. T. GAIRDNER, *The Reproach of Islam*, London, 1909; 5th edition revised as *The Rebuke of Islam*, London, 1920.

[10] Among his many books on Islam and Christian witness: S. M. ZWEMER, *Islam, a Challenge to Faith*, New York, 1907; *A Moslem Seeker after God: Sharing Islam at its Best in the Life and Teaching of al-Ghazali*, New York 1921.

[11] Report published under the title: *Methods of Mission Work among Moslems*, London, 1906.

[12] See W. T. GAIRDNER, *Edinburgh 1910: An Account and Interpretation of the World Missionary Conference*, London, 1910.

[13] Respectively, *Islam and Missions: Report of the Lucknow Conference*, New York, 1911, with S. M. ZWEMER as one of the editors, and *Conference of Christian Workers among Moslems*, (J. R. MOTT, ed.), New York / London, 1932.

Conference in Jerusalem in 1928. There the emphasis was on some form of continuity between religions such as Islam and Christianity which had crowned the religious quest of humanity[14]. John Raleigh Mott (1865-1955) from the USA was one of the driving forces of Protestant missions in the world, including those to Islam, until the Second World War[15].

Special mention should be made of Hendrik Kraemer (1888-1965), a scholar and a missionary of the Dutch Reformed Church. Having worked in Indonesia for 12 years, he dominated the debate of the third International Missionary Conference at Tambaram in 1938 for which he wrote the preparatory text[16]. A disciple of Karl Barth, Kraemer argued in favour of a radical discontinuity between revelation in Christ and any religion, including empirical Christianity. At that point, he opposed the idea of a religious dialogue with Islam, the system of which he criticized as being so mechanical and legalistic that the individual was suffocated. His position is well expressed in his phrase: "The Christian revelation, as the record of God's self-disclosing revelation in Jesus Christ, is absolutely *sui generis*"[17]. At the same time, Kraemer went further than Zwemer in acknowledging Muhammad's prophetic stature in his proclamation of unconditional monotheism. In the fifties, he spoke in favour of dialogue[18]. Continuity and discontinuity, these were the terms, on the threshold of the 1950s, of the alternative Protestant approaches towards other religions[19].

1.3 Protestant studies of Islam before 1950

It was in the 19th century that here and there Europeans began to admire Muhammad: Johann Wolfgang Goethe (1749-1832) in Germany, Alphonse Lamartine (1790-1869) in France and Thomas Carlyle (1795-

---

[14] S. M. ZWEMER, *Christianity, the Final Religion*, Grand Rapids, 1920. See also with a stress on the social Gospel, the famous report: *Re-Thinking Missions: A Laymen's Inquiry after One Hundred Years*, (by the Commission of Appraisal, W. E. HOCKING, Chairman), New York / London, 1932.

[15] J. R. MOTT, *Evangelism for the World Today*, New York, 1946; C. H. HOPKINS, *John R. Mott, 1865-1955: A Biography*, WCC, Geneva, 1979.

[16] Published as an epoch-making book: *The Christian Message in a Non-Christian World*, London, 1938.

[17] *Tambaram Series*, Volume One, Oxford / London, 1939, p.1. See C. F. HALLEN-CREUTZ, *Kraemer Towards Tambaram. A Study in Hendrik Kraemer's Missionary Approach*, Studia Missionalia Upsaliensia, Lund, 1966.

[18] H. KRAEMER, *World Cultures and World Religions. The Coming Dialogue.* London, 1960.

[19] For further details, see K. HOCK, *Der Islam im Spiegel westlicher Theologie*, Köln, 1986.

1881) in Britain. Among the Protestants, the first to update understanding of Islam was the Anglican priest Charles Forster, who published a monumental work of 900 pages entitled *Mahometanism Unveiled*[20]. Starting with the dual alliance of God in favour of Isaac and Ishmael, he established a close comparison between Islam and Christianity in the areas of ethics, doctrine, liturgy, Scriptures and culture. Despite its marked prejudice against Islam, Forster's oeuvre is a mine of information about Islam. More than a century was to pass before anything similar in scope and concern for systematic comparison was published by the British Methodist scholar, James W. Sweetman[21].

In actual fact, Protestants played a considerable role in the evolution of European attitudes towards Islam, as two almost contemporary Dutch theses have shown. The first, by Willem Abraham Bijlefeld[22], tended to prove that a post-Christian religion like Islam is not automatically antichristian and left the doors open for a more positive evaluation of Muslim faith and history. The second, by Jacques Waardenburg[23], is the story of five Orientalists, three of whom were Protestants: a German Lutheran, C. H. Becker; a member of the Dutch Reformed Church, Snouck Hurgronje; and a Scottish Presbyterian living in the USA, Duncan Black Macdonald.

2. Emergence of New Orientations Linked to Dialogue

As early as 1947, W. M. Watt asked for a radically new approach to Muslims, calling for stress on common elements, mutual recognition and acceptance of religious values in Islam[24]. As far as I know, the very term "dialogue" was first associated with Islam in the title of a book by Henri Nusslé called *Dialogue avec l'islam*, which was published by "Action Chrétienne en Orient" in Lausanne in 1949. If the author takes a resolutely conventional missionary approach with specific references to Zwemer and Gairdner, it is nevertheless possible to discern a real desire to know Islam better without any spirit of crusading.

---

[20] London, 1829.

[21] J. W. SWEETMAN, *Islam and Christian Theology*, 4 vol., London, 1945-1967.

[22] W. A. BIJLEFELD, *De Islam als Na-Christelijke Religie*, (doctoral diss. Utrecht) Den Haag, 1959.

[23] J. WAARDENBURG, *L'Islam dans le miroir de l'Occident. Comment quelques orientalistes occidentaux se sont penchés sur l'islam et se sont formé une image de cette religion*, (doctoral diss. Amsterdam) Paris / The Hague, 1961, 3rd ed. 1970.

[24] W. M. WATT, "New Paths to Islam", *International Review of Mission*, 36, 1947, p.74-80.

2.1 WCC Initiatives to Promote Islamo-Christian Dialogue

It was in the circles close to the World Council of Churches (WCC), which was officially established in Amsterdam in 1948, that the idea and introduction of inter-religious dialogue gained ground. Having started with 146 churches, the WCC comprises today about 325 churches with a constituency of 400 million people from all Christian denominations, Protestant, Anglican, Chalcedonian and pre-Chalcedonian Orthodox, except the Roman Catholic Church and a branch of Evangelical churches. Following the study entitled *Word of God and Living Faiths of Men*, which was carried out during the period 1955 to 1970[25], the Council set up a sub-unit called "Dialogue with People of Living Faiths and Ideologies" in 1971[26]. Direct contact with Muslims was first made in 1969 and has continued, through this sub-unit, bilaterally and multilaterally, for some 20 years[27].

For all that, there was still strong resistance to the initiative, notably at the General Assemblies held in Nairobi (1975) and Vancouver (1983). To appease those who, in Nairobi, had felt dialogue would betray the Christian mission and open up the door to syncretism, a meeting of theologians and missionaries in Chiang Mai in 1977 drew up a number of guidelines[28]. These were adopted by the WCC Central Committee in 1979 and augmented by two sets of ecumenical considerations in respect of dialogue with Jews in 1982 and with Muslims in 1991[29]. Since, in Vancouver, it was more the theological implications of interreligious dialogue which had been called into question, a response was prepared in the form of a study guide[30] for Christian individuals and local communities.

[25] For the chronology and bibliography of the study "The Word of God and the living faiths of men," see G. VALLÉE, *Mouvement œcuménique et religions non chrétiennes*, Tournai / Montréal, 1975.

[26] On the issue of dialogue in the WCC, see D. MULDER, "History of the Sub-unit on Dialogue of the World Council of Churches" in *Studies in Interreligious Dialogue*, 2, 1992/2, p. 136-151 and J.-C. BASSET, *Le dialogue interreligieux. Chance ou déchéance de la foi*, Paris, 1996, p.193-235.

[27] S. J. SAMARTHA / J. B. TAYLOR (ed.), *Christian-Muslim Dialogue. Papers from Broumana, 1972*, WCC, Geneva, 1973; *Christians Meeting Muslims, WCC Papers on 10 Years of Christian-Muslim Dialogue*, WCC, Geneva, 1977; S. BROWN (ed.), *Meeting in Faith. Twenty Years of Christian-Muslim Conversations Sponsored by the World Council of Churches*, Geneva, 1989

[28] S. J. SAMARTHA (ed.), *Faith in the Midst of Faiths. Reflections on Dialogue in Community*, Geneva, 1977.

[29] *Ecumenical Considerations on Jewish-Christian Dialogue*, WCC, Geneva, 1983 and *Ecumenical Considerations on Christian-Muslim Relations*, WCC, Geneva, 1991.

[30] Published under the title *My Neighbour's Faith — and Mine. Theological Discoveries through Interfaith Dialogue: A Study Guide*, WCC, Geneva, 1986.

At the same time, the meetings with the Muslims tended to concentrate on concrete aspects of co-existence within a given society, on such specific matters as development programmes (Colombo 1982), relations between religion and society (Benin 1986, Indonesia 1986, Crete 1987, USA 1988) and aid to refugees (Malta 1992). The Dialogue sub-unit was disbanded as part of a general re-organization in 1992 and dialogue with the Muslims became the responsibility of the Office on Interreligious Relations whose executive secretary is presently Tarek Mitri, an Orthodox from Lebanon, deeply involved in Christian-Muslim relations[31].

2.2 Islamo-Christian Relations in Protestant Denominations

The major denominations — the Anglicans, the Lutherans, the Reformed Churches, the Methodists and the Baptists — have all taken similar steps to revise their traditional thinking about Islam and to meet Muslims in different areas. As a number of publications testify[32], regional and international consultations have been organized for the express purpose of updating the Protestant churches' understanding of Islam and Islamo-Christian relations. This is unmistakably a way of encouraging people to think of Muslims as their *neighbours* — a term which is heard time and time again — and to look for new ways of understanding one another[33]. Nevertheless, we should not gloss over the growing divide between the people who are in favour of dialogue and those who are not. The so-called Evangelical groups and the fundamentalists are often resistant to this re-evaluation, which they see as a surrender to worldly values and a betrayal of the Christian message. Some have even no reluctance to use the word Crusade to speak of their con-

---

[31] T. MITRI (ed.), *Religion, Law and Society. A Christian-Muslim Discussion*, Geneva / Kampen, 1995.

[32] Among many others, one can quote: J. MICKSCH & M. MILDENBERGER (ed.), *Christen und Muslime im Gespräch. Eine Handreichung*, Frankfurt, 1981, with translations into Dutch, English, French and Italian; B. L. HAINES & F. L. COOLEY (ed.), *Christians and Muslims Together. An Exploration by Presbyterians*, Philadelphia, 1987; J. P. RAJASHEKAR (ed.), *Christian-Muslim Relations in Eastern Africa*. Report of a Seminar/Workshop Sponsored by the Lutheran World Federation and the Project for Christian-Muslim Relations in Africa, Geneva, 1988; *My Neighbour is Muslim. A Handbook for Reformed Churches*, John Knox Series, Geneva, 1990; J. P. RAJASHEKAR & H. S. WILSON (ed.), *Islam in Asia. Perspectives for Christian-Muslim Encounter*. Report of a Consultation sponsored by the Lutheran World Federation and the World Alliance of Reformed Churches, Geneva, 1992.

[33] See for instance G. SPEELMAN / J. VAN LIN / D. MULDER (ed.), *Muslims and Christians in Europe. Breaking New Ground. Essays in honour of Jan Slomp*, Kampen, 1993; see also "You shall love your Neighbor. Christians and Muslims in a time of fear", special issue of *Church and Society*, 1994/1.

cern for Muslims; others accept the word dialogue but with the old agenda of missionary conversion[34].

Among the factors of change, we must mention a number of Protestant-inspired study and research centres whose aim is to make Islam and the Muslim world better known to Christians, often with the active participation of Muslim teachers and sometimes students. The oldest, founded in the 1930s, is the *Henry Martyn Institute of Islamic Studies* at Hyderabad in India. Other well-known institutions include: the *Centre for the Study of Islam and Christian-Muslim Relations* in Birmingham, England; the *Duncan Black Macdonald Center for the Study of Islam and Christian-Muslim Relations* at Hartford, Connecticut and the *Zwemer Institute of Muslim Studies* at Altadena, California, both in the USA; and the *Christian Study Centre* at Rawalpindi in Pakistan. In Africa, an initial attempt was made at Ibadan, in Nigeria, under the auspices of the *Islam in Africa Project* renamend *Project for Christian-Muslim Relations in Africa* with headquarters in Nairobi. A new project is under study to meet the needs of the Protestant churches in Africa and to reinforce the network of counsellors who will work with both English- and French-speaking churches.

The end of colonialism opened a new era for Christian-Muslim relations by putting into serious question the classical one-way missionary enterprise. The arrival of Muslim migrants in traditionally "Christian countries" inaugurated a new situation of immediate encounter with Muslims in the daily life of almost every Christian. It provoked a lot of fear about what is often perceived as *Fremdkörper* or even a subversive force, as well as worries about the possible change of identity and values of the society. It also opened room for a rethinking of God's revelation, the status of Muhammad, the uniqueness of Jesus Christ and the nature of the Christian vocation.

In Europe, a good number of Protestant and Catholic churches have nowadays a working group to look after issues concerning the Muslim presence in their midst. In Great Britain, in Germany, in France, in the Netherlands, main churches have appointed one or more people responsible for the almost daily contacts that now exist with Muslims and members of other religions. It is within this framework that it has been possible in recent years to discuss such issues as the production of information about Islam for Christians, the rights of Muslim minorities,

---

[34] A good example is given in Don M. McCurry (ed.), *The Gospel and Islam: a 1978 Compendium*, MARC, Monrovia-CA, 1979.

Islamo-Christian marriage and Christian witness among Muslims in a resolutely pluralistic society.

The presence of some 12 million Muslims in Europe — 24 million if we extend Europe as far as the Urals and the Caucasus — has inspired a good number of scholarly studies[35] and has also been perceived as a new challenge by European Christians. Accordingly, the Conference of European Churches (CEC), which groups Protestant, Anglican and Orthodox Churches, has organized two major consultations held in Austria, at Salzburg in 1978 and St Pölten in 1984, in which Muslims took part each time[36]. In 1987, what had been a consultative committee for the CEC became a plain committee under the auspices of both the Conference of European Churches and the Council of European Episcopal Conferences of the Roman Catholic Church. After several preparatory studies, the "Islam in Europe" Committee organized a European consultation in Birmingham in 1991 to brief faculties of theology, seminaries and training centers of pastoral workers on the place that should be given to Islam in the training of priests and pastors[37]. The same "Islam in Europe" Committee has prepared a study document for Churches on the frequently discussed issue of reciprocity[38], which has been widely discussed including with Muslim partners; it is currently working on a directory on Christian-Muslim relations in Europe.

2.3 Protestant Positions Today

Unlike the Catholic Church, which has its own magisterium on Islamo-Christian relations in Rome, the Protestant Churches' moves

[35] Without mentioning national studies, see F. DASSETTO / Y. CONRAD (ed.), *Muslims in Western Europe. An Annotated Bibliography*, Paris, 1996; T. GERHOLM / Y. G. LITHMAN (ed.) *The New Islamic Presence in Western Europe*, London / New York, 1987; F. DASSETTO / A. BASTENIER, *Europa: Nuova frontiera dell'Islam*, Roma, 1988; J. NIELSEN, *Muslims in Western Europe*, Edinburgh, 1992, 1995; B. LEWIS / D. SCHNAPPER (ed.), *Musulmans en Europe*, Actes Sud, 1992; R. BISTOLFI / F. ZABBAL (ed.), *Islams d'Europe. Intégration ou insertion communautaire*, L'Aube, 1995; G. NONNEMAN / T. NIBLOCK / B. SZAJKOWSKI (ed.), *Muslim Communities in the New Europe*, Ithaca, 1996.

[36] *Churches and Muslims in Europe. Elements of Thought. Report from Salzburg 1978*, CEC & IAP, Geneva, 1978; *Witness to God in Secular Europe. Report from St Pölten 1984*, CEC, Geneva, 1985; and also J. SLOMP (ed.), *Churches in Europe (II)*, CEC, Geneva, 1982.

[37] J. SLOMP & H. VÖCKING (ed.), *Islam in Europe Committee. The Presence of Muslims in Europe and the Theological Training of Pastoral Workers. Birmingham, 9-14 September 1991. Final Report*.

[38] "Christian-Muslim Reciprocity. Considerations for the European Churches", 7 pages translated into Arabic, Bulgarian, Dutch, French, German, Italian, Spanish and Turkish; distributed by the Secretariat, "Islam in Europe" Committee, P.O. Box 3156, CH-1211 Geneva 3.

have been more dispersed. Characterized by an absence of hierarchy and a great doctrinal freedom left to the individual appreciation, Protestants defend positions which may be at times contradictory but keep the discussion open. At the present time, one can identify with Jean-Paul Gabus three major attitudes[39]: 1) the hard-line Evangelical stress on evangelism and conversion of others considered as lost people, in line with a more or less fundamentalist position, 2) the Ecumenical opening toward dialogue as way to witness to Christ while recognizing that others may have some elements of truth, and 3) the liberal emphasis on tolerance based on a positive appreciation of diversity while putting into question the uniqueness of Christ. These basic attitudes come close to the largely accepted nomenclature of Alan Race: exclusivism, inclusivism and pluralism[40]. As a matter of fact, the Protestant spectrum is even broader as can be perceived through the orientations of five well known Protestant Islamic scholars taken here as models for different sensitivities toward Islam.

1. A Scottish Presbyterian scholar and minister, who was an Edinburgh professor from 1947 to 1979, W. Montgomery Watt, is renowned for the excellence of his research on the life of Muhammad and the development of Islamic thought[41]. He is also greatly interested in the interaction of Islam with ancient and contemporary culture. His care for impartiality and academic objectivity caused him to shun any considerations of a theological nature. But, as already mentioned, he was at the same time eager to work for new relationships and made, in retirement, a very significant contribution to opening new paths in Christian-Muslim understanding[42].

2. J. Dudley Woodberry is a Professor at the Fuller Theological Seminary of Pasadena in California. Previously, he served as a missionary in the Lebanon, Pakistan, Afghanistan and Saudi Arabia. He is the earnest advocate of a certain type of evangelistic exclusivism. While there is no

---

[39] See J.-P. GABUS, "Approches protestantes de l'islam" in J.-P. GABUS / A. MERAD / Y. MOUBARAC, *Islam et christianisme en dialogue*, Paris, 1982; J.-P. GABUS, "A propos d'un récent colloque de la Fédération Protestante de France intitulé: «Musulman, mon prochain»", *Irenikon*, 1995/1, p. 5-15.

[40] A. RACE, *Christians and Religious Pluralism. Patterns in the Christian Theology of Religions*, London, 1983.

[41] W. M. WATT, *Muhammad at* Mecca, Oxford, 1953; *Muhammad at Medina*, Oxford, 1956; *Islamic Philosophy and Theology*, Edinburgh, 1962; *Islamic Political Thought*, Edinburgh, 1968.

[42] W. M. WATT, *Islam and Christianity Today. A Contribution to Dialogue*, London, 1983.

longer any question of demonizing Islam, the main priority is still conversion in the name of love[43]. Accordingly, dialogue is seen in a context of relentless opposition between the Christian and Islamic faiths.

3. The Anglican Bishop, Kenneth Cragg, can be considered as the Louis Massignon of Protestantism and is thereby largely inclusive. In his seminal work *The Call of the Minaret*, published in 1956, he set much store by the Muslim experience of God. Cragg attempted interpretations of Qur'anic passages and showed a deep interest for contemporary Muslim thinkers[44]. In his concern for Christian presence among Muslims, he has never failed in his numerous writings to invite Christians to remove their sandals at the door of the mosque and listen to Islam[45], so that they may testify, respectfully and credibly, to their own faith in Christ in a spirit of dialogue without necessarily sparing all criticism.

4. Wilfred Cantwell Smith is a Canadian Presbyterian scholar and pastor who was Professor of Religion at the Universities of McGill in Montreal, of Harvard in Cambridge, USA and of Dalhousie in Halifax. He was first a missionary teacher in Lahore and represents the pluralist attitude. The fundamental distinction between personal faith and historical tradition that he draws for all religions leads him to pave the way for a theology which encompasses the whole of the religious dimension of humankind[46]. An expert on Islam, he strives to explain the key concepts in such a way as to change the way people look at religions, especially at Islam[47]. He allies the positions of a scholar and a liberal theologian to formulate fresh proposals to overcome the opposition between Christians and Muslims and to encourage them to reflect together on their mutual problems.

5. If there was ever a researcher who was unclassifiable, it was Henry Corbin (1903-1978), a French Protestant who devoted his entire life to the study of Islamic philosophy, particularly Iranian and Ismaili Shi'ism.

[43] J. D. WOODBERRY (ed.), *Muslims and Christians on the Emmaus Road*, MARC, Monrovia, 1989.

[44] K. CRAGG, *The Event of the Qur'an. Islam in its Scripture*, London, 1970; *The Mind of the Qur'an*, London, 1973; *The Pen and the Faith; Eight Modern Muslims and the Qur'an*, London, 1985.

[45] K. CRAGG, *Sandals at the Mosque*, London, 1958; *Muhammad and the Christian*, London, 1984; *Jesus and the Muslim*, London, 1985; *The Christ and the Faiths. Theology in Cross-Reference*, London, 1986.

[46] Especially, W. C. SMITH, *The Faith of Other Men*, New York, 1962; *The Meaning and End of Religion*, New York, 1963; *Faith and Belief*, Princeton, 1979; *Toward a World Theology. Faith and Comparative History of Religion*, Philadelphia, 1981; *What is Scripture? A Comparative Approach*, London, 1993.

[47] W. C. SMITH, *Islam in Modern History*, Princeton, 1957; *On Understanding Islam*, Berlin 1981.

Not content with publishing several Persian texts and a masterly synthesis in four volumes on Iranian Islam[48], he endeavoured, largely via 25 lectures given to the "Eranos Circle"[49] in Switzerland, to lay the foundations of a comparative philosophy which strove for nothing less than harmony between the Abrahamic religions considered in their innermost spiritual dimension, against all kinds of stereotyped and pedantic conformity.

3. Re-evaluation in the light of Islamo-Christian Encounters

It has to be admitted that even today, at the end of the 20th century, the vast majority of Christians, and especially Protestants, continue to be ignorant of anything and everything about the Muslim religion and its practices when they are not simply mute with fear in the face of boisterous demonstrations of Islam's religious and political reaffirmation. At the same time, however, it is also true that, in the past 25 years, many churches have come to take the existence of Islam seriously, endeavouring to respond positively to the challenge it presents for both Christianity and the western pattern of society.

For all that, the Protestant perception of Islam and Muslims remains extremely diverse. Between the two extremes of rejection (even condemnation) by many people and the fascination of others (sometimes to the extent of conversion), we can discern four fundamental attitudes. These are not entirely incompatible because they all find their roots in Biblical teaching and the Christian tradition.

The first, absolutely pragmatic, approach is that of conviviality and solidarity. Basically, it consists of walking towards and besides somebody else without thinking about his religious label or which community he belongs to. As examples, one can mention the former happy days of coexistence in the Middle East or the commitment of various Christian groups in favour of the rights of Muslim immigrants and asylum-seekers in Western Europe. The criteria here are based on the UN Declaration of Human Rights and the Biblical commandment "Thou shalt love thy neighbour as thyself", and the objective is to seek a just and equitable society.

The second approach fits in with the general pattern of 200 years of Protestant evangelization and conversion: demonstrating one's faith in

---

[48] H. CORBIN, *En Islam iranien*, 4 Vol., Paris 1971-1972.
[49] Published regularly in *Eranos Jahrbuch*, Zürich, Rhein Verlag, 1950-1969 / Leiden, Brill, 1970-1976.

Jesus Christ by word and deed, to encourage others to become Christians[50]. This attitude, which has its Muslim equivalent in the *da'wa*, the call to Islam, is characteristic of Evangelicals, so called because of their assiduous adherence to Biblical teaching and their conviction that there is no salvation except in Jesus Christ. The criterion here is based on the last words of Christ as given in the Gospel according to Matthew: "Go forth and make all nations my disciples" (ch. 28: 19); the objective is to make the whole world Christian.

The third approach is centered on dialogue with people meeting each other on an equal footing and in a spirit of reciprocity so as to maintain a balance between listening to the faith and expectations of the other person and talking about one's own convictions. Today, this is the preferred orientation of ecumenical Protestant circles[51], which does not go unanswered on the part of Muslims anxious to express their understanding of God and human society. The Biblical ground is found in Christ's Word: "You will bear witness for me" (Acts of the Apostles 1: 8) understood in the line of the First Letter of Peter: "Be always ready with your defence whenever you are called to account for the hope that is in you, but make that defence with modesty and respect" (ch. 3: 15). The clear objective is to find a way for the believers to be faithful to their mission call and open to their neighbour's faith.

The fourth approach is fundamentally an apprenticeship for tolerance and mutual respect in an attempt to overcome 1400 years of antagonism — now fraternal, now fratricidal by turn — between Christians and Muslims. It consists of nothing less than a renunciation of all judgements of a negative or condescending nature about the religion of the other, accepting the plurality of the traditions not only as a fact of life but as a gift of God[52]. The criterion is the golden rule: "Always treat

---

[50] Good examples of this approach are given by a former director of Islam in Africa Project: J. P. DRETKE, *A Christian Approach to Muslims*, William Carey Library, Pasadena CA, 1979; by a former missionary in Pakistan: Phil. PARSHALL, *New paths in Muslim Evangelism*, Grand Rapids, 1980 and by an Anglican Bishop: M. NAZIR-ALI, *Islam: A Christian Perspective*, Exeter, UK, 1984.

[51] See for instance B. D. KATEREGGA / D. W. SHENK, *Islam and Christianity. Dialogue Between a Muslim and a Christian*, Nairobi, 1980; C. SH. ABASHIYA / A. J. ULEA, *Christianity and Islam. A Plea for Understanding and Tolerance*, Jos, Nigeria, 1991; and also S. BROWN, *The Nearest in Affection. Towards a Christian Understanding of Islam*, WCC, Geneva, 1994.

[52] An interesting approach has been attempted by U. SCHOEN, *Das Ereignis und die Antworten*, Göttingen, 1984, speaking of the one event of God's revelation and the many human responses to it; *Bi-Identität. Zweisprachigkeit, Bi-Religiosität, doppelte Staatsbürgerschaft*, Zürich / Düsseldorf, 1996.

others as you would like them to treat you", found in Matthew 7: 12 and Luke 6: 31 as well as in Plato and in the main religious traditions. The avowed objective to is heal the rift of ignorance and misunderstanding between Christians and Muslims and to strive for, at the very least, a peaceful co-existence, and, at best, a joint testimony in respect of the issues facing the world today.

To return to a working hypothesis formulated by Jacques Waardenburg at the beginning of the present symposium, one can illustrate briefly the method of reinterpretation brought about by encounters with the Muslims. Among many others, four aspects of the debate which is presently going on within the Protestant family at large deserve a special mention.

3.1 Living Together in a Pluralist Society

Immediately after the end of the Second World War, the issues which attracted the most theological attention were the advance of secularization and the challenge of atheism, to the point that some theologians even spoke of a theology of the death of God. Today, the main challenge is related to religious pluralism. Globally speaking, and often even within a given society, Christians and other believers find themselves in the minority or at least they constitute one group among others. If religious standards have not entirely disappeared from the preoccupations of our contemporaries, especially in the West they are no longer automatically passed on as they used to be and so they can lay no claim to monopoly. Basically, what Christians need to review is the relation between religion and society — *dîn wa daula* in Muslim terms.

In Europe, this opens a broad discussion dealing with the religious identity or identities of the continent, especially in connexion with the role religion can play in society[53]. Protestants can make a specific contribution as an active minority at ease in a democratic and secular State which guarantees the freedom and equality of all religions. Being themselves plural in many ways, they have less problems with a pluralist society than Catholics or Orthodox. On the other side, the question is how far can Muslims, who come nearly all from outside Europe, become Europeans in both senses, by getting equal rights and by keeping their own identity while accepting the rules of the game of a pluralistic

---

[53] See in French two collective works: J. BAUBÉROT (ed.), *Religions et laïcité dans l'Europe des Douze*, Paris, 1994 and G. DAVIE / D. HERVIEU-LÉGER (ed.), *Identités religieuses en Europe*, Paris, 1996.

society? The key issue is the possibility, the necessity even, of inter-religious collaboration in favour of justice, peace and human rights for both the individual and the community.

3.2 Towards New Pastoral Attitudes

As soon as Christians, Muslims and members of other faiths find themselves living together, the whole concept of pastoral care has to be re-examined. This question is already the subject of much discussion in the context of religious education in schools, both public and private. It also has very real implications for hospital and prison chaplains where new types of collaboration will be needed if they are to respond to every type of spiritual need. Already constructive encounters take place at the community level[54], but the touchy issue of conversion in both directions needs to be openly addressed in a way that respects both the individual religious quest and collective integrity.

The issue of Islamo-Christian marriages has become so acute in the last 20 years in Europe that most churches in the West have now adopted new policies to meet the expectations of those who wish to enter into such unions, to say nothing of the worries of their close families or of hesitations of the liturgically ill-equipped clergy. Just as interdenominational marriages have upset ecclesiastical practices and thus advanced the cause of ecumenism, so can churches no longer evade the reality that such marriages do take place, with or without their benediction.

3.3 Mission and Dialogue

One particularly sensitive issue concerns the relationship between mission and dialogue. Now, more than ever, Protestants are deeply divided between those who favour a conversion mission along Evangelical lines and for whom "it may be found that 'dialogue' is so ambiguous or 'loaded' that it cannot even be wisely used. Or it may be felt that the activities it implies are too risky or ineffective to have place in evangelical strategy"[55]. On the other hand, there are those who, like W. C. Smith, believe and affirm that "our mission today is to cooperate with all humankind"[56].

---

[54] See A. WINGATE, *Encounter in the Spirit. Muslim-Christian Meetings in Birmingham*, WCC, Geneva, 1988.

[55] D. R. BREWSTER, "Dialogue: Relevancy to Evangelism" in D. McCURRY (ed), *The Gospel and Islam: A 1978 Compendium*, MARC, Monrovia, 1979, p. 519.

[56] Wilfred C. Smith, "Mission, dialogue, and God's will for us" in "Tambaram Revisited", special issue of *International Review of Mission*, Nr. 307, 1988, p. 360-374. The phrase quoted is on p. 374.

Two meetings organized by the World Council of Churches are particularly illuminating examples of re-evaluation directly linked to contact with the Muslims. The first was a rather tense dialogue held in 1976 at Chambésy, near Geneva, on the theme of Christian mission and Islamic *da'wah*. In the search for a *modus vivendi*, it was suggested that "religious discussion must be divorced from any direct or indirect exploitation of people's weaknesses, or their political and social disadvantage". In the final statement, it is said: "The conference recognizes that mission and *da'wah* are essential religious duties of both Christianity and Islam, and that the suspension of misused diakonia services is to the end of re-establishing mission in the future on a religiously sound basis acceptable to both"[57]. In 1979, the Dialogue sub-unit organized a conference at Mombasa in Kenya for the Christians working among Muslims which concluded with a call to mutual witness: "We ourselves are called, Christians and Muslims, on the threshold of a new decade and a new Muslim century, to discover anew our common obligation of witness to our respective faiths, in mutual and constructive criticism, seeking always to be better servants of the God Whom we worship in the societies we share"[58].

3.4 Theological Challenge

Last but not least, Christian-Muslim encounter poses a theological challenge to the Christian faith as soon as the latter seriously considers the possibility of a post-Biblical revelation, the claim that Muhammad had a prophetic function, the affirmation of intransigent monotheism or the christology contained in the Qur'an. As already mentioned, the consultation in Birmingham in 1991 opened up the way for such an examination. In spite of all their differences, Muslims and Protestants share a deep attachment to their Scriptures, a deep sense of God's absolute transcendence — *Allahu akbar / Deus semper major* —, a common distrust for clerical hierarchy and a similar emphasis on faith in God's grace. Sooner or later, Christians will have to find a positive answer to the question of the place of Islam and the Muslim community in God's plan for humanity.

On one side, it has to be admitted that Protestant thinking in relation to Islam is not as advanced as that of some more audacious Catholics;

---

[57] "Christian Mission and Islamic Da'wah", *International Review of Mission* 260, 1976, p. 365-460; quotations p. 453 and 459.

[58] *Christian Presence and Witness in Relation to Muslim Neighbours. A Conference. Mombasa, Kenya 1979*, WCC, Geneva, 1981, p. 73.

on the other side a real and deep change is taking place. Just as a remarkable evolution, not to say a Copernican revolution[59], has taken place in the past few decades in Christian attitudes and especially the Protestant attitude towards Judaism, in the same way it will no longer be possible for present-day Protestants to look at Islam and Muslims as their predecessors did. It is to be hoped that within the large Protestant family, including Anglicans and Evangelicals, a theological and ecclesiological dialogue will go on in order to arrive at more compatible positions, while maintaining the riches of diversity, as compared with the greater uniformity of the Catholic counterpart.

---

[59] So J. HICK, *God and the Universe of Faiths*, New York, 1973, p. 120-131; *God Has Many Names*, London / Philadelphia, 1980, ch. 2 and 4.

LA SITUATION DU DIALOGUE ISLAMO-CHRÉTIEN DANS LE MONDE ORTHODOXE ET EN GRÈCE

Astérios ARGYRIOU

À la première réunion panorthodoxe pré-conciliaire (Chambésy 1976), l'Église orthodoxe avait exprimé avec force son désir «de contribuer à la compréhension et à la collaboration entre les religions pour que disparaisse le fanatisme religieux et que les peuples se réconcilient et travaillent ensemble afin de faire triompher la paix et la liberté, condition nécessaire au progrès de l'homme moderne, quelles que soient sa nationalité ou sa religion. Ce désir a été renouvelé à plusieurs reprises. L'Église orthodoxe exprime ainsi sa fidélité à sa tradition qui s'est toujours opposée à tout fanatisme religieux, considérant que le dialogue interreligieux constitue un aspect essentiel de son témoignage dans le monde. L'Église orthodoxe est beaucoup plus sensible à la coexistence pacifique avec le monde musulman avec lequel elle partage une longue expérience commune de l'histoire».

Cette importante déclaration exprime certes les sentiments et la politique de l'Église orthodoxe envers les autres religions en général et envers l'islam en particulier. Cependant, suffit-elle à rendre compte de la complexité des relations entre le monde musulman et le monde orthodoxe d'aujourd'hui?

L'Orthodoxie vit au contact direct de l'Islam dans trois grandes régions principalement:
– dans certaines Républiques situées au sud-est de l'ex-Union Soviétique;
– dans le Proche et le Moyen Orient;
– dans les Balkans.

Ma connaissance de la situation ne m'autorise pas à vous parler de la première grande région, la plus éloignée de nous, où les conflits entre peuples orthodoxes et musulmans furent graves ces dernières années, le plus récent étant celui de la Tchétchénie où la guerre sévit encore et où le peuple musulman tchétchène, luttant pour son indépendance, se trouve être la victime des armées orthodoxes russes.

Pour la raison invoquée plus haut, il m'est difficile d'entreprendre un examen exhaustif des relations islamo-orthodoxes dans les deux autres

grandes régions. Je vais donc me borner à quelques réflexions et considérations générales, avant de vous présenter, dans la seconde partie de
mon exposé, de manière plus détaillée, la situation grecque qui m'est
plus familière.

* * *

Dans les Balkans, les musulmans qui, pendant cinq siècles, étaient le
peuple dominant, vivent depuis la création des états balkaniques actuels
au début de notre siècle, en situation de minorité religieuse. Dans le
Proche et le Moyen Orient, par contre, ce sont les chrétiens qui vivent en
situation de minorités depuis les grandes conquêtes arabo-musulmanes
(7e et 8e siècles), alors même que l'Orient fut le berceau du christianisme.

Les musulmans des Balkans appartiennent, dans leur grande majorité,
aux mêmes communautés ethniques, linguistiques et culturelles, que les
chrétiens: ils sont des musulmans slaves, bulgares, croates, albanais,
grecs, turcs, pomaques, tziganes, etc. Cela signifie qu'ils vivent sur la
terre de leurs ancêtres au même titre que les autres, qu'ils ont vécu la
même expérience historique, la même histoire douloureuse et qu'ils ont
participé de la même manière que les chrétiens à la formation de la culture balkanique. Le fait donc qu'ils constituent aujourd'hui une minorité
religieuse ne doit pas les priver des droits territoriaux, politiques, culturels et religieux dont jouissent leurs compatriotes chrétiens.

Mais cette vérité fondamentale est tout aussi valable pour les minorités chrétiennes du Proche et du Moyen Orient, car ces chrétiens sont,
eux aussi, en même temps des Égyptiens, des Libanais, des Syriens, des
Jordaniens, des Irakiens, etc., au même titre que leurs compatriotes
musulmans. Et si l'arabité constitue la conscience collective des Musulmans de cette région, les Chrétiens revendiquent avec la même force
cette même référence identitaire ainsi que leur droit à participer activement au devenir politique et culturel de la région.

Orthodoxes et Musulmans se sentent étrangers à la civilisation technologique contemporaine, à la construction des sociétés modernes, aux
valeurs qui régissent notre monde dit occidental. Des raisons historiques
ont fait que nos communautés n'ont pas participé à la construction de ce
monde nouveau dont le devenir commença à l'époque de la Renaissance.
En plus avons-nous le sentiment que ce monde a été construit à nos
dépens par l'exploitation, coloniale ou autre, de nos ressources maté-
rielles et humaines. Aussi avons-nous tendance à nous méfier de l'Occi-

dent (dans le meilleur des cas) ou bien à le rejeter complètement (dans le pire des cas). Ce faisant, nous nous replions sur nous-mêmes et nous cherchons à retourner à nos sources, à revivre et à réactualiser notre passé, généralement idéalisé. Cette attitude ne signifie pas pour autant que nous refusons de nous servir, nous aussi et à notre profit, des acquis de la civilisation technologique moderne (moyens de transport et de communication, produits industriels, armement, savoir scientifique, etc.).

Pour schématiser à l'extrême, je dirais que nos sociétés chrétiennes et musulmanes orientales sont traversées par deux courants de pensée très forts, par deux idéologies tout aussi puissantes l'une que l'autre: d'une part, le désir et l'effort d'imiter l'Occident, de rattraper notre retard dans tous les domaines du savoir et de la technologie; d'autre part, notre refus du modèle occidental dans tout ce qui est ou qui paraît être étranger à la structure et aux valeurs ancestrales de nos sociétés.

Si donc on observe aujourd'hui un courant fondamentaliste puissant et dangereux dans le monde musulman, ce même courant commence également à faire son apparition dans le monde orthodoxe. Peut-être se présente-t-il sous des formes différentes (voir par exemple les nationalismes grec, serbe, russe, etc.), mais il obéit aux mêmes mécanismes d'autodéfense et de retour aux valeurs ancestrales idéalisées.

Notre fondamentalisme se définit le plus souvent par rapport à l'Occident; mais il peut aussi revêtir des formes d'agressivité et d'intolérance vis-à-vis de nos compatriotes qui appartiennent à une autre religion (par exemple musulmans, chrétiens, uniates, shiites, etc.), lorsque le contexte historique vient favoriser de telles situations (guerre du Liban et de Bosnie-Herzégovine, tensions entre Orthodoxes et Musulmans, entre Orthodoxes et Uniates, etc.).

L'histoire n'a pas à nous présenter des exemples de coexistence créatrice et de tolérance religieuse réciproque plus significatifs que celui qu'ont vécu les peuples musulmans et chrétiens en Orient et dans les Balkans. Certes leur entente fut souvent marquée par des déchirements douloureux et par des événements fratricides intolérables; par des conquêtes, par des guerres pour l'indépendance nationale et par des conflits locaux. Mais le dialogue islamo-chrétien fut toujours une réalité voulue et vécue par les uns comme par les autres. Elle l'est encore aujourd'hui. Pour me limiter au seul cas des orthodoxes, S.S. le patriarche d'Antioche Ignace IV, Mgr Georges Khodr, MM Tarek Mitri et Georges Nahas ont été des membres actifs du Mouvement de Jeunesse Orthodoxe qui avait à cœur le dialogue islamo-chrétien. Celui-ci est toujours actif au Proche Orient, même si les responsables orthodoxes ressentent davantage encore les limites de la réciprocité.

J'aimerais terminer ces réflexions avec une dernière remarque: la guerre qui sévit actuellement en Bosnie-Herzégovine n'est pas une guerre de religions. Toutes les instances religieuses l'ont condamnée et la condamnent de concert et avec force. Ce n'est pas non plus une guerre voulue par les peuples qui la subissent. Ceux-ci ont appris à vivre dans la paix et le respect mutuel. Il s'agit d'une exploitation de la religion et des peuples par des hommes politiques ambitieux et étrangers à la religion. Par ailleurs, l'Occident porte une grande responsabilité quant au déclenchement et à la perpétuation de cette guerre.

*   *
*

Des trois confessions chrétiennes, l'Orthodoxie est celle qui a vécu, à notre époque, dans le contexte politique, socio-culturel et religieux le plus insupportable, le plus douloureux: dans le monde orthodoxe slave, elle a connu les régimes communistes totalitaires; en Orient, elle vit en situation de minorité religieuse depuis de longs siècles. L'Église de Grèce (et plus récemment l'Église de Chypre) est la seule à connaître une vie normale, voire une vie privilégiée, puisqu'elle est Église d'État depuis pratiquement la création de l'État grec en 1830. Son cas ne peut donc être qu'un exemple atypique dans le monde orthodoxe; sa situation et sa pensée théologique ne sauraient être étudiées comme un modèle normatif; la Grèce constitue un cas à part et n'a de valeur que comme tel.

Par ailleurs, présenter l'image que les Grecs se font de l'Islam ces cinquante dernières années s'avère une entreprise difficile.

La difficulté réside tout d'abord dans la définition même de l'Islam. En effet, s'agit-il de la religion musulmane, des Musulmans, du monde musulman, ou bien du pouvoir politique musulman? Et encore, s'agit-il des Musulmans orientaux, nord-africains ou des Musulmans turcs et balkaniques? Car si les relations entre les Grecs et les Turcs sont généralement conflictuelles, la Grèce entretient des rapports privilégiés avec les pays arabes. De même, si le Grec n'a qu'une idée rudimentaire, voire folklorique, de la religion musulmane, son imaginaire est, par contre, nourri d'une image aussi claire que négative du monde musulman. Pour être plus clair, l'idée que le Grec se fait de l'Islam est celle du Turc ottoman, du Turc kémalien, du Turc qui a envahi et occupe une partie importante de Chypre et qui pose des problèmes graves au Patriarcat œcuménique de Constantinople, du Turc que, à l'heure actuelle, le Grec associe volontiers au fondamentalisme religieux ou à la situation balkanique. Je veux dire par là que l'image que le Grec se fait de l'islam est étroitement liée à l'histoire de son pays et que cette image lui est inculquée par les livres d'histoire, par le discours politique, par l'école et par les médias. Or cette image n'a une signification religieuse que dans le mesure où l'histoire de **son** pays est liée de manière indissociable à l'histoire de **son** Orthodoxie.

La difficulté réside aussi dans le fait que cette image se présente sous des aspects différents selon que nous la regardons sous tel ou tel angle. Par exemple, voulons-nous connaître l'image que se fait de l'Islam le peuple grec, l'intelligentsia grecque, l'idéologie politique grecque, l'Église grecque, le Grec qui vit en Grèce ou bien celui qui vit à Chypre ou en Turquie? Il va de soi que l'image n'est pas la même sous ces divers angles.

Quelle que soit cependant cette image, elle est moins négative aujourd'hui qu'elle ne l'était par le passé. Car ces dernières décennies, le peuple grec n'a pas eu à connaître ni les guerres pour l'indépendance du siècle dernier (1821-1830), ni les guerres balkaniques (1912-1913), et la catastrophe de l'Asie Mineure du début de notre siècle (1922), les événements de Chypre (1974) et la situation du Patriarcat de Constantinople ne semblent revêtir ni l'importance ni la charge émotive des événements que je viens de mentionner. Et si les relations entre la Grèce et la Turquie n'ont pas été au beau fixe au cours de ces dernières années, les tentatives de rapprochement et de collaboration politique et économique furent plus nombreux que les moments de friction. Par ailleurs les deux pays sont membres du Conseil de l'Europe, de l'OTAN et de nombreux autres organismes internationaux.

J'ai voulu insister sur cet aspect du problème, car il me paraît être d'emblée le plus important, le plus significatif; il est fondamental. Car la Grèce, les Balkans, le Proche Orient, ce n'est pas l'Occident. Chez nous, l'histoire, ancienne ou récente, pèse de tout son poids sur nos sentiments, sur notre émotivité, sur notre imaginaire. C'est notre histoire qui détermine nos rapports avec les autres, avec le monde musulman en particulier. «L'étude de l'Islam en Grèce obéit toujours à des impératifs politiques, nationaux, ecclésiastiques» (An. Yannoulatos).

Quels sont donc aujourd'hui nos rapports avec l'Islam? Quelle est l'image que nous nous faisons de l'Islam? Je tâcherai de répondre à cette question en me référant à deux domaines bien précis de la réalité grecque: a) la situation des Musulmans du pays; b) la recherche scientifique.

a) Il existe en Grèce une minorité religieuse musulmane évaluée à 120.000 personnes dont 52.000 de langue turque; elle est installée dans le nord-est du pays, en Thrace. Elle est protégée aussi bien par les traités internationaux (Lausanne 1924) que par la Constitution et la législation grecques. De ce fait, elle possède ses écoles primaires et secondaires, une école d'instituteurs, ses manuels scolaires, ses mosquées, ses chefs religieux, et même ses députés au Parlement grec.

Cette communauté est plus nombreuse aujourd'hui qu'elle ne l'était en 1924, alors qu'il ne reste que quelques quatre mille Grecs en Turquie sur les 230.000 que la communauté orthodoxe grecque comptait au moment du traité de Lausanne. La minorité musulmane grecque n'a jamais connu de difficultés majeures dans sa vie culturelle et religieuse, ni de la part des autorités, ni, surtout, de la part du peuple grec. Ce dernier comprend parfaitement bien que les Musulmans ont le droit de vivre comme ils entendent leur foi et leur culture. Par ailleurs, les Musulmans et les Chrétiens de Thrace vivent ensemble en parfaite harmonie car ils ont à se partager la même misère et les mêmes mauvais coups de l'histoire.

Les événements des dernières décennies ont fait venir et s'établir en Grèce, à Athènes notamment, un assez grand nombre de Musulmans du Proche et de l'Extrême Orient. Jusqu'à présent, le gouvernement grec, soutenu par l'Église, n'a pas autorisé la construction, à Athènes, d'un lieu de culte. Un tel lieu fonctionne dans un grand hôtel athénien pour les besoins de sa clientèle musulmane. Il existe encore un autre local de culte au sous-sol d'un immeuble des quartiers populaires. Pour les grandes fêtes, les Musulmans d'Athènes doivent célébrer leurs offices en plein air. Cependant, la Faculté de Théologie de Thessalonique a cédé aux étudiants musulmans de cette Université une salle qui fut transformée en mosquée et qui fonctionne comme telle normalement, à la grande satisfaction de tous les intéressés.

b) Il n'existe à l'heure actuelle aucun groupe de dialogue islamo-chrétien à quelque niveau et sous quelque forme que ce soit. Personne, semble-t-il, ne ressent la nécessité d'un tel dialogue, ni du côté musulman ni du côté orthodoxe. Les quelques tentatives qui ont eu lieu pour nouer le dialogue avec les Musulmans de Thrace (prof. S. Agouridis) n'ont pu aboutir à des résultats concrets.

Cependant, ce dialogue a pu être noué à un niveau beaucoup plus élevé, celui des rencontres scientifiques. En voici quelques exemples:

1. Les congrès greco-arabica (et la revue scientifique GRECO-ARABICA), organisés à l'initiative du prof. V. Christidis. Ces rencontres

réunissent périodiquement des universitaires et des chercheurs grecs et arabes des pays du Proche Orient. Elles sont en partie subventionnées par l'État grec et n'ont jamais rencontré aucune difficulté ou hostilité. Leur objet principal est certes l'histoire commune des mondes grec et arabe sans mention spéciale de la religion, mais celle-ci est examinée comme l'un des éléments de cette histoire.

2. Les congrès islamo-orthodoxes organisés à l'initiative de quelques théologiens grecs (S. Agouridis, Gr. Ziakas, N. Zacharopoulos) d'une part, de l'Ambassade d'Iran à Athènes d'autre part, et financés principalement par l'Ambassade d'Iran. Au nombre de trois, ces rencontres se sont tenues à Athènes et ont eu un caractère éminemment religieux, consacrés exclusivement au dialogue entre l'Islam et l'Orthodoxie. La participation fut toujours importante de la part des théologiens orthodoxes grecs et musulmans iraniens et les travaux se sont déroulés dans une atmosphère de cordialité et de fraternité exemplaires. Les séances étant ouvertes au public, l'auditoire a toujours été nombreux et attentif.

3. Au niveau des pays balkaniques, il existe depuis les années 1960 des Centres d'Études Balkaniques, un dans chaque pays, subventionnés par les États respectifs et déployant une grande activité scientifique: recherche, édition d'ouvrages et de périodiques, organisation de colloques bilatéraux. Un grand Congrès d'Études Balkaniques est organisé tous les cinq ans, chaque fois dans un autre pays balkanique, réunissant plusieurs centaines de participants appartenant à tous les domaines du savoir en matière de sciences humaines. Les Centres d'Études Balkaniques furent, et sont toujours, les lieux privilégiés de rencontres entre scientifiques des pays balkaniques, même si les difficultés conjoncturelles n'ont jamais été absentes. La religion est un domaine de recherche comme tous les autres et cela permet de faire des progrès dans ce domaine également et surtout d'offrir des occasions de rencontres qui seraient impossibles autrement.

4. Les congrès islamo-chrétiens organisés en commun accord par l'Académie Islamique d'Amman et par le Centre Orthodoxe de Chambésy. Ces rencontres ne concernent certes pas directement la Grèce, mais elles constituent l'engagement le plus sérieux et le plus officiel de l'Église orthodoxe dans le dialogue avec l'Islam.

5. Le pas le plus décisif dans la connaissance de l'Islam a été fait par l'enseignement supérieur grec. Des chaires de Théologie existent dans pratiquement toutes les Facultés de Lettres. Dans certaines Universités, il y a aussi un enseignement de la langue arabe. Mais la chose la plus significative fut l'occupation de la chaire d'histoire des religions dans

les deux Facultés de Théologie (Université d'Athènes et de Thessalonique) par deux spécialistes de l'Islam: Anastasios Yannulatos, l'actuel archevêque de Tirana, occupe celle de l'Université d'Athènes depuis trente ans; M. Grigoris Ziakas celle de l'Université de Thessalonique depuis quinze ans.

L'ouvrage de Mgr Yannulatos, *L'Islam* (Athènes 1975), constitue la contribution la plus importante pour la connaissance de l'Islam en milieu estudiantin et intellectuel grec. C'est un ouvrage qui s'impose par ses qualités supérieures de synthèse, par sa compréhension du fait religieux musulman, par son respect de la foi d'autrui, choses auxquelles n'est pas encore habituée la littérature grecque.

Bon connaisseur de l'arabe et de l'Islam, M. Ziakas est formé à l'école allemande (Vienne). Sa contribution à la connaissance de l'Islam fut considérable, car il est l'auteur de nombreux livres sur l'Islam, sur la pensée musulmane et sur les rapports entre la pensée grecque et la pensée musulmane.

Il me faut également mentionner deux autres noms: Monsieur le professeur Savas Agouridis, professeur de Nouveau Testament à l'Université d'Athènes, homme très ouvert au dialogue avec les autres communautés, les autres cultures et les autres familles de pensée, et Monsieur le professeur Nikos Zacharopoulos, professeur d'Histoire ecclésiastique à l'Université de Thessalonique, responsable de la revue *Kath'odon*, une revue théologique qui a largement ouvert ses pages à l'Islam et à un dialogue islamo-chrétien.

6. Il faut signaler également que les vingt ou trente dernières années ont vu paraître en Grèce un assez grand nombre d'ouvrages consacrés à l'Islam ou aux rapports historiques entre le monde orthodoxe grec et le monde musulman, arabe et turc. Même si leur niveau scientifique ou leur objectivité ne sont pas toujours ceux que l'on aurait souhaités, ces publications marquent un tournant décisif dans l'approche du fait religieux musulman faite par les intellectuels grecs, et tendent à créer un climat nouveau, une ouverture significative.

* * *

Vous me permettrez de terminer ce bref exposé par quelques réflexions me concernant, car ma situation en tant qu'orthodoxe grec engagé dans le dialogue islamo-chrétien est une situation ambivalente. D'origine, de langue et de culture grecque, formé à la Faculté de Théologie Orthodoxe de l'Université de Thessalonique, j'occupe depuis bientôt trente-cinq ans un poste d'enseignement de langue et de littérature néo-helléniques dans une université française. Engagé activement dans le dialogue islamo-chrétien depuis vingt-cinq ans, mes travaux de recherche portent sur la littérature grecque byzantine et post-byzantine de polémique et d'apologétique à l'adresse de l'Islam, c'est-à-dire la littérature qui donne de l'Islam et du monde musulman l'image la plus négative. Bien qu'orthodoxe, mon engagement s'est toujours effectué avec les Catholiques et les Protestants, en France et ailleurs. Je me dois aussi de noter que mon étude *Coran et Histoire* fut publiée en version française dans la revue *Theologia* (1983-1984), organe officiel de l'Église de Grèce, ainsi que par les éditions d'«Apostoliki Diakonia» (1992, version grecque), qui sont également les éditions officielles de l'Église de Grèce. Le geste de l'Église fut courageux dans ce cas précis et la publication n'a rencontré aucune hostilité particulière, ni de la part de la presse, ni de la part du public.

Le dialogue islamo-chrétien se trouve en Grèce dans une situation embryonnaire; il existe incontestablement une certaine curiosité et une ouverture d'esprit envers la religion musulmane, mais le dialogue islamo-chrétien n'est pas encore ressenti comme une nécessité du présent.

ISLAM ET CHRISTIANISME

DEPUIS LE MILIEU DU 20e SIÈCLE

Abdelmajid Charfi

Toutes les religions connaissent à travers leur histoire des interprétations continuelles. Celles-ci peuvent être de simples rappels exigés par la nécessité de définition de l'ordre social en termes religieux, au fur et à mesure que le temps passe, que les situations changent et que les générations se succèdent. Dans ce cas, on a souvent l'impression d'une certaine stagnation et que l'on ne fait que répéter inlassablement les mêmes discours et les mêmes arguments. Bien que cette reprise ne soit jamais à proprement parler une répétition pure et simple et qu'il y ait toujours une expression et une construction théorique ou plus riches ou plus pauvres, il est plus intéressant de remarquer que, sous la pression de l'histoire, ces interprétations peuvent également être franchement divergentes. On dirait que, au-delà des considérations personnelles, toute communauté religieuse a un besoin vital d'avoir à sa disposition un certain nombre d'options parmi lesquelles elle choisit celle qui lui semble le mieux répondre à ses aspirations et à ses conditions propres. Certes, ce choix peut s'avérer malheureux et la mener à sa perte, mais il est en général celui qui lui fournit l'équilibre qu'elle recherche à un moment donné de sa vie.

Les réinterprétations successives que l'islam et le christianisme ont connues n'échappent guère à ce schéma général, qui est resté globalement valable jusqu'à la seconde guerre mondiale. En fait, les défis que l'une et l'autre religions durent relever ont commencé avec les assauts qui leur ont été infligés par l'irruption de la modernité, à partir du 18e siècle dans l'aire chrétienne et du 19e siècle dans l'aire musulmane. Nous considérons en effet que la Renaissance et la Réforme n'ont pas posé au christianisme des problèmes insolubles et que son système général de référence pouvait lui fournir des solutions adaptées à la situation nouvelle à laquelle il devait faire face. Ce sont les Lumières et ce que Paul Hazard a appelé «la crise de la conscience européenne» qui lui ont posé les défis majeurs qui l'ont acculé à rechercher des réponses qui sortent de son cadre traditionnel. Quant à l'Islam, c'est avec un siècle et demi de retard qu'au contact de l'Occident il dut vivre la même expé-

A. CHARFI

rience, peut-être plus déchirante encore, parce que les défis n'étaient pas endogènes et qu'il n'y était point préparé par des remises en question aussi audacieuses et radicales que celles de la Renaissance et de la Réforme.

Cependant, vaille que vaille et avec des fortunes diverses, le christianisme et l'islam ont pu se maintenir dans les sociétés où ils étaient fortement implantés et n'ont pas essuyé les pertes ravageuses de crédibilité qu'ils ont connues de façon dramatique dans les cinquante dernières années. C'est donc dans les contextes d'après-guerre, culturels, politiques, économiques et sociaux que nous avons à rechercher les raisons des difficultés de tous ordres que vivent ces deux grandes religions universelles, et en même temps les perspectives nouvelles qui se sont ouvertes à leurs adhérents aussi bien en ce qui concerne la qualité de leurs croyances que dans leurs rapports avec les fidèles des autres religions. Nous ne perdons pas de vue naturellement que si certaines attitudes sont inédites, beaucoup d'autres représentent le mûrissement de positions latentes qui attendaient le moment propice pour passer sur le devant de la scène ou marginalisées et combattues plus ou moins ouvertement, soit qu'elles étaient franchement en avance sur leur temps, soit qu'elles heurtaient trop directement des intérêts établis ou des habitudes de pensée bien ancrées. En d'autres termes, nous sommes en présence d'un phénomène complexe dont l'analyse doit constamment se garder d'être réductrice et de tomber dans les stéréotypes stériles entretenus par l'ignorance et la peur et véhiculés par des médias pressés par les événements de présenter des explications toutes faites et trop enclins à tomber dans les clichés commodes et simplistes. Sans nier que ces stéréotypes correspondent quand même à une part de vérité, il est à notre avis beaucoup plus intéressant de retenir les éléments porteurs et d'examiner, par delà l'écume apparente, les vagues de fond qui sont à l'œuvre dans les processus dans lesquels sont engagés l'islam et le christianisme depuis un demi-siècle. Autant dire que notre exposé sera délibérément sélectif, non en fonction d'un a priori quelconque, mais en vertu d'une approche empirique qui essaie de dégager, dans la mesure du possible, ce qui nous semble caractériser le plus la situation de chacune des deux religions dans son évolution interne ainsi que par rapport à son contexte socio-historique et à l'autre religion.

Dans le domaine religieux qui nous intéresse ici particulièrement, six facteurs parmi tant d'autres paraissent déterminants:
– Nous placerons en premier lieu les progrès fulgurants de la science et de la technique accomplis depuis la dernière guerre mondiale. Le rythme

des découvertes scientifiques et technologiques n'a jamais été aussi rapide. Le fait que tous les domaines de la connaissances ont été concernés par ces progrès nous dispense de citer des exemples pour les illustrer. En effet, de l'infiniment grand à l'infiniment petit, de l'astronomie à la génétique et à la biologie moléculaire, de la chimie et de la physique à l'informatique et à la médecine, les frontières du savoir humain ont été poussées à des limites absolument insoupçonnés il y a à peine deux générations. Du reste, les sciences de l'homme et de la société ont, elles aussi, fait un grand bond en avant qui a vu la linguistique, la psychologie, l'anthropologie, la sociologie, l'histoire, l'économie et tant d'autres disciplines encore, acquérir un statut qui ne leur était guère reconnu auparavant.

– Les retombées de ces progrès tous azimuts n'ont pas tardé à se manifester dans tous les aspects de la vie. Le «développement» — terme galvaudé et ambigu mais commode malgré tout — est sensible partout, exceptés quelques pays qui d'ailleurs n'appartiennent pas à l'aire géographique où l'islam et le christianisme sont implantés de longue date (l'Afrique noire en particulier) et exceptée la préservation de la nature et de l'équilibre écologique. Qu'il s'agisse du P. I. B. par habitant, de l'espérance de vie à la naissance, de la consommation moyenne de calories, du niveau d'instruction, des services publics de santé, de l'infrastructure de base ou des équipements collectifs, etc., il est aujourd'hui mesuré selon des critères universels qui démontrent que l'élévation générale du niveau de vie n'est pas un vain mot, même si, par ailleurs, les fruits de la croissance économique sont trop inégalement répartis entre les nations et à l'intérieur de chaque nation et que des millions de personnes vivent dans une misère et un dénuement intolérables à côté de richesses ostentatoires et de gaspillages monstres. D'où les frustations légitimes et les solutions, parfois violentes, de désespoir.

– Nous citerons en troisième lieu l'amélioration de la condition féminine. Non que les inégalités entre les sexes aient disparu dans tous les pays ou qu'elles soient partout sensiblement atténuées, mais il est indéniable qu'un nombre de plus en plus important de femmes ont accédé au statut de citoyennes à part entière et qu'elles participent activement à la vie publique, avec tous les droits et les devoirs inhérents à cette participation dans la vie politique, l'administration, les entreprises économiques, les activités sociales et culturelles. L'histoire retiendra probablement de cette seconde moitié du vingtième siècle le fait majeur que la femme a obtenu pour la première fois le pouvoir de maîtriser sa fécondité; ce qui n'est pas sans répercussion sur son autonomie en tant que

personne libre qui ne subit plus son sort dans la résignation. L'invention
de la pilule contraceptive, la généralisation des autres procédés de
contraception et même, dans de plus en plus de pays, la possibilité d'in-
terrompre volontairement la grossesse marqueront à jamais cette période
parce qu'elles ont été vraisemblablement les facteurs essentiels dans le
changement des mentalités et des attitudes sociales liées à la sexualité.
– Notons également que l'amélioration de la condition de la femme,
comme celle de l'homme, a été favorisée par les progrès de la scolarisation. La généralisation de l'enseignement a permis à des couches
entières de la population d'accéder à la lumière du savoir qui était
naguère réservée à une élite privilégiée par les hasards de la fortune et de
la naissance. Cette démocratisation a eu pour corollaire que l'enseignement a échappé partiellement ou entièrement à la mainmise des autorités
religieuses. Les jeunes éduqués dans ce contexte ont donc un accès plus
facile à la connaissance multiforme des temps modernes et ne peuvent
plus adhérer aussi facilement à la vision du monde jadis imposée par les
religions ou simplement portée par les théodicées traditionnelles. Les
théologiens n'ont pas encore réussi à se représenter clairement les conséquences profondes introduites par ces changements au niveau des
croyances et des pratiques religieuses.
– Les supports traditionnels de la religion s'étant écroulés l'un après
l'autre, c'est à une sécularisation accélérée de la culture et de la société
que nous avons assisté pendant le dernier demi-siècle, malgré le «retour
du sacré» monté en épingle par certains et qui n'est que l'expression
d'une réaction tout à fait compréhensible à cette sécularisation qui
affecte désormais l'économie, la bureaucratie, l'art et le droit comme la
politique. La légitimation religieuse n'a plus d'impact réel sur l'ensemble de ces secteurs. Lorsqu'elle persiste c'est plutôt au niveau de la
rhétorique qu'au niveau de la réalité. Seule la famille échappe encore en
partie à ce processus.
– Le sixième facteur n'est pas le moins important, c'est la mondialisation. Les progrès des communications par satellite et des transports
aériens, la multiplication des échanges commerciaux, l'implantation des
sociétés multinationales, le mouvement des capitaux à travers les frontières, le développement du tourisme de masse... font aujourd'hui que
notre planète est devenue un «village» où les informations circulent à
une vitesse vertigineuse, où tout ce qui se passe dans le moindre recoin
peut être connu instantanément de tous les habitants du monde par
l'image et le son comme par la télécopie. Les informations recueillies
par satellite ont percé l'étanchéité des frontières politiques et achevé ce

que les lois du marché ont commencé. Les relents de nationalisme exaspéré et chauvin auxquels on assiste ici ou là ne seraient donc dûs qu'à une réaction à ce phénomène, mais il s'agit d'une réaction de peur et de repli sur des identités étroites, qui navigue manifestement à contre-courant.

Les effets cumulés de ces facteurs conjugués ont varié suivant les contextes locaux. On peut donc les suivre au niveau de chaque tradition religieuse particulière. Mais on peut également les déceler dans les réponses que l'islam et le christianisme pris dans leur ensemble ont fournies à leurs adeptes. Nous nous arrêterons ainsi dans un premier temps sur les caractéristiques principales des deux courants majoritaires dans le christianisme, à savoir le catholicisme et le protestantisme, et dans l'islam, c'est-à-dire le sunnisme et le chiisme, avant de voir dans un deuxième temps comment chrétiens et musulmans ont réagi à la fois les uns vis-à-vis des autres et les deux en commun face aux défis du monde contemporain.

Le catholicisme est bien connu pour ses structures ecclésiales rigides et fortement hiérarchisées. Son histoire depuis la Révolution française en particulier se confond avec son opposition farouche aux valeurs et aux pratiques de la modernité. C'est ainsi qu'il a mené des combats d'arrière-garde acharnés contre la séparation de l'Église et de l'État, contre le libéralisme, le socialisme, la démocratie, le rationalismee, la liberté religieuse, les résultats de l'exégèse historico-critique de la Bible et, d'une façon générale, contre toutes les nouveautés qui heurtent sa théologie traditionnelle. L'affirmation de ses thèses anti-démocratiques a culminé au concile de Vatican I (1870) avec le dogme de l'infaillibilité pontificale. Le fossé n'a cessé par conséquent de se creuser entre l'Église et la réalité, fossé durement ressenti par des individus et des groupes d'intellectuels qui se situaient en marge des structures religieuses officielles et qui entendaient rester fidèles à l'Église et en même temps voir ses attitudes évoluer en fonction des données culturelles et sociales nouvelles.

Lorsque donc le concile de Vatican II, réuni par Jean XXIII, publia ses actes en 1965 sous le pontificat de Paul VI, tout le monde — et en premier lieu les catholiques — reconnut dans ce concile un virage historique. Aussi bien sur les questions théologiques sensibles, comme la liberté religieuse et les rapports avec les autres religions, que sur les questions pastorales et liturgiques; même ceux qui auraient souhaité que le concile aille plus loin admirent facilement que l'Église catholique venait enfin d'épouser son siècle. Les intégristes ne s'y sont pas trompés puisque certains, comme Mgr Lefebvre, sont allés carrément jusqu'à la scission.

L'euphorie de l'immédiat après-concile ne dura cependant pas long-temps, car depuis l'avènement de Jean-Paul II en 1978 et sans renier expressément les décisions de Vatican II, un coup de barre à droite a été donné à l'Église. Le pape, d'origine polonaise, ne manquait aucune occasion de nommer des évêques conservateurs et de défendre, sur les problèmes politiques, sociaux et moraux, des thèses traditionnelles qui confortaient les intégristes mais ne faisaient qu'éloigner les théologiens contestataires (Küng et Drewermann, par exemple) et les représentants de la théologie de la libération, et surtout vider les églises de la masse de leurs fidèles, ou du moins accélérer le mouvement.

Le protestantisme, de par ses structures plus souples et décentralisées, n'a pas suivi une ligne parallèle à celle du catholicisme. Depuis la publi-cation par Schleiermacher en 1799 de son «*Discours sur la religion*», c'est la théologie libérale qui a dominé la pensée protestante. Caractéri-sée par un effort soutenu d'adaptation à l'idéologie libérale et nourrissant même celle-ci à certains égards, selon la fameuse thèse de Max Weber dans «*Le protestantisme et l'esprit du capitalisme*», elle n'a été détrônée que pendant la période de l'entre-deux-guerres par la néo-orthodoxie dont Karl Barth fut l'initiateur et le représentant le plus éminent.

Mais, depuis la seconde guerre mondiale, s'est dessiné de nouveau un retour à la théologie libérale, favorisé par les idées d'auteurs tels que Bultmann et sa «démythologisation», Bonhoeffer dans sa distinction entre «foi» et «religion» et Paul Tillich dans sa «*Systematic Theology*». On a même assisté, dans les années soixante, à une «dérivé» radicale ou ultra libérale dont l'échantillon le plus célèbre est le livre de John Robin-son «*Honest to God*». Puis cette tendance a été relayée, à partir du milieu des années soixante-dix et dans les années quatre-vingts, par un retour en force du fondamentalisme et un engouement pour les petites églises évangélistes. Cependant, ce qui est remarquable c'est qu'au même moment les «grandes» églises protestantes (anglicane, luthé-rienne et calviniste) ont maintenu grosso modo leur orientation libérale dont l'ordination dernièrement de femmes évêques dans l'anglicanisme est la meilleure illustration.

Quant à l'islam, dans sa version sunnite largement majoritaire, il a été fortement secoué par le choc du contact avec la civilisation occidentale et particulièrement sous sa forme expansionniste et impérialiste. Le mouvement réformiste d'Afghani et de Abduh à la fin du 19e et au début du 20e s. se voulait surtout un retour aux sources et une purification de l'islam, seuls à même de lui redonner sa vigueur originelle et sa capacité d'adaptation aux situation nouvelles. Il a donc forgé une apologétique qui essayait de récupérer le rationalisme triomphant et le scientisme en vogue. Mais il n'a pas tardé, pendant l'entre deux guerres, à être débordé sur sa droite par les «frères musulmans» et sur sa gauche par des intellectuels libéraux ayant une meilleure connaissance de la culture occidentale moderne.

Les cinquante dernières années peuvent être divisées grossièrement en deux périodes: dans la première, qui va jusqu'au milieu des années soixante-dix, l'islam a été d'abord une idéologie de combat dans les luttes de libération nationale puis une instance de légitimation des transformations introduites par les États-nations issus de ces luttes. Les représentants de l'institution religieuse traditionnelle étant généralement discrédités pour leur collaboration avec les autorités coloniales, on a assisté à l'éclosion de nombreuses thèses audacieuses tendant à actualiser la pensée islamique, à réinterpréter les textes fondateurs et à trouver des compromis entre les valeurs modernes et les prescriptions du droit religieux classique. Cet islam ouvert et tolérant ne s'est pas complètement éteint pendant la deuxième période qui va du milieu des années soixante-dix jusqu'à nos jours, loin de là, mais le devant de la scène a été occupé par les activistes islamistes, encouragés politiquement et financièrement — au moins jusqu'à la guerre du Golfe — par les régimes anachroniques de la presqu'île arabique devenus arrogants par la richesse tirée de la manne pétrolière. Pour les islamistes, et plus encore pour leurs troupes, l'islam est devenu une idéologie refuge face aux distorsions entre les promesses de l'indépendance politique et la misère de la réalité vécue par les laissés-pour-compte d'une modernisation tronquée et pervertie qui n'a profité qu'à une minorité de privilégiés.

Enfin, l'islam chiite contemporain a ressenti aussi durement le choc de la modernité. Si la tendance réformiste a pu prévaloir en son sein jusqu'aux années cinquante, c'est qu'il héritait d'une tradition philosophique spiritualiste bien vivante au moment même où le sunnisme connaissait une sclérose et une léthargie profondes. C'est la marche forcée vers l'occidentalisation imposée par le régime du dernier chah d'Iran et les méthodes autoritaires qu'il pratiquait, ajoutées à la menace qu'il faisait peser sur les privilèges du clergé, qui ont provoqué la réaction violente de la «révolution islamique» de 1978-79. Cette révolution a été préparée par les idées de penseurs rénovateurs tels que Ali Chariati, mais elle a pu être récupérée par la tendance rétrograde du clergé chiite conduite par Khomeiny, en partie parce que la formation traditionnelle de ce clergé ne le préparait guère à assumer la mutation nécessaire qu'exigeait l'adaptation aux valeurs de la modernité et des droits de l'homme, dont l'universalité est niée du fait même qu'elles ont vu le jour dans un contexte occidental.

Sans avoir constamment à l'esprit aussi bien les facteurs déterminants dans la situation des sociétés humaines dans le dernier demi-siècle que les particularités de l'évolution de chaque grande tradition religieuse au cours de cette période, il est difficile d'appréhender les perceptions mutuelles de l'islam et du christianisme, car celles-ci sont influencées par les contraintes du présent autant que par les péripéties de l'histoire de chaque religion et par la structure interne de chaque pensée religieuse. Ajoutons que ces perceptions ne sont pas toujours suffisamment pensées et ne trouvent pas par conséquent leur expression adéquate dans la production des «clercs», théologiens ou théoriciens laïcs. Néanmoins, elles sont bien présentes dans les comportements des fidèles et pèsent sur les décisions pratiques des autorités religieuses, même lorsqu'il s'agit de communautés qui coexistent épisodiquement ou en permanence sans vraiment se connaître.

En outre, quand on parle des perceptions mutuelles de l'islam et du christianisme, on a trop tendance à privilégier les positions des porte-parole officiels ou quasi officiels de chaque groupe religieux, alors que ces positions sont loin de refléter fidèlement les attitudes individuelles des croyants qui peuvent se reconnaître en tout ou en partie dans ce que proclament leurs leaders comme ils peuvent ne pas s'y reconnaître du tout. Il n'est pas rare ni vraiment exceptionnel que les affinités entre les personnes transcendent les particularismes confessionnels, que des chrétiens se sentent plus proches de certains musulmans que de leurs propres coreligionnaires et vice versa, au grand dam évidemment de ceux qui se considèrent investis de la mission de gardiens de l'orthodoxie. Ceux-ci d'ailleurs, par-delà leurs divergences, manifestent une solidarité remarquable les uns vis-à-vis des autres, à propos d'événements sacrilèges pour l'une des parties. Ainsi, les dignitaires musulmans ont pris fait et cause pour les responsables chrétiens lors de la sortie du film de Martin Scorsese «*La dernière tentation du Christ*» et ceux-ci se sont joints à ceux-là lors de la publication par Salman Rushdie de ses «*Versets sataniques*» — sans aller bien sûr, de même que leurs collègues musulmans dans leur grande majorité, jusqu'à approuver la *fatwa* de Khomeiny à son égard.

Cette solidarité est aussi à rapprocher de celle qui a été suscitée par le mouvement œcuménique chrétien et par les tentatives de rapprochement entre sunnites et chiites. Tout se passe comme si, confrontés aux mêmes défis, musulmans et chrétiens éprouvent le besoin de former un front commun de la foi contre l'athéisme et le matérialisme et, pis encore, contre l'indifférence religieuse rampante. C'est ainsi que catholiques et protestants mettent en veilleuse leurs querelles ancestrales et leurs divergences pour ne retenir que ce qui les unit et qui est à leurs yeux beaucoup plus important que ce qui les divise. Le même phénomène est perceptible chez les musulmans. Il n'y a pas si longtemps, les tenants des écoles juridiques à l'intérieur même du sunnisme entretenaient une inimitié et une exclusion réciproques, mais depuis que la loi positive a marginalisé partout dans le monde musulman, la loi religieuse, jusques et y compris sous les régimes qui se prétendent islamiques, on assiste à une fraternité retrouvée dans l'adversité commune qui les frappe sans distinction.

Doit-on situer dans ce cadre ce qu'il est convenu d'appeler le dialogue islamo-chrétien et les nombreuses rencontres qui lui ont été consacrées? De l'extérieur du moins, répondre oui à cette question ne semble pas faire de doute, bien qu'elle semble assez réductrice lorsqu'on examine de plus près les motivations des protagonistes de ce dialogue. La variété des attitudes défendues lors de ces rencontres, des horizons culturels des participants et même des recommandations émises à leur issue n'autorise pas en effet les généralisations abusives. Quoiqu'il en soit, personne ne peut nier que le dialogue est en soi une entreprise positive pour au moins quatre raisons:
– parce qu'il est aux antipodes des attitudes belliqueuses du passé qui ont été à l'origine de conflits armés entre les communautés musulmane et chétienne lors des conquêtes des débuts de l'islam et surtout des Croisades et de la Reconquista espagnole qui est allée jusqu'à la conversion forcée de musulmans:
– parce qu'il est de loin préférable au dénigrement mutuel systématique, à la diabolisation de l'adversaire et à la déformation, souvent délibérée, de ses dogmes et de sa morale qui étaient la règle dans la littérature apologétique et polémique florissante:
– parce qu'il constitue, malgré ses insuffisances et ses limites, un progrès remarquable par rapport à l'ignorance phénoménale entretenue pendant des siècles chez la masse des fidèles et aussi chez les élites cultivées, alors que l'islam et le christianisme appartiennent à la même tradition biblique et monothéiste;
– et enfin parce que dialoguer ne signifie pas être d'accord sur tout mais être à l'écoute de l'autre et situer les divergences à leur juste valeur, ce

qui est de nature à offrir des perspectives très vastes pour la collaboration et les entreprises communes dans l'action sociale et l'effort pour la paix et la justice.

Certes le dialogue islamo-chrétien a le plus souvent fonctionné sous la forme de discours parallèles et de récriminations réciproques débouchant dans la plupart des cas sur des déclarations de bonnes intentions non suivies, ou presque, d'effet. Il était alors tout à fait naturel que se substituent au dialogue des structures paritaires de recherche commune sur des sujets qui concernent les musulmans et les chrétiens. Le Groupe de Recherches Islamo-Chrétien (GRIC), qui fêtera bientôt ses vingt ans d'existence, en est à cet égard l'exemple le plus réussi. Beaucoup de chemin, cependant, reste à faire. Ces initiatives d'avant-garde ne doivent pas faire oublier que, mis à part un nombre très restreint de chercheurs, la réflexion qui se fait à l'intérieur de l'aire musulmane comme de l'aire chrétienne n'inclut pas encore le christianisme dans le premier cas et l'islam dans le second. Les «théologiens» font encore comme s'ils n'étaient pas concernés par ce que pensent et disent leurs homologues de l'autre religion. Et cela se répercute fatalement sur les «catéchismes» et les manuels d'enseignement religieux, malgré quelques efforts louables ici ou là, mais somme toute limités dans leur envergure du fait qu'ils ne dépassent guère une présentation plus objective ou moins tendancieuse de la religion sœur, tout en restant extérieure.

Il nous semble par ailleurs superflu de passer en revue toutes les représentations stéréotypées qui ont cours dans chaque religion à propos de l'autre. Qu'il nous suffise d'énumérer les plus courantes et les plus significatives:
– L'islam est la religion du fanatisme, il ignore la séparation du temporel et du spirituel qui lui sera fatale le jour où elle s'instaurera, il idolâtre un texte (le Coran), il impose un statut inférieur à la femme, il refuse la liberté religieuse, ses lois sont contraires aux droits de l'homme...
– Le christianisme est une perversion du message de Jésus, il ne porte aucun intérêt aux choses de la vie, il est de nature inquisitoriale, il ne peut se propager que par la force matérielle, il a institué des médiateurs entre l'homme et Dieu, il est l'ennemi de la raison et de la science...

Ce qu'il importe de noter c'est que ces représentations, ainsi que beaucoup d'autres, ne sont pas innocentes. Elles dissimulent des conflits d'intérêt lorsqu'elles ne sont pas l'héritage d'un passé lui aussi conflictuel. Il y a lieu également de remarquer que les considérations proprement théologiques passent aujourd'hui au second plan et laissent la place à des aspects qu'on qualifierait plutôt de sociologiques. Certaines représentations sont ainsi plus pertinentes à une époque qu'à une autre. Il est rare, par exemple, dans le dernier demi-siècle d'entendre parler du fatalisme de l'islam, s'agissant de la religion dominante dans des sociétés en mutation rapide et en pleine effercescence, alors que c'était un reproche constant dans la littérature chrétienne du 19ᵉ siècle. Le fatalisme d'antan a été remplacé par le fanatisme alimenté par l'islamisme militant. De même, le thème du christianisme synonyme d'inquisition et d'intolérance n'est plus aussi répandu depuis que le bras séculier n'est plus à la disposition de l'Église dans les pays de tradition chrétienne, il est remplacé par le christianisme agent de l'impérialisme occidental, en particulier là où il y est en concurrence avec l'islam, plus précisément la mission avec la *da'wa*.

Qu'y a-t-il à retenir de cette analyse forcément rapide et fragmentaire? Les changements d'attitude intervenus à l'intérieur des deux religions concernées, comme ceux qui affectent le regard porté par l'une sur l'autre, sont à mettre au crédit des facteurs historiques massifs qui ont bouleversé les modes de vie, les conditions d'existence et les visions du monde des individus et des groupes. En tête de ces facteurs et en plus de ceux qui ont marqué le dernier demi-siècle (progrès de la science et de la technique, élévation du niveau de vie, amélioration de la condition féminine, scolarisation, sécularisation et mondialisation) on doit certainement placer l'urbanisation et l'industrialisation, en extension dans tous les pays. Le développement de l'anonymat et de la solitude dans les grandes métropoles, la dissolution de la contrainte sociale omniprésente dans les villages, les campagnes et les cités traditionnelles, la disparition des solidarités claniques et tribales jadis très puissantes, l'individualisme inhérent à la structure sociale moderne sont responsables des mutations qui ont mis un terme au monolithisme de rigueur dans les religions anciennes et favorisé l'émergence de «sectes» chaque jour plus nombreuses qui revendiquent la fidélité à l'islam ou au christianisme par souci de se rattacher à une tradition valorisante plus que par respect pour l'enseignement et les valeurs de cette tradition.

On est tenté d'appeler ces sectes «nouvelles religions» s'il ne s'agissait pas davantage d'une mise en forme, voire d'une mise en scène, de techniques d'organisation et de communication que de l'apparition de croyances fondamentalement nouvelles. Leur bricolage des croyances et des pratiques témoignent en fait de la perte d'influence des organisations religieuses qui avaient assuré, jusqu'à un passé récent, la gestion du sacré. Elles ont l'avantage sur les structures classiques de prendre en charge concrètement les peines physiques et spirituelles de leurs membres en leur offrant la possibilité individuelle d'adhérer à un enseignement plus proche des préoccupations quotidiennes. C'est ainsi que l'islamisme assume les revendications identitaires de populations déboussolées tandis que les mouvements évangélistes proposent une expérience immédiate du sacré et un salut dans le monde présent. Leur fanatisme relatif s'expliquerait par le fait qu'elles sont en concurrence sur le même marché religieux et idéologique, en l'occurrence celui de jeunes en quête de dignité et de repères sinon fixes du moins assez stables.

Dans ces conditions, il est difficile d'évoquer les perceptions mutuelles de l'islam et du christianisme sans tenir compte du changement radical du paysage religieux contemporain. Ces perceptions sont aujourd'hui déterminées en grande partie par ce qu'offrent les moyens modernes de communication, et en particulier la télévision, lesquels sont avides de sensationnel et à la merci des groupes d'intérêt et des lobbies qui les accaparent. Le grand public occidental n'est donc informé que des agissements de quelques groupes islamistes qui recourent à la violence ou à des actes qui sortent de l'ordinaire. Les attitudes normales de piété, la vague de fond de la sécularisation à l'œuvre dans les sociétés musulmanes, la désaffection progressive par rapport aux pratiques cultuelles, les débats passionnés concernant l'application dans le contexte moderne de la loi religieuse, tout cela est laissé dans l'ombre et occulté. Seuls quelques spécialistes avertis de l'islam s'y intéressent. Les musulmans, dans leur très grande majorité, sont logés à la même enseigne. Ils ne sont informés sur le christianisme qu'à propos d'événements spectaculaires: déplacements du pape, réactions à des décisions du Vatican rappelant à l'ordre certains théologiens ou dignitaires, déclarations belliqueuses d'évêques orthodoxes dans le conflit serbo-bosniaque, etc. On y voit des relents de l'esprit des croisades, de l'inquisition et du prosélytisme. En d'autres termes, ce sont les difficultés et les manifestations négatives dans l'une et l'autre religions qui sont mises en exergue. Cela ressemble fort à un exercice d'exorcisme collectif où l'on essaie de se donner bonne conscience à moindre frais et sur le dos de l'autre.

Le tableau qui se dégage de ce constat amer et lucide peut sembler excessivement sombre. Le seul élément, et il est de taille, de nature à le nuancer est que ces perceptions et ces représentations négatives disparaissent en général très vite dès qu'une meilleure connaissance s'instaure entre les individus. Il n'en reste pas moins que, tout en écartant avec la dernière énergie la thèse du complot trop souvent invoquée de part et d'autre, on doit admettre que la pensée religieuse musulmane et chrétienne contemporaine est en crise. Elle ne s'est pas encore débarrassée de son lourd passif historique, notamment de son exclusivisme et de sa tendance à l'auto-satisfaction, et elle est encore au stade du balbutiement dans la recherche d'une expression des croyances adaptée à la connaissance et à la civilisation de cette seconde moitié du vingtième siècle et répondant à ses exigences spirituelles particulières.

ISLAMIC FUNDAMENTALIST PERCEPTIONS
OF OTHER MONOTHEISTIC RELIGIONS

Ahmad S. Moussalli

Introduction

This study aims at shedding light on the theoretical development of
modern Islamic thought, especially the phenomenon of fundamentalism as related to its views of Christianity and Judaism. While minorities have solid foundations in the Middle East, the issue of religious
minorities has been especially explosive since the rise of independent
nationalist states, specifically in the second half of the twentieth century. This study does not deal with the histories of Judaism, Christianity, missionary schools, orientalism or Islam, but focuses on the theoretical analyses of Christianity and Judaism by some Islamic
fundamentalist movements. The first objective of this paper is therefore to show the context or contexts around which Islamic fundamentalisms have arisen and their opposition to the traditionally held views
on religious minorities. The second objective is to show how a theoretical revision of traditional views has taken place because of the negative relationship with the West and its perception as a protector and
manipulator of religious minorities in the Middle East. But, on the
other hand, the third objective is to show that many Muslim fundamentalists as well as ordinary Muslims share with Christians and Jews
theoretical common concerns about pluralism, tolerance, nature of
political order, ethics, morality and co-existence.

Christianity in the Middle East has witnessed a fundamentalist revival
as well, as is the case of Lebanon, the Sudan and Egypt. The Coptic
revival, for instance, has been one of the main features of the politicization of the Egyptian Coptic Church. However, most Western and Middle
Eastern media as well as scholars have in general only treated modern
Islamic fundamentalist discourses as constituting one negative and radical interpretation of the religion of Islam. Worse than this, many analysts
and politicians even made Islam and Islamic fundamentalism exchange-
able, consequently making Islam an easy target as a strategic enemy for
the West. Now, it is widely circulated that the new green — or Islamic
— threat replaces the danger of the red — or communist — threat.

While it is true that many Islamic movements are radical in the sense that they are alienating to and alienated from their societies, others are moderate, cooperate and positively involved in their societies. Islamic 'fundamentalisms' — and even Islam — have however been read through the lenses of Islamic radicalism. But other religions are read through the lenses of their moderate views. This study therefore sets down a preliminary theoretical typology of Islamic 'fundamentalisms' regarding their view of and relationships with other religions, specifically Judaism and Christianity. It starts by outlining and analyzing radical fundamentalism, then moderate fundamentalism. It focuses on the theoretical discourses of a few important fundamentalist theoreticians and ideologues. All this is followed by a theoretical assessment of the prospects of co-existence and co-operation between Islam and other religions as well as the West.

First: Radical Fundamentalism

This trend makes the essence of Islam a negative protest against all non-Islamic phenomena. It is best represented by Sayyid Qutb whose discourse on Judaism and Christianity in the Middle East and in the world represents the intellectual framework for radical groups and movements. Qutb believes that the whole universe is living a life of paganism (*jahiliyyah*); false gods of materialism, atheism, secularism abound, and the forces that fight true religion are alive and well. For him, only the spiritually inferior Muslims, under the pressures of miserable conditions or for lack of power, look at Islam as being only a belief and not a system of life. The relationships between the Islamic society and non-Islamic ones are based on attempts for mutual annihilation or, at least, subjection. While he believes that Christians and Jews may be allowed to worship in their own ways, they have to submit to Islam as being the only universal foundation for any positive interaction — for Qutb paying a head-tax, or *jizya*, is an indication of that. Only Islamic law (*al-shari'a*) could be the legitimate law that governs the relationship of Islam with Judaism and Christianity. Any other law brings all society into a total state of disbelief. If this is applicable to Muslims, it is also applicable to Jews and Christians[1].

It is applicable to all because, for instance, Christianity, according to Qutb, has lost its true essence when it created a church that allied itself

---

[1] Sayyid Qutb, *Ma'alim fi al-Tariq* (Beirut: Dar al-Shuruq, 7th ed. 1980), p. 65.

with the Roman empire, where man became naturally a sinner. The introduction of Greek mythologies and idols into the body of Christianity corrupted its essence. Whereas Christianity looked originally at man as good by nature, it tainted him however with original sin, making the whole of the human race guilty. While the Church looks at Christ as the savior, no true salvation occurred in fact. Man's instincts and sexual desires became a sign of 'dirtiness', and self awareness, a sign of sin[2].

According to Qutb, paganism and polytheism have been introduced by the hypocrites who pretended to be Christians and held high positions in the Roman Empire. Also, the emperor Constantine was unjust and did not follow sincerely the teachings of the Church. Christianity then could not uproot paganism but became mixed with it, which produced a new Christianity — but Islam radically uprooted paganism. Constantine manipulated Christianity for the sake of his own personal power and therefore combined both Christianity and paganism into a new paganistic Christianity whose political manifestation was the Roman empire, and religious manifestation, the Roman Catholic Church[3].

However, this new Christianity could not, adds Qutb, move Europe away from its materialistic and paganistic life. It led to unnatural reaction represented by monks who repressed human natural and instinctual desires and energies and created spiritual conflicts and led as well to social and cultural apathy. Finally, Europe revolted against the Church and its doctrines in particular and moved away from dogmatism to reason. But reason was made the new god that must control all aspects of life. Positivism followed reason in the 19th century and blew away the power of reason. Now it was believed that matter created man's ideas and his reason, and man was nothing more than an imprint of nature. Darwin, Freud, and Marx dealt the final blow to any religious conception of life by arguing either that all man's impulses were sexual in nature or that man was only an economic instrument of production, the real source of all history and ideas[4].

Thus, the dislike of Westerners for religion is in general due both to the Church and its misuse of authority and to its view of man. But Islam has not had the problem that the West has had whether in politics or ethics. This is, for Qutb, because Islam has not from its beginning

[2] Sayyid Qutb, *Al-Islam wa Mushkilat al-Hadarah* (Beirut: Dar al-Shuruq, 8th ed. 1983), p. 54.

[3] Sayyid Qutb, *Al-Islam wa Mushkilat al-Hadarah*, pp. 58-59.

[4] Ibid., pp. 60-64 & 54-57. See also on the church in the United States of America, pp. 80-88. Qutb, *Khasa'is al-Tasawwur al-Islami wa Muqawwimatuh* (Beirut: Dar al-Shuruq, 6th ed. 1979), pp. 68-69.

looked down on man's needs and desires nor allowed any religious institution to rule in God's name. Nor has it sanctioned life isolated from
social interaction[5]. The original status of Protestantism is closer to Islam
from Qutb's perspective. For Protestantism as advocated by Martin
Luther in the 16th century has attacked "the teachings of the devil" or
the teaching of Popism, trinity and the Catholic Church and denied the
validity of salvation through the authority of the Pope. Luther made the
highest authority the text (the Bible) and called for freedom of interpretation as well as arguing for the priority of faith over reason or nature.
Like Luther, Calvin, Qutb adds, made the Bible the highest Christian
authority and denied the doctrine of trinity. But by this, religion became
a topic of contention for the Europeans[6].

Thus, it is obvious that Sayyid Qutb builds his discourse on the
premise that Christian theology is paganistic in origin. The Roman
Catholic Church has been opposed throughout history because it does
not represent "true Christianity." It does not represent the divinely
inspired Christianity but a human development within certain periods
and for specific political goals. It even went against the essence of religion and used the worst kinds of tyranny and torture. The conflict
between faith and reason is indeed the conflict between human thought
and Catholicism in European life.

While all messengers of God, from Noah to Jesus, have, according to
Qutb, taught pure oneness of God (*tawhid*) and the centrality of man's
position in the universe, only Islam stayed pure and true to its origin.
Those who do not follow Islam are, in his opinion, holders of incorrect
religious views. As an example he discusses the essence of Judaism, or
the religion of the people of Israel. Like Christianity, it is full of paganistic and nationalistic features. While the children of Israel received a
pure message of *tawhid* along with the Law of Moses, they have however corrupted them by including in the Old Testament myths that are
not better than Greek myths. While Abraham called for pure *tawhid*,
only few Jews followed him, but the rest insisted on worshipping idols
and broke the Covenant with God. Furthermore, they believed that their
God is a national God and not universal; thus, justifying using one
moral code among themselves, and another with non-Jews. The Old Testament is full of references to selectiveness (the God of Israel) and

[5] Qutb, *Mushkilat al-Hadarah*, pp. 178-181. see also Qutb, *Khasa'is al-Tasawwur al-Islami wa Muqawwimatuh*, pp. 34-39.
[6] Qutb, *Khasa'is al-Tasawwur al-Islami wa Muqawwimatuh*, pp. 70-71. Qutb attri-butes Luther's revolt against the Church and other principles as being effected by Islam whose teachings were carried to the West through the Crusaders and Spain.

unseemingly graphic description of God (Adam hiding from God, God's sadness and feeling of guilt and the like)[7].

Thus, Sayyid Qutb uses the purity of *tawhid* as the only measure of the truth of any divinely inspired religion. While he acknowledges the divine origins of both Christianity and Judaism, he nonetheless equates them in modern times with unbelief. He believes that Islam is the only religion that has protected its message from theological myths and economic and political corruption. The Islamic text for Qutb is beyond any doubt the word of God and divinely constructed, but other divine texts are beyond any doubt, at best, dubious and man-made constructions[8].

In this sense, Muslims are, for Qutb, called on to apply an Islamic method that brings man to his true nature by worshipping God alone and liberating him from all other methods and religions. In Islam God is the only universal law-giver and governor; no other gods or law-givers or governors are legitimate. Both Jews and Christians — and actually most of the Muslims — have committed the gravest sin by mixing the divinely ordained texts with human interpretations, by accepting legislation from political authorities and representative bodies. As an example, he argues that when priests and rabbis legislated or made laws, they and the people who accepted their legislation and laws deviated from the oneness of God. Only Islam did not give this right to any group of human beings. It is incumbent upon "true" Muslims to achieve God's pure method on earth by adhering to divine governance (*hakimiyya*) and by negating human paganism (*jahiliyya*). For human acts of legislation cannot be by definition neutral or universal, since human legislation is affected by time and place. Thus, Christianity, Judaism, and non-textual Islam should not be observed or even respected but must be demolished[9].

Al-Jihad (struggle) — which is commonly and wrongly translated as holy war — for Qutb becomes the instrument for purity of mankind and its submission to God. While Islam may tolerate Christianity and Judaism, it does that, for Qutb, only under its umbrella, for its main objective is the unity of mankind under the doctrine of *tawhid*. This is why it does not acknowledge any sort of difference as a source of distinction, be it color, race, language or wealth. But its distinction, and therefore, rights and duties, revolve around the purity of doctrines and adherence to divine governance and negation of paganism. Therefore,

---

[7] Qutb, *Khasa'is al-Tasawwur al-Islami wa Muqawwimatuh*, pp. 28-33.
[8] Qutb, *Khasa'is al-Tasawwur al-Islami wa Muqawwimatuh*, pp. 214-220.
[9] Sayyid Qutb, *Hadha al-Din* (Beirut: Dar al-Qalam, n.d.), pp. 17-23.

jihad, including war, is conducted by the believers in order to establish the just and straight system of Islam; individuals are allowed to be equally Muslims or non-Muslims. For while Islam prohibits forcing people to believe in God, the superiority of an Islamic system and the need to establish it is not contended by Sayyid Qutb. For the abode of Islam (*dar al-Islam*) is the land whose law is Islam, whether the citizens are Muslims or non-Muslims; conversely, the abode of war (*dar al-harb*) is any land whose law is not Islam, whether the citizens are Muslims or non-Muslims. Interestingly enough however, Qutb allows peace treaties and non-belligerence between the two abodes, if the intentions of the abode of war are good, non-aggressive, and non-treacherous. But, if any of these intentions is entertained — and for Qutb, these are the characteristics of the West — then it is only war that becomes decisive in resolving conflicts between the two[10].

But how is the "abode of war" of today seen by Qutb? If one brings together his political views about the Christian world or now the West and about Judaism or now Israel, one can predict the prospects of relationships between Muslims on the one hand, and Christians and Jews, on the other hand. His political discourse about Christians and Jews is more exclusive than his theological views, for while he tolerates the existence of Christianity and Judaism under an Islamic order, he believes that Islam cannot co-exist under a non-Islamic political order and especially under Zionist, imperialist and colonialist domination. He argues that Western colonialism has almost occupied all of the Muslim world and imposed itself on it. Colonialism has attempted by all means to eradicate the Islamic creed but to no avail. Now the Islamic creed is being revived in order that the Muslim world regains its power. This requires however sublimation (or psychological superiority) because dignity is related to belief and not to superior material force. Muslims must resist and struggle to establish this sublimation or superiority, because God is the ultimate power. All of the Islamic world has fought the colonialists and worked for its liberation, because the unity of the Muslims and their independence are inseparable[11].

Qutb further argues that the West has even created Western Orientalism in order to re-write Islamic history in a manner suitable to the mentality and objective of the colonialist West. Europe is made the historical center of civilization, while other civilizations are intellectually subordi-

---

[10] Ibid., pp. 84-92.

[11] Sayyid Qutb, *Fi al-Tarikh... Fikra wa Minhaj* (Beirut: Dar al-Shuruq, 9th ed. 1991), pp. 7-10.

nated to the West, even when it was backward and without any major scientific and intellectual achievements. Thus, political domination created intellectual domination[12].

But the Muslim world cannot get rid of this Western intellectual domination, according to Qutb, without first getting rid of Western political domination. The West has "eaten up" Muslims individually, torn their world apart into dependent states and created within each a fifth column or a minority which is allied with the West and its interests rather than the people and their interests. The modern West has gone so deep in its destruction of the Muslim world in a manner unprecedented in history; an act not even committed by the Tatars or the Crusaders. Moreover, the Eastern bloc which pretended to be without religion, has still been carrying out the objectives of the Russian Empire. While the Muslim population was around 42 millions during Russian imperial rule, under Marxist rule it diminished during a period of thirty years to 26 millions — on Russian soil alone 16 million were annihilated. Also, Yugoslavia and Albania witnessed religious and ethnic cleansing unprecedented in history. Qutb argues therefore that "the spirit of Crusadism" — a reference to the Crusaders — is still alive and behind the dealing of the West — both the Eastern and Western blocs — with the Muslim world. To prove this he quotes a French Marshal who represented General Catroux, saying while entering Jerusalem in 1917, "We are the offspring of the Crusaders, whoever does not like our rule can leave." For Qutb, this is the spirit of Europe, as well as the United States and the communist countries. They all hate Islam and adhere to the Crusaders' discrimination. The West sucks Muslim blood, and the national state serves its interests. He even goes back to 1909 and tell us that at a conference held by missionaries at the Mount of Olives in Palestine the conference coordinator said "Our efforts have failed miserably, because no one converted to Christianity except one or two...." Then a priest, continues Qutb, stood up and said "Our mission is not to convert Muslims to Christianity, our mission is to make them non-Muslims... .In this sense, we have succeeded completely, for every school graduate, and not only the graduates of missionary schools, left Islam..."[13].

For Qutb, in a case like this, *jihad* becomes a necessary tool to defend the Muslim world as well as the spread the true message of God. From his perspective, all modern wars have been made for nationalist interests

[12] Ibid, pp. 51-61.
[13] Ibid., 62-68.

and exploitation, taking away from people their natural resources and making them dependent on and markets for the West. The two world wars for Qutb were direct results of spiritual bankruptcy of mankind[14]. While the first objective of *jihad* is to protect Muslims so that they are not attracted away from Islam by thought and power, they must, which is the second objective, maintain the freedom of propagating Islam. The third objective is to establish God's authority over the globe and to defend it. Therefore, Islam does not look for peace at any price, but requires, in addition to the above, total justice. This means that Muslims should not placate the tyrants of the earth, whether represented in individuals or groups or classes, or accept enslavement or exploitation. Thus, what Muslims should accept from non-Muslims is one of three doctrines: conversion to Islam, *jizya* or war[15].

For Qutb, *jizya* indicates stopping resistance, the establishment of a free Islamic call and the abolition of the material force that stands against it. As to war, it is a reaction to resisting the Islamic call. Those individuals who surrender after fighting became *ahl al-dhimma* (or those who have a protection contract) and are treated equally with Muslims. But the *jizya* that is imposed on non-Muslims is equivalent to *zakat* imposed on Muslims, both of which are needed for covering the expenses of the state so that all citizens of the Islamic state enjoy justice, medical care and retirement benefits. While *zakat* is an Islamic duty, *jizya* is not, but is an alternative tax imposed on non-Muslims. Also, non-Muslims do not have to fight the enemies of the state, since fighting is a religious duty, and non-Muslims do not have to yield to it. However, if Christians and Jews want to fight with the Muslims, then they can do that and do not have to pay *jizya*. Therefore, to bring about concerns and doubts about the status of minorities in the Islamic community under Islamic rule is, for Qutb, a propaganda against Islam administered by some stupid groups among minorities. At other times, it is brought about by people who have "Islamic names" — Muslims — but whose interest is not Islam but certain material gains received from foreign "Crusadism"[16].

Qutb's discourse on the general status of Christians and Jews is the text that underlines the view of Islamic radicalism. But this text should be contextualized in order to understand why Qutb and later other radi-

---

[14] Sayyid Qutb, *Nahwa Mujtama' Islami* (Beirut: Dar al-Shuruq, 6th ed. 1983), pp. 94-96.

[15] Sayyid Qutb, *Al-Salam al-'Alami wa al-Islam* (Beirut: Dar al-Shuruq, 7th ed. 1979), pp. 167-175.

[16] Ibid., pp. 173-177.

cal fundamentalists adopt such an attitude towards Judaism and Christianity. The study of Qutb's thought, the founder of radicalism in the Arab world, would show us why many Islamic groups moved to radicalism and rejection of the other. Qutb himself was its first victim; he was transformed under 'Abd Al-Nasir's regime from a very liberal writer in Egypt to the most radical fundamentalist thinker in the Arab world. His imprisonment and ferocious torture are reified into a radical political theology of violence and isolation. Maybe, this was his psychological compensation for the violence of the regime.

Sayyid Qutb, born to a middle class family, received his B.A. from Dar al-'Ulum. Then he worked as a teacher and columnist and was associated with Taha Hussein and 'Abbas Mahmud al-'Aqqad and other liberal thinkers. Since he started writing in journals and magazines, he showed a general tendency to be in opposition to the government and critical of the state of affairs in Egypt. He was very daring in his opposition to the government and in his 'radical liberalism' manifesting in writing free love stories and calling for nudity. His writing showed existential, skeptic and liberal bents. Because of his opposition to the government he was first sent away to the countryside; and the two journals whose editor-in-chief he became, al-'Alam al-'Arabi and al-Fikr al-Jadid, were closed down. Then in 1948 he was sent by the Ministry of Education to the United States of America to continue his studies on education[17].

His first book that adopted fundamentalism as a way of life along with a political agenda, Al-'Adala al-'Ijtima'iyya fi al-Islam (Social Justice in Islam), which appeared while he was still in the United States, was far removed from radicalism and closer to al-Banna's discourse — discussed below. His stay in the United States, 1948-51, made him review his previous attitude and adoption of Westernization. His dislike of the materialism and racism and the pro-Zionist feelings of the West that he personally experienced in the United States seems to be the beginning of his alienation from the Western culture and the return to the roots of the culture that he was born into. Upon his return to Egypt, that is after the death of Hasan al-Banna and the First Ordeal of the Brotherhood, he joined the Brotherhood and became very active in its intellectual and publishing activities and wrote numerous books on "Islam as the solution." However, until that point no radicalism and violence were

---

[17] Ahmad Moussalli, Radical Islamic Fundamentalism: The Ideological and Political Discourse of Sayyid Qutb (Beirut: American University of Beirut, 1992), pp. 19-24 and passim.

involved. His priority was to rewrite a modern understanding of Islam and the solutions that Islam provides to the basic political, economic, social and individual problems of Egypt, the Arab world and the Islamic world[18].

In 1953 Qutb was appointed editor-in-chief of the weekly *Al-Ikhwan al-Muslimun* which was banned along with the dissolution of the Brotherhood in 1954 after the fall-out between the Brethren and the Free Officers' regime. He was put in jail, then released. In fact, the Brotherhood in general, and Qutb in particular, were instrumental to the Officers in paving the way for the Revolution of 1952. But the Brotherhood refused to accept the absolute power of the Officers and called for a referendum that would show the kind of constitution that the people want. Furthermore, it supported General Najib against Colonel 'Abd al-Nasir. After major disagreements between the Brotherhood and 'Abd al-Nasir, the Muslim Brethren were accused of cooperating with the communists to overthrow the government. In 1954 their movement was again dissolved and many Brethren, including Qutb, were jailed. He was released that year and arrested again after the *Manshiyya* incident where an attempt was made on 'Abd al-Nasir's life, and Qutb and others were accused of being from the secret military section. In 1955, Qutb, who was sentenced to 15 years in prison, along with thousands of the Brethren and their supporters was subjected to ferocious torture that left unhealed scars up till today. In this context, he moved to radical fundamentalism and exclusiveness. His most important books or the gospels of radicalism, *Fi Zilal al-Qur'an, Ma'alim fi al-Tariq, Hadha al-Din* and *Al-Mustaqbal li Hadha al-Din* and others, were written because of and despite the torture that he and others endured for year after year — Qutb was released in 1966, then arrested on charges to overthrow the government and was executed that year. Again, isolated from the outside world, under tremendous daily pressures such as witnessing the slaughtering of tens of the Brethren in a jail hospital, Qutb could not but blame those who were free outside the jail but would not defend the unjustly imprisoned and ferociously tortured; they became for him accomplices in the crimes of the regime and therefore, like the regime, infidels[19].

[18] Ibid., pp. 24-30. See also Sayyid Qutb, *Nahwa Mujtama' Islami*, pp. 11-12, *Al-Mustaqbal li Hadha al-Din* (Cairo: Maktabat Wahba, 1965), pp. 71-90, *Al-Islam wa Mushkilat al-Hadara*, pp. 77-78 & 83-87.

[19] Moussalli, *Radical Islamic Fundamentalism*, pp. 31-39. See Mitchell, *The Society of Muslim Brothers*, pp. 103 & 187-189. Badrul Hasan, *Milestones*, (Karachi: International Islamic Publishers, 1981), pp. 7-13 & 30-31; Asaf Hussain, *Islamic Movements in Egypt, Pakistan, and Iran* (Great Britain: Mansell Publishing Limited, 1983), pp. 7-11 & 91.

In order to tolerate his pain and poor prison conditions, he reified his thought into an exclusivist discourse so that it was not the state and society that were excluding him; he, as the leader of the believing vanguard, was excluding individuals, societies and states from true salvation. The whole world and all religions — except 'true' Islam — became a target of his condemnation and isolation. The state's vengeful exclusion and repressive intolerance to any sort of even popular opposition was counteracted by his desperate spiritual, moral, social and political exclusion and intolerance. This is a clear contextual and historical example of how the parameters of radical fundamentalism developed. From there on and from his cell, he starts developing his exclusivism. Religions were viewed from what he described as the international crusade (imperialism and colonialism) and Zionism against the Muslim world. People like Mustafa Kemal Ataturk, the founder of modern Turkey, were serving the interest of the West by secularizing the Muslim world. The creation of Israel, adds Qutb, has made the Arab disenchanted with the West, for the British, for instance, promised the Arabs to give back their land, all the while they were giving it to Jews. Also, the United States has betrayed the Arabs by siding with Zionism in the United Nations about the creation of the Jewish state and by discriminating against the Arabs because of its anti-Arab and pro-Jewish propaganda[20].

He argues that divine governance or *hakimiyya,* the essential political component of *tawhid*, must be upheld at all times, when forming a virtuous and just society or providing personal or social freedom and under all conditions — in prison or outside it. Freedom is perceived in a negative way: the people are free insofar as the choice of social and political systems does not violate divine governance and does not hinder religious life. The state is perceived as the moral agent for creating and maintaining morality, both individually and collectively. Because of the divinity of legislation, religions, individuals, societies and states cannot legitimately develop normative rights and duties whether related to religious freedom, pluralism or political parties. Universal divine laws as outlined in the Qur'an must be viewed as the bases for all sorts of freedom and relationships. In other words, all people, Muslims and non-Muslims alike, must link their views of life with the Islamic worldview, and Islamic and non-Islamic countries must finally submit to the divine laws without exceptions[21].

---

[20] Moussalli, *Radical Islamic Fundamentalism*, pp. 29-30.
[21] Qutb, *Hadha al-Din*, pp. 32 & 123; and Qutb, *Ma'rakat al-Islam wa al-Ra'si-maliyyah* (Beirut: Dar al-Shuruq, 4th. ed. 1980), pp. 49 & 60.

Qutb's implementation of a vanguard program of Muslim radicals ended in his execution by hanging in 1966. Once out of jail in 1964, he started forming a "party" that adhered to the above-mentioned rationalizations and included the following principles: Human societies do not follow Islamic ethics, system and *shari'a* and are in need of essential Islamic education. Those individuals who respond positively to this education should undertake a course of study of Islamic movements in history in order to set a course of action to fight Zionism and colonialism. Also, no organization was to be established until a highly ideological training was undertaken[22].

Most of the radical fundamentalist groups in the Arab world and specifically in Egypt have been influenced both directly and indirectly by this Qutbian radical exclusivist discourse and by his notions of paganism of the "other," personally, socially and politically as well as culturally and philosophically. A few examples may suffice here.

The *Liman Tarah* prison in Egypt played an important role in Qutbian radical education of himself and of others. Mustafa Shukri, an inmate with Sayyid Qutb, accepted Qutb's views and established the exclusivist *Jama'at al-Muslimin* (the community of the Muslims), notoriously known as *Al-Takfir wa al-Hijra,* as a fulfillment of the Qutbian vanguard. Shukri denies the legitimacy of pluralistic religious understanding and calls on people to adhere only to the Qur'an and the *sunna.* In his trial before the martial court in Egypt, he explains the exclusivity of his group in its rejection of theories and philosophies that are not textually derived; the Qur'an and the *sunna* are the only criteria of legitimacy and truth; therefore the Egyptian government is in violation of God's governance. Furthermore, Shukri brands as unbelievers all other Muslims who do not view Islam in his own manner and turns migration (*hijra*) from the Egyptian society into a religious duty — thereby making his isolated community the only true Muslim society[23].

[22] On these issues and his life, see Muhammad T. Barakat, *Sayyid Qutb: Khulasat Hayatih, Minhajuhuh fi al-Haraka wa al-Naqd al-Muwajah ilayh* (Beirut: Dar al-Da'wa, 197?), p. 19; Salah A. Khalidi, *Sayyid Qutb, al-Shahid al-Hay* (Amman: Dar al-Firqan, 1983), pp. 147-149; Qutb, "Limadha 'A'damuni?" *Al-Muslimun,* March, No. 4, pp. 6-9; Moussalli, *Radical Islamic Fundamentalism,* Chapter One.

[23] On the prison experience see Rif'at al-Sa'id's article in *Qadaya Fikriyya: al-Islam al-Siyasi: Al-'Usus al-Fikriyya wa al-'Ahdaf,* p. 15 and *passim.* See also, Moussalli, *Radical Islamic Fundamentalism,* pp. 34-36,. On a first-hand and sympathetic account of the torture that Shukri, Qutb and others were subjected to as well as the movement itself see, Muhammad Mahfuz *Alladhina Zulimu* (London: Riad al-Rayyis Books Ltd., 1988), pp. 7-141. On Shukri's thought as put forward in his trial, see Rif'at Sayyid Ahmad, Second Document in *Al-Nabiy al-Musallah: Al-Rafidun,* pp. 53-57.

Shukri believes that the Qur'an exhorts Muslims to fight the people of the book (*ahl al-kitab* or Jews and Christians) because many of them want to turn Muslims against their religion. Fighting them stops only after they pay *jizya*. For him, Jews and Christians like pagans deserve death. Thus, when the Qur'an orders Muslims to kill the infidel, then Jews and Christians are included. When the Qur'an talks about their toleration, it is the exception from the general rule and for specific reasons. For Islam accepts nothing less than Islam, and the complete religion is no more than Islam. Muslims can co-exist with non-Muslims either under their rule or when Muslims are in a stage of weakness or when non-Muslims pay *jizya* or when an agreement is reached. As to the verses that call for non-coercion in religion, Shukri states that they have to be linked to the more general verses — for him those verses that call for fighting. For him, formal submission to Islam is necessary, whether people believe in it or not. So when Islam calls for allowing people to believe in whatever they want, this for Shukri does not include the formal aspect of religion, but the conscience. Therefore, there is no freedom in expressing unbelief; when the Qur'an speaks of that freedom to the prophet Muhammad it is telling him that he cannot force them to believe because he does not know their intentions, but still they have to conform to the rituals of Islam[24].

Thus, belief at heart is for Shukri different from formal submission, nonetheless outside conformity is called for. While Muslims may not be able to make others believers, because no one can force faith, Islam calls for the spread of its message, whether people like it or not. Islamic law must as well be maintained whether people are Muslims or not and Islamic rituals must be exercised. Muslims can fight non-Muslims who may not want to fight, because Muslims fight for the spread of the Islamic message; also killing is permitted if the message of Islam reaches non-Muslims and they reject it. For Shukri, domination over the world should be the objective of Muslims so that the divine law and doctrines become supreme. This is why "true" Muslims must isolate themselves from their societies, then defend themselves and finally overtake others — Jews, Christians and, even Muslims. Interestingly enough, Shukri argues that the Jewish occupation of Palestine is no different from any other land that has been occupied by infidels, which is a characteristic of the whole world today. He does not even believe that fighting Jews is a priority, because the war between the Arabs and the Jews is not

---

[24] Ibid., pp. 85-86.

an Islamic war. An Islamic war is not launched to regain a land, Shukri goes on, but it is the war the spreads the message of Islam. The wars that are going on today in the world are human wars. While fighting Jews is a legal duty for Shukri, he makes fighting them similar to fighting Egyptian Intelligence services and he denies the legitimacy of fighting Jews under the current conditions in Egypt. He even prohibits his fellow members from joining the Egyptian army; for him all existing societies, Muslim, Christian and Jewish, are equally infidels and should not be dealt with positively[25].

Salih Sirriyya, originally associated with *Hizb al-Tahrir*, the leader of *Tanzim al-Fanniyya al-'Askariyya*, another radical and militant fundamentalist group, was influenced by Qutb as well. His exclusivity can be seen in his categorization of mankind into only three groups: Muslims, infidels and hypocrites. Any neglect of an Islamic duty makes the individual an apostate and subject to death[26]. While Shukri turned his back on the *jahili* society, Sirriyya allows the temporary use of democracy in order to set up an Islamic state. For the struggle to topple un-Islamic governments and any irreligious institutions is a religious duty until the day of judgment. The defense of un-Islamic governments and participation in un-Islamic ideological parties and holding foreign philosophies and ways of life are obvious instances cited by Sirriyya of unbelief that incurs death. That sovereignty belongs to God is used by him to divide mankind into the exclusive *hizb shaytan*, consisting of all individuals and institutions and religions that do not believe or even practice Islam, and the exclusive *hizb Allah*, consisting of those who struggle to establish the Islamic state. He believes, for instance, that the Jews who followed their law were Muslims — submitted to God — and those who were expelled from Egypt, for instance, believed in Moses. Pharaoh — in reference to Egyptian nationalism — was an infidel and his camp was made up of unbelievers. He also believes that the first Jewish state established by David and Sulaiman (Solomon) was an Islamic state, while those who fought it were unbelievers. But later Islam has annulled all previous legal codes and became the center of belief and unbelief. Out of this logic, Sirriyya attempted a coup d'état against Anwar al-Sadat — the new Pharaoh! — which resulted in the former's execution in 1974 as happened later to Shukri in 1977[27].

---

[25] Ibid., pp. 86-87 & 97-100.

[26] Salih Sirriyya, Second Document (1973), "Risalat al-Iman," *Al-Rafidun*, pp. 31-32.

[27] Ibid., pp. 36, 42-44 & 48; and, Mahfuz, *Alladhina Zulimu*, pp. 83, 120-123, 222 & 233 & 242.

Sirriyya even refuses to see religion as only a way of worshipping God. Now the Christian concept of religion as being a private relation between man and God is becoming current in the Muslim world, but this understanding of religion is wrong because it denies the appropriateness of Islamic law to life. Those who believe in such a thing are unbelievers. He argues that the West wants to separate religion from politics, because it wants to isolate Islam from political life, as happened to Christianity in the West. But unlike Christianity, Islam will not be cornered[28].

Also, 'Abud al-Zumar, a former army intelligence officer, the military leader of *Tanzim al-Jihad* and the leader and one of the founders of *Jama'at al-Jihad al-Islami*, follows Sayyid Qutb's rationalization in stressing the importance of active involvement in total opposition to the state and society. An active program of action should focus on an applicable Islamic vision that helps in uniting Islamic movements in one framework and leads to forgoing individual and public differences. Employing a Qutbian political key term, *ma'alim al-tariq* (signposts of the road), he urges the Islamic movement to concentrate on its basic objective, the Islamic state. This requires an uncompromising and exclusive attitude toward the *jahili* systems, societies and religions as they relate to all aspects of life. Islam's objective is to eradicate unbelief and paganism, including nationalism, patriotism, and incorrect religious creeds. He rejects the idea that *jihad* is launched for defensive purpose and argues that Muslims have agreed to defend themselves from as well as to invade the unbelievers in order to force them either to accept Islam, pay *jizya* or be killed. This is why God sent his messenger, that is, in order to raise the banner of *jihad*. Peace or co-existence is not allowed if Muslims can fight them; however, their temporary deception is permitted. But *jihad* will stay as a permanent Islamic duty till the day of judgment[29].

The alternative to al-Zumar is to employ a radical transformation or total Islamization of all facets of life and the unstinting rejection of secularism, nationalism, parliamentary life and others. All this change has to start, however, with dethroning current rulers who are not obeying the *shari'a*. In line with his exclusive radical ideology, al-Zumar tried but failed to kill President Sadat who was killed, however, with al-Zumar's aid, by members of *Tanzim al-Jihad*. [30]

---

[28] Ibid., pp. 44-45.

[29] 'Abud al-Zumar, Third Document, in *Al-Rafidun*, pp. 122-123.

[30] 'Abud al-Zumar, Third Document, in *Al-Rafidun*, pp. 113-121; and Mahfuz, *Alladhina Zulimu*, pp. 226, 254, 267-268, 271 & 273.

Muhammad Abul Salam Faraj, the general secretary of *Tanzim al-Jihad*, believes that the reason why Islam lost its universal place is because Muslims no longer apply *jihad*. Tyranny on this earth will not disappear without force, and it is the Muslim's religious duty to establish God's rule on earth as a way for establishing God's law. He also argues that the abode of Islam is that land that is ruled by God's law, and the abode of unbelief is the land that is ruled by other laws. Thus, the so-called Muslim land or Christian land are both the abode of unbelief. Today, the law that rules over the whole earth is the law of unbelief; rulers are brought up by "Crusadism, communism or Zionism", and are like the Tatars who borrowed law from Judaism, Christianity and Islam[31].

As to *jihad*, which relates to the self, the devil and the unbelievers and hypocrites, he, again like the previous thinkers, argues that it is made for the spread of the divine message, and it could be both defensive and offensive. But first, the message of Islam should be allowed to be spread peacefully so that people can adopt Islam willingly; if not, then it is either *jizya* or war. Fighting is a duty on all Muslims without exception. Those who do not do that lose their faith[32].

Al-Jama'a al-Islamiyya al-Jihadiyya, a branch of *Tanzim al-Jihad* in upper Egypt, which is headed by 'Umar 'Abd al-Rahman, is no less exclusive. 'Abd al-Rahman divides the Islamic movements into two trends: one spearheaded by the Muslim Brotherhood — discussed below — which accepts the existing regime as legitimate and therefore accepts the rights of minorities, pluralism and democracy as legitimate tools of political action and the establishment of the Islamic state; the other, spearheaded by *al-Jama'a al-Islamiyya*, denies the rights of minorities, the legitimacy of the regime and publicly follows a course of total confrontation. He accuses the Brotherhood of complacency because of its work with Sadat and Mubarak, its condemnation of Sadat's death and violence and its visits to "the enemies of religion" like the Coptic Pope and other Christians. He further rejects its inclusive and compromising attitude in allying with the *Wafd* party as well as *Amal* and the *'Ahrar*. He calls on replacing the inclusivity of the Brotherhood with the exclusivity of the *Jama'at*, which rejects integration in democratic institutions and adopts a course of forceful resolution to basic issues of identity, ethics, value system and the like[33]. Also, in line with Qutb's argument,

---

[31] Muhammad Abdul Salam Faraj, "Al-Farida al-Gha'iba,"pp. 127-131.
.[32] Ibid., pp. 132-141.
[33] Fifth Document, *Al-Rafidun*, pp. 150 & 160-164; and 'Abd al-Khabir, "Qadiyyat al-Ta'aduddiya," pp. 118-120. See also Sa'id, *Qadaya Fikkriyya*, pp. 30-31. Sixth Docu-

he describes any system that adopts foreign principles as belonging to *kufr* and the *jahiliyya* and legalizes its overthrow.

Such a view leads *Tanzim al-Jihad* to declare war against the Egyptian Parliament; for the Parliament has given itself (Article 86 of the Constitution) the right to legislate and permitted democracy, a concept that treats the believer and non-believer equally as citizens[34]. The "assumed democratic system" in Egypt wants us to enter in party politics in order to equate Islam with other ideologies and religions, 'Abd al-Rahman explains. However, the Islamic movement believes in its distinctive superiority and does not respect the *jahili* positive law. He further rejects any role for representative bodies as being an instrument of Qur'anic interpretation and adjudication. Qur'anic legitimacy stands on its own. Thus any violation of Qur'anic texts leads a ruler to *kufr* punishable by death. 'Abd al-Rahman himself was viewed as the instigator for Sadat's assassination because he argued that illegitimate rulers deserve death[35].

Furthermore, Salim al-Rahhal, a leader of a branch of *Tanzim al-Jihad*, argues that Muslims today are confronting the whole world and the enemies of virtue like International "Crusadism", international communism and international Zionism and their secular agents. The United States of America stands at the top of the list of the enemies of Islam because of its strategic alliance with Israel and its oppression of the people of the world. His analysis of the objectives of the USA in the Islamic world leads him to attribute to the US the deep "Crusaders' hatred" of Islam and interest in raw material. For the USA belongs to the Christianity of the Crusaders and continues along the historical enmity between Islam and Christianity. Hatred is what regulates the US behavior towards Islamic movements. After a detailed analysis of this, he argues that the US supports religious minorities against Muslims, and gives the example of the Copts in Egypt. For while Egypt is an ally of the US, still the US supports the Orthodox Coptic Church and its illegal political

ment, *Al-Rafidun*, pp. 165, 169 & 173-174. On the organization itself, see Rif'at Sayyid Ahmad, *Al-Nabiy al-Musallah: Al-Tha'irun* (London: Riad al-Rayyis Books Ltd., 1991), pp. 185-186.

[34] "Wathiqat 'I'lan al-Harb 'ala Majlis al-Sha'b," *Al-Tha'irun*, pp. 187-189. For a description of how this organization views each political party and the political system in Egypt, see pp. 193-197.

[35] "Wathiqat Muhakamat al-Nizam al-Misri," *Al-Tha'irun*, pp. 273-275 and see pp. 290-291 where the diverse kinds of rulers are specified. On similar views see "Wathiqat al-'Ihya' al-Islami" from *Jama'at al-Jihad al-Islami* written by Kamal al-Sa'id Habib, pp. 199-229. On *Tanzim al-Jihad* and its splits and offshoots, which are many and numerous, see Mahfuz, *'Alladhina Zulimu*, pp. 213-283.

party (which is legal in the United States). Also, the US uses Egypt in order to bring about an Arab peace with Israel and to fight Islamic movements in the area. For Islam does not fit the US interests in the Muslim world[36].

Second: Moderate Fundamentalism

The discourse of the Muslim Brotherhood's founder and first supreme guide in Egypt, Hasan al-Banna, lays down the bases of inclusionary views of the theological and political doctrine of God's governance or *hakimiyya*. While it has been used at times historically and presently to exclude whatever is considered un-Islamic and, for some, even non-Islamic — as explained above — al-Banna turns it into a source of pluralism and tolerance — a feature that has been followed more or less by the majority of moderate fundamentalist political movements. For the Egyptian society in the first half of this century enjoyed relative freedom, and radicalism was not a priority for the Brotherhood. Though interested in the Islamization of government, state and society, al-Banna aimed essentially at participating in the political order and competing as well with other political parties. Al-Banna ran twice for elections along with his party, the Brotherhood. Some of the Brotherhood's founding members were simultaneously members of other political parties; and the same applies to contemporary Brethren. The peaceful involvement of the Muslim Brotherhood in the political life of Egypt is well-documented. It was involved in the struggle of the Azhar during the twenties and thirties and it has sided with the King against the government. Al-Banna during that period cooperated at times with Isma'il Sidqi, the on and off prime minister, and involved himself in teaching and lecturing. The Brotherhood built its headquarters from voluntary donations, then it built a mosque and schools for boys and girls. In 1946, the government provided financial aid and free books and stationery to the Brotherhood schools, then the Ministry of Education paid all its educational and administrative expenses. Concerned with the spread of missionary schools in Egypt, the Brotherhood called on King Faruq to subject this activity to governmental supervision. But after a meeting with a father in a church, al-Banna wrote on the necessity for the unification of men of religion against atheism[37].

[36] Salim al-Rahhal, "Amrika wa Misr wa al-Haraka al-Islamiyya" Seventh document, pp. 179-184.
[37] Rifa'at al-Sa'id, *Hasan al-Banna, Mu'assis Harakat al-Ikhwan al-Muslimin* (Beirut: Dar al-Tali'a, 4th ed., 1986), pp. 93-94, 99-100 & 112-16. Al-Sa'id's leftist account is not favorable but still the facts mentioned in it minus the author's analysis

Al-Banna never denied that the Brotherhood was a movement that sought the revival of religion with political and educational and economic aspirations. But this did not mean that the Brotherhood isolated itself from society. In 1936, the Brotherhood participated, for instance, in the coronation of King Faruq. By 1948, the Brotherhood had set up 500 branches for social services, and also established medical clinics and hospitals and treated about 51,000 patients. Again, al-Banna set up a women's organization in the forties whose membership in 1948 reached 5000 — a high number according to the standards of the time. The active membership of the Brotherhood was around half a million, the supporters, another half, and it had by the time of its dissolution, one thousand branches in Egypt[38].

In politics, the Brotherhood did not originally resort to violence but played the game as long as it was allowed, and then played with violence when it became the name of the game. It was not only the Brotherhood that established secret apparatuses, but that was a common denominator with other parties as well as the state which used political assassination to resolve many problems. This violence manifested itself against the Brethren in jailing thousands of them as well as dissolving the organization and liquidating its assets and in assassinating al-Banna.

Before that, the Brotherhood played by the rules. More importantly, the Brotherhood has always accepted the legitimacy of the existing regime, and al-Banna described King Faruq as the legitimate ruler. Al-Banna developed his organization into a political party with a specific political agenda in order to compete with other parties that were corrupt in his opinion. Al-Banna became a powerful player; for instance, he was called to the Palace in 1946 for consultation on the appointment of a new prime minister. At the time the Brotherhood was especially encouraged in order to stand against the communists and the *Wafd*[39]. Again, his condemnation of Egyptian parties was based not on

---

serve to show that the Brotherhood has not officially sanctioned or employed violence. On the active involvement of al-Banna and his organization in civil society and their cooperation with other civil segments, see, for instance, Ishaq Musa al-Husseini, *Moslem Brethren* (Beirut: Khayat's College Book, 1956), Richard Mitchell, *The Society of Muslim Brothers* (London: Oxford University Press, 1964), and Charles Adams, *Islam and Modernism in Egypt* (N.Y.: Russell and Russell, 1986). See also the views of 'Umar al-Tilmisani in Rif'at Sayyid Ahmad, *Al-Nabiy al-Musallah: Al-Rafidun* (London: Riad al-Rayyis Books Ltd., 1991), pp. 199-200. On al-Banna's ideology, see Ahmad Moussalli, "Hasan al-Banna's Islamist Discourse on Constitutional Rule and Islamic State," *Journal of Islamic Studies*, vol. 4, no. 2, 1993, pp. 161-174.

[38] Sa'id, *Hasan al-Banna*, pp. 101-107, 112, 117 & 122-124.

[39] Ibid., pp. 129, 132-39 &169-179.

religion but on their widespread corruption and collaboration with the British[40].

In the seventies the Brethren were used by Sadat in order to add legitimacy to his government, though still not allowed to form their own political party. They broke with him over his trip to Jerusalem in 1977 and the Camp David agreement and its aftermath[41]. Their protest led to the imprisonment of hundreds of Brethren in addition to the radical groups — discussed above. But the Muslim Brethren have not officially sanctioned or used violence to achieve any political or religious objective. Since 1984, the Brotherhood in Egypt and elsewhere, and similar movements like al-Nahdah in Tunisia, have been trying to be included in the political process and have been involved in setting up civil institutions and opening up dialogues with non-Muslims and with the West. Because in Jordan the Brotherhood has functioned as a political party since the fifties, some of its members have been well placed in the government and the parliament.

Inclusion and recognition in the state's hierarchy as well as the Brotherhood's attempts to become part of state administration, made the hakimiyya basically a doctrinal organizing principle of government and a symbol of political Islam, all the while allowing pluralistic interpretative policies. Al-Banna's emphasis on the proper grounding of political ideology does not exclude individual and collective social and political reformulations of Islamic political doctrines in accordance with modern society's needs, aspirations, and beliefs[42].

While Islam contains basic legal substance, its denotations and connotations cannot be restricted to or derived from past historical conditions only. More importantly, al-Banna attempts to show that it must account for and deal with modernity as a worldview, not only as a law. Both the law and worldview must deal with the real world, not in abstract terms, but essentially in practical terms and therefore must take

---

[40] Banna, *Majmu'at Rasa'il al-Shahid Hasan al-Banna* (Beirut: Dar al-Qur'an al-Karim, 1984) (hereafter cited as *Rasa'il al-Imam*), pp. 48 &56-60; Banna, *Majmu'a*, pp. 14, 169, 309, 331-322 &335-337; Banna, *Kalimat Khalida* (Beirut: n.p., 1972), p. 45.

[41] Henry Munson, *Islam and Revolution in the Middle East* (New Haven: Yale University Press, 1988), pp. 78-79. See also Dilip Hiro, *The Rise of Islamic Fundamentalism* (New York: Routledge, 1989), pp. 69-72.

[42] Hasan al-Banna, *Din wa-Siyasa* (Beirut: Maktabat Huttin, 1970), pp. 40-45; and Banna, *Majmu'at Rasa'il al-Shahid Hasan al-Banna* (Beirut: Al-Mu'assasa al-Islamiyya, 4th. ed. 1984) (hereafter cited as *Majmu'at Rasa'il*), pp. 161-165. On al-Banna's biography, see, for instance, *Memoirs of Hasan al-Banna Shaheed* translated by M. N. Shaikh (Karachi: International Islamic Publishers, 1981), and Rif'at al-Sa'id, *Hasan al-Banna, Mu'assis Harakat al-Ikhwan al-Muslimin*.

into account and include other interpretations, political ideologies, philosophies and religions. Because Islam is both religion and society and a mosque and a state, it must deal effectively with religion and the world by the inclusion of diverse substantive and methodological pluralistic interpretations, while maintaining the basic doctrines of religion[43].

Because the *shari'a* is viewed as a social norm, al-Banna frees its application from past specific methods and links its good practice to the maintenance of freedom and popular authority over the government, and the delineation of the authorities of the executive, the legislative and the judiciary. Western constitutional forms of governments do not contradict Islam, if grounded in both constitutionality of Islamic law and objectivity. Constitutional rule is turned into *shura* or consultation by a subtle reinterpretation in light of modernity and in a spirit not contradictory to the Qur'an. *Shura* as the basic principle of government and the exercise of power of society becomes inclusionary by definition and employed to empower the people to set the course of its political actions and ideology. If the ultimate source of the legitimacy of *shura* is the people, its representation cannot be restricted to one party that may represent only a fraction of the people. Continuous ratification by the community is required because governance is a contract between the ruled and the ruler[44]. Al-Banna's theoretical acceptance of political pluralistic, democratic and inclusionary interpretations implants the future seeds for the Muslim Brotherhood's further acceptance of political pluralism and democracy, not withstanding its link to *tawhid* and its political connotation, unity. This acceptance does not exclude even the existence of many states. Recognizing the legitimacy of party politics and political systems leads al-Banna to the acceptance of substantial differences in ideologies, policies and programs. But an Islamic state does not include atheistic parties[45]. The illegitimacy of atheistic parties is not in al-Banna's view an infringement on freedom of expression or freedom of belief insofar as the majority and the minority accept religion as the truth. Such parties

---

[43] Banna, *Majmu'at Rasa'il,* p. 165, Banna, *Majmu'at Rasa'il al-Imam al-Shahid Hasan al-Banna* (Beirut: Dar al-Qalam, n.d.) (hereafter cited as *Majmu'a*), pp. 304 & 343-47; and Banna, *Din wa-Siyasa,* pp. 57-59.

[44] Banna, *Majmu'at Rasa'il,* pp. 160-161 & 317-318; and Banna, *Al-Imam Yatahadath ila Shabab al-'Alam al-Islami* (Beirut: Dar al-Qalam, 1974), p. 99; and, Banna, *Majmu'a,* pp. 99 & 332-337.

[45] Al-Banna, *Majmu'at Rasa'il,* pp. 95-96,165-167, 317, 320-323, 325 & 328-330; al-Banna, *Minbar al-Jum'a* (Alexandria: Dar al-Da'wa, 1978), pp. 78-79 & 136; al-Banna, *Al-Da'wa,* No. 7, 1979, p. 9. On centrality of this demand, the Islamic state, in the fundamentalist thought, see Bruce Lawrence, *Defenders of God: The Revolt against the Modern Age* (San Francisco: Harper and Row, 1989), pp. 187-226.

would be outside the consensus of the society and therefore threaten its unity. If Islam is chosen as the basis of government and society, then its opposition is a matter of anarchy and opposition to society, not freedom. Still, this is not a negation of pluralism in Islam since foreign ideas and systems of thought can be included[46]. The state must reflect social agreement and provide a framework for resolving conflicts peacefully[47].

Again, al-Banna includes into an Islamic system different religious groups such the Christians and Jews who along with the Muslims are united by interest, human good, and belief in God and the holy books. Where religion is acknowledged as an essential component of the state, political conflicts ought not to be turned into religious wars, and must be resolved by dialogue. Individuals also enjoy equal religious, civil, political, social, and economic rights and duties. This principle of individual involvement, to enjoin the good and forbid evil, is the origin of pluralism leading to setting up political parties or social organizations or, simply, democratizing the social and political process[48].

Al-Banna argues further that while Islam fights colonialism, it does not accept dominating other people, for people are born free. Islam calls for *jihad* in order to defend the nation and to secure the peaceful spread of the message of God, if it is opposed by force. Again, Islam encourages peaceful solutions when there is good will, and the Prophet accepted peace agreements and accepted the arbitration of non-Muslims[49]. For al-Banna, the original condition of life is peace, not conflict. But at times, one has to fight in order to push away individual and collective ambitions and greed. Thus, defense of the self or the nation is legitimate, so that people's life and property as well as religion are not wasted. Also, Muslims may defend their creed from ideological attacks and can fight those who break their contracts and agreements. In addition, Muslims may launch war in order

---

[46] Al-Banna, *Majmu'at Rasa'il*, pp. 96-97, 161-163 & 167-169; and; al-Banna, *Rasa'il al-Imam*, p. 53.

[47] Al-Banna, *Nazarat fi Islah al-Nafs wa al-Mujtama'* (Cairo: Maktabat al-'I'tisam, 1969), p. 194; al-Banna, *Minbar al-Jum'a*, pp. 24-25, 63, 72 & 347; al-Banna, *Majmu'at Rasa'il*, pp. 317; al-Banna, *Majmu'a*, pp. 63, 72, 101, 104 & 317; al-Banna, *Rasa'il al-Imam*, pp. 53-55; and al-Banna, *Al-Imam al-Shahid Yatahadath*, pp. 15-17.

[48] Al-Banna, *Al-Salam fi al-Islam* (Beirut: Manshurat al-'Asr al-Hadith, 1971), pp. 27-29. On his acceptance of pluralism, see 'Abd al-Khabir Mahmud 'Ata, "Al-Haraka al-Islamiyya wa Qadiyat al-Ta'addudiyya," *Al-Majallat al-'Arabiyya li al-'Ulum al-Siyasiyya*, Nos. 5 & 6, April, 1992, pp. 115-116; on al-Banna's own declaration of accepting equal rights and pluralism, see *Al-Islam wa al-Salam*, p. 37 and *passim*. For similar views in Jordan, see Taqiy al-Din al-Nabahani, *Al-Takatul al-Hizbi* (Jerusalem: n.p., 2nd ed., 1953), pp. 23-57 and *Nizam al-Hukm* (Jerusalem: Matba'at al-Thiryan, 1952), pp. 56-59.

[49] Al-Banna, *Majmu'at Rasa'il*, pp. 308-310.

to defend oppressed people wherever they are. Apart from this, Islam prohibits war — whether for national interests or raw material[50].

On the other hand, Islam calls for respecting contracts, agreements and pacts. But *jizya* is a tax collected from people of the book for the services provided by the state, protection and defense and was levied from the land that was lost in war, since Muslims became responsible for their state affairs. Islam in this regard is like Christianity and Judaism which do not reject *jihad* and war[51].

For Islam acknowledges the unity of mankind as being the offspring of Adam, and therefore it is only piety that distinguishes one individual or group from others. For the Qur'an addresses all mankind equally and establishes the divine origin of religions. The religious holy books are inspired by Him, and the sincere believers in his books are saved wherever they are. Thus, people should not fight each other in God's name and must unite by religion. A Muslim should believe not only in the Qur'an but also in the other holy books and in all prophets without distinction. The bases of the teachings of Moses, Jesus and Muhammad are the Abrahamic traditions. The Torah is a legitimate holy text, so is the Old Testament and the Bible (N.T.). The children of Israel are the nation of Moses and Christians are the followers of Jesus. Therefore, the relations between the three religions should be based on their common beliefs and interests, especially when no one overpowers the other and occupies its land. Muslims are asked to use good argument with the people of the book because of the unity of the message. Islam does not want to create enmity with the believers, be they Christians or Jews. Al-Banna goes on to say that Islam has given all people spiritual rights, in addition to the political and others[52]. However, the conflict with Western civilization is not religious in nature but political. The West is not fighting the East because it is Muslim, for the West fought within itself more severe wars than those with Muslims. It supports Jewish Zionism because it serves its colonialist objectives, but in fact the West dislikes it and committed murders against the Jews. Put simply, the West wants to control the East politically and economically. The materialist West wants to appropriate raw material and oppresses the rest of the world after it has taken the leadership from the Prophetic traditions of Moses, Jesus and Muhammad. The West is now unjust, repressive and aimless[53].

---

[50] Al-Banna, *Al-Salam fi al-Islam*, pp. 49-56.
[51] Ibid., pp. 63-74.
[52] Al-Banna, *Al-Salam fi al-Islam*, pp. 21-29.
[53] Al-Banna, *Majmu'at Rasa'il al-Imam al-Shahid*, pp. 168-169 & 342-343.

Al-Banna rejects the notion that an Islamic system denies religious minorities the right to exist or practice their rituals. On the contrary, he believes that all groups of society should cooperate in order to set up a good and virtuous society. For Islam postulates the need for protecting minorities and prevents Muslims from fighting others for no legitimate cause; for all believers, Muslims, Christian and Jews, constitute one community[54].

Along the same line, 'Umar al-Talmasani, the former guide of the Muslim Brotherhood in Egypt argues that while the implementation of Islamic law in Egypt is necessary, he does not look at minorities and the West as being the enemies. As to the Christians and Jews residing outside the Muslim world, he believes that Islam makes international relations dependent on good will and justice. The Jews are included within this framework, but the conflict with the Israelis is a political conflict, and insofar as they do not hurt Muslims, normal and cordial relations can be developed and maintained. Now, the Jews have expelled the Palestinians and are enemies of peace and have controlled some Islamic holy places. In other word, they are the aggressor right now. But minorities in the Islamic world have the right to conduct their lives according to their own laws[55].

Yusuf al-Qaradawi, one of the leading contemporary thinkers of the Muslim Brotherhood in Egypt and the Arab world, bases the relationship with non-Muslims on, again, good will and justice, and this is applicable, of course, in the absence of war and the persecution of Muslims. For Jews and Christians have a more favored position in Islam than others, even though some of them have made some changes in their holy books. The Qur'an, adds al-Qaradawi, calls on Muslims to dialogue with the people of the book, allows eating the animals they slaughter and allows marrying their women, which means mixing Muslims and non-Muslims and by this making non-Muslim women head of Muslim families. This applies as well to those Jews and Christians that do not reside in Muslim territories[56].

But those Jews and Christians who do reside in Muslim territories, are, al-Qaradawi goes on, *ahl al-dhimma,* which refers to non-Muslim citizens of an Islamic society. *Al-dhimma* means security, guarantee and contract, which are provided for them so that they can live peacefully. It

---

[54] Ibid., pp. 184-186

[55] 'Umar al-Talmasani, an interview, *Al-Rafidun,* pp. 199-202.

[56] Yusuf al-Qaradawi, *Ghayr al-Muslimin* (Beirut: Mu'assasat al-Risalat, 2nd ed., 1983), pp. 5-7.

is similar to today's naturalization where a foreigner becomes a citizen. In this sense, *ahl al-dhimma* belong to the abode of Islam and carry an Islamic citizenship. This contract is eternal and guarantees that Muslims protect *al-dhimmiyin* if they pay *jizya* and accepted Islamic law in their non-religious issues. Their rights include internal and external protection, physical, financial and legal aspects, as well as, for instance, retirement guarantees. More importantly, their religious freedom, whether in terms of rituals or belief, is also protected and they should not be forced to change any of it. They also enjoy economic freedom, whether in terms of work or selling and buying — excluding usury, pork and alcoholic drinks. On another level, they have the right to occupy any governmental post, except those that are of Islamic religious nature, like the imamate and presidency because these institutions represent the Prophet Muhammad, and non-Muslims cannot represent him. But they can be appointed as ministers and work as deputies[57].

Al-Qaradawi then explains the duty of the people of the book and delineates three basic duties; 1) to respect the rituals of Muslims, 2) to adhere to Islamic law in civil interaction, and 3) to pay *jizya* and other taxes. *Jizya* is a compensation for not serving in the defense of the community against external enemies, because fighting others may involve some religious aspect, which the non-Muslims do not want to honor. *Jihad* is in particular a religious duty that non-Muslims are not asked to perform, and if non-Muslims fight for Islamic causes, this would be unjust. But those Jews and Christians who fight with Muslims do not pay *jizya* in addition to clergy, women, children, the elderly, the blind and the sick[58].

As to tolerance, al-Qaradawi believes that Islam extended it to a point where those who do not believe in Islam are allowed by textual authorities to hold their divergent views. Islam has never sanctioned forcing people to adhere to Islam and has always respected the rituals of others. He argues that while Islamic law has, for instance, prohibited specific activities like drinking wine or selling pork, the prohibition of doing that does not infringe on non-Muslims. For while wine-drinking is not prohibited by Christians, drinking itself is not a religious duty; also eating pork is not a religious duty. Thus, by not eating pork or drinking wine, they are not committing any religious crime but they are considering the feelings of Muslims. Therefore, he concludes that non-Muslims ought to respect the feeling of Muslims in matters that do not involve breaking a religious law. Tolerance of each religious group should go beyond the specifics of legal

---

[57] Ibid., pp. 8-25.
[58] Ibid., pp. 31-41.

issues to include good will, gentle interaction, justice, mercy and benevo-
lence, most of which fall outside the scope of law[59].

On the other hand, al-Qaradawi gives historical examples of others'
intolerance of Muslims. He asks his reader to study what the Muslims
did when they invaded Spain, and what Christians did when they over-
came Muslims eight hundred years later. He also discusses the Crusades
and their consequences, which are like the communist revolution in Russia and Nazism in Germany. Muslims in Ethiopia, Russia, Yugoslavia,
China and other countries are today oppressed and killed. Even the history of Christianity testifies to the intolerant attitudes of Christians to
each other, which led to many wars and crimes. Al-Qaradawi's exposition is made in order to show that Christianity has historically been less
tolerant than Islam, and that the charges that are brought against Islam
are the very charges that can be brought against Christianity. All the
while, Islam is essentially tolerant of the other religions, but the others
are intolerant of Islam[60].

Al-Qaradawi calls on Islamic movements to extend their discourse to
include the others, especially their opponents, intellectually and politically. He believes that it is high time for the movements to enter into a
fruitful dialogue with all, including the opponents and the enemies. The
West as well should be a party to this dialogue, notwithstanding the religious differences that exist. For the West is dominant and rules over the
Islamic world, directly and indirectly. Moreover, it is impossible to build
the 'Virtuous City' in isolation from the world, given the high techno-
logical advancements that have been taking place. It is the Muslims'
duty to open up to the West in order to explain the true message of
Islamic movements. For the West still looks at Muslims from a perspective developed by the Crusades, in addition to the West's support of
Israel and the suppression of Muslims in, for instance, France, Sudan,
and the Philippines. Even Turkey, which has followed in the footsteps of
the West, is not allowed to join the European common market because
its population is Muslim. Nonetheless, this does not mean for al-
Qaradawi that Muslims should not try to present their case and develop
good relations with the West or between civilizations. For him, mankind
is destined to live together and therefore cooperate and co-exist[61].

---

[59] Ibid., pp. 43-50.
[60] Ibid., pp. 69-78.
[61] Yusuf al-Qaradawi, *Awlawiyat al-Haraka al-Islamiyya* (Beirut: Mu'assasat al-
Risala, 13th ed., 1992), pp. 160-178.

Sa'id Hawwa, the Syrian Muslim Brotherhood's leader and thinker, argues that in an Islamic state all citizens are equal and protected from despotism and arbitrariness. The distinction between one individual and another should not center around race or belief. As to the exercise of power, it should be based on *shura* and freedom of association, specifically, minorities, political parties, unions, associations and civil institutions. The rule of law should reign supreme, and people should be able to have access to courts to redress their grievances. More importantly, freedom of expression should be guaranteed, whether on the personal or the public level[62].

In particular, Hawwa shows sensitivity to the importance of arguing for equal rights for Syrian minorities with the majority. While ultimate authority should be within the confines of Islamic teachings, and while individuals from minorities can be members of cabinets or parliaments, political representation must be proportionate. But, the administration of their internal affairs or building educational institutions and religious courts are the domain of minorities themselves and should not be subjected to others[63].

Other thinkers, like Muhammad S. al-'Awwa, a prominent Egyptian intellectual of the Brotherhood, go beyond these general statements and directly address the standing issues of democracy and rights. Starting from al-Banna's discourse, al-'Awwa elaborates further the absolute necessity of both pluralism and democracy. Islam to al-'Awwa is falsely accused of being opposed to pluralistic societies. For him, a society is civil when institutions that aim at effecting political life are free to function and develop without interference form the state. In other words, the existence of a particular form of association is in itself not a guarantee that a pluralistic society exists. Because the institutions of society change from one time to another, al-'Awwa does not specify the kinds of institutions that make a Muslim society pluralistic, but links this to the function of institutions. In the West, unions, clubs, and parties function as such, in the Muslim world, the mosque, the church, religious endowments, teaching circles, professions and craft organizations and the neighborhood functioned similarly[64].

---

[62] Sa'id Hawwa, *Al-Madkhal ila Da'wat al-Ikhwan al-Muslimin bi-Munasabat Khamsin 'Aman 'ala Ta'sisiha* (Amman: Dar al-Arqam, 2n. ed., 1979), pp. 13-18. On the Muslim Brotherhood's participation in elections in Syria, see al-Habib al-Janhani, "Al-Sahwa al-Islamiyya fi Bilad al-Sham: Mithal Suriyya," *Al-Harakat al-Islamiyya al-Mu'asira fi al-Watan al-'Arabi* (Beirut: Center for the Studies of Arab Unity, 2nd. ed. 1989), pp. 105-120.

[63] Hawwa, *Al-Madkhal*, p. 282.

[64] Muhammad S. al-'Awwa, *Al-Hayat*, August 3, 1993, p. 19. See also "Awwa, Al-Ta'addudiyya min Manzur Islami,' *Minbar al-Hiwar*, Vol. 6, No. 20, Winter 1991, pp. 134-136.

That despotism was the general practice of the historical Arab-Islamic state is accepted by al-'Awwa as a general description, but this does not mean that Islam, by its very nature, is opposed to pluralism and democracy. Again, he uses historical examples, like the first state in Islam founded by the Prophet that included Jews and others, to show that despotism, as a political concept of politics, has not had credibility, though tolerated by the general populace. Again, the historical state could not claim the sole legitimacy to impose on the people its own opinions. For al-'Awwa the first step to induce major changes is to reorganize society in a way that allows civil institutions to develop freely[65].

Pluralism for al-'Awwa is the tolerance of diversity, religious, political, economic, linguistic and others. Such diversity is a natural human tendency and an inalienable right because the Qur'an itself allows differences of belief, identity and belonging[66]. Al-'Awwa identifies six doctrines that make Islam tolerant and pluralistic, among which are the freedom to develop a particular social and political system; the election of the ruler through *shura*; and religious freedom; for all people are equal in terms of both rights and duties[67].

Hasan al-Turabi, the leading and influential fundamentalist thinker of today's Islamic movements, the former general guide of the Muslim Brotherhood and the head of *al-Jabha al-Qawmiyya al-Islamiyya* and now the head of the Popular Arab and Muslim Congress in the Sudan, breaks theoretically many taboos relating to society. He drops many conditions and imposes more "Islamic" limitations on the power of the state and equates them to those of liberalism and Marxism. The state must not go beyond putting down general rules enabling a society to organize its affairs. Accepting the idea that the *shari'a* limits the powers of the state and, instead, frees society he grounds it in the religious command "to enjoin the good and to forbid the evil."[68]

---

[65] Ibid., p. 19. On the Islamic movement in Egypt, see Muhammad A. Khalafallah's article in *Al-Haraka al-Islamiyya fi al-Watan al-'Arabi,* pp. 37 and *passim.* See also Rislan Sharaf al-Din, "Al-Din wa al-Ahzab al-Siyasiyya al-Diniyya," *Al-Din fi al-Mujtama' al-'Arabi* (Beirut: Center for the Studies of Arab Unity, 1990), p. 180 and *passim.*

[66] Al-'Awwa, "Al-Ta'adudiyyah al-Siyasiyyah min Manzur Islami," pp. 129-132 and *passim.*

[67] Al-'Awwa, *Fi al-Nizam al-Siyasi,* p. 77; and al-'Awwa, "Al-Ta'addudiyya al-Siyasiyya min Manzur Islami," pp. 133-137 & 152-153.

[68] Hasan al-Turabi, "Islam, Democracy, the State and the West: Summary of a Lecture and Roundtable Discussion with Hasan al-Turabi," prepared by Louis Cantouri and Arthur Lowrie, *Middle East Policy,* Vol. 1, No. 3, 1992, pp. 52-54.

Pluralism for al-Turabi is obviously of communal nature, because *shura* and *ijma'* are the prerogatives of the people, which requires diversity of opinions. This task is more urgent today since Muslims are beset by dire conditions and unprecedented challenges — a situation that demands a new understanding of religion that transcends mere addition and subtraction of particulars here and there, to provide new organizing principles appropriate for modernity[69].

Al-Turabi theoretically justifies such a need by arguing that both the specifics and organizing principles of religion are historically developed and consequently subject to change in terms of the need of the community. Their historical nature means that no normative standing is attributed to them or that their replacement with new specifics and principles is not a violation of religion. While this replacement does involve the Qur'an and the *sunna*, a new set of *'usul* or organizing principles must be the outcome of a new *ijma'* itself the consequence of a popular choice in the form of contemporary *shura*[70].

Ultimate political authority is reserved by al-Turabi to the community, which makes a contract with an individual to lead the community and organize its affairs. But this is done only through delegation of power for the well-being of the community. The ruler must never transgress against the individual and communal freedom provided for by the Qur'an whose discourse is directed to people and the individual. A proper Islamic constitution must guarantee all sorts of individual and communal freedom[71].

While the *shari'a* is pivotal to al-Turabi, it does not exclude non-Islamic doctrines and institutions[72]. This kind of change cannot take

[69] Hasan al-Turabi, *Tajdid 'Usul al-Fiqh* (Jedda: Al-Dar al-Su'udiyya li al-Nashr wa al-Tawzi', 1984), pp. 10-16; and Turabi, *Qadaya al-Hurriyya wa al-Wahda, al-Shura wa al-Dimocratiyya, al-Din wa al-Fan* (Jedda: Al-Dar al-Su'udiyya li al-Nashr wa al-Tawzi', 1987), pp. 17-18.

[70] Al-Turabi, *Tajdid al-Fikr al-Islami* (Jedda: Al-Dar al-Su'udiyya li al-Nashr wa al-Tawzi', 2nd. ed. 1987), pp. 20, 73 & 132-133; al-Turabi, "Awlawiyyat al-Tayyar al-Islami," *Minbar al-Sharq*, No. 1, March 1992, pp. 21-26, 69-72, 81-82, 136-138, 167-169 & 198-199.

[71] Al-Turabi, *Qadaya*, pp. 51-57; and al-Turabi, *Tajdid al-Fikr*, pp. 45, 66-68, 75, 93-97 & 162-163. On al-Turabi's definition of religion and the need for revolution, *Tajdid al-Fikr*, pp. 200-203 & 106-119; on the general bonds and the Islamic ones that make the establishment of society worthwhile, see al-Turabi, *Al-Iman wa 'Atharuhu fi Hayat al-Insan* (Jedda: Al-Dar al-Su'udiyya li al-Nashr wa al-Tawzi', 1984), pp. 181-261; on the social connotations and their fulfillment, see pp. 112-121, on the role of science in society, see pp. 269-301, and on the importance of the unity of society for general interests, see pp. 325-329.

[72] Al-Turabi, *Usul al-Fiqh*, pp. 27-29.

place by minor adjustments, but requires a comprehensive mental and social restructuring of the experience of the community within a modern program that leads to redressing not only peculiar grievances but all of contemporary problems. The beginning of all of this relates however to freeing individuals and groups to pursue what they consider as new means toward development[73].

Al-Turabi postulates further comprehensive freedom as a fundamental right and formative principle in the life of people. More specifically, he denies the government any right even to impose recognized legal views on the community. For such an action constitutes un-called-for interference of the state in the life of the community and a breach of *shura*[74]. The community should not be one and the same; for the existence of only one public opinion may constitute an obstacle to progress. A democratic interpretation of Islam requires for al-Turabi the proper and free basing of relationships between the state, individuals, the community and its institutions[75].

Without freedom man loses, according to al-Turabi, his and religion's true nature and becomes indistinguishable from animals. The original freedom includes freedom of belief and expression. For God convinces and does not force man to believe, all the while providing individuals with freedom that may not be legitimately given to institutions and to society[76]. But such freedom should not lead to breaking the Muslim society into combating ideological groups, such as happened in the history of Islam, where the community is basically split into Shi'ism and Sunnism. While pluralism is recommended by al-Turabi, its good practice revolves around its consensual context where a set of principles is agreed upon that will guarantee the indivisibility of society[77].

The leader of *Al-Nahda* in Tunisia, Rashid al-Ghannushi, steers a similar course to that of al-Turabi. Al-Ghannushi argues for the need for maintaining public and private freedoms and human rights, which are both called for by Qur'anic teachings and ratified by international covenants. For they are not contradictory to Islam and involve primarily the freedoms of belief, expression and association as well as political participation and independence and the condemnation of violence and

[73] Al-Turabi, *Tajdid al-Fikr al-Islami*, pp. 108-109, 164-165, 133-139 & 160-163.
[74] Al-Turabi, *Usul al-Fiqh*, pp. 36-37 & 42-45; al-Turabi, *Tajdid al-Fikr al-Islami*, pp. 26-31, 36-49, 54-63, 76-77, 148-149 & 172-143.
[75] Al-Turabi, *Tajdid al-Fikr al-Islami*, pp. 68-71; for a discussion of the forms of *shura*, see al-Turabi, *Qadayah*, pp. 72-77 & 80-81.
[76] Turabi, *Qadaya*, pp. 10-19 & 22-28.
[77] Ibid, pp. 34-37 & 44-47.

the suppression of free opinion. Such principles for al-Ghannushi may become the center of peaceful co-existence and dialogue between society and the state and between and rulers and the ruled[78].

Al-Ghannushi believes that popular authority, grounded in God's governance, is the highest authority in society. Accepting the freedom of association leads him even to accept those parties that do not believe in God such as the communist[79]. Some citizens may find it in their best interest to form parties and other institutions that might be irreligious or to change its political systems. This does not constitute a breach of religion since pluralism — or to believe or not — itself is sanctioned by religion. For the sacred text represents a source for, a reference to and an absorption of the truth, while its human interpretations are grounded in diverse methods representing different understanding of changing social, economic, political and intellectual complexities[80].

Al-Ghannushi recognizes the rights of minorities to run for election and to be represented in the parliament of an Islamic state. For an Islamic state does not mean that all political institutions are limited to Muslims. It means that the law should be of Islam and that the powers of society ought to be represented in parliament; and a non-Muslim minority should participate in the administration of the state within the law of Islam. Islam thus is not a condition for political representation. For citizenship as well as its rights and duties is not the result of faith, but belongs to man as such. Of course the overall acceptance of the political parameters of the state is needed[81].

Dialogue between Muslims and non-Muslims and between the West and the East becomes a must for al-Ghannushi; it must be extended not

[78] Al-Ghannushi, *Bayrut al-Masa'*, 15 May, 1993, p. 15; and al-Ghannushi, "Mustaqbal al-Tayyar al-Islami, *Minbar al-Sharq*, Vol. 1, No. 1, March 1992, pp. 3-32. On a general discussion of al-Ghannushi and *Harakat al-Itijah al-Islami*, see 'Abd al-Khabir Mahmud 'Ata,"Qadiyat al-Ta'addudiyya,"pp. 116-117.

[79] Al-Ghannushi and al-Turabi, *Al-Harakah al-Islamiyya wa al-Tahdith* (n.d,. n.p., 1981), pp. 34-35. See also Muhammad 'Abd al-Baqi al-Hirmasi, "al-Islam al-Ihtijaji fi Tunis," *Al-Harakat al-Islamiyya al-Mu'asira*, pp. 273-286.

[80] Al-Ghannushi, "Hiwar," *Qira'at Siyasiyya*, Vol. 1, No. 4. Fall 1991, pp. 14-15 & 35-37; and, al-Ghannushi, "Al-Islam wa al-Gharb," *Al-Ghadir*, Nos. 10 & 11, 1990, pp. 36-37. On his and other fundamentalists' acceptance of democracy, see also John Esposito and James Piscatori, "Democratization and Islam," *Middle East Journal*, Vol. 45, No. 3, Summer 1991), pp. 426-434 & 437-438. On his political life see al-Ghannushi, "Hiwar," p. 5, and 'Abd al-Qadir al-Zugul, "Al-Istratijia al-Jadida li Harakat al-Itija al-Islami," in *Al-Din fi al-Mujtama'*, pp. 346-348. See also on the possibilities of liberalization, Gudrun Kramer, "Liberalization and democracy in the Arab World," *Middle East Report,* January-February, 1992, pp. 22-25.

[81] Rashid al-Ghannushi, *Al-Huriyyat al-'Amma fi al-Islam* (Beirut: Center for Arab Unity Studies, 1993), pp. 25-28.

only on the internal level or the Muslim world but to all of the world, and the West in particular. Any objective analysis, according to al-Ghannushi, shows the fact that the negative and positive values and forces of goodness exist in the East and the West. The forces of goodness are invited to dialogue and to search for avenues for intercourse[82].

A pact was published and distributed by Muhammad al-Hashim al-Hamidi, a Tunisian fundamentalist, as to what an Islamic movement should do after it rules. Its program must include the rights of minorities, life, equality, justice, fair trial, and political participation as well as freedom of thought, belief, expression, religion and women. The basic principles governing the formation of parties and associations include the freedom to form parties and political associations for all citizens without exception and must be guaranteed by an Islamic constitution. Furthermore, secular citizens, including communists, have the right to form parties, to propagate their ideology and to compete for power. Finally, racial, tribal, sectarian or foreign affiliations cannot be the base of a legitimate political propaganda[83].

Assessment

This discussion has attempted to show that although fundamentalisms are looked at as being one single phenomenon in both practice and theory, in fact they are not. But still it is only Islam that is identified with radical fundamentalism in an essentialist manner. It seems that the concurrence of terminology used by both radicals and moderates that involves the superstructure of Islam is the source of confusing not only radical fundamentalism with moderate fundamentalism but also with Islam. At a superstructural level all committed Muslims might seem therefore fundamentalists.

Islamic fundamentalism is not therefore a theoretically and politically unified movement. Of course, the discussion on a superstructural level enjoys certain common terminological underpinnings: the supremacy of *tawhid* as the pivotal doctrinal and political foundation, the superiority of the *shari'a*, the necessity of establishing an Islamic state and other very important issues.

But a distinguishing feature of a radical view from a moderate one is to be derived around the conditions and principles of transforming a

---

[82] Al-Ghannushi, "Al-Islam wa al-Gharb," *Al-Ghadir*, Nos. 10-11, pp. 37.

[83] Muhammad al-Hashimi al-Hamidi, "Awlawiyyat Muhimma fi Daftar al-Harakat al-Islamiyya: Nahwa Mithaq Islami li al-'Adl wa al-Shura wa Huquq al-Insan," *Al-Mustaqbal al-Islami,* No. 2, November 1991, pp. 19-21; the quotation is from pp. 14-15.

political agenda into daily life. It has been made clear that even fundamentalisms employ diverse methodological and practical processes to intellectual and political formulas. One of these is based on conceptual exclusivity of the other, whether religiously or politically — a concept that condones all means for self-fulfillment, including violence. Because radical fundamentalism perceived its own real and imagined isolation as a result of social disunity and exploitation resulting from colonialism and imperialism as well as their "agents" or the minorities, in addition of course to the political violence and illegitimacy of regimes, it has transformed, mostly under torturous and inhuman conditions, its political discourse into a rejectionist puritan theology of politics and violence. For any religion becomes a political system, and all systems are competing with each other for world domination. This is why Islam, according to radical fundamentalism, thrives on its political contextualization, which necessarily means the clash of systems and therefore religions.

While *shura* is essentially a religious concept and a mechanism for elections, it is used by the radicals to mean the Islamically-derived religious public will, which means that any other concept, including religious tolerance and pluralism, is subordinated to it. More essentially, this will is the carrier of the divine will, and as such any deviation from Islamic doctrines becomes an act of revolt against Islam, even if it is a religious doctrine held by Jews or Christians. Therefore, every individual, and not only the Muslim, must yield to this will. While this will sets up a contractual political order, it cannot permit pluralism, religious, political or philosophic, since such a multiplicity of opinions ends up in political disunity or theological unbelief. An Islamic state becomes for radicalism the fulfillment of this divine will, and again individuals and groups are consequently subordinated to the state. Politics and theology become interchangeably one and the same.

Processed through the lenses of the *shari'a*, the institutionalization of *shura* provides the state, which expresses public will, a normative role in making basic choices in people's life. The formal legitimacy that the state acquires makes it in fact unaccountable to anyone but God or obedience to *shari'a*, itself institutionalized in the state. Thus, henceforth, legitimacy becomes an internal state affair and not a social and public issue, though originally it was. Therefore, insofar as the state is not going against the *shari'a*, no one can legitimately overthrow it, and it supervises in this context the morality of people and the application of *shari'a*. Thus individual religiosity is transformed into communal public will, itself transformed into state control, both moral and political. Religions, other than of course Islam, as well as other forms of association and expression, have no intrinsic validity in this hierarchy, and may only operate in a supplementary manner and under the control of Islamic law and rule.

Such a view of other religions seems ultimately to demand exclusivity: no possibility of pluralistic understanding of religions, the politicization of Islam as the proper Islamic interpretation, itself cannot be represented but by an exclusive Islamic state. In this context, the establishment of pluralistic democracies and ways of life and, more importantly, the freedom of other religions are not theoretical and practical possibilities.

But to use Islamic radicalism as representative of Islamic and Arab culture is both factually erroneous and culturally biased — other religions suffer from very similar phenomena but are never treated in the same manner. One has to keep in mind that the employment of violence by this group is not theoretical in origin, but their theory is historically developed against a background of imperialism, colonialism, Zionism, tyrannical regimes and the like. In other words, they have not been committing violent acts because of their theories, but their theories justifying violence have been derived from the violence that they and the Muslim world have been subjected to or that they have perceived as such. In fact, practice has been reified into theory, which has now a life of its own. Both radical groups and most of the regimes are committed to recycling intellectual and practical violence and exclusivity, which spills out and even involves minorities, most of whom seem to support the regimes and are uncomfortable, to say the least, with Islamic movements. Violence, by both secular and religious groups, has been exercised most of the time in reaction to the tyrannies of political regimes. 'Abud al-Zumar, serving a forty-year term in jail, attributes, incorrectly or not, the violence of the radical groups to the violence of the Egyptian regime and questions the effectiveness of death sentences in curbing Islamic movements. For him fundamentalist violence is directed against those who have already liquidated fundamentalists and worked against Islam[84].

However, once these doctrines are translated into a religiously developed political philosophy, they are, in fact, processed by an extremely radical methodological and intellectual formula. This formula is grounded in a few exclusive concepts: authenticity, one-sidedness of truth, purity,

---

[84] *Al-Safir*, 25 September, 2993, p. 10 and *Al-Diyar*, 25 September, 1993, p. 14.

superiority and above all salvational knowledge. In turn these concepts lead their adherents to be self-righteous and undemocratic. For claiming the exclusive, authentic, scriptural, salvational and superior knowledge will force them, and will force any one who has similar concepts, to essentially marginalize *other* religions and philosophies of life.

Thus, minorities, special interest groups, private organizations and the like are subjected to the communal social interest. The communal interest is reified again to represent the divine will. With such an argument any breaking away becomes a theological crime which is severely punished. Social mutual responsibility forces the individual not only to accommodate but also to subject the individual interest to the communal interests. Consequently, the regulator of interests becomes for the radicals their specific interpretation of Islam.

Islamic radicalism views minorities suspiciously not only in political terms but also in religious terms; therefore, tolerance of and coexistence with other religions are not part of their vocabulary. Their views are more radical than traditional views, which tolerated other religions as being divine in origin but humanly corrupted. They turn the traditional views upside down, where they make the Qur'anic verses that call for tolerance the exception, and the verses that call for war, the principle. They therefore turn political conflicts that took place between religions into theological conflicts between political systems. The original stance towards Judaism and Christianity is therefore a state of permanent conflictual interactions. For the radicals, these religions carry within them the seeds for corruption of the divine pure creed, and thus their destruction is a religious duty. In other words, religious conflicts are divine, systematic and eternal.

On the other hand, and under the pressures to conform to democracy which have become a universal demand, the absence of a pluralistic society and of democratic institutions are cited by moderate fundamentalism as the real cause for violence against the state and against other religions. While this trend has for long been excluded from political participation and fought by minorities — like the Copts in Egypt — it still calls for its and others' inclusion into politics and formal institutions. Its involvement in civil society and its call for pluralism are still seen as the road to salvation of the community, religions and individuals. Their inclusionary views do not postulate an eternal and divine enmity between Islam and its institutions and systems, and other religions as

well as the West and their institutions and systems. Properly grounded,
what is Western becomes indeed Islamic. Here, I think, the moderate
fundamentalists may blend the culture of the East with the culture of the
West and can propel, given certain conditions, mutual religious and
political tolerance. For they are providing Islamic arguments for inclusion of other religions, not mutual exclusivity — as some secular and
religious radicals do in the East and West. The conflicts between Islam
and other religions and between the East and West are viewed primarily
as political and economic, not religious or cultural. For Islam and other
religions along with the West have common monotheistic grounds upon
which multi-cultural and religious cooperation and co-existence might
be built.

Jews and Christians residing in Islamic societies are believed to be
part of the community itself and enjoy similar religious and political
rights and duties. For moderate fundamentalism makes the Qur'anic
verses that call for tolerance and co-existence the basis of its attitude
towards other religions. It even extends the traditional theological and
juristic tolerance to cover political rights, parties, elections and representation. In other words, equal citizenship becomes a must for the setting of a modern Islamic state that should provide its citizens qua citizens with their legal, economic, religious and political rights.

A form of popular and representative democracy, grounded in Islamic
law, is adopted so that all groups in society can be rightfully represented.
More importantly, this form of democracy could become a political
bridge between the East and the West and a source for co-existence of
Islam and other religions and philosophies. For authoritarianism and
despotism are ultimately not specific to any culture or Islam. They have
existed in both the West and the East, but are more prominent now in the
Arab world and the East. The moderate trend adopts an Islamic interpretation of liberal democracy as opposed to the religiously exclusive
democracy of radical fundamentalism or the authoritarian nationalist
state in the Arab world. Whereas radical fundamentalism proclaims the
constitutionality of Islam even in the non-Islamic states and as such
requires no prior popular approval and excludes the possibility of dialogue and cooperation with other religions, the Arab regimes and the
West, moderate fundamentalism seems more amenable and eager to be
included in dialogue and cooperation on issues of politics, ideology and
religion in a context of a civil society. If the weakness of fundamentalism, both in its minor radical and, especially, major moderate trends
might lead to free liberal, pluralistic, tolerant and democratic societies,

why has not this happened while Islamic activists were at their lowest ebbs and packed up in jails?

Of course the moderate fundamentalist thinkers are not, strictly speaking, Western liberal democrats, but still they are, loosely speaking, liberal and democratic enough in a context like the Middle East, plagued with nationalist totalitarian rule or traditional despotic kings. For they believe that the government enjoys executive power as delegated willingly by popular social forces. They postulate as well the division of power into the three well-known institutions, the executive, the legislative and the judiciary. Furthermore, they make consent and contract the legitimate means of selecting a ruler. Last and not least, basic human rights such as those of association, expression and belief are mostly accepted as both natural and religious rights. No inherent contradiction or superiority of one right over the other is developed but all are viewed as emanating from God. Here Islam becomes the constitutional reference only if the people have chosen it as such. Therefore, if radical fundamentalism proves resilient to dialogue and cooperation with other religions and the West in general, moderate fundamentalism, which is often lumped together with the radical trend, because of political expediency, easiness of targeting Islam as the new **green threat**, and the interests of certain circles in the East and West along with most of the governments in the Middle East, is open to dialogue, tolerance and more importantly to universal rights, freedom, pluralism, and civil society. If this does not form the basis of cultural and political platforms for dialogue, what does? For moderate Islamic fundamentalism seems to have adopted at the theoretical level most of the modern Western political principles, such as election, representation, democracy, human rights and even capitalism. Its discourse can therefore converse with Western democratic discourses and the core ideas of both may constitute a positive opening for the peoples of both the West and the East.

LE CHRISTIANISME ET LES CHRETIENS
VUS PAR
DEUX AUTEURS ARABES MUSULMANS

Waheed HASSAB ALLA

Il faut avouer que la tâche n'est pas facile pour un musulman de percevoir la foi et la place des chrétiens dans la société musulmane, et inversement. De plus, la plupart des musulmans qui participent au dialogue ou écrivent à ce sujet ne font pas du christianisme ou du judaïsme leur spécialité[1]. Cela est encore plus difficile quand ils le font sous la pression et la menace de groupes extrémistes qui veulent imposer leur interprétation de la religion musulmane à l'ensemble de la société. C'est dans ce contexte qu'on trouve beaucoup d'ouvrages musulmans qui visent à démontrer l'inconsistance de certaines interprétations des textes coraniques au sujet des non-musulmans.

Il y a deux méthodes intimement liées pour comprendre le contenu de la foi d'une autre religion. La première est la rencontre et le dialogue avec les croyants de l'autre religion. La seconde est la lecture d'ouvrages qui exposent la foi de l'autre religion. Les deux méthodes sont complémentaires et indispensables. L'expérience de la rencontre avec des gens de l'autre religion facilite la compréhension que l'on peut avoir de ce qu'ils ont écrit au sujet de la foi de leur religion. Cela permettra à chaque groupe de rapprocher les points de convergence et de discerner les points de divergence.

Ces deux approches du dialogue doivent être «*basées sur la liberté intellectuelle <ou de la pensée> et le respect mutuel entre les partenaires. L'Islam insiste sur la nécessité d'arriver à la vérité par le dialogue d'une manière rationnelle et objective. Même si cela contredit la doctrine générale des gens <hattâ wa law hâlafa l 'aqîdata al-'âmmata li-n-nâs* حتى ولو خالف العقيدة العامة للناس>», «*personne n'a le droit d'empêcher l'autre de jouir de cette liberté en l'accusant d'incrédulité*» (Fadlallâh s'inspire des versts coraniques suivants: *S. 3:78; 18:56; 22:8*[2].

---

[1] AS-SAYYID, Radwan, «Les relations islamo-chrétiennes – le dialogue islamo-chrétien», رضوان السيد: العلاقات الإسلامية – المسيحية والحوار الإسلامى المسيحى: قراءة من وجهة نظر إسلامية», In *Les relations islamo-chrétiennes: lecture référentielle dans l'histoire, le présent et le future*, Beyrouth: Centre des études stratégiques et des recherches 1994, pp. 62-63.

[2] FADLALLAH, Muhammad Hussein, فى آفاق الحوار الإسلامى المسيحى *Fî âfâq al-hiwâr al-islâmî al-masîhî* (Dans l'horizon du dialogue islamo-chrétien), éd. Dâr-Al-Malâk, Bey-

Nous savons qu'il y a deux façons de percevoir l'autre religion: la première est polémique et négative, l'autre «*offre à chaque groupe la connaissance des racines de l'autre groupe et de ses particularités à partir des sources qu'il accepte. Cette méthode permet de sauvegarder la pureté de l'idée dans sa source d'origine. Mais cela ne doit pas s'arrêter à des questions théologiques par lesquelles les musulmans et les chrétiens diffèrent. Au contraire, le dialogue doit s'étendre aux conceptions générales liées à la valeur de la vie, de l'homme et de la conduite morale dans la réalité du mouvement humain. Cela permettra au musulman comme au chrétien de comprendre l'arrière-pensée qui réside derrière les comportements de l'homme musulman dans ses relations personnelles ou publiques <et inversement pour le chrétien>. Les savants musulmans ou chrétiens doivent être conscients du contenu de la foi de l'autre selon ses sources d'origine.*»[3]

La perception objective et exacte d'une autre religion est devenue une nécessité fondamentale dans les pays à majorité musulmane où existe un pluralisme religieux et ethnique qui rend indispensable de prendre en compte «*la nouvelle philosophie de notre monde <qui> est la reconnaissance de l'autre par le moyen de l'échange verbal: <dialoguer> avec lui, comprendre ses problèmes et ses objectifs, d'être sur le même pied que l'autre. Si le dialogue est le résultat d'une évolution culturelle et humaine <en Occident>, il est pour nous une nécessité, un besoin existentiel.*»[4]

Mon essai consiste à présenter la perception du christianisme et la place des chrétiens au sein de la communauté musulmane du point de vue de deux auteurs musulmans: Muhammad Hussein Fadlallâh[5] محمد فهمى فضل الله حسين, qui est un Libanais shî'ite شيعىّ, et Fahmî Huwaidî[6] هويدى qui est un Egyptien sunnite سَنىَ. Le choix de ces deux auteurs

routh 1994, p. 14. Nous avons utilisé l'édition coranique de: Cheikh HAMZA BOUBAKEUR, Le Coran: texte, traduction française et commentaire. Paris: éd. Fayard, 1979, 2 vol.

[3] Ibid., p. 92.

[4] AS-SAYYID, Radwan, رضوان السيد: العلاقات الإسلامية – المسيحية والحوار الإسلامى المسيحى: «Les relations islamo-chrétiennes et le dialogue islamo-chrétien». In *Les relations islamo-chrétiennes: lecture référentielle dans l'histoire, le présent et le futur.* العلاقات الإسلامية – المسيحية: قراءة مرجعية فى التاريخ والحاضر والمستقبل. بيروت: مركز (الدراسات الإستراتيجية والبحث والتوثيق، ١٩٩٤، صفحة ٦٩). Beyrouth: Centre des études stratégiques et des recherches, 1994, p. 69.

[5] Il est né le19.02.1934 à Nejef en Irak, de mère libanaise: Bint Jubayl et de père descendant de la noblesse de la Mecque: As-sayyid 'Abd al-Ra'ûf Fadlallâh bin Hasan bin 'Alî ibn Abî Tâlib. Il a émigré au Liban en 1967.

[6] Il est âgé de 50 ans environ. Il est considéré comme l'un des penseurs musulmans du mouvement réformiste en Egypte, a écrit plusieurs ouvrages et travaille comme journaliste au journal égyptien al-Ahrâm.

n'est pas dû au hasard. Les deux auteurs ont une place très influente dans leur société respective. Muhammad Hussein Fadlallâh est un homme religieux populaire auprès des musulmans du Liban. Il est l'auteur de nombreux ouvrages[7]. Huwaidî est un journaliste à *Al-Ahrâm*, un grand quotidien égyptien, et il est l'auteur de nombreux ouvrages[8].

Leur perception du christianisme est certes tirée de leur contexte local. Les deux auteurs vivent en effet avec des chrétiens orientaux. Il est à noter en outre que les rapports islamo-chrétiens en Egypte ne sont pas les mêmes qu'au Liban. Par ailleurs, les chrétiens en Orient appartiennent soit à des Eglises indépendantes et autochtones, soit à des Eglises dont le centre de référence se trouve à l'étranger. Fadlallâh et Huwaïdî ont grandi avec des chrétiens. Leur perception du christianisme se situe dès lors à deux niveaux différents: une perception plutôt positive en ce qui concerne les chrétiens orientaux, et plutôt négative vis-à-vis du christianisme et des chrétiens occidentaux.

I. Muhammad Hussein FADLALLAH[9]

INTRODUCTION

L'ouvrage et les relations de l'auteur avec les milieux chrétiens

L'ouvrage de Fadlallâh se divise en neuf chapitres qui touchent à des sujets comme le dialogue, le Christ dans la pensée musulmane, le dialo-

---

[7] Par exemple A. Al-Haraka al-islâmiyya…humûm wa qadâyâ همّوم … الإسلامية الحركة وقضايا (Le mouvement islamique… Soucis et problèmes), Beyrouth: Dar al-malâk,199?; B. Al-Islâm wa mantiq al-quwwa القوة ومنطق الإسلام (L'Islam et la logique de la force), Beyrouth: Dar al-ma'ârif, 1987; C. Al-masa'il al-fiqhiyya الفقهية المسائل (Les questions jurisprudentielles), Beyrouth: Dar al-Malâk, 1995.

[8] a. Al-'Arab wa-Irân: wahm as-sirâ' wa-hamm al-wafaq وهمّ الصراع وهم : وإيران العرب الوفاق (Les Arabes et l'Iran: l'illusion de la lutte et le souci de l'entente). Le Caire: Dâr al-shurûq, 1991; b. Azmat al-wa'y al-dînî الديني الوعى أزمة (La crise de l'éveil religieux). San'a: Dâr al-hikma al-yamaniyya, 1988; c. Hattâ lâ takûna fitna فتنة تكون لا حتى (Afin qu'il n'y ait pas de dissension). Le Caire-Beyrouth: Dâr al-shurûq, 1989; d. Irân min al-dâkhil الداخل من إيران (L'Iran de l'intérieur), Le Caire: Markaz al-Ahrâm, 1991; e. Al-Qur'ân wa-l-sultân والسلطان القرآن (Le Coran et le pouvoir),Le Caire-Beyrouth: Dâr al-shurûq, 1982; f. At-tadayyun al-manqûs المنقوص التدين (La religiosité incomplète). Le Caire: Markaz al-Ahrâm, 1988; g. Tazyîf al-wa'y الوعى تزييف (La falsification de la conscience). Le Caire-Beyrouth: Dâr al-shurûq, 1987. h. Muwâtinûn lâ dhimmiyyûn لا مواطنون ذميّون (citoyens et non des protégés). Le Caire-Beyrouth: Dâr al-shurûq, 2ème éd., 1990. i. Al-islâm fî l-Sîn الصين فى الإسلام (L'islam en Chine). Kuwayt: Al-majlis al-watanî li-l-thaqâfa wa-l-funûn wa-l-âdâb, 1981.

[9] FADLALLAH, Muhammad Hussein, *Fî âfâq al-hiwâr al-islâmî al-masîhî* الحوار آفاق فى المسيحى الإسلامى (Dans l'horizon du dialogue islamo-chrétien), Liban, 1994.

gue et la coexistence au Liban, les relations islamo-chrétiennes dans la
réalité présente et future, les chrétiens sous le régime islamique (ch. 1-5).
Sont traités ensuite les dialogues de l'auteur avec des prêtres et des moines (ch. 6), les discours de l'auteur à l'Université Américaine de Beyrouth (ch. 7), les différentes rencontres de l'auteur avec des journalistes
(ch. 8), et enfin les résultats effectifs du dialogue (ch. 9).

Nous présentons donc en premier lieu les opinions Muhammad Hussein Fadlallâh. Celui-ci a eu, et a encore, beaucoup de contacts avec des
personnalités ecclésiastiques. Il cite, à titre d'exemple, ses rencontres, à
Damas, avec différents patriarches, le Nonce Apostolique en Syrie, et
quelques métropolites influents à Damas et au Liban. Ces rencontres ont
eu pour objet de discuter autour de quelques problèmes généraux de la
région. A ce sujet, il avait lu quelques écrits du métropolite orthodoxe
Georges Khodr qui en fait mention dans ses écrits. Ce fait, nouveau, ne
s'était pas produit depuis deux mille ans[10].

Fadlallâh préfère que ses rencontres avec les personnalités chrétiennes
se déroulent de façon non protocolaire, par le biais d'une invitation sociale et sur la base d'un désir mutuel de se rencontrer en toute amitié.
D'ailleurs, il a entretenu des liens avec le patriarche maronite Sfeir par
l'intermédiaire d'amis communs[11].

Quant à sa relation avec le Vatican, elle s'est développée à deux niveaux:

– le premier niveau est celui de l'évolution de la pensée catholique
exprimée par le Vatican et ses discours religieux, qui sont ouverts au
dialogue et concernent beaucoup de problèmes humains. Il trouve que la
pensée catholique au sujet de l'homme est proche de la sienne. De ce
fait, il adopte une attitude positive envers le discours du Vatican;

– le deuxième niveau est le cercle de quelques amis théologiens, spécialement le Nonce Apostolique qui lui transmet régulièrement des messages du Pape, et inversement. Pour le moment, il n'a pas eu de contact
direct avec lui, mais il est ouvert et reste prêt à un contact direct[12].

Notre auteur a des amitiés dans les différentes confessions chrétiennes, spécialement avec des théologiens, des intellectuels et des hommes
politiques. Mais il regrette, pour des raisons de sécurité, de ne posséder
qu'une liberté relative qui l'empêche d'élargir le cercle de ses rencontres. Les rencontres qui sont possibles avec ses amis chrétiens lui appor-

---

[10] Ibid., p. 316.
[11] Ibid., p. 317.
[12] Ibid., pp. 358-9.

tent beaucoup de tranquillité, de paix et de bonheur: si leurs opinions divergent beaucoup, cela ne l'empêche pas de les rencontrer et de dialoguer[13]. D'autre part, il reconnaît qu'il n'a jamais eu l'occasion jusqu'à présent d'aller dans une église, mais il est prêt à y aller si l'occasion se présente[14].

Fadlallâh se considère comme une personnalité religieuse indépendante n'agissant au nom de personne, ni d'aucun parti. Il est ouvert à l'Orient comme à l'Occident, il se compte parmi ceux qui croient que la pensée, la science et les principes n'ont pas de patrie[15].

La connaissance du christianisme et du judaïsme est une partie intégrante de sa connaissance de l'islam[16].

Fadlallâh rejette catégoriquement l'accusation selon laquelle il est le guide spirituel du Hizbollah pro-iranien au Liban.

1. LE DIALOGUE ISLAMO-CHRÉTIEN

1.1. *Analyse philologique*

Fadlallâh analyse, dans un premier temps, les deux termes coraniques حِوار *hiwâr (dialogue) et* جِدال *jidâl (discussion).* Quant au premier terme, حِوار *hiwâr,* on le trouve dans S. 58:1 et 18:34; tandis que le second, جِدال *jidâl,* se trouve dans nombre de références coraniques (S. 4:107; 11:32; 18:54; 22:8; 29:46; 40:5). L'A. pense que même si حِوار *hiwâr* convient mieux que جِدال *jidâl* au contexte du dialogue, cela ne veut pas dire que ce dernier terme soit entièrement négatif. Au contraire, il exprime plutôt le dynamisme de l'homme dans sa lutte rationnelle et affective. Cela lui permet de s'ouvrir, de se transformer et de changer, sans donner l'occasion à quiconque d'enfermer ou encadrer dans un stéréotype[17].

1.2. *Le dialogue*

Fadlallâh suggère qu'il est d'abord nécessaire que le dialogue commence avec soi-même. Cela donne à l'homme dialoguant une identité, une personnalité équilibrée et logique. Car l'homme qui refuse de dialoguer avec lui-même ne sera pas en mesure de dialoguer avec autrui

---

[13] Ibid., p. 361.
[14] Ibid., p. 369.
[15] Ibid., p. 226.
[16] Ibid., p. 137.
[17] Ibid., pp. 7-8.

(S.3:191; 29:20; 46:3)[18]. Quant au dialogue avec l'autre, nous constatons à travers l'histoire des prophètes dans le Coran que ceux-ci étaient des hommes de dialogue (S. 2:30; 16:24,103; 34:46; 36:78-79). D'ailleurs, dans la conception islamique, le dialogue n'exclut aucun objet ni domaine. Tout est susceptible de devenir sujet de dialogue, rien n'est exclu, car chacun a le droit de connaître la vérité[19].

Il est indispensable, en outre, que ce dialogue soit basé sur la liberté que suppose la pensée rationnelle et sur le respect mutuel entre les partenaires du dialogue. L'islam insiste sur la nécessité d'arriver à la vérité par le dialogue d'une manière rationnelle et objective, même si cela contredit la doctrine générale des gens. Et personne n'a le droit d'empêcher l'autre de jouir de cette liberté en l'accusant d'incrédulité (S. 3:78; 18:56; 22:8)[20].

1.3. *Le style du dialogue*

Fadlallâh remarque que le Coran a invoqué deux styles de dialogue: l'un est violent et manque de respect à l'égard de l'adversaire. Ce style n'arrange évidemment rien; au contraire, il provoque plutôt la haine et l'agressivité en empêchant en même temps de parvenir à des résultats positifs. Tandis que l'autre, non-violent et pacifique, se fonde sur l'amour et la souplesse comme fondement de l'effort rationnel, comme les textes coraniques le suggèrent « وجادلهم بالتى هى أحسن *Discute avec eux de la meilleure façon.*» (S. 16:125);

«ولا تجادلوا أهل الكتاب إلا بالتى هى أحسن إلا الذين ظلموا منهم وقولوا أمنا بالذى أنزل إلينا وأنزل إليكم وإلهنا وإلهكم واحد ونحن له مسلمونَ»

«Et ne discute que de la meilleure façon avec les gens du Livre, sauf ceux d'entre eux qui sont injustes. Et dites: Nous croyons en ce qu'on a fait descendre vers nous et descendre vers vous, tandis que notre Dieu et votre Dieu est le même (Un Dieu Unique), et c'est à Lui que nous nous soumettons»(S. 29:46)[21].

Fadlallâh est convaincu qu'en matière de dialogue, la méthode islamique a l'avantage sur la méthode rationnelle, parce que cette dernière se fonde sur le principe de la probabilité minimale d'erreur. Cela se résume

---

[18] Ibid., pp. 8-11.
[19] Ibid., pp. 11-14.
[20] Ibid., pp. 11-16.
[21] Ibid., pp. 16-18.

ainsi: «*mon opinion est juste, mais elle peut être fausse; l'opinion de l'autre est fausse, mais elle peut être juste*».

Par contre, la méthode coranique suit la règle suivante, conformément au verset coranique: «وإنآ أو إياكم لعلى هدى أو فى ضلال مبين» «*C'est nous ou bien vous qui sommes sur une bonne voie, ou dans un égarement manifeste*» (S.34:24). C'est dire l'égalité entre les partenaires devant l'erreur ou la vérité; en outre, elle nous libère du fanatisme et n'oblige pas à essayer de convaincre l'autre par des arguments acceptables rationnellement (S.28:49)[22]. La méthode de l'Islam dans le dialogue cherche l'objectivité, le rationalisme et la discussion de la meilleure façon sur la base de la confiance et le respect mutuel.

Dans ce contexte, Fadlallâh met en garde contre les islamistes à cause de leur style agitateur dans le dialogue, un style qui n'a rien en commun avec l'islam. En même temps, il rappelle aux non-musulmans que l'islam est une religion qui a des affinités avec la raison et l'esprit de la science. En partant du verset coranique 3:64, il nous est donc nécessaire d'affronter les murs qui séparent les deux communautés ou religions. Il considère qu'il y a entre le christianisme et l'Islam plus de 90% des opinions qui sont communes, mis à part les détails théologiques[23].

Fadlallâh refuse que le dialogue soit exploité à des fins politiques, mais qu'il doit se dérouler dans un environnement rationnel et neutre (S.28:49;34:24)[24].

Fadlallâh refuse, d'autre part, la tendance d'une espèce de dialogue qui veut faire une religion qui rassemble les points communs entre l'islam, le christianisme et le judaïsme, en laissant de côté les différences. Cette méthode est un contournement du problème et non pas une solution. On ne peut accepter le principe d'éliminer les différences — afin d'éviter les problèmes — comme une solution. Nous sommes pour le dialogue qui vise à faire comprendre aux musulmans ce qu'est le christianisme pour le penser, et inversement[25].

Fadlallâh reconnaît qu'il y a une méconnaissance des musulmans de l'essence du christianisme, et inversement. Il préconise pour remédier à cela un dialogue progressif autour des concepts moraux généraux, la question de la Sharî'a (الشريعة) et son application, le sujet des dhimmîs (الذميين), les problèmes communs d'une société diversifiée et la recherche de la complémentarité de l'un dans l'autre[26].

---

[22] Ibid., pp. 18-20.
[23] Ibid., pp. 20-22.
[24] Ibid., pp. 22-24.
[25] Ibid., p. 194.
[26] Ibid., pp. 24-26.

1.4. *Le dialogue entre Libanais*

Fadlallâh voit qu'il est nécessaire de présenter l'image authentique du christianisme et de l'islam dans l'opinion des croyants des deux religions, afin de bâtir une base solide permettant aux deux communautés de se comprendre mutuellement. D'ailleurs, il ne faut pas que le dialogue soit un instrument mis en mouvement par des volontés politiques ou des services de renseignements[27].

1.5. *Les gens qui participent au dialogue*

Ils doivent posséder l'esprit du dialogue, sa culture, sa confiance et son dynamisme. Ils doivent aussi avoir la volonté d'arriver à des résultats positifs. Ils doivent, en outre, être spécialisés dans le domaine qu'ils vont aborder dans le cadre du dialogue. Fadlallâh n'oublie pas de souligner la différence théologique entre l'Eglise Orientale et Occidentale[28].

1.6. *Le dialogue avec les juifs*

Fadlallâh insiste, d'une part, sur la nécessité de différencier le judaïsme et Israël, car le judaïsme — comme le christianisme — est une religion du Livre et l'islam a appelé au dialogue avec ses adeptes. Il évoque, d'autre part, l'existence de l'Etat d'Israël sur une terre islamique, sur la base d'une promesse biblique. C'est pourquoi les juifs correspondent à ce que le Coran les qualifie: «*sauf ceux d'entre eux qui sont injustes*» (S.29:46); «لتجدن أشد الناس عداوة للذين أمنوا اليهود والذين أشركوا» «*Tu trouveras certainement que les Juifs et les associateurs sont les ennemis les plus acharnés des croyants*» (S. 5:82)[29].

1.7. *Obstacles au dialogue*

Fadlallâh aborde la question des obstacles au dialogue en constatant la vision négative qu'adoptent des chrétiens à l'égard de l'islam, et des musulmans à l'égard du christianisme. C'est clair en ce qui concerne les aspects théologiques de l'une ou de l'autre religion, comme la nature divine du Christ, l'Unicité et la Trinité, la Rédemption, ou la reconnaissance du caractère prophétique de Muhammad et de l'islam, ce qui est interdit et permis dans l'islam. Ces points constituent des obstacles au dialogue. Mais il nous faut les affronter avec un style rationnel et une compréhension humaine[30].

---

[27] Ibid., pp. 28-30.
[28] Ibid., pp. 31-32.
[29] Ibid., pp. 32-34.
[30] Ibid., pp. 34-35.

Fadlallâh pense qu'il est naturel qu'on trouve parmi les musulmans quelques savants et personnalités fermées, même en ce qui concerne la diversité confessionnelle islamique, de même que parmi les chrétiens[31]. Un grand obstacle pour le dialogue islamo-chrétien est aussi constitué par les grandes puissances, parce que la réalisation de la paix entre les deux religions et communautés ne servira pas leurs intérêts dans la région. Mais, pour arriver à contourner cela, il nous faut peut-être «tromper les grandes puissances et les induire en erreur»[32].

1.8. *Caractère du dialogue*

Pour Fadlallâh, le dialogue libère les nouvelles générations d'une sclérose rationnelle et culturelle et de troubles politiques. Mais il reconnaît qu'on a besoin de beaucoup de temps pour éliminer la haine héritée et accumulée de l'histoire et le fossé qui existe entre les deux religions et les deux communautés[33]. Fadlallâh ne voit pas d'autre moyen que le dialogue comme un instrument possible pour que l'Appel islamique ou la Mission chrétienne percent la raison de l'homme. «Car l'épée âpre et l'arme tranchante ne peuvent que soumettre le corps, mais on ne peut convaincre la raison qu'avec l'arme de la parole et de la pensée»[34]. Fadlallâh affirme que le dialogue avec les chrétiens ne s'inspire pas des situations occasionnelles qui font surgir la politique d'un côté, l'ambition d'un autre côté, les intérêts personnels d'un troisième côté[35].

1.9. *La question théologique et la réalité*

Le Coran associe la question de Dieu à la question de l'homme[36] et la Sharî'a est la démonstration du lien entre les deux. Nous comprenons — dit Fadlallâh — la doctrine de la foi comme un dynamisme qui met en mouvement les spécificités de la vie de l'homme. Cela au point que l'homme sent à travers la Sharî'a que Dieu est avec lui dans sa vie personnelle, son environnement intime et les singularités de ses relations privées. Dieu n'est pas inintelligible et abstrait, vivant dans l'inconscient de l'homme comme une chose séparée de Lui-même, qui le regarde d'en haut. Dieu est miséricordieux, absolument compatissant[37]. De là, nous

---

[31] Ibid., pp. 218-9.
[32] Ibid., p. 340.
[33] Ibid., pp. 35-38.
[34] Ibid., p. 196.
[35] Ibid., p. 197.
[36] Ibid., p. 45.
[37] Ibid., p. 46.

remarquons que le Coran, en instaurant un environnement de dialogue avec les gens du Livre, insiste sur la parole commune qui s'ouvre sur deux lignes qui ne s'éloignent pas de la dynamique de la réalité:

Première ligne: «قل يأهل الكتاب تعالوا إلى كلمة سواء بيننا وبينكم ألا نعبد إلا الله ولا نشرك به شيئاً» «*Dis O gens du Livre, venez à une parole commune entre nous et vous: que nous n'adorions qu'Allah, sans rien Lui associer*» (S.3:64). Il faut croire en Un Seul Dieu, et ne pas adorer la force injuste, oppressive et orgueilleuse en la considérant comme associée à Dieu.

Deuxième ligne: «ولا يتخذ بعضاً بعضاً أرباباً من دون الله» «*Que nous ne nous prenions point les uns les autres pour seigneurs en dehors d'Allah*» (S.3:64). Un refus absolu que l'homme soit hautain et orgueilleux à l'égard de son frère l'homme, au point que l'un devienne le seigneur de l'autre. Dans cet esprit le Coran affirme la liberté politique, rationnelle et sociale. A tel point par exemple que même un souverain ne doit pas oppresser un gouverné[38]. Fadlallâh évoque l'expérience historique de la coexistence de l'islam et des musulmans avec les juifs et les chrétiens comme une réalité enracinée dans leur vie commune, depuis l'apparition de l'islam jusqu'à nos jours. Même s'il y a eu quelques problèmes entre chrétiens et musulmans d'une part et entre juifs et musulmans, d'autre part, ce sont des problèmes accidentels, comme c'est le cas dans beaucoup de sociétés[39]. Nous n'avons pas de problème, dit-il, avec la foi chrétienne, même si nous avons quelques différents dans quelques-unes de ses particularités. Fadlallâh insiste sur le fait que musulmans et chrétiens sont libres de proposer ce qu'ils veulent. Mais l'essentiel est que cette liberté s'exerce par des moyens civilisés qui respectent tout le monde[40].

1.10. *La méthode rationnelle dans le dialogue*

Il est indispensable pour les croyants conscients et les responsables des communautés de revoir comment motiver le sentiment religieux chez les croyants et leur offrir les spécificités de la doctrine religieuse. Ainsi le dialogue entre ce groupe-ci et celui-là se transforme-t-il en un mouvement de recherche de la vérité et de réforme des idées doctrinales. Au point que l'homme du dialogue porte d'une manière involontaire en s'ouvrant sur l'autre et le rencontre[41].

---

[38] Ibid., p. 46.
[39] Ibid., p. 50.
[40] Ibid., p. 51.
[41] Ibid., p. 90.

Fadlallâh propose, pour renforcer le dialogue, la création d'un programme rationnel pour des études communes dans le cadre culturel islamique ou chrétien. Celui-ci peut offrir à chaque groupe une connaissance des racines de l'autre groupe et de ses singularités à partir des sources qu'il accepte. Cela permettra tant au musulman qu'au chrétien, de comprendre l'arrière-fond qui réside derrière les comportements de l'homme musulman ou chrétien dans ses relations personnelles ou collectives. Car il n'y a pas de ligne séparant le dialogue «الدعوة أو التبشير» de la Da'wa ou de la Tabshîr», c'est-à-dire de l'Appel islamique ou de la Mission chrétienne, puisque personne ne peut être neutre devant la pensée de l'autre dans la conversation[42].

1.11. *Le sérieux du dialogue, son objectivité et sa souplesse*

Le dialogue rationnel doit être basé sur la compréhension mutuelle de la nature des idées — à travers la démonstration des points communs et des différents — ou d'une position de force ou de faiblesse. Fadlallâh suggère que le dialogue ne doit pas se dérouler dans un contexte de courtoisie, en donnant des concessions ou en tenant compte des sensibilités, des complications psychologiques et sociales. Car la question est liée à Dieu à travers la Vérité ouverte sur Lui[43].

1.12. *Les principes du dialogue (S. 3:64)*

Il est important que le dialogue se déroule autour de la rencontre d'une pensée avec une autre. Il est fondamental d'aborder les points de différence sur la base d'une atmosphère positive qui soulage l'homme de la pression et l'inspire à la rencontre, la coopération et l'ouverture spirituelle sur l'autre. C'est ainsi que le verset 5:82 exprime l'amour profond dans la spiritualité de la rencontre[44].

1.13 *Fondements des relations Islamo-chrétiennes*

Fadlallâh croit que Dieu a réuni les chrétiens et les musulmans dans la responsabilité partagée pour l'effort (الجهاد *al-jihâd*) commun et avec des valeurs spirituelles, et que des circonstances occasionnelles ne doivent pas les diviser. En outre, il faut une planification pour l'unité ou la complémentarité, ou une collaboration face aux problèmes de l'injustice et

---

[42] Ibid., p. 92.
[43] Ibid., pp. 92-3.
[44] Ibid., pp. 93-5.

de la justice entre le christianisme et l'islam dans la région et dans le monde en général. C'est pourquoi le mouvement des chrétiens et des musulmans donne à la rencontre un dynamisme vivant dans la conscience de l'être et dans la profondeur de l'esprit[45].

2. LE CHRISTIANISME

Fadlallâh donne une description de Jésus et de la Vierge Marie à partir des textes coraniques. Toutefois, on peut remarquer que ses commentaires portent l'empreinte du langage chrétien. Il considère, d'ailleurs, sans tenir compte des détails théologiques, qu'il y a entre le christianisme et l'islam plus de 90% de points communs[46]. Cependant, il recommande aux savants musulmans et chrétiens d'être plus conscients du contenu de la foi de l'autre et de ses sources.

Fadlallâh voit que le problème de la rencontre se situe autour d'une parole commune comme un principe fondamental. Ce dernier se fonde dans l'unicité de Dieu, dans Son adoration sans association, et dans le désir d'unir l'homme dans sa relation avec l'autre sans orgueil.

Fadlallâh cite, comme la plupart des auteurs musulmans, les questions théologiques constituant des divergences, telles que la nature divine du Christ, la Trinité, la Crucifixion avec son mystère, la Rédemption. Ces questions sont toujours en discussion entre le christianisme et l'islam, et entre les chrétiens eux-mêmes. Plus d'une fois, Fadlallâh pose la question du besoin qu'avait Dieu de souffrir afin de Se sacrifier et d'expier le péché originel. Pourtant, il réaffirme que les religions se rencontrent autour de l'Unicité de Dieu dans l'horizon de l'unité, et autour de l'unité humaine (S. 3:64)[47].

Fadlallâh croit qu'il n'y a pas de contradiction — au sens strict du terme — entre l'islam et le christianisme. Parce que l'islam et le christianisme se différencient entre eux par des détails doctrinaux. Les chrétiens croient que Jésus est Dieu Incarné dans l'homme. Mais ils ne reconnaissaient pas le prophète Muhammad. Alors que les musulmans croient en Jésus comme prophète, au prophète Muhammad et aux autres prophètes[48].

L'islam et le christianisme, poursuit-il, ont des points communs dans la doctrine, dans les lignes morales et spirituelles, et dans le dynamisme

---

[45] Ibid., p. 99.
[46] Ibid., pp. 20-22.
[47] Ibid., pp. 24-28.
[48] Ibid., p. 60.

de vie. Ainsi l'islam et le christianisme s'appuient-ils l'un l'autre par beaucoup de concepts communs. Fadlallâh croit que l'islam se dirige vers un processus d'harmonisation avec le christianisme. Cependant, la lutte entre les concepts chrétiens et islamiques dans les détails <théologiques> — par exemple — ou d'autres problèmes doctrinaux, demeure une lutte rationnelle, non pas une lutte armée et militaire[49].

La connaissance du christianisme et du judaïsme fait partie intégrante de notre connaissance de l'islam[50], même s'il est vrai que nous avons quelques différences avec le christianisme dans les détails de la théologie[51]. Néanmoins, dit-il, les lignes générales sont la foi en un Dieu Unique, l'adoration d'un Dieu Unique. Tu adores le Dieu Unique! L'un met peut-être l'image du Christ devant lui quand il adore Dieu dans sa pensée et l'autre ne met pas cette image[52].

Fadlallâh expose la foi chrétienne en Jésus qui représente dans la foi des chrétiens «l'Incarnation vivante de Dieu dans l'homme, Il est venu pour porter les souffrances de l'humanité, afin d'expier le péché du Premier Homme. On parle de la souffrance de l'homme dans la personne de Dieu et de la manifestation de Celui-ci à l'homme, afin de lui accorder Sa miséricorde à travers les souffrances qu'Il supporte à sa place. Les chrétiens discutent cette idée dans leur théologie qui ne s'éloigne pas de la réalité dans sa dynamique.»[53] En résumé, les questions théologiques liées à la personne de Dieu, à la nature messianique du Christ, à l'Unicité et la Trinité sont des questions intellectuelles qu'il est nécessaire d'intégrer au dialogue rationnel précis. Car celles-ci représentent les principes fondamentaux de la pensée chrétienne et islamique. Pour cette raison, Fadlallâh trouve préférable de discuter ces questions dans une deuxième étape.

2.1. *L'unicité de Dieu*

Fadlallâh répète qu'on peut s'unir en Dieu, même si nous avons des différences dans le détail de nos conceptions[54]. Nous n'avons aucune différence quant au fait que nous croyons en Un Seul Dieu[55]. Abraham est le point commun de la foi dans l'Unicité de Dieu du judaïsme, du

[49] Ibid., p. 61.
[50] Ibid., p. 137.
[51] Ibid., p. 142.
[52] Ibid., p. 247.
[53] Ibid., p. 47.
[54] Ibid., p. 133.
[55] Ibid., p. 143.

christianisme et de l'islam. De là, les chrétiens, les juifs et les musul-mans croient en Un Seul Dieu, et ils n'ont aucune différence quant à l'origine de l'Unicité de Dieu[56]. Même dans la Trinité, les chrétiens par-lent de l'Unicité dans leurs prières quotidiennes: «بسم الآب والابن والروح القدس إله واحد» *«Au nom, du Père, du Fils et du Saint-Esprit, Un Seul Dieu»*[57].

2.2. *La différence théologique*

Fadlallâh aborde la question de la divinité du Christ par rapport au qualificatif des chrétiens dans le Coran et dans les croyances populaires de الكافرون *kâfirûn* (incroyants) ou المشركون *mushrikûn* (associateurs /po-lythéistes). Fadlallâh pose la question de savoir comment cela peut être en harmonie avec notre discours du point commun de la foi en Un Seul Dieu, et la complémentarité dans l'Appel aux valeurs spirituelles de la foi? Il se peut que la vision coranique soit présentée à partir des exem-ples chrétiens de l'époque de l'Appel islamique qui ne se concordent pas avec la compréhension religieuse du christianisme primitif ou contem-porain! Car le Coran parle des chrétiens disant que: «أن الله هو المسيح *Dieu est l'Oint»* (S.5:72). Mais le Coran le nie en affirmant l'Unicité de Dieu: «أنى يكون له ولد ولم تكن له صاحبة *Comment aurait-Il un enfant alors qu'Il n'a point de compagne»* (6:101) *ou* «لم يلد ولم يولد *Il n'a ni enfanté, ni été enfanté»* (112:3)[58].

2.2.1. La filiation du Christ

C'est ainsi que le Coran refuse catégoriquement la question de البنوة *al-bunuwwa*, la filiation du Christ. Ce refus se fonde sur la compréhen-sion d'une filiation sensible dans le sens charnel de ce terme, en ce qu'il exprime la «naissance». Mais les chrétiens ne parlent pas de ولد الله *walad Allâh*, «enfant» de Dieu; ils parlent de إبن الله *ibn Allâh*, «fils» de Dieu. Cela en vue de préciser que le sens entendu de la filiation n'est pas toujours lié à l'idée d'un compagnon, etc. De cette façon, le Coran rejette aussi ce que les chrétiens n'ont pas affirmé, parce qu'ils sont d'accord avec l'opinion islamique qui refuse l'enfantement au sens sen-sible. La filiation concerne alors l'aspect conceptuel (figuratif) qui est le mystère de Dieu. Ainsi le Fils est-il du Père, comme la parole de celui qui parle est de l'idée de sa pensée, en multiplicité, sans contredire l'uni-

---

[56] Ibid., p. 245.
[57] Ibid., p. 246.
[58] Ibid., p. 99.

cité de celui-ci. Quant aux versets 4:171;5:116, les chrétiens diront qu'ils ne sont pas concernés par leur contenu. En effet, personne d'entre eux ne prend Maryam pour une divinité, mais peut-être que quelques Arabes le disaient. Il n'est pas permis en conséquence de faire porter au christianisme le fardeau de ce reproche[59].

2.2.2. La question de la crucifixion et de la mort de Jésus-Christ

Quant à la question de la mort de Jésus, Fadlallâh répond ainsi: le Coran parle du futur. Peut-être quelques musulmans disent que Dieu l'a élevé et qu'il reviendra sur terre à la fin des temps. En tout cas le problème est constant entre musulmans et chrétiens. Si nous voulons provoquer le débat autour de ce sujet: les chrétiens disent que le Christ est mort et puis ressuscité. Où est-il allé après avoir été ressuscité? Dieu l'a élevé auprès de Lui. Quelques musulmans disent qu'il n'est pas mort. D'autres disent qu'il est mort naturellement et que Dieu l'a élevé auprès de Lui d'une manière naturelle. L'essentiel est que nous sommes d'accord que Dieu l'a élevé auprès de Lui. Pourquoi différons-nous? Que Dieu l'ait élevé auprès de Lui après sa mort et sa ressurrection, ou sans qu'il soit mort, c'est une étape terminée. Que nous soyons d'accord sur le fait que le Christ se trouve auprès de Dieu et que Dieu l'a élevé! Nous honorons tous le Christ: Je l'honore d'une manière et toi, tu l'honores d'une autre manière, mais nous sommes d'accord autour de lui. Pourquoi nous concentrons-nous sur les points de différence au lieu des points d'accord[60]?

2.2.3. La signification du terme كفر *kufr*

Fadlallâh clarifie le terme الكفر *al-kufr* qui ne signifie pas nier la foi des chrétiens en Dieu. Mais le terme كفر *kufr* désigne le rejet par les chrétiens du prophète Muhammad en tant qu'Envoyé de Dieu. Car الكفر *al-kufr* (incroyance) et الإيمان *al-îmân* (foi) sont deux notions qui ne sont pas absolues, mais relatives[61]. En outre, le terme الكفر *al-kufr* (incroyance) signifie la méconnaissance d'une chose quelconque. Rejeter une chose signifie la nier. De cette façon, l'incroyance est une notion relative, comme la foi. Pour cette raison, il n'y a pas de problème proprement dit entre l'islam et le christianisme. Nous verrons qu'il y a plu-

---

[59] Ibid., p. 100.
[60] Ibid., p. 234.
[61] Ibid.

tôt une confusion autour du christianisme dans l'esprit du musulman[62]. Il faut tenir compte du fait que le Coran ne transcrit que quelques lignes du christianisme; c'est aussi le cas pour le judaïsme.

2.2.4. La question de la Trinité

La conception de la Trinité peut conduire à «الشِّرْكُ l'association» au sens philosophique seulement, sans qu'elle soit fondée sur l'«association» au sens coranique. C'est dans ce sens que l'islam ne considère pas les chrétiens comme des associateurs. Le Coran a fait une différence entre l'associateur et les gens du Livre:

«لم يكن الذين كفروا من أهل الكتاب والمشركين منفكين حتى تأتيهم البينة» (S. 98:1). Nous ne pouvons pas considérer les gens du Livre comme des associateurs au sens coranique, *sauf* au cas où le sens philosophique conduit à l'«association» dans le fond[63].

D'ailleurs, Fadlallâh souligne que la tradition chrétienne recommande ce discours quand elle dit: «Au nom du Père et du Fils et du Saint-Esprit, *Un Seul Dieu*». L'explication de la question se base sur des notions qui sont au-dessus de la raison. Parce que nous ne pouvons pas raisonner sur ces choses, il nous est donc nécessaire de les sentir, de les vivre et de les imaginer dans ces horizons spirituels. C'est pourquoi, quand il s'agit d'«incroyance» que reflètent certains mots dans le Coran, il ne s'agit que d'une incroyance indirecte, philosophique, qui émerge à travers le discours de l'Incarnation de Dieu dans le Christ. Le concept d'Incarnation ne concorde pas avec la perception islamique de l'Unicité de Dieu, même si ce concept est un terme d'approche[64]. Si les théologiens chrétiens disent que leur perception de la Trinité ne signifie pas multiplicité, ils nient ainsi le problème dans sa nature apparente. C'est pourquoi il y a là un accord en substance, même s'il y a un différend quant à son aspect philosophique[65].

En outre, même si la question de la Trinité est une question philosophique qui se place dans le cadre de la compréhension du Mystère de Dieu et de la personnalité du Créateur, il y a là, peut-être, des idées qui parlent du Fils par l'Incarnation et du Père par l'Incarnation. Pourtant, l'idée qui prévaut dans la conception chrétienne est que le concept de l'Incarnation n'a pas le même sens que l'incarnation humaine quand il y

---

[62] Ibid., p. 292.
[63] Ibid., p. 293.
[64] Ibid., p. 294.
[65] Ibid., p. 295.

a un fils qui se sépare de son père. Mais elle est semblable à la parole quand elle s'incarne dans un livre, et peut s'incarner dans une personne[66]. Il y a une discussion autour de ce sujet entre les chrétiens eux-mêmes et avec les musulmans.

2.2.5. Une vision différente

Fadlallâh explique les origines du problème de ces différentes visions. Celles-ci résident dans le fait qu'il y avait beaucoup de notions religieuses simples et compréhensives à leur point de départ. Mais ces notions sont devenues complexes par l'accumulation et l'interaction culturelles qui ont introduit beaucoup d'altérations et de choses superflues dans les différentes doctrines. Ainsi, la doctrine s'est transformée d'une chose simple à une forme plus complexe[67].

D'ailleurs, nous avons besoin d'étudier les conceptions et les notions courantes dans le cadre de l'imagination populaire et de sa déviation des principes rationnels[68]. Du reste, Fadlallâh pense que la nature de la diversification de la croyance entre les musulmans et les chrétiens impose cet échange de l'incroyance relative. Les chrétiens considèrent les musulmans comme des incroyants, parce qu'ils ne croient pas au Christ de la même façon qu'eux. Les musulmans ne considèrent pas les chrétiens incroyants en ce qui concerne la foi en Dieu, bien qu'ils discutent les détails de cette foi. Ainsi, les chrétiens ne peuvent dénier aux musulmans leur vénération du Christ et de la Vierge Marie. Ce genre d'incroyance n'empêche pas le dialogue[69]. Car, l'utilisation du terme كُفْر *kufr* dans le dialogue scientifique d'une manière objective ne provoque pas de sensibilité défavorable[70].

2.2.6. Les valeurs spirituelles et morales dans le christianisme et l'islam

Fadlallâh propose de se mettre d'accord sur un ordre moral inspiré de deux religions mises ensemble, par rapport à ce qui a été dit dans le Coran et l'Evangile. On pourra donner un enseignement religieux moral dans le cadre d'un programme unifié en rapport avec ceux dont l'opinion, l'effort et les conceptions spirituelles et morales s'accordent. Quant aux différences, dans les limites réelles et selon les inspirations

---

[66] Ibid., p. 246.
[67] Ibid., pp. 100-103.
[68] Ibid., p. 91.
[69] Ibid., p. 321.
[70] Ibid., p. 322.

spirituelles, nous pouvons continuer le dialogue et l'effort de chercher le sens du texte avec ces questions. L'idée de l'effort offre la possibilité au savant musulman de chercher à faire parler (اِسْتَنْطَاقَ/يستنطق yastantiq) le texte de l'Evangile dans un mouvement d'effort personnel (اجتهاد ijtihâd). De même pour le savant chrétien, en ce qui concerne le texte coranique, s'il possède la capacité de la lecture et de l'étude[71].

Fadlallâh croit d'ailleurs que la complémentarité dans la question de la force et de la faiblesse sur terre représente la ligne réelle de la perception du croyant, chrétien ou musulman. La religion ne parle pas seulement du Paradis et de l'Au-delà, mais elle montre un exemple pour la vie sur la terre. Les valeurs spirituelles et morales ne sont pas les idées magiques d'une pensée idéaliste. Mais elles sont des idées réalisables qui poussent l'homme à défendre les faibles, les déshérités, les sans-abri, les opprimés, à mourir (accepter le martyre) pour eux, et à faire de cet acte un témoignage de Dieu. Quelques-uns trouvent dans cette méthode un appel à la violence qui ne concorde pas avec l'entité de l'amour. Nous ne la proposons pas comme le seul choix possible. Mais, dans la situation où le faible a usé de tous les moyens pacifiques pour récupérer ses droits, éliminer l'injustice, réaliser sa liberté, il pourra agir ainsi. L'homme est placé entre deux choix, subir la déchéance de l'humanité par la violence de l'autre sans agir lui-même, ou affronter l'autre par la violence pour éliminer son injustice[72].

L'idée islamique est que la bienveillance, comme moyen d'affronter les problèmes difficiles, est la base. Mais la violence représente un moyen humain pour l'équilibre de l'humanité dans la vie, face à ceux qui détournent le sens de la vie au profit de leur injustice impérialiste[73].

3. LA PLACE DES CHRÉTIENS AU SEIN DE LA COMMUNAUTÉ MUSULMANE

3.1. *Les fondements des relations islamo-chrétiennes*

Fadlallâh affirme que «ce que Dieu a réuni dans la responsabilité partagée pour l'effort (الجهاد al-jihâd) commun et avec des valeurs spirituelles, les mauvaises circonstances occasionnelles ne peuvent pas le diviser». En outre, il voit que musulmans et chrétiens doivent tendre à l'unité et à la complémentarité et s'organiser pour faire face aux problè-

---

[71] Fadlallâh, op. cit., p. 95.
[72] Ibid., p. 96.
[73] Ibid., pp. 97-98.

mes d'injustice dans le monde. C'est pourquoi le mouvement des chrétiens et des musulmans donne à la rencontre un dynamisme vivant dans la conscience de l'être et dans la profondeur de l'esprit[74].

3.2. *La coexistence islamo-chrétienne*

Fadlallâh présente l'expérience historique de la coexistence de l'islam avec les juifs et les chrétiens comme une réalité qui s'enracine dès l'apparition de l'islam jusqu'à nos jours. Il reconnaît qu'il y a eu quelques problèmes entre les chrétiens et les musulmans, d'une part, et entre les juifs et les musulmans, d'autre part, mais ce sont des problèmes accidentels, comme c'est le cas dans beaucoup de sociétés. Il insiste d'ailleurs sur le fait que musulmans et chrétiens sont libres de proposer ce qu'ils veulent. Mais l'essentiel est que cette liberté doit être exprimée par des moyens civilisés qui respectent les êtres humains[75].

3.3. *Le problème est politique plus que rationnel*

Fadlallâh réaffirme qu'il n'y a pas de contradiction — au sens strict du terme — entre l'islam et le christianisme.

Dans le domaine pratique, les chrétiens disent qu'ils n'ont que des conceptions spirituelles, des pratiques cultuelles et des valeurs de la foi. C'est pourquoi ils ne s'occupent pas de politique. En plus, ils disent qu'ils n'ont pas de الشريعة *Sharî'a*, pas de Loi. Ce principe se base sur les paroles de Jésus (Lc. 20:25; Jn. 18:36)[76].

Il faut comprendre les musulmans quand ils proposent la الشريعة *Sharî'a*, l'Etat islamique et la ligne politique islamique. Les chrétiens n'en possèdent pas d'équivalent: ils ne possèdent ni الشريعة *Sharî'a*, ni théorie politique, ni, non plus, une conception du pouvoir.

C'est pourquoi nous croyons — dit Fadlallâh — que les chrétiens peuvent vivre sous le régime d'un Etat islamique sans avoir aucun problème. L'islam reconnaît le Christ, Marie et l'Evangile, il reconnaît aussi la Torah et le Coran. L'islam ne s'élève pas contre les chrétiens et

---

[74] Fadlallâh, op. cit., p. 99.

[75] Ibid., pp. 50-51.

[76] Lc. 20:25 «Rendez donc les choses de César à César, et les choses de Dieu à Dieu.»; Jn 18:36 «Jésus répondit: 'Mon royaume n'est pas de ce monde. Si mon royaume était de ce monde, mes serviteurs auraient combattu, afin que je ne fusse pas livré aux Juifs; mais maintenant mon royaume n'est pas d'ici'» (La Sainte Bible: version de J.N. BARBY. Strasbourg: Ed. La Bonne Semence, 1970.

leur loi, puisqu'ils n'en ont pas. Ce qui provoque un problème entre le christianisme et l'islam, ce n'est qu'une situation politique, ethnique <élémentaire> ou tribale et historique, et non pas un état de pensée spirituelle, comme quelques-uns essaient de le dire.

Dans ce domaine, nous disons que les responsables des affaires du christianisme peuvent être rassurés quant à l'islam. Ils doivent plutôt avoir peur de la domination de la grande puissance des USA, qui travaille pour faire tomber toutes les valeurs spirituelles dans le monde. De ce point de vue l'Amérique représente un plus grand danger pour le christianisme que l'islam. Car l'islam reste — quelque soit le point de vue de ceux qui ont peur de lui — une religion céleste qui reconnaît le Christ, la sainte Vierge, l'Evangile et beaucoup d'autres concepts[77].

3.4. *Description du problème*

Fadlallâh pose le problème de la crise dans les relations islamo-chrétiennes dans le présent et le futur. La question est celle de savoir comment lire ses impacts négatifs et positifs sur notre vie tout en restant ouvert sur les conditions extérieures de la réalité humaine. Comment remédier à ces problèmes au niveau culturel, politique et social?

Ensuite, y a-t-il là réellement deux identités vivantes et différentes dont l'une serait l'entité islamique et l'autre l'entité chrétienne? L'une comme l'autre vit enfermée dans ses particularités culturelles et réelles en plein milieu de la crise qui secoue le Proche-Orient. La question essentielle est celle d'une réalité humaine qui doit survivre dans des équilibres de force et de faiblesse dans la région et dans le monde en général. Cela représente l'entité des arrogants et celle des méprisés (الإستكبار والإستضعاف *al-istikbâr wa 'l-istid'âf*), la richesse et la pauvreté, le Nord et le Sud dans le dynamisme des intérêts internationaux. Ces divergences conduisent aux disparités dans le monde pour le transformer d'une manière ou d'une autre en un instrument de déchirement, de désaccord conduisant à des luttes entre groupes. Cette situation peut conduire à la guerre motivée par l'objectif de faire disparaître les soucis de problèmes généraux. Ainsi les haines passées reprennent et accentuent les complications du présent[78].

3.5. *La réalité des mouvements islamistes radicaux*

Fadlallâh expose le problème actuel qui est posé par le fondamentalisme (الإصولية *al-'usûliyya*) islamique dans son expression politique. Il

---

[77] Ibid., pp. 61-62.
[78] Ibid., p. 87.

pense que celui-ci présente un problème pour l'impérialisme et le sionisme international, mais qu'il n'a pas d'influence négative sur le christianisme[79].

La peur qui entoure le fondamentalisme islamique, provient du fait qu'il entre dans le jeu de la politique internationale, offrant à chaque groupe une identité distincte et réveillant à l'intérieur de chaque groupe des complexes historiques à l'encontre de l'autre. Ainsi le mouvement islamiste devient-il le jeu de la politique internationale d'une manière directe ou indirecte, au lieu d'être un mouvement commun avec des notions diversifiées d'après la religion ou des particularités régionales. Dans la géopolitique on cherche à traiter les grands problèmes tout en gelant les petits mouvements qui bougent ici et là. Le pluralisme religieux, ethnique ou politique est alors menacé par des rivalités et des comportements de violence afin de pouvoir survivre[80].

Fadlallâh estime que le mouvement islamiste, tout au moins dans le monde musulman, a pu se régénérer par la persécution dont il fait l'objet. Cette persécution a permis au mouvement d'approfondir ses racines auprès des peuples opprimés et persécutés. Il s'est révélé unique dans son affrontement avec l'impérialisme mondial, de sorte que l'islam a commencé à attaquer l'impérialisme de l'intérieur. Cela a commencé à présenter un problème pour les pays impérialistes qui veulent préserver leur situation et leur identité[81].

D'après Fadlallâh, les islamistes (الإسلاميون *al-islâmiyyûn*) pensent l'islam d'une manière rationnelle et logique. Ils sont proches des musulmans modérés, parce que les uns et les autres se rencontrent autour de l'Unicité de Dieu et l'unité de l'humanité, contre les impérialistes[82].

Fadlallâh pense que la compréhension du fondamentalisme en Orient est entièrement différente de celle de l'Occident officiel ou ecclésiastique. Le fondamentalisme chrétien consiste, définit-il, à être chrétien comme le christianisme l'était dans la pensée du Christ et de l'Evangile, c'est-à-dire le retour aux sources propres existant dans la profondeur de l'homme[83].

Les islamistes ne songent pas à anéantir l'autre et à résoudre les problèmes par la violence, mais par la manière dont pensent les groupes civilisés dans le monde. Ils comprennent le christianisme dans l'esprit de

[79] Ibid., p. 88.
[80] Ibid.
[81] Ibid., p. 338.
[82] Ibid., p. 113.
[83] Ibid., p. 157.

son message, et non pas en tant que sectarisme. A partir de là, le dialogue entre musulmans et chrétiens ne sera pas dirigé entre les deux partis pour marquer des points, mais plutôt pour consolider des concepts et pour rapprocher des convictions. Cela exige que nous nous méfiions des médias occidentaux et de leur méthode agressive. Il faut que nous étudiions nos problèmes rationnellement avec conscience et équilibre, en vue de pouvoir dessiner les sujets de la rencontre et du dialogue et comprendre les sujets d'après les interprétations différentes qui en sont données[84]. C'est ainsi qu'à travers le dialogue on peut découvrir que le chrétien n'est pas un «loup-garou» pour le musulman, et inversement[85].

L'Occident part en guerre contre les mouvements islamiques avec une conception uniquement coloniale et non pas chrétienne. C'est pourquoi la lutte entre l'islam dynamique et l'impérialisme n'est pas une lutte islamo-chrétienne. L'Occident n'est pas chrétien dans son régime, sa politique et ses valeurs. Il est laïc et se trouve dans le cercle vicieux du pouvoir, de l'oppression et de la violence[86].

La question de la violence n'est pas une chose typiquement islamique. Elle est une réaction contre une autre violence, celle des régimes en place. Ceux-ci empêchent les islamistes de jouir pacifiquement de leur liberté politique. Nous voyons que les islamistes sont victimes de la violence et ne sont pas ses guides[87].

Il y a dans le monde actuel une grande agitation, par exemple dans les pays orientaux où des chrétiens vivent comme minorités. Cette agitation est causée par le mouvement islamiste radical qui, elle, a pour objectif l'islamisation du monde. Ce mouvement-là fait pression sur les chrétiens dans leur religion ainsi que dans leur réalité sociale, culturelle et politique. Cela a poussé quelques-uns à constituer un radicalisme chrétien contre la nouvelle réalité islamique dynamique[88].

Certains parlent des incidents violents commis contre les Coptes en Egypte par des islamistes radicaux. D'autres parlent des incidents sauvages commis contre les musulmans par des Serbes ou des Croates. Tout cela est une manifestation agressive des mouvements radicaux islamistes ou chrétiens. Le danger d'une telle lutte sanguinaire est qu'elle peut transformer le monde en un champ de guerre violente entre l'islam et le christianisme[89].

[84] Ibid., p. 113.
[85] Ibid., p. 326.
[86] Ibid., p. 49.
[87] Ibid., p. 113.
[88] Ibid., p. 112.
[89] Ibid.

3.6. *Les chrétiens à l'ombre du régime islamique*

Fadlallâh aborde à sa manière la place du christianisme et des chrétiens au sein de l'Etat islamique. A son avis, le christianisme, comme les chrétiens le reconnaissent eux-mêmes, n'a pas de pensée législative capable de légiférer, ni de projet politique relevant de sa conception profonde de la foi. Il est différent du projet islamique avec sa planification concernant le pouvoir ou la loi. Dès lors il est possible de concevoir l'idée de fonder un Etat islamique au Liban ou ailleurs.

Quand les musulmans proposent l'idée de l'Etat islamique, c'est en vue de faire sortir l'islam et le christianisme de leur frontières confessionnelles, et non pas dans le but d'utiliser la violence, le terrorisme, le fanatisme. C'est par cette proposition qu'on désire se présenter aux autres pour discuter, penser. S'ils le reconnaissent, un tel Etat peut se réaliser encore dans notre vie; sinon, il restera au stade du projet sans provoquer la haine, l'animosité ou la peur.

L'islam considère le christianisme, par sa conception spirituelle, plus proche de lui que d'autres courants sectaires ou athées[90]. Fadlallâh affirme que l'islam a pris soin du christianisme et des chrétiens au cours de son histoire, tandis que le régime chrétien en Andalousie anéantissait la présence musulmane en Espagne.

Quand on propose l'Etat islamique, on affronte des libéraux et des marxistes qui prétendent appartenir au christianisme.

3.6.1. L'Islam est Religion et Etat دين ودولة <dîn wa-dawla>

Fadlallâh, en comparant les différentes approches faites par les musulmans de la conception d'un Etat islamique, avoue qu'il y a une divergence entre les interprétations des textes coraniques ou des hadîths (النصوص القرآنية أو الأحاديث) et les méthodes d'application. C'est le cas des mouvements islamiques contemporains[91].

La question se pose si des chrétiens peuvent assumer de hautes fonctions au sein de l'Etat islamique. Fadlallâh répond ainsi: chaque Etat dans le monde suit une ligne particulière. Il n'accepte pas dans son centre de décision quelqu'un ne croyant pas en son système de pouvoir. A titre d'exemple on peut penser à des Etats marxistes ou à des gouvernements composés par un parti politique particulier. Ceux-ci n'offrent pas de place à quelqu'un qui appartient au parti opposé. C'est le cas dans les

---

[90] Ibid., p. 117.
[91] Ibid., pp. 47-48.

pays dits libéraux. L'islam suit la même règle en ce qui concerne le système de pouvoir. Mais en dehors de ce cadre, chrétiens et musulmans ont les mêmes droits et devoirs[92].

3.6.2. Le régime de l'Etat entre le christianisme et l'islam

Fadlallâh, de son côté, discute les arguments des penseurs chrétiens qui contestent l'instauration de l'Etat islamique et l'application de la Sharî'a الشريعة. Fadlallâh explique qu'il ne discute pas le caractère sacré de l'Etat islamique à l'intérieur duquel les chrétiens vivent. C'est pourquoi la soumission des chrétiens à un régime islamique ne contredit pas leur foi chrétienne. La foi chrétienne ne représente en aucun cas une contradiction avec un régime politique donné. Tandis que la foi islamique sera en contradiction avec un régime laïc et positiviste, parce que celui-ci diffère de la Sharî'a islamique dans ses principes et dans les détails. Cela représentera un problème pour le musulman qui vivra alors une dualité pratique entre la Sharî'a الشريعة et la loi civile en vigueur. Ainsi, le musulman enfreindra la Sharî'a الشريعة. Cela reste illicite (حرام – *harâm*) pour le musulman, même s'il vit dans une réalité juridique non islamique, par exemple dans un Etat laïc. Ce n'est pas le cas pour le chrétien, parce que le chrétien n'est pas lié à des lois édictées par le christianisme. Mais c'est un choix personnel de celui-ci, d'être socialiste, libéral ou autre, ce qui n'a rien à voir avec le christianisme en tant que religion. Fadlallâh suggère que le chrétien étudie par exemple le droit civil dans la Sharî'a الشريعة comme dans d'autres systèmes juridiques sans qu'il soit obnubilé par le caractère islamique du régime. Car la mentalité étroite et fanatique se base sur le refus a priori de l'autre, en général et dans les détails[93].

Le christianisme pur ne contient pas de négation à l'encontre de l'islam et de sa loi. La sharî'a الشريعة islamique n'est pour les chrétiens qu'une loi comme les autres lois qui existent dans le monde. Quand le chrétien se sépare de la loi islamique, il ne se sépare pas tellement de cette loi en tant que telle, mais il veut se distinguer plutôt de sa source, l'islam en tant que religion. Pour cette raison, cela ne constitue pas une lutte entre le chrétien, avec son identité chrétienne, et le musulman, avec son identité islamique. Sauf sur les points où les musulmans diffèrent des chrétiens en matière théologique, il n'y a pas de différence véritable[94].

---

[92] Ibid., pp. 118-119.
[93] Fadlallâh, op. cit., pp. 103-105.
[94] Ibid., p. 428.

3.6.3. Les chrétiens dans le cadre de l'Etat islamique

Fadlallâh reconnaît que les chrétiens ne se sentent pas à l'aise avec le contenu juridique de l'Etat islamique. La cause de ce malaise réside dans les mouvements islamiques qui tendent à instaurer un Etat Islamique dans la pratique. Ceux-ci n'offrent pas l'égalité dans les droits et les devoirs entre les musulmans et les non-musulmans. Ils prévoient de traiter ces derniers comme des citoyens de deuxième classe. Ainsi, ils n'auront plus la possibilité de participer à la prise de décision, ni à la législation. Ils seront considérés comme des gens protégés (ذمّة *dhimma*), comme une entité humaine autonome. Les non-musulmans n'acceptent pas ce statut en tant qu'hommes libres, vivant dans un Etat libre, sans différence entre les citoyens. Fadlallâh rejette cette image sombre de l'Etat islamique. Les non-musulmans peuvent, dit-il, participer aux décisions politiques, sociales et économiques, *sauf* celles concernant les aspects militaires et la guerre, qui peuvent heurter et contredire leur conscience[95]. Il pense, par contre, qu'il n'y a pas de régime qui protège les minorités autant que le régime de l'islam[96].

3.7.1. الذمّة Al-Dhimma

Fadlallâh voit le système de ذمّة *dhimma* comme une protection symbolisant l'ouverture de l'Etat islamique sur ses responsabilités à sauvegarder l'humanité des non-musulmans contre toute agression. Ce statut organise également la relation des «minorités protégées» (ذميون *dhimmiyyûn*) avec les autres gens avec qui ils partagent la citoyenneté, mais qui se différencient d'eux sur la base de la pensée religieuse[97].

3.7.2. الجزية Al-Jizya[98]

Fadlallâh justifie, à sa façon, la capitation (الجزية *jizya*, S.9:29):

«Combattez ceux qui ne croient pas en Dieu ni au jour dernier et ne s'interdisent pas ce que Dieu et son envoyé ont prohibé, [Combattez] également ceux, parmi les gens du Livre, qui ne professent pas la religion de la vérité, à moins qu'ils ne versent la capitation directement et en toute humilité»

---

[95] Ibid., p. 106
[96] Ibid., p. 335.
[97] Ibid., p. 106.
[98] Fadlallâh, op. cit., pp. 107-108.

«قاتلوا الذين لا يؤمنون بالله ولا باليوم الآخر ولا يحرمون ماحرم الله ورسوله
ولا يدينون دين الحق من الدين أوتوا الكتاب حتى يعطوا الجِزْية عن يد وهم
صاغرون»

Cela concerne l'impôt que le non-musulman (ذِمِى *dhîmmî*) doit payer
pour avoir la protection de l'Etat. Ainsi, il n'est pas obligé de participer
à la défense et de payer l'aumône (زَكاة *zakât*). Fadlallâh ajoute que si les
non-musulmans veulent l'égalité totale avec les musulmans, ils doivent
accepter les conséquences de celle-ci. C'est-à-dire qu'ils paieront l'aumône islamique et accepteront de s'harmoniser avec la ligne du الجهاد
jihâd dans le cadre de la sécurité générale de l'Etat. De ce fait, ils paieront plus que la *jizya* الجِزْية .

Quelques-uns émettent une réserve à l'encontre de ce verset en disant
que la *jizya* الجِزْية ne concerne pas les gens du Livre, puisque ceux-ci
croient en Dieu et au Jour Dernier[99].

3.8. *Le mariage mixte*[100]

Fadlallâh explique la raison pour laquelle les gens du Livre ne peuvent pas se marier avec une musulmane, tandis que le contraire est autorisé. C'est que le musulman respecte tout ce qui est sacré chez le chrétien et le juif, la Torah et l'Evangile, Moïse, Marie et tous les prophètes
du Livre. Par contre, le juif ne croit ni en Jésus, ni à l'Evangile, ni en
Muhammad, ni au Coran; et le chrétien ne croit ni à Muhammad ni au
Coran. Cela peut provoquer un effet négatif pour la vie de la femme
musulmane vivant sous le toit d'un juif ou d'un chrétien. C'est la règle
légale générale, mais il peut y avoir des exceptions.

3.9. الحِجاب *Le voile: Hijâb*

L'Islam regarde le voile (حجاب *hijâb*) dans sa forme raisonnable, et
non pas dans sa forme repliée; d'ailleurs, le christianisme représente le
voile sur la personne de la Vierge et de la moniale. «Je ne dis pas que le
christianisme impose cela», dit Fadlallâh. La conception soutenant que
le chrétien possède une liberté absolue n'est pas un concept chrétien, mais
un concept occidental. Si les occidentaux sont des chrétiens, cela ne veut
pas dire que leurs valeurs sont des valeurs chrétiennes[101].

---

[99] Ibid., pp. 119-121.
[100] Fadlallâh, op. cit., p. 313.
[101] Ibid., p. 325.

3.10. *La liberté de pensée dans le cadre de l'islam*

Fadlallâh invoque le discours des penseurs chrétiens au sujet de la liberté de conscience, de pensée et de recherche, en se référant au texte
coranique. Il veut suivre les chrétiens sur la base de leurs théories ration-
nelles[102].

Fadlallâh considère que les savants musulmans ont toujours mené une
discussion ardue et pénible concernant le contenu de la foi musulmane,
soit du côté historique, soit du côté doctrinal. Il fait mention du problème du matérialisme et du fatalisme[103].

Il nous faut distinguer la vérité rationnelle qui s'impose sur un texte
quelconque et la théorie rationnelle qui reste toujours une supposition. Il
nous est impossible de soumettre le texte à l'intérêt d'une théorie rationnelle, mais cette théorie rationnelle peut constituer la base d'une
réinterprétation du texte. Le texte révélé reste, dans ce cas, acquis, sauf
dans le cas où il affirme, à travers la critique historique ou la réflexion
rationnelle, une autre volonté, différente[104].

Fadlallâh explique sa vision islamique des Droits de l'Homme en disant que ceux-ci ne sont pas des choses absolues suspendues en l'air. A
partir de là, il n'accepte pas que la Révolution française ou les Nations
Unies décident des droits de l'homme. L'islam a sa théorie particulière
des droits de l'homme. C'est pourquoi l'islam assure ces droits selon sa
théorie, comme les autres les assurent selon leur théorie. Il peut y avoir
un dialogue entre les droits de l'homme des musulmans et les droits de
l'homme chez les autres. L'islam n'exclut rien dans le monde du dialogue[105].

3.11. *L'islam et l'activité missionnaire*

Le christianisme est une religion de Mission (التبشير *tabshîr*) comme
l'islam est une religion d'Appel (الدعوة *da'wa*). L'un comme l'autre appellent les gens d'autres religions à adhérer à leurs croyances. Il y a tout
un complexe chez les musulmans en ce qui concerne l'œuvre mission-
naire chrétienne et ses liens avec la question de la colonisation des pays
musulmans[106]. Fadlallâh propose de discuter ce problème dans le cadre

---

[102] Ibid., p. 108.
[103] Ibid., p. 109.
[104] Ibid., p. 110.
[105] Ibid., p. 335.
[106] Ibid., p. 110.

des dialogues islamo-chrétiens, dans le présent et le futur. Ce dialogue vise à organiser ces activités de part et d'autre, et à éviter en même temps les conséquences néfastes pour la sensibilité. Car on ne peut pas interdire, ni التبشير al-tabshîr, ni الدعوة al-da'wa, qui sont enracinés dans la profondeur de la foi. Nous devons arriver à ce que la question devienne une question de concurrence et non pas une lutte[107].

II. Fahmî HUWAIDI[108]

INTRODUCTION

Nous donnons d'abord quelques pensées d'ordre général de Huwaïdî avant de décrire le contenu de son ouvrage.

---

[107] Ibid., p. 111.

[108] Fahmî HUWAIDI, *Muwâtinûn lâ dhimmiyûn: Mawqi' ghayr al-muslimîn fî mujtama' al-muslimîn* مواطنون لا ذميون: موقف غير المسلمون فى مجتمع المسلمين (Des citoyens et non des protégés: la position des non-musulmans dans la société musulmane), 2e éd. Le Caire-Beyrouth: Dâr al- shurûq, 1410 /1990. Comp. sa contribution dans شكرى غالى Ghâlî Shukrî, *Aqni'at al-irhâb: al-bahth 'an 'lmâniyya jadîda* أقنعة الإرهاب : البحث عن علمانية جديدة (Les masques du terrorisme: à la recherche d'une nouvelle laïcité), Le Caire: Matba'at al-hay'a al-'âmma li-l-kitâb, 1992.

Muhammad Jalâl KISHK محمد جلال كشك, dans son ouvrage *A-la fî l-fitnati saqatû: tahlîl 'ilmî..* إلا فى الفتنة سقطوا: تحليل علمى.. (Ne sont-ils pas tombés dans la dissension: analyse scientifique...) Le Caire: Maktabat al-turâth al-islâmî, 1992, fait une critique à l'égard de Huwaïdî et son ouvrage sujet de notre étude. Nous devons noter l'opinion de Kishk formulée à l'encontre de Huwaïdî. Cette critique réside dans le fait que Kishk ne trouve pas qu'il y a une contradiction entre le système de la *dhimma* et la citoyenneté. Première remarque: Kishk pense que Huwaïdî est un des responsables de la dissension confessionnelle, d'une part, et que le titre de son ouvrage est une insulte à l'encontre de Dieu et du prophète de l'islam d'autre part. Deuxième remarque: Kishk ne voit aucune raison de revenir au système de *dhimma* et de *jizya* aujourd'hui (p. 24). D'autre part, Kishk rappelle qu'il était le premier à écrire sur ce sujet en 1950, dans un livre intitulé طوائف لا مصريون *Egyptiens et pas des confessions*. En ce temps-là, Kishk était le secrétaire du Parti communiste égyptien à Malâwî en Haute-Egypte.

Nous pouvons aussi ajouter que Kishk se vante d'être le premier à dire «...*qu'il est possible qu'un Copte puisse devenir le président d'un Etat islamique souhaité s'il était élu et s'il jurait de respecter sa Constitution islamique*» (p. 24). Bien plus, Kishk cite ce qu'il a déjà écrit, le 13.01.1990, dans le journal *Al-Wafd*, en demandant un congé officiel pour tous à l'occasion des fêtes chrétiennes, comme c'est le cas pour les fêtes musulmanes (p. 84). Plus encore, Kishk invoque la question de l'apostasie en envisageant la nécessité de décréter une loi interdisant la conversion dans les deux sens, d'une part, et, d'autre part, le respect de la liberté de croyance sans intervention étrangère et le moyen unique de la connaissance mise à disposition librement (p. 170).

– Huwaïdî affirme qu'il y a une crise relationnelle entre les musulmans et les non-musulmans. Les causes de cette crise ne datent pas d'aujourd'hui. Il cite parmi elles les guerres des croisades et l'expulsion des musulmans hors de l'Andalousie et de la Sicile, après la Reconquista. A l'époque moderne, ce sont les colonies anglaises, françaises et autres, les problèmes des minorités musulmanes en Asie et en Afrique. Il rappelle aussi les attitudes de certaines tribus juives et chrétiennes à l'encontre de Muhammad, ce qui a influencé la jurisprudence islamique qui a légué «...un héritage jurisprudentiel» qui n'exprime pas nécessairement «...l'esprit des enseignements célestes et leurs textes». Pour cette raison, cet héritage a besoin «d'être révisé» en vue d'éliminer tout ce qui est en contradiction avec l'esprit coranique. Huwaïdî fait remarquer que «...cette anomalie intellectuelle n'a pas seulement touché les non-musulmans, mais aussi les musulmans». En outre, certains écrits de quelques auteurs non-musulmans critiquent l'Islam sous prétexte de défendre les droits des non-musulmans. Ils ne font qu'élargir le fossé entre musulmans et non-musulmans. Il est donc difficile, lance-t-il, «...de rester inactif devant une telle situation si nous voulons exister ensemble». Les deux partis, musulman et non-musulman, portent une part de responsabilité réciproque «...avec l'esprit d'un partenaire fidèle qui est intéressé par la réussite du projet commun par lequel l'avenir de l'un est lié par l'autre»[109].

– Huwaïdî ne croit pas qu'il y a réellement une guerre entre l'islam et le christianisme ou le judaïsme. Une guerre résidera plutôt dans les luttes d'influence et de pouvoir, entre le progrès et la régression. La véritable guerre est dès lors le combat pour le progrès et l'indépendance, et le seul ennemi est le déclin et la subordination[110].

– Chercher les racines de cette crise relationnelle dans les religions serait une erreur. Il faut séparer désormais le problème de son cadre «théologique» et le mettre dans son cadre «humain». Car la question est plus proche de la politique que de la religion[111].

Il n'est pas sans intérêt de noter l'opinion de Kishk au sujet du mouvement de dialogue islamo-chrétien. Kishk considère ce mouvement comme «... une idée satanique inventée par le Conseil Oecuménique des Eglises, lié à la C.I.A. Américaine». Kishk justifie son rejet du dialogue pour les raisons suivantes: d'abord, le dialogue arrive en retard de 14 siècles; ensuite, il n'y a pas de nécessité de dialogue entre musulmans et chrétiens sur des sujets dogmatiques ou des croyances; enfin, si un dialogue doit avoir lieu, il doit avoir pour sujet: l'organisation des différents aspects de la vie commune (p. 157).

[109] Ibid., pp. 7-10.
[110] Ibid., p. 13.
[111] Ibid., p. 14.

– La position géopolitique du Proche-Orient conduit à un état de tension continue dans cette partie du monde. En effet, les puissances étrangères sont en lutte pour la possession de cette région. Ceci a eu des répercussions sur les relations entre les musulmans et les autres gens du Livre qui vivent là. En outre, cela a détérioré aussi les rapports entre le christianisme et l'islam en général[112]. Mais nous devons rappeler que la plupart des chrétiens de la région ont combattu avec les musulmans contre les colonisateurs, sans tenir compte du fait que ces colonisateurs partageaient avec eux la même religion. Aux yeux des chrétiens qui vivent dans les pays musulmans, ces puissances étrangères s'intéressent plutôt à leurs propres affaires et au pouvoir qu'à la défense des chrétiens.

– Huwaïdî[113] distingue la loi (الشريعة *sharî'a*) qui vient de Dieu et la jurisprudence الفقه *fiqh*) qui vient des hommes. La sharî'a se divise pourtant en deux parties. La partie principale constitue l'aspect cultuel (عبادات *'ibâdât*) qu'il est obligatoire de suivre (إتباع *ittibâ'*); la partie secondaire touche aux affaires (معاملات *mu'âmalât*) et a besoin continuellement d'être mise à jour (إبتداع *ibtidâ'*). S'il y a dans la jurisprudence des textes péremptoires (قطعية *qat'iyya*) et putatifs (ظنية *zanniyya*), il reste néanmoins pour l'homme une tâche herméneutique importante soit en s'appuyant sur les règles juridiques qui préconisent que les lois changent par rapport au changement des temps, des lieux, des circonstances et des coutumes, soit en donnant une appréciation dans ce que quelques jurisconsultes appellent «*vérification de rôle*», en d'autres termes «... *mettre le jugement légal dans sa place et dans ses conditions correctes*»[114].

– Huwaïdî considère que l'expression «Etat religieux» est le résultat d'expériences non-islamiques. Quant au caractère de «droit divin» du Président dans un Etat islamique, cela n'a pas, dit Huwaïdî, de rapport, ni de près, ni de loin, avec l'islam. Il n'y a pas de «procuration divine» absolue du pouvoir à quiconque gouverne au nom de l'islam. Aucun gouvernement musulman ne peut prétendre que sa légitimité vient de Dieu. Le fondement juridique de régime est son appui sur les valeurs islamiques[115].

---

[112] Ibid., p. 47.

[113] Fahmi HUWAIDI in Ghâlî SHUKRI, *Aqni'at al-irhâb: al-bahth 'an 'ilmâniyyah jadîdah* (Les masques du terrorisme: à la recherche d'une nouvelle laïcité), Le Caire: Matba'at al-hay'a al-misriyyah al-'âmma lil-kitâb, 1992.

[114] Ibid., p. 99.

[115] Ibid., p. 100.

– Le Coran est pour Huwaïdî un livre céleste destiné à convertir des gens. Il est donc hors de question d'attendre que le Coran nous donne des théories politiques, économiques ou juridiques. Le Coran ne définit que des principes généraux en politique, en économie et dans le domaine législatif. A la question de savoir si ces principes généraux sont suffisants pour élaborer une théorie, Huwaïdî répond que le Coran organise la vie du musulman, et que celui-ci peut déduire ce qu'il veut du Coran. C'est une sagesse dans la législation quand il est dit que le fondement du régime politique est la consultation et que le but du message et du régime islamique, c'est de réaliser un ensemble d'objectifs. Les jurisconsultes les ont définis comme suit: sauvegarder la religion, la raison, la procréation, l'honneur et la richesse[116].

– Huwaïdî aborde le problème de l'avenir du Tiers-Monde et des mouvements islamistes. Il voit qu'il y a des dangers très graves qui entourent l'avenir du Tiers-Monde au point que nous ne pouvons pas parler de l'an 2000 comme les Européens en parlent. Quant au problème du réveil islamiste en général, et en Egypte en particulier, Huwaïdî ne donne pas une opinion précise. Il pense que beaucoup dépend de la manière dont les autorités traitent ces mouvements. Il est nécessaire, préconise Huwaïdî, de traiter ces mouvements d'une manière saine et il faut leur offrir des conditions naturelles pour se développer, en les conseillant, pour qu'ils deviennent un facteur positif. Car si on traite ces mouvements d'une manière violente ou si on ignore leur existence, ils deviendront un facteur négatif et destructif. Dans l'état actuel des choses, Huwaïdî craint un avenir plutôt sombre s'il n'y a pas un changement radical dans l'attitude de chaque parti concerné[117].

– Huwaïdî discute le problème des expressions islamiques, spécialement le réformisme (السلف *Al-salafiyya*), qui signifie le retour aux sources et aux racines principales de la loi islamique que sont le Coran et la Sunna. Le réformiste (السلفى *al-salafî*) est appellé à l'effort personnel (إجتهاد *ijtihâd*) et au renouvellement. Huwaïdî signale que le problème réside dans le fait qu'une expression commence normalement par une signification précise, mais qu'elle finit par acquérir une autre signification qui est souvent très différente. Le vrai musulman, d'une part, est réformiste par nécessité, s'il veut respecter les enseignements dans ses racines, mais il doit, d'autre part, être futuriste là où le musulman s'oriente par nature vers l'au-delà, c'est-à-dire vers le futur. La source du musul-

---

[116] Ibid., p. 102.
[117] Ibid., pp. 104-105.

man est réformiste et son embouchure est futuriste. Pour arriver au futur, le musulman s'appuie sur les sources d'origine.

– Huwaïdî trouve que les expressions إنبعاث *inbi'âth* (renaissance), أصولى *usûlî* (fondamentaliste) et أصولية *usûliyya* (fondamentalisme) ainsi que الصحوة *al-sahwa* (le réveil), ne sont pas des expressions islamiques, mais qu'elles sont répandues dans les milieux des mouvements islamistes. On peut d'ailleurs trouver ces mouvements de réveil également chez les coptes et les juifs. Par contre, la seule expression proprement islamique connue dans ce domaine, c'est celle de la revivification: الإحياء *al-ihyâ'*[118].

– Huwaïdî cite de nombreux textes indiquant la foi des gens du Livre en un seul Dieu[119].

1. LA DIGNITÉ HUMAINE DANS LES TEXTES CORANIQUES

1.1. *Témoignages du Coran et de la Tradition*

Huwaïdî fonde sa critique à l'égard de la jurisprudence (الفقه *fiqh*) au sujet de la dignité humaine dans le Coran. Cette dignité ne concerne pas uniquement les musulmans, mais elle englobe tout le genre humain.

Il montre que chaque créature a une inviolabilité et une «immunité naturelle» dans l'islam. Cette inviolabilité ne se restreint pas à quelques êtres, mais elle est illimitée. On t'interrogera sur l'âme. Dis: «L'âme relève de l'ordre de mon Seigneur ويسئلونك عن الروح قل الروح من أمر ربى» (S. 17:85); selon le texte coranique, chaque être a son honneur, qui ne doit pas être humilié sans raison valable[120]. En outre, les textes coraniques S. 2:30; 7:11; 15:29; 17:70; 95:4, honorent l'homme et l'élèvent au-dessus des autres créatures. Ils visent l'homme en tant que tel, non pas à cause de sa croyance, mais comme créature humaine. Cela est vrai avant même de savoir s'il est musulman, chrétien, juif ou bouddhiste, ou encore s'il est blanc, noir ou jaune. Les textes coraniques sont très nets sur ce point-ci; tantôt ils parlent de l'«être humain», tantôt ils parlent des «fils d'Adam», tantôt ils s'adressent aux «gens». Cette généralisation sert de preuve à quiconque est raisonnable, juste. Dans le discours coranique, il y a des expressions qui s'adressent à l'homme et aux gens

---

[118] Ibid., pp. 92-98.
[119] Huwaïdî, *Muwâtinûn lâ dhimmiyyûn*, p. 85.
[120] Ibid., pp. 79-80.

en général, tandis que d'autres s'adressent aux croyants et aux musulmans seulement. Ceux qui prétendent que cette description coranique est
réservée uniquement aux musulmans ont tort[121].

Huwaïdî voit dans le verset 5:32 «ومن قتل نفساً بغير نفسٍ أو فسادٍ فكأنّما
قتل الناس جميعاً» «Quiconque tue une personne non convaincue de meurtre ou de dépravation sur terre est à assimiler au meurtrier de tout le
genre humain», une description très forte du caractère monstrueux d'un
meurtre injuste pour la personne d'un homme sans droit. Ce texte ne
considère pas seulement le meurtre comme une agression contre un seul
homme, mais contre l'humanité toute entière. Huwaïdî parle aussi de
l'âme humaine et des gens sans distinction de couleur, de race ou de religion, comme le dit Ibn Kathîr: «...*parce qu'il n'y a pas de différence
pour lui entre une âme et une autre âme*»[122]. Ainsi, la valeur de
l'homme reste un des piliers fondamentaux de la pensée musulmane. La
transgression de cette valeur reste comme un heurt et une contradiction
directe avec l'esprit du texte[123]. Il ne faut pas dans ce sens perdre de vue
que les textes islamiques ont étendu une multitude de ponts relationnels
à partir de cette grande vérité. Cette doctrine ouvre une voie très large
pour la fraternité des fils de l'homme, en vue de bâtir une vie d'amitié et
de miséricorde.

Huwaïdî appuie son opinion en se basant sur les textes coraniques et
la Tradition (الحديث):

1. Il y a quelques textes qui s'adressent à tous les êtres vivants, de
toutes races, couleurs ou religions: S. 49:13; 4:1; 31:28. Ajoutons à
cela le discours d'adieux du Prophète: «*O gens! Votre Allah est Un,
votre père est un, vous êtes tous comme Adam, et Adam est de la poussière. Le plus honoré auprès d'Allah est celui qui a plus de piété. Il n'y a
pas de préférence pour un arabe par rapport à un non arabe (persan),
un non arabe par rapport à un arabe, un rouge par rapport à un blanc,
un blanc par rapport à un rouge, sinon par la piété. Je vous ai fait part,
Dieu est témoin, celui qui présent fait part à celui qui est absent*». Et
dans la prière de la fin de la nuit, il disait: «*Je professe que c'est Toi
Dieu, et qu'il n'y a pas d'autre dieu que Toi, et que les adorateurs sont
des frères*» (أبو داؤود Abû Dâwud).

Ces textes insistent sur l'origine unique des fils de l'homme. En outre,
ils attirent l'attention sur une sagesse divine qui a mis de la diversité

---

[121] Ibid., p. 81.
[122] Ibid., p. 83.
[123] Ibid.

dans la création, en genre et en position. Ils affirment, enfin, qu'il n'y a pas dans ce monde un homme meilleur par nature qu'un autre. En résumé, tous les humains sont d'une seule âme, leur père est Adam et leur mère est Eve. La préférence devant Dieu a seulement une seule mesure, la piété, née de la foi, et les bonnes œuvres.

2. Certains textes coraniques s'adressent aux gens des autres religions qui croient en un seul Dieu: S. 2:32; 5:69.

3. D'autres textes appellent les musulmans et les mettent en éveil (S. 2:136,285; 4:151; 42:13) en ouvrant la porte de la rencontre entre eux et les non-musulmans. D'ailleurs, l'essence des messages célestes est une, sans contradiction ou discordance[124].

4. D'autres catégories de textes s'adressent à Muhammad renforçant (le sens de) l'unité des religions, l'humanité du Message et le grand but de la Mission (S. 6:158; 21:107; 34:28; 41:43). L'ensemble de ces textes permet en réalité de trouver des points de rencontre entre les musulmans et les autres. Ils jettent des ponts capables de porter tout effort sincère pour construire un monde préservant à l'homme sa dignité, son bonheur et son bien-être[125].

1.2. *Témoignages de l'histoire*

Huwaïdî a procédé à une comparaison des visions respectives de l'homme dans l'islam et dans les autres religions et croyances de l'époque. Cette comparaison va d'Aristote jusqu'au christianisme, en passant par le judaïsme. Elle constitue le fondement de la démonstration par laquelle Huwaïdî cherche à démontrer que la conception islamique du respect de la dignité humaine est supérieure aux autres[126].

Quelles sont les textes qui font le pont selon les textes coraniques et les hadîths, qui font le lien entre les musulmans et les non-musulmans?

La première clef se trouve dans la liberté de la croyance qui jouit d'une immunité selon le verset coranique: «لا إكراه في الدين قد تبين الرشد من الغي *point de contrainte en religion. La vérité se distingue de l'erreur.*» (S. 2:256) Donc, toute violation de cette immunité devient une violation de la règle coranique. Ce verset ouvre les portes au dialogue par la sagesse et la bonne prédication. C'est la fraternité humaine qui en est la base, et la bonne parole en est le moyen.

[124] Ibid., p. 85.
[125] Ibid., p. 86.
[126] Ibid., pp. 86-87.

La deuxième clef est dans le verset 2:190 «ولا تعتدوا إن الله لا يحب المعتدين Ne dépassez pas les limites permises, car Dieu n'aime pas les transgresseurs». Les musulmans sont appelés à coexister avec «leur semblable dans la création». Car Dieu a créé les gens, peuples et tribus, pour se connaître et non pas pour s'entretuer et se détester, comme le pensent certains. La seule exception à cette règle est le cas où les musulmans deviennent la cible d'une injustice ou d'une agression de la part des autres.

La signification la plus importante à laquelle nous conduit cette règle dans la conception islamique, c'est la reconnaissance «de la légitimité des autres», une reconnaissance basée sur la valeur de l'homme et sur la fraternité des fils de l'homme.

Les non-musulmans ne sont pas des diables ni des démons, encore moins l'enfer, comme le font croire d'aucuns. Ils ne sont pas des «hérétiques» qui méritent l'anéantissement et le feu, comme cela a été le cas en Europe au Moyen-Age. Ils sont humains, nos semblables dans la création, même si leur couleur, leur race et leurs croyances sont différentes; ils sont acceptés — même si nous nous différencions- tant qu'ils n'ont pas transgressé des interdits comme l'injustice et l'agression.

Huwaïdî continue à affirmer que la légitimité des non-musulmans n'est pas basée sur leur croyance, vraie ou fausse, mais qu'elle est fondée sur leur nature humaine proclamée par l'islam dès le début. Ils ont le droit à l'immunité, à la dignité et à la protection. C'est pourquoi, s'il y a une lutte entre les deux partis, celle-ci ne doit pas — dans la conception islamique — annuler la légitimité de l'autre parti ou pousser les musulmans à violer les limites de l'immunité proclamée par le Coran pour l'homme. Car la liberté de choix — même en matière de religion — est un droit garanti par l'islam à chacun, même s'il est un ennemi ou un comploteur (S. 5:8)!

Dieu a blâmé Son Envoyé car son sentiment s'est dirigé vers l'un des musulmans contre un juif opprimé par lui (S.4:105-113).

1.3. *Principes de la rencontre*

Huwaïdî pense que la règle qui commande de rejeter la contrainte en matière de religion incite à la rencontre des autres. Celle-ci élargit les ponts de la compréhension entre les musulmans et les non-musulmans. L'appel à l'Islam doit respecter dès lors les principes suivants:

1. Le prophète, ainsi que chaque musulman, est chargé uniquement de l'annonce et de la prédication selon les textes coraniques (S. 29:18; 34:28; 88:21-22).

2. Ceux qui sont chargés de l'Appel (الدعوة *da'wa*) doivent être liés par des conduites particulières (S. 3:64,; 4:148; 6:108; 16:125; 29:46; 41:34).

3. En cas du refus, c'est Dieu qui est le Juge (S. 3:20; 9:129; 39:46; 42:48; 88:20. 26).

4. La différence des voies ne signifie pas la perte des droits des autres et elle n'empêche pas la continuation de la collaboration de la part des musulmans (S. 5:8; 9:6; 42:15).

Huwaïdî constate donc que le fondement de la pensée islamique donne aux autres un libre choix, spécialement en ce qui concerne la foi et la croyance, ce que quelques-uns appellent la liberté de «*conscience*» (S. 20:44). Le musulman respecte la pensée des autres, en raison de leur humanité. C'est pourquoi il ne doit y avoir ni grossièreté, ni injure, ni orgueil. Le musulman est au contraire dominé par l'esprit de fraternité et par les lumières de la sagesse. A cet effet, le musulman doit recourir à l'argument et à la preuve rationnelle qui sont l'unique arme du croyant pour l'Appel (الدعوة da'wa). C'est le fondement auquel on doit se conformer vis-à-vis des autres (S. 2:111; 6:148; 34:24). Après l'annonce du message coranique, tous doivent retirer leur main de la conscience des gens. Fouiller dans la conscience des autres est une agression contre le pouvoir de Dieu qui a annoncé à tous «ثم إن علينا حسابهم *Il nous incombera de leur demander compte*» (S. 88:26).

Si le résultat du dialogue et le choix sont négatifs — c'est-à-dire si l'autre ne donne pas suite à l'appel qui lui est —, cela ne doit pas altérer l'amitié des fils de l'homme, ni toucher l'inviolabilité garantie par l'islam à toutes les créatures de Dieu. Fonder la valeur de la justice parmi tous les hommes est un ordre divin et un signe de piété envers Dieu. L'indication divine procède, d'une façon très particulière, en appelant à tendre la main aux autres (S. 6:9). Il n'appelle pas seulement à protéger l'associateur, mais à l'aider s'il le demande, jusqu'à ce qu'il ait traversé ses difficultés. S'il en est ainsi pour l'associateur, combien plus en est-il alors en ce qui concerne les gens du Livre qui croient en Dieu?

1.4. *Les autres entre la vérité et l'identité*[127]

Huwaïdî utilise souvent le terme «الآخرين *les autres*» pour désigner les non-musulmans. Il est donc impératif de définir clairement ce qu'on

[127] Ibid., pp. 97-98.

entend par cette expression et de vérifier si celle-ci est conforme à l'esprit de l'islam et de ses textes. Cela est indispensable parce qu'il est nécessaire de formuler cette problématique d'une façon qui soit à la fois actuelle et fondée sur un fond islamique qui correspond à la réalité du XXᵉ siècle et de ce qui y fera suite. Les ponts déjà mis en place pour lier les musulmans aux autres ont besoin d'être revus: tantôt par la restauration, tantôt par une nouvelle définition, tantôt par la suppression.

Huwaïdî établit des comparaisons entre la préoccupation des jurisconsultes musulmans au sujet des droits des autres, conformément à l'ordre de Dieu au sein de la nation musulmane, et l'attitude des Européens jusqu'à la moitié du XIXᵉ siècle. On a considéré, en Europe, que les droits internationaux ne doivent être appliqués qu'aux pays chrétiens. Ce n'est qu'en 1856 que le monde occidental a été forcé d'accepter l'Empire Ottoman, le pays du «Khalife islamique» «دولة الخلافة الإسلامية», comme un partenaire traité sur un pied d'égalité avec les pays chrétiens dans les droits et les devoirs.

Néanmoins, Huwaïdî reproche aux successeurs des premiers jurisconsultes de répéter ou de copier ceux-ci, au point que les fruits des efforts des trois premiers siècles sont restés dominants jusqu'à aujourd'hui, en dépit des changements de temps et de lieux.

Les droits de l'homme, ses libertés fondamentales et l'égalité entre tous les hommes, musulmans ou non, sont promulgués par l'islam et édictés par les textes coraniques. Il y a donc une base doctrinale à ces droits. Ces droits eux-mêmes ne dépendent pas de la jurisprudence et de l'opinion des jurisconsultes. Ceux-ci ne s'occupent que de leurs limites dans les détails et dans l'application. La base doctrinale de ces droits ne laisse pas aux musulmans la liberté de choisir entre ce qu'il faut prendre et ce qu'il faut écarter de ces droits.

Huwaïdî cite le principe coranique «ولا تَزِرُ وَازِرَةٌ وِزرَ أُخرَى» *Aucune âme ne portera le fardeau d'une autre âme*» (S. 6:164). S'il arrive qu'une violation de ces droits soit commise, cette injustice n'affecte pas seulement les autres, mais elle affecte en premier lieu le Livre de Dieu et Son Droit.

1.5. *La tolérance*[128]

Huwaïdî juge inconcevable de qualifier de «tolérance» islamique la simple jouissance par les non-musulmans de leur droit naturel dans les

---

[128] Ibid., pp. 100-103.

pays musulmans. Le terme «tolérance» (تسامح *tasâmuh*) n'a pas la même
résonance en Orient qu'en Occident. En Orient il est perçu d'une façon
péjorative, car il représente une relation liant un supérieur à des infé-
rieurs. Il est acceptable que l'on use de ce terme à titre de comparaison
avec l'intolérance des autres et leur fanatisme, voire leur persécution des
musulmans. Mais il n'est pas permis de faire usage de ce terme quand
nous parlons de la relation des musulmans avec les non-musulmans selon la doctrine islamique, sur la base coranique des droits naturels du
genre humain. Dès lors, il n'y a plus de place pour une telle terminologie. Huwaïdî se demande encore: «*depuis quand l'obligation pour les
croyants de respecter les droits 'naturels' des non-musulmans édictés
par la doctrine (coranique) est-elle devenue une sorte de 'tolérance'?*»

D'ailleurs, l'usage du terme «tolérance» laisse supposer que l'attitude
normale des musulmans qui consiste à respecter les droits des non-musulmans ne constitue pas un principe islamique fondamental. Cet usage
impliquerait que cette attitude pourrait être changée à tout moment, puisqu'elle ne représente qu'une attitude extra-coranique. Donc, l'usage de
ce terme provoque indéniablement une crainte de la part des non-musulmans. Le terme «tolérance» ne devrait donc plus être utilisé pour parler
des Droits fondamentaux de l'homme dans le langage contemporain.
Huwaïdî renforce encore sa conviction en recourant à des textes du Coran et à des hadîths. En somme, nous ne pouvons pas qualifier de «tolérance» une relation toute naturelle entre les musulmans et les non-musulmans.

2. LA PLACE DES CHRÉTIENS

Huwaïdî pose certaines questions avant de parler de la place et du rôle
des chrétiens au sein de la société musulmane:

Est-il acceptable qu'une personne musulmane dirige un pays dont la
majorité est non-musulmane? Est-il acceptable que des mosquées se
trouvent sur les places principales des villes de caractère et de population chrétiens? Est-il acceptable qu'un groupe de musulmans fasse l'appel à la prière cinq fois par jour à travers un haut-parleur, et cela dans
une société européenne non-musulmane?

Certes, dit Huwaïdî, il faut tenir compte d'un équilibre nécessaire
dans les relations entre une majorité et une minorité, relations basées sur
le respect de l'ordre public «النظام العام», de ses sensibilités et des sentiments de la société. Le «public», «العام» ici se place sur deux niveaux:

l'un concerne la société toute entière, tandis que l'autre touche aux valeurs de la majorité et de leurs lois particulières, tirées soit de sa doctrine, soit de sa tradition. Cette logique implique l'obligation pour la majorité de respecter les sentiments de la minorité.

Respecter les valeurs et les sentiments de la majorité ne signifie pas diminuer les droits de la minorité. S'il y a des limites pour exercer la liberté, il y a aussi des limites pour utiliser le droit. Un équilibre doit être préservé, puisqu'il est le seul garant de la stabilité d'une société qui connaît un pluralisme religieux, confessionnel, politique ou ethnique[129].

Une question se pose: Que veut une minorité? Huwaïdî ne voit qu'une seule réponse, c'est qu'une minorité ne demande que l'assurance de la liberté des croyances, et l'égalité des droits et des devoirs vis-à-vis des autres. Il évoque la discussion autour de la pratique rituelle et des lieux de culte, qui restent encore un point de discorde. Il mentionne trois principes à prendre en considération:

1. Dans les textes du Coran et de la Tradition, il n'y a aucune restriction au droit des non-musulmans à pratiquer leur culte. La reconnaissance par le Coran des gens des autres religions appelle à respecter leur droit de pratiquer leur culte et de construire leurs lieux de culte[130].

2. Les réalités et les pratiques historiques dans ce domaine ne manquent pas de glissements et d'inventions. A ce propos, nous devons être très prudents. Huwaïdî cite l'exemple de ce qu'on a appelé le «traité de 'Umar», «عهد عمر أو الشروط العمرية» attribué à 'Umar ibn al-Khattâb, dont la critique scientifique a montré qu'il n'est pas authentique et qu'il date d'une époque beaucoup plus tardive[131]. Néanmoins, la majorité des jurisconsultes a repris les conditions de ce traité et les a mis en vigueur pour les non-musulmans. C'est pourquoi on doit être prudent avec des textes de la jurisprudence (الفقه fiqh) des jurisconsultes. Ceux-ci doivent être en accord avec le Coran et la Tradition authentique, autant textuellement qu'en esprit.

3. Une partie de la question de la pratique cultuelle et des lieux de culte reste à gérer par des considérations d'ordre et de sensibilité publiques. C'est une question d'appréciation soumise aux conditions de temps et de lieux. C'est pourquoi il est impossible de donner une formu-

---

[129] Huwaïdî, op. cit., p. 148.
[130] Ibid., p. 149.
[131] Ibid., pp. 150,203-212.

lation définitive ou de déterminer les modalités pour résoudre cette question[132].

Huwaïdî[133] précise que l'égalité en droits et en devoirs entre la minorité et la majorité est consolidée par nombre de textes juridiques du Coran et de la Tradition. La jurisprudence a assuré l'égalité entre les musulmans et les non-musulmans et elle a, de surcroît, cédé aux non-musulmans le droit de gérer les affaires qui relèvent de leur propre loi religieuse.

Cependant, Huwaïdî fait remarquer que la mise en place dans un pays d'un système social et politique qui est basé sur une doctrine particulière, a pour conséquence le droit pour le pays d'engager à sa tête les partisans de sa doctrine. En outre, c'est aussi son droit de protéger les spécificités de ceux qui croient en sa doctrine. Cela n'est pas spécifique à l'Etat islamique, mais c'est le système qui est pratiqué partout dans le monde sur un plan politique.

Nous comprenons l'idée principale de cette orientation: donner le droit à un Etat de confier l'exécution de sa direction à ceux qui croient dans sa doctrine. C'est dans ce contexte qu'on peut comprendre l'attitude de l'islam. S'il opte pour l'égalité de tous, il a cependant fait une exception à cette règle, non pas en partant du principe de la supériorité de musulmans sur les autres, mais plutôt en partant du fait que la croyance de l'islam assure plus d'harmonie au sein de la direction du pays. La condition de l'islam ici ne doit pas être comprise comme une sorte de discrimination religieuse ou confessionnelle.

Huwaïdî[134] sait qu'il y a des musulmans qui ne partageront pas sa façon de voir la question de la place des non-musulmans. Ceux-ci protesteront en se référant aux trois versets cités ci-dessous, avec l'appui de quelques jurisconsultes donnant la préférence aux musulmans dans la direction de la société musulmane en général:

«لا يتخذ المؤمنون الكافرين أولياء من دون المؤمنين ومن يفعل ذلك فليس من الله فى شئ إلا أن تتقوا منهم تقاية ويحذركم الله نفسه وإلى الله المصير»

– «*Que les croyants ne prennent pas, en dehors des croyants, d'alliés parmi les infidèles. Quiconque contractera une telle alliance aura rompu avec Dieu, à moins que vous n'ayez quelque méfait à redouter de leur part. Dieu vous avertit d'être circonspects à son égard. C'est vers Lui qu'est le devenir*» (S. 3:28)

---

[132] Ibid., p. 151.
[133] Ibid., pp. 154-156.
[134] Ibid., pp. 156-159.

«يأيها الذين أمنوا لا تتخذوا بطانة من دونكم لا يألونكم خبالاً ودوا ماعنتم
قد بدت البغضاء من أفواههم وماتخفى صدورهم أكبر قد بينا لكم الآيات إن
كنتم تعقلون»

– «Croyants! Ne prenez pas de confidents en dehors de vous. [Ceux
que vous prendriez comme tels parmi les infidèles] mettraient tout en
œuvre pour vous corrompre. Ils voudraient que vous soyez en difficulté.
La haine est exprimée par leur bouche; mais ce que dissimule leur cœur
est encore pire. Nous vous avons clairement exposé les versets, si [toute-
fois] vous [êtes aptes] à raisonner» (S. 3:118)

«يأيها الذين أمنوا لا تتخذوا اليهود والنصارى أولياء بعضهم أولياء بعض ومن
يتولهم منكم فإنه منهم إن لله لا يهدى القوم الظالمين»

– «Vous qui croyez! ne prenez point les juifs et les chrétiens pour alliés. Ils sont alliés les uns les autres. Quiconque parmi vous s'alliera
avec eux [finira] par être des leurs. Dieu ne mettra point sur la bonne
voie les gens injustes» (S. 5:51)

Selon Huwaïdî, ces trois versets concernent l'attitude à prendre vis-à-
vis d'agresseurs. Les deux premiers versets ne mentionnent pas les gens
du Livre de toute façon. Quant au troisième verset, il ne vise que le
groupe des gens du Livre qui a déclaré la guerre aux musulmans. Il est
donc normal d'exiger de rompre toute relation avec des gens en état de
guerre contre les musulmans. C'est une pratique générale. Huwaïdî signale, en outre, que des chrétiens ont dirigé les armées musulmanes à
Baghdad et en Andalousie. En conséquence, il est injuste que certains
interprètent ces versets, en les sortant de leur contexte, dans le sens qu'il
y aurait une interdiction générale de traiter avec les non-musulmans.

Huwaïdî fait deux remarques à l'encontre des opinions des jurisconsultes:

La première, c'est que les droits et les devoirs des non-musulmans,
ainsi que leur participation à la marche et à la direction d'un Etat islamique occupent une grande place dans le dialogue et la discussion;

La deuxième, c'est que dans les autres domaines de la vie de tous les
jours — comme l'industrie, l'agriculture et le commerce — il n'y avait
aucune distinction entre non-musulmans et musulmans. De toute manière, les opinions de la jurisprudence (فقه fiqh) n'ont pas le dernier mot.
Certaines opinions peuvent être développées, d'autres éliminées, ou bien
encore être adaptées en fonction du temps et du lieu. Malgré le respect

qu'on a pour les jurisconsultes, leur opinion n'a pas constitué l'élément fondamental qui a dirigé les relations avec les non-musulmans à travers l'histoire. D'ailleurs, on peut remarquer que les théories de la jurisprudence n'étaient pas nécessairement conformes à la réalité. En fait, la réalité était plutôt en avance sur la jurisprudence[135].

Huwaïdî souligne, à titre d'exemple, que dans l'Egypte contemporaine, il y a eu trois premiers ministres chrétiens: Nûbâr Pasha en 1878, Butrus Pasha Ghâlî en 1908, et Yûsuf Pasha Wahba en 1919[136].

Huwaïdî[137] suggère dès lors qu'il faudra examiner les textes du Coran et de la Tradition qui sont cités dans les livres de jurisprudence. En fait, la plupart de ces livres ont besoin d'être vérifiés et revus. A cet effet, il nous faut d'abord avoir la certitude que ces textes ont bel et bien été prononcés par le Prophète ou l'un de ses compagnons. En cas de doute, on doit les traiter en tant que tel, ou les éliminer. Ensuite, si un tel texte est authentique, on doit le lire à la lumière des circonstances de son temps. Puis il faut savoir si le texte en question a répondu simplement à une situation temporaire qui ne lui donne aucune portée pour l'avenir. Enfin, on doit prendre en considération le fait que certains textes ont été prononcés par le Prophète selon sa nature humaine et d'autres concernent sa personne seulement, comme la question de ses mariages avec plus de quatre femmes.

A titre d'exemple, Huwaïdî[138] évoque le texte du hadîth suivant attribué au Prophète au sujet des juifs et des chrétiens: «لا تبدأوا اليهود والنصارى بالسلام. وإذا لقيتموهم فى طريق فاضطروهم إلى أضيقها *Ne commencez pas par saluer les juifs et les chrétiens. Si vous les rencontrez sur le chemin, forcez-les à l'étroit*». Ce hadîth a été répandu parmi la population musulmane ces dernières années par les islamistes. C'est la raison pour laquelle Huwaïdî essaie d'y donner une réponse critique.

Pourquoi le Prophète a-t-il dicté un tel comportement? Pourtant, sa façon d'être et ses déclarations dans d'autres hadîths sont en contradiction avec celui-ci. L'histoire nous rapporte que cela n'a été qu'une mesure temporaire à l'encontre des juifs et des chrétiens d'Arabie d'alors, vu leur comportement vis-à-vis du Prophète et de son Appel (دعوته *da'wa*).

Il est grave de constater que beaucoup de jurisconsultes ont consacré un chapitre dans leurs ouvrages au sujet de la salutation des gens de

---

[135] Ibid. pp. 161-176.
[136] Ibid., p. 172.
[137] Ibid., pp. 177-180.
[138] Ibid., pp. 181-196.

dhimma أهل الذمة (protection). Ainsi découvre-t-on que ce qui était particulier est devenu général, avec des répercussions à travers les siècles. Ce qui est encore plus étrange, c'est de trouver aujourd'hui des gens qui essaient de faire passer ces idées pour un enseignement islamique.

Huwaïdî continue de décrire la situation des musulmans à l'époque du Prophète, surtout en ce qui concerne l'attitude des juifs et de certains chrétiens et de leur hostilité à l'encontre de l'Appel (الدعوة da'wa) islamique. Cela implique la décision de faire sortir les juifs et les chrétiens en dehors de certaines régions du Hijaz, afin d'assurer la sécurité intérieure. Mais cela n'a pas empêché qu'ils pussent y venir et résider quelques jours en raison de leur commerce. Cela démontre que la décision d'éloigner les juifs et les chrétiens était temporaire. A ce sujet, Huwaïdî fait trois observations:

1. Ces textes de la jurisprudence reflètent un climat de méfiance entre musulmans et non-musulmans. Devant ce fait, on ne doit pas perdre de vue la ligne principale que l'islam a édictée et qui est basée sur le respect de la dignité de l'homme, musulman ou non, ami ou ennemi.

2. Tous ces textes doivent rejoindre la liste des témoignages historiques démontrant le fossé entre la jurisprudence et la réalité sociale.

3. Souvent ces textes de la jurisprudence ne s'appuient pas sur des textes légaux authentiques et sûrs du Coran et de la Sunna القرآن والسنة. S'il y a des gens qui protestent en disant que la guerre entre le vrai et le faux continue de même que la guerre entre le bien et le mal, Huwaïdî leur répond que l'arme première des musulmans dans cette guerre est le dialogue et la preuve rationnelle, selon le texte coranique. Huwaïdî cite le cas du Prophète qui a accueilli les chrétiens de Najran, qui a dialogué avec eux à l'intérieur de la mosquée, et qui leur a même permis de prier à côté des musulmans[139].

3. LES CHRÉTIENS ENTRE LE STATUT DE DHIMMA ET LA CITOYENNETÉ

Huwaïdî remarque que le qualificatif «أهل الذمة *ahl al-dhimma*» (les gens protégés) a besoin d'être révisé. Il commence par voir la place de cette expression dans la *sharî'a*, afin de discuter ensuite de son utilité dans la société musulmane contemporaine.

Il repère ce terme deux fois dans le Coran: S. 9:8 et 10. Par contre, les références coraniques aux non-musulmans utilisent d'autres expres-

---

[139] Ibid., pp. 197-203.

sions, tels que: «الكتاب أهل *ahl al-kitâb*» (les gens du Livre) ou «المشركون *al-mushrikûn*» (les associateurs)[140].

Huwaïdî[141] trace l'historique de l'expression «الذمة *dhimma*». Elle fait partie du discours propre au rapport avec les tribus arabes avant l'islam. Le traité de protection (ذمة *dhimma*) et l'immunité était le produit de la coexistence que les tribus arabes préislamiques ont connue. Cette formule ne s'appuie donc pas sur un texte coranique, et son utilisation dans la *Sunna* السنة (tradition du prophète) n'était faite qu'à titre de description, et non pas d'identification.

Huwaïdî appelle à la révision de la formulation أهل الذمة *ahl al-dhîmma*, ce qui demande de déterminer la nature de la place des *dhimmiyyûn* ذميون dans la communauté musulmane. Il est alors nécessaire de différencier entre ce que Dieu a «légiféré» et a transmis à son Prophète, et la jurisprudence qui s'en est suivie plus tard. La formulation des jurisconsultes doit être vue sous l'angle de leur vision particulière en rapport avec le temps et le lieu dans lesquels ils écrivaient. On ne doit pas perdre de vue les nombreux textes coraniques qui ont élevé la place de l'homme et lui ont accordé l'honneur, en affirmant son origine céleste et l'égalité entre les hommes.

Huwaïdî[142] continue la discussion sur la question de la citoyenneté des gens du Livre. Certains chercheurs ont répondu par la négative. C'est-à-dire qu'ils les considèrent comme des citoyens de deuxième classe. Si cela était limité à des ouvrages édités en Occident, cela n'aurait pas mérité d'attention. Mais cette conception vient d'être citée par un grand chercheur tel que Majid Khadduri, et dans le même sens par Hisham Sharabi. Le premier donne un jugement dans un problème très précis et sensible, sans donner une preuve légale pour appuyer ses paroles. Quant à Hisham Sharabi, il ne fait que décrire une situation et dessiner une image. Il semble que Majid Khadduri se réfère à al-Mâwardî qui a cité l'opinion des shâfi'ites au sujet de la *jizya* الجزية.

Ce qui provoque l'inquiétude, selon Huwaïdî, c'est qu'il y a pour ces opinions anciennes des adeptes dans la pensée islamique et arabe de nos jours. Il est donc dangereux de laisser ces opinions circuler librement, de sorte qu'elles peuvent se propager parmi les jeunes dont la foi est profonde, mais dont la connaissance de la religion et de la vie est faible.

---

[140] Huwaïdî, p. 110.
[141] Ibid., pp. 111-117.
[142] Ibid., pp. 117-122.

Huwaïdî présente alors les opinions de 'Abd al-Karîm Zaydân et de Mawdûdî à ce sujet, en faisant la critique suivante à l'encontre de la prise de position de ces auteurs:

1. Ils traitent les gens de la *dhimma* أهل الذمة en tant qu'identité séparée de la communauté musulmane, en raison du souvenir historique des traités de *dhimma* ذمة d'une part, et parce qu'ils prennent les religions comme critère de division entre les hommes, d'autre part. De cette manière ils considèrent les musulmans comme les seuls citoyens de l'Etat islamique. En conséquence, la responsabilité du régime incombe aux musulmans uniquement, ce qui annule la valeur d'une patrie appartenant à tous: ceux qui la défendent à partir d'une doctrine aussi bien que ceux qui la défendent en tant que terre commune.

2. En donnant ces opinions ils s'adressent à un autre monde que le nôtre. Ils écrivent pendant que leurs yeux et leurs pensées se dirigent vers l'époque du grand Etat islamique des premiers siècles, mais cela ne concerne pas les musulmans dispersés maintenant dans le monde entier.

3. Ceux qui prétendent que le non-musulman doit être considéré comme un citoyen de deuxième classe n'ont pas fourni de preuve légale pour étayer leur opinion, même s'ils se basent sur le discours des shâfi'ites الشافعين. Ce discours n'est qu'un effort juridique (*ijtihâd* إجتهاد) et n'est pas un texte légal. Par ailleurs, les opinions de Mawdûdî manquent de précision et ne conduisent pas nécessairement aux conclusions qu'il présente.

Huwaïdî[143] affirme avec fermeté la citoyenneté entière des non-musulmans dans la communauté musulmane. Cette affirmation se trouve dans de nombreux textes et des références l'appuient:

1. Les versets coraniques qui honorent l'homme;

2. Les discours du prophète qui interdisent qu'un musulman porte atteinte à un *dhimmî* ذمى, commette une injustice à son égard, ou l'humilie;

3. Le traité de Médine où le prophète a défini les fondements de la relation entre les musulmans et les autres dans la communauté de Médine et où il parle d'une «*seule nation*»;

4. Les paroles de 'Alî ibn Abî Tâlib et de la majorité des jurisconsultes selon laquelle «leur sang est comme notre sang et qu'ils ont les mêmes devoirs et droits que nous». Comment peut-on leur nier ensuite leur droits politiques?

5. N'est-il pas étrange que les jurisconsultes autorisent les musulmans à faire la guerre pour défendre *ahl al-dhimma* أهل الذمة et qu'ensuite ils

---

[143] Ibid., pp. 123-126.

veulent les empêcher de voter dans les élections de l'Assemblée de la Consultation, par exemple?

Huwaïdî ne voit aucune obligation de revenir à l'expression de «*ahl al-dhimma* أهل الذمة» avec ses conséquences néfastes, étant donné les changements qui ont hypothéqué les intentions originales. Il faut ajouter cette expression à la liste des formes du passé et l'éloigner du vocabulaire des problèmes de la communauté musulmane contemporaine;

6. L'expression *ahl ad-dhimma* أهل الذمة est tombée hors du code juridique dans le monde arabe depuis la déclaration de la première Constitution Ottomane en 1876. Celle-ci a édicté l'égalité en droits et devoirs de tous les citoyens de l'Empire, quelle que soit leur religion;

7. Appeler les non-musulmans des citoyens de première classe est superflu car ils le sont déjà d'après l'islam;

8. Les non-musulmans sont devenus des associés réels dans les pays musulmans, et les relations avec eux ne sont plus basées sur le voisinage de tribu à tribu, ou sur la soumission d'une tribu à une autre;

9. Les pays musulmans doivent rester la propriété des musulmans et des non-musulmans qui y habitent, sans privilège, ni domination de l'un sur l'autre.

4. LES CHRÉTIENS ET LA JIZYA[144]

Huwaïdî compte la *jizya* الجِزْية (la capitation) parmi les sources de malentendus dans les relations des musulmans avec les non-musulmans. Il constate, d'après le verset S. 9:29, que la capitation ne concerne qu'un groupe des gens du Livre qui répond à une description déterminée.

La discussion qui a eu lieu dans le passé et dans le présent ne concerne pas seulement la capitation. Elle touche aussi au problème de l'humiliation (*al-saghâr* الصغار). Cette expression a pris une dimension disproportionnée dans le cadre des machinations pour agrandir la divergence entre les musulmans et les non-musulmans. Huwaïdî constate, comme Fadlallâh, que la *jizya* الجِزْية était une indemnité payée par des non-musulmans pour la protection et l'immunité garanties par les musulmans.

Huwaïdî[145] établit que la plupart des jurisconsultes ont dit que les non-musulmans sont dispensés de payer la capitation en cas de participation au devoir de défense. Ceux qui payaient la capitation étaient ceux

---

[144] Huwaïdî, op. cit., pp. 128-136.
[145] Ibid., pp. 136-138.

qui remplissaient les conditions du service militaire. C'est pourquoi ce n'était pas une injustice de leur demander de payer, s'ils ne participaient pas à la guerre. Cela a été pratiqué d'ailleurs en Egypte jusqu'à la moitié du vingtième siècle autant pour les musulmans que pour les non-musulmans: celui qui ne voulait pas faire le service militaire payait ce qu'on a appelé l'«indemnité de la conscription», qui était une somme symbolique.

Les conditions de paiement de la capitation étaient les suivantes:
a- avoir la raison et la majorité et être de sexe masculin;
b- être en bonne santé;
c- être libre;
d- n'être ni pauvre ni invalide;
e- ne pas être moine.

Huwaïdî[146] invoque l'expression «sâghirûn صاغرون» (S. 9:29) qui a été mal interprétée, affirme-t-il, par de nombreux jurisconsultes. Nous ne pouvons pas séparer ce verset des principes fondamentaux édictés par l'islam, soit dans sa vision de la dignité humaine, soit dans son appel à la bienfaisance envers les gens du Livre. C'est une grave erreur d'isoler ce verset et de lui faire prendre une signification en contradiction avec les principes fondamentaux de l'islam. Ce qui a justifié cette attitude, c'est l'influence des circonstances historiques et de certains comportements des gens du Livre à l'égard des musulmans. Toutefois, cela ne justifie pas de généraliser cette faute, quelle qu'en soit la raison.

Huwaïdî[147] s'interroge alors sur la nécessité de la *jizya* الجِزْية dans la société islamique contemporaine où les factions intégristes réclament la réintroduction de cette pratique. Il réaffirme que la *jizya* الجِزْية n'a plus de place dans la société islamique contemporaine, étant donné que le motif principal de cette institution a disparu, puisque tout le monde participe maintenant à la défense et au maintien de l'inviolabilité <du pays>, quelle qu'en soit la raison, religieuse ou patriotique. Quant à la participation des non-musulmans aux revenus financiers de l'Etat, c'est la responsabilité de tous les citoyens, qu'ils soient musulmans ou non.

Huwaïdî[148] aborde un dernier point qui concerne les conditions dans lesquelles la jurisprudence islamique a été conçue et développée. L'Appel (الدعوة *da'wa*) de l'islam a dû affronter, à l'époque, divers ennemis:

---

[146] Ibid., pp. 139-141.
[147] Ibid., pp. 142-145.
[148] Huwaïdî, op. cit.,pp. 103-105.

les associateurs de la péninsule arabe, les tribus juives, les Persans à l'Ouest, les Byzantins à l'Est. Cette réalité a divisé le monde en deux camps selon la terminologie suivante: دار الإسلام ودار الحرب *Dâr al-islâm* et *Dâr al-harb*, la terre de l'islam et la terre de la guerre. Les livres de jurisprudence et d'histoire donnent trois opinions à ce sujet:

1. A partir de la conception de دار الإسلام ودار الحرب *Dâr al-islâm* et *Dâr al-harb*, certains jurisconsultes ont opté pour définir ce qu'on veut dire par «les autres», en s'appuyant sur le fait de leur croyance et notamment s'ils sont musulmans ou non.

2. D'autres, dans cet effort de définition, ont opté plutôt pour «l'élément de la sécurité» pour ceux qui résident à l'intérieur de la frontière de la «terre de l'islam».

3. D'autres encore affirment que l'islam n'a pas établi de différence entre les musulmans et non-musulmans sur la base de la religion, mais plutôt sur le fait s'ils sont en paix ou en guerre avec les musulmans. Cette troisième position est plus proche de celle du Prophète qui a signé le premier traité avec «les autres» où on peut trouver cette formule: «*Les juifs de Banî 'Awf sont une nation avec les croyants, les juifs ont leur religion et les musulmans leur religion*». Si la division avait eu lieu sur la base de la religion, on aurait pu faire sortir les الذميون *dhimmiyyûn* de la terre de l'Islam, ce qui n'a pas été fait.

Ces anciennes formules ne sont pas de la pure invention de la part des musulmans. D'ailleurs, on trouve les mêmes formulations chez les Romains avant l'islam et après. Huwaïdî fait remarquer que les théologiens en Occident ont eu l'habitude d'utiliser l'expression «la terre chrétienne et la terre d'incroyance».

5. CONCLUSION

Huwaïdî[149] attire l'attention sur les points suivants concernant les opinions données dans la jurisprudence au sujet des non-musulmans:

1. Ces opinions ne s'appuient pas toutes sur des textes légitimes du Coran ou de la Sunna. Elles ne sont que des efforts proposés par les jurisconsultes à la lumière de leur lecture de la réalité qu'ils ont vécue.

2. La plupart de ces opinions s'adressaient à un monde différent du monde actuel. Car à l'époque, l'idée de la patrie composée d'hommes de différentes religions et ethnies n'existait pas.

---

[149] Ibid., pp. 106-107.

3. La terre de l'islam dont parlent les jurisconsultes n'a plus d'existence que dans les livres de l'histoire.

4. La terre de la guerre n'est plus seulement dans le camp des non-musulmans, car nombre de guerres dans notre temps ont lieu entre les pays musulmans mêmes, et moins entre des musulmans et des non-musulmans.

III. SYNTHESE

La consultation de quelques autres ouvrages de Fadlallâh et Huwaïdî en rapport avec notre sujet nous conduit à apporter quelques précisions pour mieux situer nos deux auteurs. Notons d'abord l'ambiguïté et même des contradictions dans leur position tant sur la question des mouvements islamistes que sur la place des chrétiens dans la société musulmane, ainsi que sur la question de la liberté de pensée et de croyance. Ensuite, il faut voir de plus près leur réflexion au sujet des mouvements islamistes. Fadlallâh d'une part désapprouve la violence qui n'est pas propre à l'islam, d'autre part il considère le recours à la violence comme le dernier moyen légitime pour réaliser la justice. En plus, Fadlallâh croit que le mouvement islamiste est un mouvement de progrès vers une société juste, morale et croyante qui vise aussi à barrer la route aux courants matérialistes et athées. Quant à Huwaïdî, il adopte d'une part un ton très violent envers les penseurs égyptiens laïcs. Il les accuse d'éléments non-démocratiques qui visent à détruire l'islam et sa tradition. D'autre part il critique les comportements des islamistes ou des groupes avec un mode de vie trop stricte du point de vue religieux, en considérant que leur connaissance de l'islam est déformée. Il essaie de justifier l'attitude des islamistes en tant que réaction à la pratique du régime et l'attitude du pouvoir vis-à-vis de toute opposition sérieuse. Devant ces constatations, nous n'avons d'autre choix que de rester prudents à l'encontre d'un genre d'écrits qu'on peut, à la limite, qualifier plutôt de démagogique.

Résumons maintenant, sous forme de synthèse, une comparaison entre nos deux auteurs dans les dix points suivants.

1. Fadlallâh et Huwaïdî décrivent les gens du Livre, juifs et chrétiens, comme des gens croyant au Dieu Unique. Huwaïdî n'entre pas dans les détails des différences théologiques concernant les questions de la Divinité du Christ, de l'Incarnation de Dieu, de la Trinité et de la Crucifixion

du Christ. Par contre, Fadlallâh a traité toutes ces questions en essayant de rapprocher ce qui peut être rapproché[150]. Quant à la question de la Trinité, Fadlallâh la place sur un plan plutôt philosophique que théologique. En outre, Fadlallâh décrit le christianisme comme une «religion d'amour» dont le rôle serait de résoudre les problèmes des gens en barrant la route à la violence.

2. Les deux auteurs insistent sur le fait que les gens du Livre ne sont ni des associateurs, ni des incroyants au sens que le Coran donne à ces termes. Huwaïdî affirme, en outre, que les autres — les non-musulmans — ne sont ni des diables ni des démons, ni l'enfer comme l'imaginent même certaines personnes. Ils sont des êtres humains, nos semblables dans la création, même si leur couleur, leur ethnie et leur croyance sont différentes.

3. Les gens du Livre, aux yeux de nos auteurs, sont des partenaires à part entière des musulmans. Vis-à-vis de ces derniers, ils sont des citoyens égaux tant en droits qu'en devoirs. Mais Fadlallâh met quelques réserves quant à l'égalité entre les gens du Livre et les musulmans. L'égalité n'empêche pas, dit Fadlallâh, que les gens du Livre paient la capitation, d'une part, et qu'ils ne puissent pas accéder à certaines hautes fonctions au sein de l'Etat islamique. Par contre, Huwaïdî ne partage pas du tout cette opinion de Fadlallâh. Il tente de démontrer historiquement que les gens du Livre ont toujours eu accès à de hautes fonctions comme par exemple chef d'une armée composée majoritairement de musulmans, ou chef de trésorerie. Cela a été fait en accord avec l'idée coranique de l'égalité entre tous les hommes, sans distinction religieuse, raciale ou ethnique.

La différence entre les deux auteurs repose sur leur appartenance confessionnelle au sein de la religion musulmane. Fadlallâh est un shî'ite dont la conception de l'imamat a influencé sa vision vis-à-vis des non-musulmans. Huwaïdî est un sunnite. La vision sunnite diffère quant au concept de l'Etat islamique. Mais nous savons, d'autre part, que chaque musulman sunnite ne représente que son opinion personnelle.

4. Quant à la jurisprudence (الفقه *fiqh*), Fadlallâh reconnaît qu'il y a des divergences entre les jurisconsultes au sujet des non-musulmans. Huwaïdî, pour sa part, ne se contente pas seulement de signaler qu'il y a des divergences, mais il entame une critique à l'encontre de la jurisprudence même. Huwaïdî souligne que la jurisprudence reste un acte humain conditionné par le temps et le lieu. Par contre, cela n'est pas le cas

---

[150] Fadlallâh, op. cit., p. 234.

du texte coranique ni des hadîths authentiques. Bien plus, continue Hu-waïdî, on doit être prudent, même devant certains textes coraniques qui nous obligent à bien les situer dans leur contexte historique du temps du Prophète. Cette même méthode doit être appliquée aussi à certains hadîths.

5. Fadlallâh et Huwaïdî mettent l'accent sur la nécessité de libérer les sociétés et les gens de la domination nouvelle de l'impérialisme contem-porain. Les deux auteurs trouvent que la coopération entre musulmans et non-musulmans est nécessaire afin de faire face au déclin moral et au sous-développement dans la majorité des pays du monde. Fadlallâh cla-rifie un point essentiel autour des moyens à utiliser pour résoudre les problèmes de l'injustice: «*L'idée islamique est la bienveillance comme moyen d'affronter les problèmes difficiles. Mais la violence représente un moyen humain pour garder l'équilibre de l'humanité dans la vie, de-vant ceux qui abattent le sens de la vie par leur injustice impéria-liste*»[151].

6. Les deux auteurs se prononcent en faveur d'un dialogue entre mu-sulmans et non-musulmans, en vue de rebâtir une relation islamo-chré-tienne solide basée sur le respect mutuel et sur la liberté de pensée. Huwaïdî fait remarquer que, s'il y a des limites pour exercer la liberté, il y a également des limites pour utiliser les droits. Cela veut dire qu'il faut respecter l'équilibre entre la majorité et la minorité. Ce qu'il faut enten-dre par là, c'est que le respect des valeurs et des sentiments de la majo-rité ne signifie pas qu'on peut diminuer les droits de la minorité. Mais cela oblige plutôt la majorité à respecter les sentiments de la minorité[152].

7. Fadlallâh note que la compréhension du fondamentalisme en Orient est entièrement différente de celle de l'Occident. Le fondamentalisme chrétien signifie, en Orient, être chrétien comme était le christianisme dans la pensée du Christ et de l'Evangile. En d'autres termes, c'est un retour aux sources. Il est évident qu'on trouve dans le camp chrétien, comme dans celui des musulmans, des fanatiques.

8. Le problème de la réalité humaine aujourd'hui, selon Fadlallâh, c'est de garder un équilibre dans les mouvements de la force et de la fai-blesse (الإستكبار والإستضعاف *al-istikbâr wa'l-istid'âf*) dans la région et dans le monde en général, entre la richesse et la pauvreté, entre le Nord et le Sud, dans le dynamisme des intérêts internationaux. Devant cette réalité les chrétiens et les musulmans doivent coopérer pour faire face

---

[151] Ibid., pp. 97-98.
[152] Ibid., pp. 147-148.

ensemble aux problèmes de l'injustice et de nouvelles formes d'escla-
vage. Cette coopération doit se faire en vue de réaliser ici-bas les valeurs
spirituelles et morales de leurs Messages respectifs, sur lesquels ils concordent étroitement. Une telle réalisation aiderait à défendre les faibles
et les déshérités, les sans-abri et les opprimés. C'est par le dialogue entre
les musulmans et les chrétiens que nous pourrons parvenir à remédier à
la déchéance actuelle de l'humanité, en usant de tous les moyens pacifiques. Il faut libérer l'homme de la violence afin qu'il réalise sa liberté.

9. Quant à la question des Droits de l'homme, Fadlallâh considère
que ce n'est ni la Révolution française, ni les Nations Unies qui doivent
en décider. L'islam a sa théorie particulière des droits de l'homme. Mais
Fadlallâh assure «...qu'il peut y avoir un dialogue entre les droits de
l'homme chez les musulmans et les droits de l'homme chez les autres.
L'islam n'exclut rien dans le monde du dialogue»[153].

Contrairement à Fadlallâh, Huwaïdî voit, d'une part, que chaque créature a une inviolabilité, une immunité et des droits en islam. Ces droits
sont assurés «...avant de savoir si <l'homme> est musulman, chrétien,
juif ou bouddhiste, s'il est blanc, noir ou jaune»[154]. Pour Huwaïdî, ce
sont les textes coraniques, les hadîths du Prophète, et la déclaration de
'Umar ibn al-Khattâb qui confirment ces droits édictés par Dieu. C'est
aussi sur ces fondements que le Coran déclare «لا إكراه فى الدين Nulle
contrainte en religion!» (S. 2:256). Cela donne à la croyance une immunité dont la violation est inadmissible. C'est la fraternité humaine qui
est la base et la bonne parole est le moyen. D'autre part, Huwaïdî justifie
la méthode de l'Etat qui fait recours à des lois très sévères contre les
apostats et les brigands, afin de protéger sa sécurité intérieure et l'ordre
public[155].

Nous avons vu ci-dessus que Fadlallâh a affirmé que «.... l'islam insiste sur la nécessité d'arriver à la vérité par le dialogue d'une manière
scientifique et objective. Même si cela contredit la doctrine générale des
gens (hattâ wa-law khâlafa l-'aqîdata l-'âmmata li-l-nâs), personne n'a
le droit d'empêcher l'autre de jouir de cette liberté en l'accusant d'incroyance» (S. 3:78; 18:56; 22:8)[156]. Bien plus, Fadlallâh a confirmé
que «...l'épée âpre et l'arme tranchante ne peuvent que soumettre le
corps, mais non pas la raison de l'homme. C'est seulement l'arme de la

---

[153] Ibid., p. 335.
[154] Huwaïdî, op. cit., pp. 79-80.
[155] Ibid., p. 244.
[156] FADLALLAH, Muhammad Hussein, Fî âfâq al-hiwâr al-islâmî al-masîhî (Dans l'horizon du dialogue islamo-chrétien), Liban 1994, p. 14.

parole et de la pensée qui peuvent mettre en mouvement le dialogue et convaincre l'homme»[157].

Cependant, Fadlallâh parle de certains chrétiens ou musulmans qui revendiquent le droit de penser librement sans aucune obligation religieuse, soit chrétienne, soit musulmane. Mais le musulman est contraint par la loi de l'apostasie, et le chrétien l'est par la loi de l'anathème[158]. Il est vrai que le châtiment islamique appliqué au musulman est plus sévère que le châtiment chrétien appliqué au chrétien[159]. Fadlallâh justifie la position islamique sur ce point de la façon suivante: Tout d'abord, nous savons que le christianisme ne permet pas qu'un chrétien embrasse l'islam. Le christianisme fait recours à l'arme de l'anathème comme un moyen de pression afin d'empêcher cette conversion. Pour la même raison, l'islam fait recours à l'arme de la loi afin d'empêcher l'apostasie[160]. Ensuite, la liberté de pensée ou de croyance n'empêche pas que l'islam codifie des lois pour protéger son territoire d'une manière juridique; le christianisme fait la même chose en sens inverse. Enfin, personne ne peut empêcher l'autre de devenir musulman ou chrétien, mais on peut diminuer les conséquences négatives que cette liberté a pour la réalité sociale et l'ordre public[161]. On peut dès lors constater que la liberté de pensée ou de croyance n'a pas un caractère absolu. C'est encore au nom de la sécurité et de la protection de l'ordre public qu'on limite la liberté de l'homme.

10. Fadlallâh a fait un rapprochement au sujet du voile entre l'islam et le christianisme[162].

11. Fadlallâh différencie entre l'Église catholique romaine et l'Église orientale orthodoxe[163].

[157] Ibid., p. 196.
[158] Ibid., p. 45.
[159] Ibid., p. 111.
[160] Ibid., p. 177.
[161] Ibid., p. 283.
[162] Ibid., p. 325.
[163] L'Église catholique ne représente pas le monde chrétien, mais uniquement les chrétiens catholiques et uniates. Quoique l'Église orientale orthodoxe ait des points communs avec l'Église catholique, elle diffère de cette dernière dans sa vision spirituelle qu'elle a acquis par sa présence sur la terre où le Christ est né. L'Église orthodoxe considère que le Vatican et l'Église catholique se sont éloignés d'une façon générale de l'élément spirituel et qu'ils se sont rapprochés plus de l'élément matériel... Peut-être elle a assimilé quelque chose du paganisme matériel de l'Occident. Voir Ali Hasan Sorour, على حسن سرور: «العلمة فضل الله: تحدى الممنوع» (Fadlallah, le défi de l'interdit). Beyrouth: Dar al-malâk, 1992, pp. 111-118. Sur Fadlallah, voir par exemple Khalid Al-Lahhâm: خالد اللحام قضايا اسلامية معاصرة: حوار مع السيد محمد حسين فضل الله (Problèmes islamiques contemporains. Dialogue avec Muhammad Hussein Fadlallah). Beyrouth: Dar al-Malâk, 1993.

CHRISTIANITY FROM THE MUSLIM PERSPECTIVE: VARIETIES AND CHANGES

Hugh GODDARD

Introduction

Any investigation of variety and change in Muslim perceptions of Christianity during the last half century or so cannot be completely separated from what has gone before, and although it will not be possible, for obvious reasons, to look in great detail at that earlier history, it is important at the outset to make one or two general observations concerning it[1].

Most importantly, and most obviously, in looking at the long history of Muslim perceptions of Christianity, it is important to remember that variety and change are no strangers there either. This is true firstly with reference to the Qur'ān, where on the one hand quite positive statements about the Christian faith and about Christians can be found in some, earlier, *sūras* and yet on the other hand more negative judgements about each of those things can be found in different, later, *sūras*. By way of explanation for this variety and change it has been argued, for example by Professor Jacques Waardenburg in a paper entitled "Towards a periodization of earliest Islam according to its relations with other religions"[2], that the different statements need to be seen in the context of Muḥammad's own immediate relationships with other religious communities, so that the earlier more positive statements perhaps spring from a context of deteriorating relationships with the Jewish community alongside continuing hopes of a positive response to Muḥammad's message from Christians, while the later more negative statements may come from a context in which it had become clear that those hopes were not to be fulfilled. Variety is thus to some extent explained by change of the most practical experiential kind.

---

[1] A fuller account of the development of Muslim perceptions of Christianity may be found in my *Muslim Perceptions of Christianity*, London, Grey Seal, 1995.

[2] This paper was read at the 9th Congress of the Union Européenne des Arabisants et Islamisants held in Amsterdam in 1978, and later published in the Proceedings of the Congress, edited by R. Peters, by Brill in 1981, pp. 304-326.

Secondly, something similar is also true with reference to the classical period of Islamic thought, where on the one hand relatively positive comments about Christianity can be found in the writings of, for example, the Shī'ī historian al-Ya'qūbī or the group known as the Ikhwān al-Ṣafā, and yet on the other more critical comments are to be found in the works of, for example, Ibn Ḥazm or 'Abd al-Jabbār. In seeking an explanation for the diversity in this period, attention should be paid both to the existence of different streams of thought in the Muslim scripture itself, which were developed in different ways by later Muslim thinkers, and to the shifting nature of the relationships between the Christian and Muslim communities in the Umayyad and 'Abbasid periods as the hold of the Islamic state was consolidated and as the process of conversion to Islam, resulting in Muslims becoming less of a numerical minority in the population as a whole, began to accelerate. Context is thus equally as important as text here, but both certainly point to the existence of both variety and change in Muslim perceptions of Christianity in this period.

Thirdly, in looking at the development of Muslim thinking about Christianity in the period before the last half century or so, it is important to remember that the early modern period, that is from roughly 1800 CE/1200 AH, has seen the addition of a number of new themes to the range of traditional Muslim ideas in this area, largely as a result again of the changing nature of the relationship between the Muslim and Christian worlds. Put very crudely, prior to 1800 CE/1200 AH the initiative in that relationship tended to lie with Muslims, so that Christians were in a situation of simply responding to Islam (with some obvious exceptions such as the Crusades, but these were peripheral to the Muslim world as a whole), but since around that time this situation has been reversed, so that the initiative tended to lie with Christians, with Muslims being driven to being reactive rather than pro-active. The balance of power between the two communities, in other words, had changed, and so in this period Muslim thinking about Christianity came to include new arguments about the links between Christian mission and Western imperialism, that is the identification between Christianity and the West, and also to make use of the strong critique of Christian convictions and practices which grew up inside the West in this period. These arguments can be seen in the nineteenth/thirteenth century works of, for example, Jamāl al-dīn al-Afghānī and Raḥmat Allāh al-Hindī in the Middle East and the Indian Subcontinent respectively. In looking at the whole history of

Muslim thinking about Christianity there is thus a kind of change of gear, a major change of tone, at what might be called the start of the modern era, leading both to further variety and further change in Muslim opinion.

What has evolved since 1950?

As we move into the period which is the main focus of our concern, here too, not surprisingly, we will find further change and further variety. In order to illustrate this what I propose to do is firstly to examine in some detail the writings of two very significant Muslim thinkers who wrote mainly in the earlier part of the last half century or so, and then move on to look at the ideas of a number of other rather younger Muslim thinkers who are still writing today. The distinction here, in other words, is one of generations, between two thinkers who were born in the first decade of this century (more or less the 1320s) and underwent their training in higher education between the two World Wars and a larger group of thinkers who were born between the two World Wars and underwent their training in higher education after the Second World War. Our purpose is thus to try and highlight how we can see both change and diversity even within the period of the last fifty years, let alone as compared with the earlier period.

a) The first generation

The first two thinkers whom I would like to discuss are Muḥammad Kāmil Ḥusain from Egypt and Syed Vahiduddin from India, both of whom, I think, are already widely-known, who represent a stream of Muslim thinking which was widely influential in the 1950s and 1960s (1370s and 1380s), and who also, of course, serve to represent thinking in two rather different parts of the Muslim world, namely the Middle East and the Indian Subcontinent.

Muḥammad Kāmil Husain, first of all, is, I think, best-known for his book *Qarya ẓālima*, first published in Cairo in 1954, winner of the Egyptian State Prize for Literature in 1957/1376, and subsequently translated into English (by Kenneth Cragg) under the title of *City of Wrong: a Friday in Jerusalem* (Amsterdam, Djambatan, 1959), and also translated into French and Spanish. The English translation has recently been reprinted by Oneworld in Oxford (in 1994).

Essentially this book is a kind of historical novel which explores the problem of human motivation through a series of meditations on the thoughts and feelings of some of the characters who were involved in the series of events leading up to the crucifixion of Jesus in Jerusalem on the first Good Friday. After the magnificent introduction, simply called "Friday" (and probably the only piece ever written by a Muslim which could be used constructively as part of a Good Friday service), the book proceeds to look at the thoughts in the minds of some of the Jews, some of the disciples and some of the Romans involved in the events and then, in a final section, the disciples and another character, the Magus, look back with the benefit of hindsight at the events and reflect upon their meaning. The interest of the book, therefore, is partly in its probing analysis of human motivation, and especially the ease with which different people, as a result of group pressure, do what their individual consciences tell them quite clearly to be wrong, and more especially in the choice of historical event which the author selected as the focal point for his analysis.

In addition to *Qarya ẓālima*, Dr Ḥusain is also well-known for his work *Al-wādī al-muqaddas*, first published in 1968, and again translated by Kenneth Cragg into English under the title *The Hallowed Valley* (American University in Cairo Press, 1977). As the subtitle of the English version (which was added with the approval of the author) explains, this is essentially a "Muslim philosophy of religion" which ranges in its discussion over human intention — conscience and purity of heart; different types of religion — dominated by fear, love and hope, depending on an individual's temperament and corresponding in a sense to the types of religion represented by Moses, Jesus and Muḥammad; relationships between different religious communities — especially focusing on the tendency of power to corrupt such relationships; and more general discussion of human well-being. It is therefore a wide-ranging book, but in different places it demonstrates both an understanding of and sympathy for Christian opinions.

Finally, some of Dr Ḥusain's smaller works, articles and papers, are also germane to an outline of his perception of Christianity. These include firstly four pieces from his two volume collection of miscellaneous essays (*Mutanawwi'āt*, published in 1958), two from Volume I, on the Exodus and on two rather similar theological debates in Christian and Muslim history (the Incarnation of Christ and the createdness or otherwise of the Qur'ān) respectively, and two from Volume II, on the meaning of *ẓulm* (sin/wrong-doing) in the Qur'ān, and on the story of

Adam respectively[3]. Secondly, there is a short story, *Jarīma shan'ā'* (an appalling crime), published in *al-Hilāl* in 1962, a story which probes the motivations of all who are involved in the trial of a young man for rape and which has a particularly positive portrait of a Coptic priest[4]. In many of these pieces the focus is on humanity and human nature rather than on Christianity *per se*, but in many cases this leads to constructive comment and reflection upon different aspects of the Christian faith, views which were more systematically outlined in Muḥammad Kāmil Ḥusain's contribution to the volume *Verse et controverse 14: les musulmans*, edited by Youakim Moubarac and published by Beauchesne in Paris in 1971, to which we will return later.

The works of Syed Vahiduddin, secondly, are perhaps less well-known in the West than those of Dr. Ḥusain, but some of them at least are readily accessible in Volume 3 of the series *Islam in India: Studies and Commentaries*, edited by Professor Christian Troll and published by Chanakya Publications in Delhi in 1986, and which is a collection of articles by Syed Vahiduddin, under the general title "Islamic experience in contemporary thought". Two sections of Part I of the book, which groups seventeen articles under the general title "Islam: self-awareness" are of particular relevance to us. The significance of the first, which was published for the first time in this volume, is obvious from the title of the chapter, "What Christ means to me" (Chapter 15, pp. 182-186).

> "Christ as he appears to me through the Quranic perspective is a mystery which unfolds itself at different levels, and the termination of his earthly career on a fateful Friday in Jerusalem is equally wrapped in mystery." (p. 182).

The element of mystery is returned to later:

> "Our focus ought not to be on the question of the historical authenticity of the events, but rather on the mystery that haunts the life of Christ from beginning to end." (p. 183).

---

[3] English translations of the first, third and fourth of these articles may be found as follows: A.K. Cragg "The Exodus: an Egyptian view" in *Muslim World*, 49 (1959), pp. 30-40; id. "The meaning of *ẓulm* in the Qur'ān" in *Muslim World*, 49 (1959), pp. 196-212; and K.E. Nolin "The story of Adam" in *Muslim World*, 54 (1964), pp. 4-13.

[4] This has been translated into English under the title "Atrocity" in M. Manzalaoui (ed.) *Arabic Writing Today: Vol. I, The Short Story*, Cairo, American Research Center in Egypt, 1968, pp. 54-75.

A number of particular details of Jesus' life are emphasised: the special status of his Virgin Mother; his healing powers, which break through the laws of mechanical causation and have deep symbolic significance if applied to spiritual as well as physical malaise; his role as comforter and also as exposer of hypocrisy and cant; and supremely as the bearer of a Gospel which abounds with love:

> "Christ's Gospel abounds with the love that overflows itself (*agapē*). The call to forgiveness, unlimited and without reservation, resounds throughout his teaching.... Christ reflects in every act of His God's *jamāl* in all its fullness. He is the embodiment of that tender aspect of the divine which the Quran calls *rahma*, and this is what Rudolf Otto calls *mysterium fascinans...*[5]" (p. 184).

This view is founded, Vahiduddin suggests, not simply on the writings of Sufis such as Ibn 'Arabī, who is mentioned on p. 182, but also on the Qur'an itself, which bears witness to the fact that Christians display characteristics of mercy (*Sura* 57:27) because this was an attribute of Jesus.

The paragraphs on the end of Jesus' life are very interesting not least because of the extent to which some of them may call to mind some of Muhammad Kāmil Husain's language on the subject in *Qarya zālima*, though with the significant addition of some specific references to the New Testament accounts of events:

> "The treatment that was meted out to him makes the saddest chapter of human history. He was spat on his face, humiliated and insulted, mocked and laughed at and was condemned to be crucified, with two confirmed criminals. 'And the light shineth in the darkness and the darkness apprehendeth it not' (John 1:5). He is forsaken and betrayed. Those who stand close to him flee! But there is no complaint. It is a state of perfect surrender to God's will, of *rida* and grace, 'not what I will, but what thou wilt' (Mark 14:37)........

> "What greater ignominy and disgrace could there be than which Christ suffered. But it is here that Christ appears in all His glory, and the world and all that it stands for is exposed in all its vanity. Whether we see the end and the culmination of his earthly course in the Christian or the Muslim perspective, death is not allowed to prevail and Christ appears to be ascending to supreme heights defying death. Perhaps it is due to my Muslim background that what strikes me most, is not the suffering through which he passes but his triumph through suffering.

> "What looks like defeat, subjection to mortality, the brute success of worldly power and of hard-headed priesthood lose their relevance (sic).

---

[5] *jamāl* means beauty and *rahma* mercy.

Death is vanquished once for all, and Christ's life serves as a beacon to those who are laid low, who 'labour and are heavy laden' (Matthew 11.28)....[6]" (pp. 184-185).

These are remarkable words, and the author ends by drawing out the consequences that follow from this view of Jesus, namely that Muslim and Christian are bound together by a shared devotion to Christ and to His Holy Mother. This is a view which is further developed in Chapter 10 (pp. 137-144), of the book, "The Quranic understanding of inter-religious harmony", (first published in *Studies in Islam*, 15 (1978), pp. 205-212). Here the author argues as follows:

"Religion... cannot afford to engage in interminable theological disputes. Followers of one religion should try to understand what the other stands for and have a 'feel' for the experience which is not theirs. However difficult it may be to accept theological positions which seem to be completely at variance with one's own, it is not as difficult to share in the experience of which dogmas are inadequate conceptual formulations." (p. 137).

He continues:

".. if we wish to be true to the spirit of the Quran we should remain conscious of the continuity of the prophetic tradition and cherish with as much fervour the memory of pre-Islamic piety as its post-Islamic manifestation..." (p. 141).

This understanding of reconciliation is based on what the author calls "Quranic humanism", and although it has to be conceded that such an attitude has often been conspicuously absent in history, nevertheless if Muslims are able to return to the sense of transcendence which the Quran itself inculcates, then

"... we can make a common cause with all those who believe, be they Christians or Sabaeans or people of other faiths, and even with those who fight for the cause of Allah anonymously, without knowing that they are doing so, as is possible today in a way which could never have been thought of before." (p. 144)[7].

Both Muḥammad Kāmil Ḥusain and Syed Vahiduddin, then, seem to represent a new approach to the understanding of different aspects of the Christian faith on the part of Muslim writers, and despite their hailing from widely-separated parts of the Muslim world they both seem, for

[6] *riḍa* means grace or goodwill.
[7] The use of the word 'anonymously' here is particularly interesting, calling to mind as it does a similar use of the word by the Roman Catholic theologian Karl Rahner in his phrase 'the anonymous Christian'.

example, to display firstly a deep concern for the establishment of good relationships and mutual understanding between the Christian and Muslim communities and secondly a new awareness of and sympathy for some of the affirmations of the Christian faith which have traditionally been at best problematic and at worst anathema to Muslim thinkers, especially the events at the end of Jesus' life.

The important question which we need to ask now involves the reasons for these two thinkers developing their ideas in these directions: why did they succeed in breaking new ground and establishing new Muslim perceptions of Christianity? I suggest that there are three main reasons for this. One obvious factor, whose importance cannot be stressed enough, is simply their own biographies and life experiences. Muḥammad Kāmil Ḥusain, born in 1901/1318 in the village of Sabq in the Manūf district of Egypt, trained as a medical doctor at the Qaṣr al-'Ainī medical school in Cairo between 1917/1335 and 1923/1341 and then went to study in England in 1925/1344 at St Bartholemew's Hospital in London. There he read furiously in order to become conversant with English literature and also to develop a deeper understanding of Western thought and religious and social structures. The historian Edward Gibbon was a particular focus of his attention. In 1931/1350 he became Professor of General Surgery at Qaṣr al-'Ainī, and in 1950/1369, at the request of Ṭāḥā Ḥusain, he became Rector of the new Ibrāhīm University, which later became 'Ain Shams University. He resigned from this post after only two years, to return to private medical practice, but he maintained a wide range of interests and contacts until his death in 1977/1397. As well as the State Prize for Literature, which he won in 1957/1376 (for *Qarya zālima*), he also won the State Prize for Research in Science and Medicine in 1967/1376, and he is the only person to have received both of these prizes.

Syed Vahiduddin, born in 1909/1327 in Hyderabad in South India, studied first at the Osmania University in Hyderabad and then, in 1933/1352, left to undertake postgraduate study in Germany. There he studied in the Universities of Berlin (under Prof Nicolai Hartmann), Heidelberg (where he attended a seminar of Karl Jaspers) and Marburg (where he took a doctorate in philosophy under Prof Erich Jaensch. He also visited Freiburg im Breisgau to hear Martin Heidegger and Edmund Husserl. One of the main influences on him, however, was Rudolf Otto, the Professor of Protestant Theology in Marburg, who was noted for many things including the foundation of the Inter-Religious League in 1921/1339, and with whom Syed Vahiduddin stayed as the paying guest of his widowed sister. Otto's influence is clear from a number of references to his thinking in *Islamic Experience in Contemporary Thought*, (e.g. p. 28 [on God as mystery], p. 118 [on the numinous core of religion], p. 184 [on the *mysterium tremendum et fascinans*] and pp. 189-190 [on the influence of Goethe on Otto]). After his time in Germany Vahiduddin spent six months in Paris, making contact with Jacques Maritain and Étienne Gilson, the scholars of medieval western Christian philosophy, and the Islamicist Louis Massignon (whose influence we will see recurring at a later stage of this paper too), and he also visited Russia and Italy during his time in Europe. On his return to Hyderabad in 1937/1356 Vahiduddin taught first in the Department of English and then in the Department of Philosophy, and during this time he developed a network of contacts in the United States, including both Boston and California. After his retirement he then moved to Delhi to become Head of the Department of the Philosophy of Medicine and of the Department of Comparative Religion at the Indian Institute of Islamic Studies at Hamdardnagar.

Secondly, partly because of their education in what has been called a "liberal age", both scholars had a broad range of intellectual interests, which included both a comprehensive knowledge of the Western intellectual tradition and, very importantly, familiarity with the whole range of the Islamic tradition. In the case of Muḥammad Kāmil Ḥusain this may be seen in his avid reading of English literature during his time in London and in his writings on such groups within the Islamic community as the Ismāʿīliyya (*Ṭāʾifat al-ismāʿīliyya*, Cairo, Al-maktaba al-taʾrīkhiyya, 1959), and with respect to Syed Vahiduddin it is perhaps seen even more clearly, in the references in his works to such authors as Schiller, Kant and Goethe, as well as Otto, and to figures such as Ibn ʿArabī within the Islamic tradition. Both thus represent what might be called an "inclusive" or "universal" view of knowledge, whereby useful insights may be obtained from any source in any part of the world and truth should not be seen as being exclusively located in one community or tradition.

Thirdly, as mature scholars, both enjoyed deep and enduring friendships with Christian scholars. In the case of Muḥammad Kāmil Ḥusain this was most particularly Kenneth Cragg, who did much to make Dr Ḥusain's work more widely-known through translating it and who was also a significant contributor to the development of his thought, but it also included a number of Coptic Christian thinkers; and in the case of Syed Vahiduddin it was particularly Louis Gardet and later Christian

Troll: Chapter 12 of *Islamic Experience in Contemporary Thought*, entitled "Muḥammad Iqbal's approach to Islam: some critical reflections", was originally published in a volume entitled *Recherches: articles offert à Georges C. Anawati et Louis Gardet par leurs collègues et amis* (Louvain, Éditions Peeters, 1977), and it was, of course, Christian Troll who by editing the volume of Syed Vahiduddin's articles did so much to make his work more widely accessible and thus better-known. The importance of human relationship and friendship cannot be emphasised enough in accounting for the development of these two thinkers' ideas about Christianity.

These are perhaps the three most important factors in explaining how it was that Muḥammad Kāmil Ḥusain and Syed Vahiduddin both contributed to the evolution of fresh Muslim thinking about Christianity. Let us now move on to look at what might be called the next generation of Muslim scholars who have written about different aspects of Christianity and see to what extent and for what reasons they too have managed to push forward Muslim understanding of the Christian faith.

b) The next generation

In this area it is clearly much more invidious to have to make any kind of selection of writers to discuss since there is a greater number of figures who could be referred to and most are still active in writing in this field. It is with some diffidence, therefore, that I have chosen the following ten figures to discuss (in alphabetical order according to the Latin alphabet): Shabbir Akhtar (born in Pakistan, educated in Cambridge and Canada, formerly a Race Relations Officer in Bradford, was lecturing in the International Islamic University in Malaysia), Muḥammad Arkoun (born in the Berber region of Algeria in 1928/1346, now Emeritus Professor of Islamic Studies in Paris), Ḥasan Askari (born in India in 1932/1351, formerly Professor of Sociology at Osmania University, Hyderabad (the same University as Syed Vahiduddin), later Professor of Islamic Studies in Birmingham, now retired in Leeds), Maḥmūd Ayoub (born in the Lebanon in 1935/1354, later a teacher at McGill University, Toronto, and now Professor of Islamic Studies at Temple University in Philadelphia), 'Abd al-Majīd Charfi (born in Tunisia in 1942/1361, now Professor of Islamic Studies in Tunis), Saad Ghrab (born in Tunisia in 1940/1359, until 1995 Professor of Islamic Studies in Tunis), Prince Ḥasan of Jordan, the heir to the throne of the Hashemite Kingdom of Jordan, 'Alī Merad (born in Algeria, Emeritus

Professor of Islamic Studies in Lyon and Paris), Seyyed Hossein Nasr (born in Iran, former head of the Imperial Academy of Philosophy in Teheran, now Professor of Islamic Studies at George Washington University in Washington, D.C.), and Muḥammad Talbi (born in Tunis in 1921/1339, Emeritus Professor of History in Tunis). There are undoubtedly many others whose contribution merits discussion, but in order to make this paper manageable discussion will be confined to these ten figures.

The range of work of these ten scholars is, I think, broadly-speaking fairly well-known, but by looking at a selection of their works I hope to illustrate something of the varieties and changes in modern Muslim perceptions of Christianity, although such a brief review runs the risk of reading like a kind of extended bibliography and thus not doing full justice to the thinkers concerned.

Shabbir Akhtar, first of all, is perhaps best known in Britain for his appearances on television and writings in the press at the time of the controversy concerning Salman Rushdie's novel *The Satanic Verses*, in which he sought to explain the sense of outrage felt by many Muslims concerning the novel and to persuade those in positions of influence to do something about it. Alongside these activities, however, in a number of publications he has sought to outline his views on Islam and in many of these there are some interesting observations concerning Christianity. His two most substantial works were both published in 1990: *The Light in the Enlightenment: Christianity and the Secular Heritage* (London, Grey Seal) owes something to an earlier book, *Reason and the Radical Crisis of Faith*, which was published in North America in 1987, and is quite critical of much modern Christian thought, and then *A Faith for all Seasons: Islam and Western Modernity* (London, Bellew) is a more positive outline and commendation of Islam.

The Light in the Enlightenment is essentially an attempt to outline the interaction between modern philosophical thought and Christian theology, the attempts, in other words, of Christians to make their faith comprehensible in the Age of Reason. Some of Akhtar's comments are very complimentary about this venture: "Christian thinkers, particularly in the Protestant wing, have produced what may be described as possibly the finest essay in intellectual probity in the history of ideas" (p. 7). But there are also deep criticisms of particular Christian schools of thought. The fideism of Kierkegaard and Barth, with its argument that faith is its own authority so Christianity cannot be judged on the basis of rationality, is rejected on the basis of the assertion that Christianity is not immune from rational scrutiny: both St. Thomas Aquinas and Ibn Rushd are referred to as supporters of the view that belief in God is subject to rational investigation and even proof. Different opinions concerning the essence of Christianity, which Christian theologians have argued remains valid even in the Age of Reason, are then examined, and a distinction is drawn between what Akhtar calls 'reductionists' (those such as Bultmann and Cupitt "in... (whose) hands... the traditional theistic content of Christian belief has been excessively eviscerated" (p. 64)) and 'revisionists' (the 'sophisticated Christians' such as Swinburne and Hick who seek to allow Christianity to "make its case before the tribunal of post-Enlightenment culture" (p. 93)). The latter is viewed much more positively than the former by Akhtar, but even it is regarded as disowning too much of the Christian tradition. Akhtar's prescription at the end of the book, is for the renewal of natural theology, a religious vision of the world, which would be of benefit to all the monotheistic religions.

Akhtar is thus by no means uncritical of modern Christian thought, but there is no denying that he has wrestled with its main ideas, and presented them on some occasions even with wit, as in note 2 on page 198, where he writes: "On my definition, the sophisticated Christian Club currently has the following membership: Terence Penelhum, Basil Mitchell, John Hick and Richard Swinburne. Anglicans are often tempted to become members." But it is interesting to note that the opening quotation, opposite the Contents page, is a Biblical one: "Where is the philosopher of this age? Has not God made foolish the wisdom of the world? (1 Corinthians 1:20)", and also interesting to note the extent to which much of the argument is presented in very similar terms to that of the Christian missiologist and theologian Lesslie Newbigin, whose 1986 booklet *Foolishness to the Greeks* (London: SPCK) is referred to on p. 93 and, indeed, almost seems to have given rise to the argument and even the title of Akhtar's book: "'The "light" in the Enlightenment was', as one distinguished Christian missiologist reminds us, 'real light'", Akhtar writes, quoting p. 43 of Newbigin's book. Perhaps most interesting of all is a small note on p. 200 (note 28), where Akhtar writes: "I do think, however, that if the doctrine of the Incarnation were free of certain fatal logical infirmities, it could provide useful conceptual resources, lacking in Judaism and Islam, for explaining the nature and origin of evil. And if Christianity could explain the mystery of evil, it would, other things being equal, be explanatorily superior to its related religious rivals."

A Faith for all Seasons goes over some of the same ground, even to the extent of repeating some phrases from *The Light in the Enlightenment* almost *verbatim*, for example the sentence about the group of 'sophisticated Christians' (*Faith* n. 51, p. 227; cf. *Light* n. 2, p. 198), and the statement about Lesslie Newbigin (*Faith* p.70; cf. *Light* p. 93). But the central theme of this book is much more the commendation of Islam, though the intended audience seems to be as much Muslim as non-Muslim. The Preface ends rather wistfully: "Suffice it to say that I have not found many allies in contemporary Islam or Christianity for most of the views expressed here" (p. viii.). In the course of the book Akhtar spends some time discussing themes such as human nature and the need, in the Christian view, for salvation (pp. 154-158), a section in which there is substantial reference to the writings of Kenneth Cragg on this theme. The penultimate chapter, Chapter 9, entitled "Choice and destiny", is then, in a sense, an outline of why people should choose Islam rather than Christianity. It includes some remarkably positive statements about aspects of Christianity traditionally rejected or even mocked by Muslims: "... let us look now at the two related doctrines of the Incarnation and the Trinity. These are, by any standards of religious originality, among the most fertile and indeed influential ideas in the history of religious conviction." (p. 174). "... the doctrinal complexity of Christianity is intimately tied up with its concern to record and partly resolve a central perplexity, namely, the riddle of God's moral involvement with a human nature that is so strikingly recalcitrant to divine guidance. It is very much to the credit of the Christian faith that it recognises — feels and lives in creative tension with — this puzzle. The scandalously intricate collection of Christian doctrines is in fact the direct result of taking seriously the characteristically human threads of the theological fabric: sin, suffering, our moral sense, and the human demand for a divine accountability to the human." (p. 175). "Among the monotheisms of Hebrew origin, Christianity alone fully explores the issue of God's implied normative engagement with creation." (p. 176). But doubts are then raised concerning the historicity of the Christian faith, including the reliability of the New Testament accounts of Jesus' ministry, and the conceptual complexity of Christianity: "It may fairly be said.... that among monotheistic creeds, embrace of Christianity requires assent to the largest collection of highly implausible beliefs, requiring at times.... an unusually dramatic suspension of critical powers." (p. 179). Akhtar adds later: "Complexity.... is one thing, incoherence another. Paradox is one thing, nonsense another. The doctrine of the Incarnation does appear, even in the eyes of sympathetic critics, to be incohe-

rent." (p. 179). There follows a detailed discussion of the potential for and
the obstacles in the way of dialogue between Christians and Muslims, and
some reference to the matter of conversion between the two traditions, a
theme which is reflected in the final chapter, entitled "The road to
Mecca", which echoes the title of Muḥammad Asad's autobiographical
account of his conversion to Islam (from a Jewish background).

Akhtar thus seems to enjoy a kind of love-hate relationship with
Christianity, admiring the subtlety and integrity of some of its modern
thinkers and yet exasperated by the complexity and incoherence of some
of its traditional doctrines. More recently he has turned his attentions to
more practical matters, not only in connection with the Rushdie Affair
but also related to ethical questions, especially those of power. His most
recent book is *The Final Imperative: an Islamic Theology of Liberation*
(London, Bellew, 1991), a work in which there is much discussion of
Christian as well as Islamic political thought and reflection upon power,
and considerable reference to Kenneth Cragg's comments on the relationship between the thinking of the two traditions in this area. On a
practical as well as a theological level, therefore, Akhtar is one interesting example of fresh Muslim thinking about different aspects of Christianity, and it is certainly to be hoped that his pen has not run dry in the
aftermath of the Rushdie Affair.

Muḥammad Arkoun comes from a very different background, being
as he is a Berber, originally from Algeria, and formed in the French
intellectual tradition. He has written widely on different aspects of
Islam, including the Qur'ān, classical Islamic thought with a special
emphasis on the ethical tradition, as represented by such writers as
Miskawayh, the history of Islam in the Maghrib, and modern Islamic
thought and the issues confronting Muslims today. Most of this material
was originally written in French, and although a number of his articles
have been translated into English, only recently has one of his books
appeared in that language, and it is not surprising, therefore, if he is not
particularly well-known in the English-speaking world. He has recently
retired from the Chair of Islamic Studies at the Sorbonne in Paris.

The book by Arkoun which has recently been translated into English
is his *Ouvertures sur l'islam* (Paris, Grancher, 1989), which appeared in
an English translation entitled *Rethinking Islam: Common Questions,
Uncommon Answers* (Boulder, Colorado, Westview, 1994). This takes
the form of 24 questions to which Arkoun provides an answer, and the
seventeenth question is on the subject of Judaism, Christianity and

paganism: "What did Islam retain from the previously-revealed religions Judaism and Christianity? And what in addition did it retain from
the religions and customs of pre-Islamic Arabia?" In addressing these
questions Arkoun stresses that the position of the Qur'ān with reference
to Judaism and Christianity is quite different from the Qur'ān's view of
paganism, since Jews and Christians are recognised as peoples of the
Book who received revelation through a number of prophets in earlier
history. "Jesus, son of Mary, enjoys a special status: he is the Word of
God.... but not the son of God, and he was not crucified." (p. 71). Up
until this point this may seem a pretty traditional account, but Arkoun
immediately adds: "To understand the Qur'anic definition of Jesus the
person, we must come back to the theological disputes dividing Eastern
Christians in the fifth and sixth centuries. It took time for the Christian
dogma of the Trinity to assert itself in the now familiar standard
Catholic form. Current debates between Muslims and Christians do not
take account of the historic dimension of the problem. Beliefs elaborated
later are projected backwards by both sides." (p. 71). And this insistence
that all texts must be seen in their historical context is repeated later with
reference to discussion of the Qur'anic texts (*Sura* 9) which insist that
Jews and Christians be humiliated and pay the *jizya* (tax on non-Muslims): "These verses.... warrant a long historical and theological commentary. They have fed an interminable polemic from which there is no
escape because it is conducted at the dogmatic level. I cite them here not
to touch off new controversies but to attract attention to the urgent need
for a modern rereading of these sacred texts that takes account of historical context and doctrinal struggles aggravated by the appearance of the
Qur'an at the beginning of the seventh century." (p. 72).

Arkoun has also produced a number of articles which serve to illustrate both variety and change in Muslim perceptions of Christianity. For
example an article on revelation, first published in 1988 in *Die Welt des
Islams* (Vol 28, pp. 62-89), under the title "The notion of revelation:
from Ahl al-kitāb to the societies of the book", moves from discussion
of traditional Islamic concepts of revelation to a revised reading of the
concept, which is then applied to the traditional concept of the "Ahl al-
kitāb" (People of the Book). Arkoun thus insists that the fundamental
teachings of Muslim tradition must be submitted to the requirements of
modern historical analysis, the philosophical evaluation of the implicit
or explicit postulates of these teachings and the benefit of modern rationality and scientific thought (p. 63). A distinction is then drawn between
the two levels of revelation in the minds of Muslims: on the one hand

there is the Word of God related to the Heavenly Book, the *Umm al-kitāb*, which guarantees the authenticity and transcendence of the manifested book, the *Muṣḥaf*, which is the physical book, commonly used among Muslims, and on the other hand there is the literature produced by successive generations of Islamic scholars on the basis of that Word of God. In the Christian community, it is observed, Jesus Christ corresponds to the *Muṣḥaf* (p. 66).

There follows a detailed investigation of Sura 96 of the Qur'ān, with particular attention to its semiotic structure. It is argued that three participants are involved in the chapter, namely God, the prophet, and man, that the chapter is dominated by a technique of persuasion so that, rather like Jesus' parable of the sower in the New Testament, God announces a judgement or message, some people accept it while others reject it, and then at the Day of Judgement the believers are rewarded and the others are punished by God, and that this semiotic structure is shared by the Bible, the Gospels and the Qur'ān (p. 72). Professor Arkoun's terminology here is a little confusing, since he seems to use the term "Bible" to correspond to the *tawrāt* (Torah), but the main point, that Judaism, Christianity and Islam share something in this respect is surely valid. More detailed analysis follows of revelation in later Islamic thought, and it is suggested that in the main body of the Muslim community the Qur'ānic text came to be used not as text but as pretext, according to modern definitions, being rewritten in different contexts (pp. 77-78). All of this analysis is then applied to the concept of the *Ahl al-kitāb*, with the intention of illustrating "a pluralist reading of the Revelation manifested in the Qur'ān" (p. 82).

The article is an expanded version of a lecture delivered in 1987 at the Claremont Graduate School in California, and it contains much learned analytical discourse and abstract technical terminology, which the author insists is necessary "not for the sake of complexity or 'Parisian mode', but in order to accomplish a specific intellectual task" (p. 71). One thing which is very clear, however, is the author's constructive use of studies of different aspects of Islamic thought by Western scholars: there are references to "the still-valid studies of Geo Widengren" on the concept of the Heavenly Book (p. 65), the works of Paul Ricoeur and Northrope Frye on metaphor and metonymy in religious language (p. 70), W.M. Watt's insistence on taking into account the political, social and cultural situation in which early Islamic thought developed (p. 73), D.S. Powers' work on the science of Islamic Law (p. 79), and the works of Watt, W.C. Smith and Cragg on the Qur'ān (p. 88).

Some of these ideas are also referred to in a short article first published in the *Journal of Ecumenical Studies* (Vol 26, 1989, pp. 523-529), under the title "New perspectives for a Jewish-Christian-Muslim dialogue". Here Arkoun laments both the persistent tendency of Western journalists to give no attention to liberal Islam and the deeply-ingrained tradition in Western academic institutions for religious traditions to be taught quite separately, with little opportunity for fruitful dialogue even between the adherents of the three monotheistic traditions of the world. "Theological references are... used as *cultural systems for mutual exclusion*, never as tools to cross the traditional boundaries and to practice *new* religious thinking" (p. 524, author's italics). The author goes on to plead for the promotion of a new teaching of history, culture, religion, philosophy, theology, literature and law on a comparative basis, and this is illustrated with reference to the concept of revelation, which is explicated here as having *three* levels, rather than simply the two of the article referred to above, namely the transcendent word of God (e.g. the *Umm al-kitāb*), the historical manifestations of that word (e.g. through the Israelite prophets, Jesus of Nazareth and Mohammed), and the official closed canons of the communities which grew up around those manifestations (p. 526). There is further discussion of the theory of texts, and at the end of the article there is a plea for us "to be emancipated from inherited traditions not yet studied and interpreted with controlled methods and cognitive principles" (p. 528), which is reinforced in the final paragraph as follows:

> "Muslims are currently accused of being closed-minded, integrists, fundamentalists, prisoners of dogmatic beliefs. Here is a liberal, modern, humanist, Muslim proposal. I await the response of Jews, Christians, and secularists to my invitation to engage our thoughts, our endevors (sic), and our history in the cause of peace, progress, emancipation, justice through knowledge, and shared spiritual values." (pp. 528-529).

In a more recent pair of articles Prof. Arkoun has returned to these themes, but with some significant new emphases added. First of all, in an article originally published in *Revue des deux mondes* in April 1993, and reprinted, with a brief postscript in *Islamochristiana* (Vol 19, 1993, pp. 43-54), under the title "Réflexions d'un musulman sur le 'nouveau catéchisme'", he comments in a rather more focused manner on a specific document emanating from the majority branch of the Christian community today. Amidst considerable reference to global political issues and the involvement of Christian churches in past injustices in the second and third worlds, the main criticism voiced involves the whole tone in which the contents of the Catechism are expressed: it seems to reflect the views of theologians who claim a privileged position as spokesmen for God, and this, the author suggests, could have some interesting consequences with reference to Islam:

> "In these conditions, the rigid formulation of orthodox catholic doctrine in the 'new' Catechism can only accentuate the need of Muslims too to seek refuge in the same doctrinaire, intransigent reaffirmation of the ancient professions of faith." (p. 45, my translation).

Prof Arkoun even goes on to draw a comparison between the new catechism and *al-farīḍa al-ghā'iba* (The Neglected Duty) of Muḥammad 'Abd al-Salām Farag, the work which inspired the Jihād group in Egypt which was responsible for the assassination of President Sadat in Egypt in 1981[8]. He is careful to add in a footnote that this comparison refers only to the "closed, ahistorical and normative" structure of the discourse, and not to its contents, but this is clearly still a strong judgement. The exclusivist definition of revelation, which is assumed in the catechism, is then condemned, allied as it is with the old view of truth as one, which results in the assertion that the only historically authentic revelation is that accomplished in Jesus Christ. Prof. Arkoun then calls for a comparative approach to be adopted, where no form of reason can claim hegemony, so that a more inclusive approach is adopted and all people can be involved in investigating the claims which are made.

Most interesting, perhaps, is the final section of the article, in which Prof Arkoun comments on the place of Jesus of Nazareth in all of this. He makes it clear that these are personal ideas, but they are no less interesting for that:

> "... I think that what is communicated to the human conscience by the *incarnation* or word made flesh to live among us (the *logos* emanating from God, says the Qur'ān, *kalima min allāh*), the *passion* or suffering on the cross by love identifying itself with the finite and unhappy condition of man, the *resurrection* or rejection or denial of absolute, irreversible death, without trace or meaning; the reclaiming, on the contrary, of the unyielding desire to endure and to reach out towards the fullness of being, the *communion* in the sacrificial meal linking mystically, indefectibly, eternally (cf. the most trustworthy link, *al-'urwa al-wuthqā* of which the Qur'ān speaks), the living and the dead..., I think that this whole set of paradigms which try to make man fit for God are not superseded or exhausted

---

[8] On this group see J.J.G. Jansen *The Neglected Duty — the Creed of Sadat's Assassins and Islamic Resurgence in the Middle East*, London, Macmillan, 1986, and M. Youssef *Revolt against Modernity — Muslim Zealots and the West*, Leiden, Brill, 1985.

so much as put into language, symbol, parable, metaphor and action of the last resort and ultimate stakes for all human existence." (p. 52, author's italics, my translation).

The author adds that the gratuity of these paradigms must be preserved in the face of established orthodoxies, and in the final paragraph he poses a challenging question: how is it is that Christian societies have managed to become so far removed from such profound paradigms?

Some of these themes were developed further in an article in the 1994/3 volume of *Concilium*, which took the theme of "Islam: a challenge for Christianity". Prof Arkoun's contribution (pp. 48-57) was entitled "Is Islam threatened by Christianity?" After expressing some amazement at the title, since terms such as "threat" are surely not appropriate for use in connection with religions, it is argued that since both Christianity and Islam include much diversity it is hard to see how one can threaten the other. It is not denied, however, that under certain circumstances each *feels* the other to be a threat (e.g. 19th century Christian mission in North Africa, 20th century Islamic Revolution in Iran), but it is argued that in these settings "'Islam' and 'West' have ceased to refer to their objective contents... (and have come to)... function as powerful conglomerates of images, of prejudices..." (pp. 49-50). Today, Prof Arkoun suggests, Christianity bears the historical responsibility of being the only religion to have been associated, since the 18th century, with the hegemonic enterprises of capitalist Europe, but the loud voice of John Paul II, which is omnipresent in today's broken, divided and violent world, is a kind of exception to this. A more worthwhile task than the examination of "fantasy questions about the threat that Islam and Christianity might pose to each other" (p. 53), is the critical examination of the situation in Europe today whereby Enlightenment reason and religious reason confront each other in a rather intransigent manner.

Prof Arkoun's proposal for finding a way out of this apparent impasse is a highly original one: he suggests the convening of a Vatican III, which "would attempt to articulate a new language of hope, a semantic order which would be compelling for all consciences of the twentieth century, both those of the arrogant and cynical triumphalists... and those of the marginalized, the frustrated, the exploited, the dominated, the victims of uncontrolled forces". (pp. 53-54). This does not involve somehow setting Christianity above other religious traditions; on the contrary it would involve the explicit renunciation of all theological privilege and the recognition of the plurality of human articulations of meaning. The primary role allocated to Christianity in convening such an assembly is thus simply a result of that tradition's continuous exposure to the challenges of modernity:

> "It is this historical position which confers on Christianity not so much an intrinsic superiority as an intellectual responsibility, which in my view also implies a moral and spiritual responsibility". (p. 54).

In particular, a future Vatican III would have the cultural, intellectual and institutional resources, moral credit, and historical and symbolic capital necessary to make the realisation of such a task possible.

In slightly more detail the programme which Prof Arkoun suggests consists in outline of four main points: to move from an era of inter-faith dialogue to an era of thought and action founded on the historical solidarity and integration of the peoples; to move from theologies founded on themselves, and intended to promote reciprocal exclusion, to a radical criticism; to surmount the division between religious reason and Enlightenment reason or, in a pleasing phrase, between revelation and revolution; and to open up institutions of teaching and research to true comparative study of religion, so that both "the concern for orthodoxy and edification in establishments controlled by the religious authorities... (and)... the agnostic indifference and cold erudition of the state universities are removed from positions of dominance" (p. 56). This call for a Vatican III, the author suggests, is an implicit refutation of all discourse which presents Islam as a threat to the West, and partly for that reason may seem a rather utopian vision, but it represents the attempt of at least one Muslim intellectual to move on from the tragic confrontations of the past.

In Muḥammad Arkoun, then, we see a Muslim thinker who writes passionately about the need for the application of the methods and discoveries of new disciplines of thought to the religious domain. The social sciences in general, perhaps anthropology in particular, with its stress on the significance of religious traditions as sources of meaning, and literary criticism and hermeneutical theory, in his view, should all be taken up and used to illuminate and challenge different religious traditions of all kinds, including both Christianity and Islam.

Our third author, Ḥasan Askari, hails originally from the southern part of India, and differs from each of the authors discussed so far by virtue of the fact that he is a Shī'ī Muslim. His contribution to fresh Muslim understanding of Christianity may be illustrated through a brief review of three papers, some of which have been reprinted on a number of different occasions. Firstly, in a paper entitled "The dialogical relationship between Christianity and Islam", first published in *The Journal of Ecu-*

menical Studies, 9 (1972), pp. 477-488, and later reprinted in *Inter-religion* (Aligarh, Printwell Publications, 1972, pp. 62-71), and *Spiritual Quest*, (Leeds, Seven Mirrors, 1991, pp. 80-88), and also in L. Swidler's volume on Muslims in dialogue, pp. 37-47, Prof Askari argues clearly and specifically that there is a special relationship between the two faiths on the basis of the fact that they share so much of each other. Jesus, in particular, is a sign common to both, and by virtue of that commonality the relationship between the two communities should necessarily be one of dialogue:

> "All creeds, even the best of them, might turn their truth into a monologue. To me, personally, Christ, as Sign of God, liberates man from the dead circle of monological religion and restores unto him his genuine dialogical existence." (*Spiritual Quest*, p. 84).

Christ, indeed, is a symbol par excellence of the dialogical relationship between God and man, reminding us not to make a fetish of the revealed word, the book, since in this context the Word is supremely a person (pp. 85-86). This understanding, the author argues, may be helpful to Islam in balancing the stress there on word as book:

> "The truth is that Christianity and Islam constitute one complex of faith, one starting with the Person, and another with the Word. Their separateness does not denote two areas of conflicting truths, but a dialogical necessity." (p. 86).

An easy syncretism is thus clearly avoided, and the differences between the two traditions are not ignored, but what is stressed is their mutual dependence or complementarity. The differences are themes for conversation rather than confrontation.

A second contribution by Prof Askari has not, as far as I know, appeared in published form, but it was widely-influential among students in Birmingham during the period when he taught there and deserves to be better-known[9]. It consists of a simple but effective outline or schema of the Qur'ānic teaching about Jesus in terms of what it affirms and what it rejects. Sixteen points are referred to, as follows: the Qur'ān affirms Jesus as son of Mary, Jesus as prophet and messenger to the Children of Israel, the miracles of his birth and life, his moral teaching, his rejection by the Jews, his "ascension" into heaven, his being uplifted, his being word/sign/spirit, his role as Messiah, his special status as being "confirmed by the Holy Spirit", his prophecy of the Para-

---

[9] It is discussed in more detail in Chapter One of my forthcoming book *Muslim Perceptions of Christianity*, London, Grey Seal, 1995.

clete (understood as Aḥmad), the last supper, his disciples as "anṣār Allāh" (helpers of God), the Injīl (the Gospel in the form of a book), Christians as "People of the Book", and Christian piety. It rejects, however, Jesus as son of God, his universal/eternal mission, the incarnational understanding of his miracles, the doctrines of his redemptive power, his crucifixion, his death on the cross, his rising from the dead, his status as word made flesh, the implications of the title of Messiah in Christian theology, the uniqueness of Jesus, the doctrine of the Holy Spirit, the sacramental significance of the last supper, the disciples as being united "in Christ" by the power of the Spirit and the Eucharist, the authenticity of the Injīl in its Biblical form, the church as the body of Christ, and Christian belief about the divinity of Christ and the Trinity. Clearly there is no underestimation here of the differences between the two traditions, but on the other hand there is also a clear indication of how much is affirmed by the Qur'ān.

Thirdly, as an example of Prof Askari's positive appreciation of many of the aspects of Christian spirituality, he has written appreciatively of the Sermon on the Mount in particular. This was the theme of a lecture delivered at the Free University of Amsterdam in September 1977, subsequently published in *Spiritual Quest* (pp. 89-97), and it was also the theme of his inaugural lecture in Birmingham in 1978, under the title "The Sermon on the Mount: a Muslim view". Parallels are drawn between some of the themes of the Sermon and those associated with the death of al-Ḥusain in the Shī'ī Muslim tradition, and also between Sufi and Christian ideals, for "it is in the Sermon that the mystical streams of both Christianity and Islam converge" (p. 92). But this is not taken to mean that the message of the Sermon is somehow idealistic and otherworldly, for there is also an insistence that the Sermon's ethical and eschatological perspectives be taken seriously too.

Here, therefore, we have a fresh approach to Christianity which may be seen as being heavily influenced by Shī'ī and Sufi ideas, but it is none the less Islamic for that, and by his insistence on the inter-relationship between Christianity and Islam, not just historically but also existentially today, and on the need for differences of understanding to be reviewed through dialogue rather than through monologue, Prof Askari has significantly contributed to the development of new Muslim thinking about Christianity.

Maḥmūd Ayoub shares with Ḥasan Askari membership of the Shī'ī Muslim community, but the communities from which they come are rather different since for Askari it is the Shī'ī community of South Asia, whereas for Ayoub it is the Arabic-speaking Shī'ī community of south Lebanon. Ayoub is perhaps best-known for his compilation and editing of an extremely useful series of volumes consisting of English language translations of extracts from classical Muslim commentaries, both Sunnī and Shī'ī, on the Qur'ān, under the title *The Qur'ān and its Interpreters*. Two volumes have been published so far, Volume I, covering Suras One and Two, having been published in 1984, and Volume II, covering Sura Three, in 1992, both by the State University of New York Press. He is also well-known for his study *Redemptive Suffering in Islam: a Study of the Devotional Aspects of 'Ashūra in Twelver Shī'ism* (The Hague, Mouton, 1978).

In addition to these works, however, Ayoub has also written a number of articles reviewing modern Muslim understandings (or misunderstandings) of Christianity, for example an article on Muḥammad 'Abdūh (*Humaniora Islamica*, 2 (1974), pp. 121-137) and an article outlining the views of 'Abdūh, Rashīd Riḍā, Muḥammad Abū Zahra and Aḥmad Shalabī (*Islamochristiana*, 10 (1984), pp. 49-70). Each of these articles ends with a plea for Muslim thinking about Christianity to move on from, rather than simply reproduce, the polemical, or at best apologetic, approach represented by these authors.

He has also produced a number of articles calling for the development of better relationships between Christians and Muslims in today's world. Thus in "Roots of Muslim-Christian conflict" in *Muslim World*, 79 (1989), pp. 25-45, Ayoub reviews the history of Christian-Muslim misunderstanding, including such movements as the Crusades, Colonization, Evangelization and Orientalism, but then points to some more hopeful trends emerging in the modern period, such as the work of the British Council of Churches, as seen in the publication of *A New Threshold: Guidelines for the Churches in their Relations with Muslim Communities*, by David Brown (London, British Council of Churches, 1976), the Second Vatican Council's Declaration on non-Christian religions, and the much greater objectivity, sensitivity and appreciation of Islam among western academic scholars. And in "Islam and Christianity between tolerance and acceptance" in *Islam and Christian-Muslim Relations*, 2 (1991), pp. 171-181, after a review of the history of Christians (and Jews) under Islam Ayoub goes on to argue that in the medieval period "the ideals of love, universalism and openness which are basic to both faiths gave way to ideas of exclusivism and hostility on both sides" (p. 178). For today, however, "the challenge of the Qur'ān, I believe, and more to Muslims than to Christians, is to regard the people of the

Book as a large family of faith, speaking different languages, but worshipping the same God" (p. 179).

Even more interesting still are some articles relating to more specific
aspects of Christianity. In a 1985 article in *Islamochristiana* 11 (pp. 91-98)
Ayoub addresses the topic of Christian holiness, or spirituality, under the
title "A Muslim appreciation of Christian holiness". This article is significant for two main reasons: firstly because of the depth of knowledge
which the author reveals on the subject, so that the sacraments of baptism and the Eucharist are discussed in some depth, including the rather
different understandings of them which are evident among Eastern and
Western Christians; and secondly because of the warmth which it is evident that the author felt for Christian thought and practice in this area.
This is evident even in the title, for the paper was originally given at a
Colloquium on the subject of Holiness in Islam and Christianity, at
which six papers were delivered, two on the concept of holiness in the
two traditions, two on models of holiness and two evaluating and commenting on the other tradition's ideas. The fifth paper, by Jean-Marie
Gaudeul, is thus entitled "A Christian *critique* of Islamic holiness" (my
emphasis), but the sixth, by Ayoub, is entitled "A Muslim *appreciation*
of Christian holiness". The choice of word is surely significant.

Finally, in a pair of very interesting articles, Ayoub has put forward
some ideas for the development of an Islamic Christology. The first of
these is entitled "Towards an Islamic Christology: an image of Jesus in
early Shī'ī literature" (*Muslim World*, 66 (1976), pp. 163-188), and the
second "Towards an Islamic Christology II: the death of Jesus, reality or
delusion?" (*Muslim World*, 70 (1980), pp. 91-121). The two articles are
quite different. The first looks at the general picture of Jesus presented
in a number of Shī'ī texts in an attempt to illustrate the fact that knowledge of the Qur'ān alone is not sufficient to grasp the understanding of
Christ in Islam, for "the Christ of Muslim piety has continued to be a
living personality, humble and pious, forever thundering against the
wrongs of society, and full of wisdom and the Holy Spirit" (p. 163). The
second then focuses quite specifically on the disputed question of the
death of Jesus. Here Ayoub investigates the opinions of a number of
Muslim writers, both classical and modern, on this issue. There is a particular concentration on the Qur'ān commentary of Ṭabarī. On the basis
of this survey Ayoub then comes to an interesting conclusion:

> "The substitutionist theory will not do, regardless of its form or purpose.
> First, it makes mockery of divine justice and the primordial covenant of
> God with humanity, to guide human history to its final fulfillment. Would

it be in consonance with God's covenant, his mercy and justice, to deceive humanity for so many centuries? Or, can it be said that the argument of the commentators would really be meaningful to Christians? Muslim commentators have generally assumed an attitude of overconfident superiority towards the Christians whom they were supposed to guide to the truth. This attitude has been generally a polemical one in that it assumes... that the Christian witness to the Cross of Christ is based on a divine deception, and is therefore false." (pp. 104-105).

"The Qur'ān... does not deny the death of Christ. Rather, it challenges human beings who in their folly have deluded themselves into believing that they would vanquish the divine Word, Jesus Christ, the Messenger of God. The death of Jesus is asserted several times and in various contexts." (p. 106).

Here, then, Ayoub moves away quite dramatically from the most widely-accepted Muslim account of the end of Jesus' life, namely that not he but rather someone else was crucified, so that someone else was substituted for him on the cross.

The two articles together therefore seem to be attempting to do two things: firstly, particularly in the second article, to put right some widespread misunderstandings about Jesus within the Muslim community; and secondly, and perhaps more importantly, to ensure the recognition of the existence of a valid and legitimate Christology outside the Christian tradition, as argued in the first article. In a sense there has always been an Islamic Christology, or at least "Jesus-ology", but Ayoub's contribution is to use the term publicly and officially in a way that it has not really been used in before, and then to argue for this Christology to be given serious consideration more widely. This is a significant new departure[10].

Our next two authors both come from Tunisia and, indeed, are both members of staff in the Arts Faculty of the University of Tunis. 'Abd al-Majīd Charfi, first of all, is noteworthy firstly as the editor of the section on Muslim authors in the extremely useful Bibliography of Christian-Muslim dialogue published in *Islamochristiana* (1 (1975), pp. 152-169, 2 (1976), pp. 196-201, and 4 (1978), pp. 249-260). He has also written two very useful survey articles, one on "Christianity in the Qur'ān commentary of Ṭabarī" (*Islamochristiana*, 6 (1980), pp. 105-148) and the

---

[10] There are one or two books by Christian authors about Christology which do take some account of the existence of Islamic opinions on the question, but they very much represent the exception rather than the rule. One such book is F.F. Bruce's *Jesus and Christian Origins outside the New Testament*, London, Hodder and Stoughton, 1974, but this is clearly in the context of an investigation of "non-canonical" opinion on the question.

other on "L'islam et les religions non-musulmans — quelques textes
positifs" (*Islamochristiana*, 3 (1977), pp. 25-45), which contains translated extracts from the Ikhwān al-Ṣafā, al-Ghazālī, the al-Manār commentary, and Muḥammad Kāmil Ḥusain's *al-wādī al-muqaddas*. His
most substantial work is his thesis *Al-fikr al-islāmī fi'l-radd 'alā'l-
naṣārā ilā nihāyat al-qarn al-rābi'/al-'āshir* (*Islamic thought on the
refutation of the Christians to the end of the fourth/tenth century*, Tunis,
Maison Tunisienne de l'Édition, 1986). No English translation of this is
yet available, but there is a French translation of the Conclusion of the
thesis in *Islamochristiana*, 13 (1987), pp. 61-77, entitled "Pour une nouvelle approche du Christianisme par la pensée musulmane".

Here Prof Charfi argues quite simply that religious polemic is point-
less. This is as true of Byzantine polemic against Islam, on which he
quotes Adel-Théodore Khoury's judgement, as it is of Muslim polemic
against Christianity.

> "If one opens the New Testament and reads in the gospels the Sermon on
> the Mount, Jesus' meeting with the Samaritan woman, his attitude towards
> the woman caught in adultery, the Sabbath, the publicans and sinners, the
> Pharisees and the doctors of the law, one cannot but be astonished to see
> anyone, whatever their religion and narrowness of spirit, think for an
> instant to criticise the sublime teachings of these texts. They are nothing
> other than an ideal worthy of urging every man, whatever he be, to strive
> to realise them. What therefore happened that these people believed them-
> selves constrained to refute those who believed in these teachings? What
> happened was that those who considered themselves disciples of the Mes-
> siah have not, in reality, been faithful to his message, in the eyes of others.
> They have, in effect, created a theological and ecclesiastical system which,
> in the way that it functioned, is not attributable to him.
>
> "It is for these innovations that the Muslims refuted the Christians, on the
> basis of their conviction that the Muslim system is a divine system, based
> on the Qur'ān and the Tradition of the Prophet, not to mention its rational
> and logical foundation." (p. 64, my translation).

Prof Charfi then goes on to argue that questions of interpretation and
hermeneutics are important here, a view supported by references to Paul
Ricoeur. Each faith thus has its own logic and rationale.

> "The reader of these Muslim refutations could perhaps get the impression
> that Christians and Muslims lived on different planets. This impression is
> correct if one considers the theories of the two parties in themselves: no
> hope in effect of them agreeing without falling into a false syncretism. But
> this impression must be corrected by taking into consideration the agree-
> ment between the two parties with respect to mentality and methodology.
> They agree, despite everything, on faith in the existence of one God and

creator of all humankind; both have recourse to Greek categories to explain their faith and to Greek logic to prove it; in short both are dependent on the same epistemological framework." (p. 67, my translation).

The polemicists' whole discourse is thus a product of its own period and is therefore obsolete today. What is needed now, among other things, is a more subtle reading of the Qur'ān, taking into account the three elements inevitably involved in reading a text — the text itself, the context, and the personality of the reader — something which many contemporary Muslim writers about Christianity conspicuously fail to do. Study of classical Muslim polemic against Christianity thus reveals some things which should be rejected and some which should be retained:

> "What should be rejected is especially the contempt for the opposite party, the deformation of its views and the contents of its scriptures, and the desire to confound it by means of formal logic and sophist proofs. What should be kept is the finality of these refutations: the concern for the other, the wishing good for him, the effort to know with precision and detail what he believes, the defence of what the controversialist himself believes to be the truth, without thinking of forcing the other to accept it..." (p. 77, my translation).

In a more recent article, "La fonction historique de la polémique islamochrétienne à l'époque abbasside" in S.K. Samir and J.S. Nielsen (eds.) *Christian Arabic Apologetics during the Abbasid period (750-1258)* (Leiden, Brill, 1994) Prof Charfi outlines in rather more detail some of the functions which this Muslim polemic was intended to carry out. Again, therefore, we see the prominence given to the importance of looking at context as well as text. Six points in particular are referred to: demographic factors (the fact that Muslims were in a minority in this period); the concern for the integration of converts without syncretism; the theological elaboration of Islam (the need to conserve boundaries); research concerning the roots of the faith of Islam (as seen in the search for the authentication of Muḥammad in the Bible); the need for a solution for social antagonism between the communities; and the defence of Islamic civilization against other civilizations. These works of polemic therefore "fulfilled a rich and multiple function which must be put in its particular historical context, that of a culture and a civilization which were right in the middle of elaboration at the start of the Abbasid period..." (p. 56, my translation)[11].

---

[11] See also Prof Charfi's paper in this volume, in which once again he refers to six factors which need to be kept in mind, but this time in looking at the contemporary relationship between Islam and Christianity.

Prof Ghrab is included in our discussion particularly because of an article entitled "Islam and Christianity: from opposition to dialogue", originally delivered at a Colloquium in Tunis in 1984 on the subject of "Islam facing today's challenges", and subsequently published in *Islamo-christiana*, 13 (1987), pp. 99-111. In this paper a certain contrast is drawn between relationships between Jews and Muslims on the one hand, and between Christians and Muslims in the other. With respect to the former relationship, initial hostility in the time of Muḥammad grad-ually gave rise to an improvement in the relationship, which has only been threatened in recent times by the creation of the state of Israel. Concerning the latter relationship, however, it is the other way around: initial warmth gave rise to increasing tension. This resulted in part from the fact that both Christianity and Islam proclaim universal messages, so that each has universal aspirations. There are also clashes over their creeds, notably over the Trinity/the divinity of Jesus, the question of the cross of Jesus, and the announcement of Muḥammad's coming. And there are also examples of overt conflicts, such as the Crusades, the cap-ture of Constantinople in 857/1453, the Reconquista in Spain, and mo-dern colonialism, in reaction to which "... in general the Islamic religion played an active role in strengthening the resolve to resist the intruder" (p. 106).

On the other hand there are also more positive aspects to the relation-ship. In the twelfth century of the Christian calendar some Western Europeans began to develop a more positive appreciation of Islamic cul-ture, and in the current century Christians have begun to develop a new attitude towards Islam. Vatican II's statement concerning the relation-ship of the Roman Catholic Church to Muslims is quoted extensively.

> "To some this new attitude appears insignificant, but to our mind it is important when a comparison is made with that which predominated in bygone days. It is necessary in my opinion for this new attitude to be appreciated fully on the part of Muslims. For it is always difficult for a prior religion to recognize in one way or another a subsequent religion..." (p. 107).

It is true that not all Christians share this move towards a more posi-tive attitude towards Islam; some Arab Christians in particular have been very mistrustful of it. Many Muslims have also been cautious towards the idea of dialogue with Christians. But the author is clear con-cerning his own attitude to the question:

> "We have to be honest with ourselves and say that dialogue today must move away from the style of the ancient disputation. For its aim in fact is

not invitation to Islam… or mission… or loathsome byzantine controversy. Its fundamental goal is knowledge of the other as the other wishes to be, and not as it pleases us to imagine him, and on the basis of *his* texts and *his* heritage and not merely on the basis of *our* texts." (p. 109, author's italics).

The author freely concedes that there are not many Muslim scholars whose knowledge of Christianity goes beyond what can be found in classical literature, but he adds that there is still widespread ignorance of Islam among Christians, despite the existence of many Christian scholars who know Islam and Muslims better than the Muslims themselves, so both communities have some way to go to reach mutual understanding. But the hope is there of this happening.

Our next writer, the seventh under consideration, is the one who stands a little on his own in our list, simply because unlike all the others he is not an academic but a figure who is actively involved in the political realm. He is Crown Prince Hasan of Jordan, and he is included in virtue of his book *Christianity in the Arab World*, published in 1994 by Arabesque in Amman. The author freely acknowledges at the start of the book that the research for it was carried out by the staff of the Royal Institute for Inter-Faith Studies in Amman, and a particular debt is acknowledged to the Director of the Institute Kamal Salibi, who is well-known for his writings on the history of the Lebanon in particular. The book is essentially historical in its treatment of the subject, with four chapters looking at the history of the Christian church in the Middle East prior to the coming of Islam, two chapters then looking at the Iconoclast Controversy and the Schism between East and West, one chapter investigating the position of Christians under the early centuries of Islam, and the remaining chapters then tracing more modern developments — the Maronite Union with Rome and the emergence of Uniate and Protestant churches, with the final chapter then surveying the position of Christians in the modern Arab world. This acknowledges the key role played by Christians in the Arab renaissance of the nineteenth century, not least in laying the intellectual foundations for the idea of Arab nationalism, and also the prominent role taken by many Christian Arabs in presenting the views of the nations to which they belong on the international stage in the twentieth century. The view is then expressed that despite the considerable concern about the future of Christian Arabs expressed both in international circles and among Arab Christians themselves, especially with respect to "the waves of Islamic fundamentalism which have been sweeping a number of Arab countries during the last decade" (p. 97), reassurance may be provided, as follows:

"People who entertain such concern or fear rarely take into account that it is in the nature of waves, no matter what their apparent enormity, to subside once they have consumed their initial driving force, especially in the case of waves of social behaviour driven by ephemeral emotion rather than by solid reason." (pp. 97-98).

The book is not particularly original or profound in its description and analysis, but despite this it is surely worthy of note that the designated heir to the throne of the Hashemite kingdom of Jordan has been prepared to put his name publicly to the production of such a book and to sponsor the Institute which has done much of the work for it[12].

Our next writer, like a number of others we have already looked at, comes originally from North Africa. 'Alī Merad was born in Algeria, and after a number of years as Professor of Arabic Literature and Civilisation in the University of Lyon he has recently moved to Paris to take up the post recently vacated at the Sorbonne by Professor Arkoun upon his retirement.

Prof Merad's contribution to the development of new Muslim thinking about Christianity comes in two main places. The first is an article published in the *Revue de l'occident musulman*, 5 (1968), pp. 79-94 and later translated into English in *Encounter*, No. 69, November 1980, under the title "Christ according to the Qur'ān". The author begins by stating clearly that "To Muslims, the figure of Christ is certainly the most fascinating among those in the Qur'ān. But to the extent to which it invokes in Muslims an interest tinged with admiration, to the same extent it gives rise to questions which disturb them..." (p. 2). It is acknowledged that Muslim commentaries do not shed light on the figure of Christ in the way he deserves and that Muslim exegesis "whether traditional or of modern reformist authors, does not satisfy our desire for knowledge." (p. 3). The author therefore explains his intention of presenting "a personal perusal of the Qur'ān around the central theme of Christ" (p. 3) which, he writes, must include taking the Qur'ān as a whole since it has its own logic and coherence, so the different Qur'anic passages about Christ will be examined, in an interesting phrase, "Synoptically" (p. 4).

---

[12] Partly as a result of the work of the Institute Crown Prince Hasan was invited to preach a sermon in Christ Church Cathedral in Oxford on 4th June 1995, the first person who is not a Christian ever to have been given such an invitation. There were a number of Christian protests against the invitation, and one interruption took place at the start of the sermon itself, but on the whole the Prince's call for mutual tolerance and interfaith dialogue was well received.

Prof Merad then goes on to examine firstly what the Qur'ān denies of Christ and then what it affirms of him, firstly about his identity and secondly about his nature. Thus Christ is designated Messiah, prophet, and servant of God, and with respect to his nature it is clearly denied that he is God. But this does not mean that he is simply man (*bashar*), for his miraculous birth and his status as word (*kalima*) and spirit (*rūḥ*) from God "would suggest a spiritual nature infinitely more eminent than ordinary natures" (p. 10). Not only that but the term *bashar* is never actually applied to Christ in the Qur'ān, so "Through all that the Qur'ān has to say about Jesus, we cannot fail to recognise an unquestionable convergence: everything it gives leads to the declaration of Christ's surpassing greatness." (p. 11).

Christ is placed above the ordinary level of the Envoys of God by virtue of the fact that he alone brings the dead to life. This does not mean that Christ shares the sovereign freedom of God or participates in the omniscience of the Creator, but it does indicate that his mission is without precedence. The mystery of Christ's death, moreover, is the crowning point of his surpassing greatness, since the elevation of Christ is a gratuitous act of God, and affirms the final triumph of hope despite all trials. On this basis the Qur'ān's picture of Christ is completely coherent. Christ is:

"A dominant figure among the Envoys of God, an exceptional being, whose creation is given the same significance as that of Adam; for both represent unique points in the destiny of mankind on earth; Adam's creation indicates its beginning, that of Christ its spiritual consummation." (p 15).

A final section then points to a further lesson from the whole teaching of the Qur'ān concerning Jesus, namely an appeal for a united search for truth. Some elements of the Qur'ān "are proposed as a subject of reflection for Muslims and for the People of the Book, that is in this context for Christians" and "what it (the Qur'ān) seeks to do in this domain, seems to be to provoke reflection rather than to furnish final answers." (p. 16). On this basis "how can we fail to wish that, with the help of this essential theme of Christ, Christians and Muslims be increasingly imbued with the desire for dialogue, with a view to mutual understanding and appeasement." (p. 17).

This same spirit is manifested in an article Prof Merad wrote in the first volume of *Islamochristiana* (1975, pp. 1-10), entitled "Dialogue islamo-chrétien: pour la recherche d'un langage commun". After a review of some of the misunderstandings which have been evident in the history of the relationship between Christians and Muslims, the author asks whether the result is simply an impasse, and part of his answer is to suggest that perhaps the Qur'ān is not so radical concerning the demythologisation of divinity as many Muslims think, and on the other hand perhaps Christianity runs the risk of idolatry in its teachings about Christ. On this basis there is a need for a new language and a new mode of communication, so that the stage of parallel monologues is superseded by the stage of true dialogue on themes such as Abraham and Christ. The appeal to move on to a new level of understanding is thus clearly presented here.

Our next writer, Seyyed Hossein Nasr, comes from a part of the world which we have not referred to so far, namely Iran, and he is therefore a Shī'ī Muslim, but in that he is not unique among our authors for others whom we have discussed already are also Shī'ī. Nasr is perhaps unique, however, in his knowledge of the whole philosophical tradition in Islam, which was preserved in Iran even when it had become weakened among Sunnīs, and this gives him a particular perspective on Christianity.

Among other things Nasr is the author of perhaps one of the simplest and yet most profound accounts of the real differences which exist between Christianity and Islam. This can be found in his *Ideals and Realities of Islam*, 2nd ed., Allen and Unwin, 1975, pp. 21-22:

> "Christianity is essentially a mystery which veils the Divine from man. The beauty of Christianity lies in the acceptance of God as mystery, and in bowing before this mystery... In Islam, however, it is man who is veiled from God. The Divine Being is not veiled from us, we are veiled from Him and it is for us to try to rend this veil asunder, to try to know God... Islam is thus essentially a way of knowledge; it is a way of gnosis (*ma'rifah*)."

This view has been amplified in a number of other more recent publications. In the first part of the Postscript to Nasr's *Islamic life and thought*, Allen and Unwin, 1981, there is a brief section entitled "Jesus through the eyes of Islam" (pp. 209-211). Here Nasr states clearly that Islam does not accept the idea of incarnation or filial relationship, and that the Qur'ān does not accept that Jesus was crucified, the one "irreducible 'fact' separating Christianity and Islam, a fact which is in reality placed there providentially to prevent a mingling of the two religions." (p. 209). "All the other doctrines, such as the question of the nature of Christ or the Trinity, can be understood metaphysically in such a way as to harmonise the two perspectives." (pp. 209-210). Jesus' three main functions, according to the Qur'ān, are to preserve the Torah, celebrate and perpetuate the Eucharist, and announce the coming of the Prophet of

Islam; these functions thus represent the past, present and future aspects of his ministry. "… the Islamic conception of Christ… could enable Christians to realise that the sun of their spiritual world which they so love is also a shining star in the firmament of another world and plays an important role in the religious and spiritual economy of another human collectivity." (p. 211).

"The Islamic view of Christianity" in *Concilium*, No. 183 (Feb. 1986), pp. 3-12, takes this a little further and there are some interesting shifts of opinion evident here. After insisting that the traditional Islamic view of Christianity is founded on the acceptance of Christianity as a religion revealed by God, Nasr continues: "There is, however, on the basis of the acceptance of the Divine Origin of the Christian message and reverance (sic) of an exceptional character for Christ and the Virgin, a rejection in the Quran itself of both the doctrine of the Trinity and the incarnation." (p. 5). Nasr thus seems to have moved away from any allowance for the possibility of these ideas being amenable to harmonisation through metaphysical understanding to outright rejection. These doctrines, he now writes, are aspects of the Christian religion which Islam came to abrogate. Muslims also have difficulties with Christian ethics, because of the absence of a divine law and an approach which is rather idealistic. But Muslims appreciate Christian piety, especially in their mystical literature, and so the problems of the history of Christian-Muslim relations, the Crusades and modern Christian mission, must not be allowed to over-ride the need for co-existence and mutual acceptance. Nasr is harsh in his judgement on fundamentalism at this point: "The fire of hatred burns bonds of amity and shrivels the soul of the faithful, whether they be Muslim or Christian." (p. 9). And with respect to those Muslims who do seek mutual acceptance, "The voice of such Muslims might seem to be drowned out at the moment by the cry and fury of those who preach hatred in the name of justice and who even insult other religions in direct opposition to the injunctions of the Qur'ān. But the voice of understanding and harmony cannot but triumph at the end…" (p. 10).

A more detailed examination of common ground between the two traditions may be found in Nasr's article on "The prayer of the heart in Hesychasm and Sufism" in *Greek Orthodox Theological Review*, 31 (1986), pp. 195-203. This ends with the following challenge: "More than ever before what matters is the prayer of the heart which has been miraculously preserved to this day in the Orthodox tradition while it continues as the central practice of Sufis throughout the Islamic world.

To understand the significance of this prayer in Hesychasm and Sufism is to grasp the profound inner resemblances between Christian and Islamic spirituality. To practice the prayer of the heart is to enter that sacred sanctuary where all diversity returns to unity and where every divine message is seen as a reflection of the face of the Beloved who is One although speaking many tongues." (p. 203). Even if, therefore, in some respects, Nasr seems to have become more rigid over his understanding of certain Christian teachings such as Incarnation and Trinity, there is no denying his continuing commitment to the existence of significant common ground in the area of spirituality.

Our final author once again comes from North Africa. Muḥammad Talbi is now Emeritus Professor of History in the University of Tunis, where he taught for a number of years and where among his pupils were 'Abd al-Majīd Charfi and Saad Ghrab, whom we have looked at earlier. His article "Islam and dialogue" is regarded by many people as one of the most important works yet written about Christian-Muslim dialogue.[13]

Prof Talbi begins by stating that dialogue is necessary and vital for Islam so that it can re-establish its contact with the world. This is all the more urgent and salutary for Islam than for other religions since many of them never really lost this contact. Islam, moreover, is called to dialogue with other people, and especially with the People of the Book, by its scripture, no less. This dialogue is not without its problems — issues such as *jihād* in the past, and today the problem of the disparity which exists between the partners in the dialogue, especially because of the relative underdevelopment theologically of the Muslim world. Islam, therefore, must surmount these difficulties and get involved in the dialogue. That dialogue should eschew polemic and renounce the goal of conversion, for God alone converts. The plurality of the ways of salvation should be acknowledged since God is the proper judge of human beings, and they should not set themselves up in God's place.

The object of dialogue is thus the disinterested service of God, of the Good and of Truth. In a nice phrase it is observed that intellectual protectionism is as vain as economic protectionism. To retreat into oneself is regarded as being like taking morphine in order to die more quietly.

---

[13] First published in 1972 by Maison Tunisienne de l'Édition, translated into English in *Encounter*, Nos. 11 and 12, February 1975, and reprinted in R.W. Rousseau (ed.) *Islam and Christianity: the Struggling Dialogue*, Scranton, Pennsylvania, Ridge Row Press, 1985, pp. 53-73.

Dialogue, then, is to prevent people becoming stuck in their own convictions. Dialogue cannot be avoided. It involves listening, and it involves new exegesis, not in order to destroy the riches of past exegesis but in order to restore the climate of exchange and tension, even of adventure. If the Word of God is eternal, it transcends time and space, so there is always a need to hear it afresh. Muslims need to be aroused from their false comfort and respond afresh to that Word of God. The vocation of religion is to be perpetually in crisis, for truth is not something which we can grasp but rather something which guides us. Dialogue, therefore, serves to re-animate our faith. This will not, to be sure, be easy. It will need much patience. But it will enable all who participate in it to go beyond their current certainties. "The road to the kingdom of God will be long and God has willed it enveloped in mystery." The final call, then, is to get up and start work.

Prof Talbi has returned to many of these themes in a whole series of articles, some published in *Islamochristiana*, to which he has been a regular contributor, and some in other journals too. Just to take one example, in an article in the *Journal of Ecumenical Studies*, 25 (1988), pp. 161-193, and reprinted in L.E. Swidler's volume on Muslims in dialogue, pp. 111-153, entitled "Possibilities and conditions for a better understanding between Islam and the West", he has investigated the problem of the misunderstandings which have grown up during the long history of interaction between the West and Islam, in part at least because of some of the fundamental differences between Islam and Christianity. The different approaches towards politics and towards the position of women in society are therefore examined.

> "... the misunderstandings between Islam and the West are not the product of mere chance or the result of miscellaneous and transitory facts but are deeply rooted in quite different or frankly contradictory social options. They are reflections of oppositions with respect to dogma, ethics, culture and civilization... (and)... they continue to underlie the judgments and discourses on the other, as well as both individual and overall reactions." (p. 168).

Caricatures therefore persist on both sides, but if there is a readiness on both sides to treat the other partner as an equal, then there is hope of a dialogue emerging. Some in each community try to disguise or disown the fact that in the course of history there has sometimes been positive exchange between the two communities and that ideas have sometimes been passed from one to the other. There is therefore a long history of symbiosis and exchange.

"At the level of faith, in a world that is becoming everywhere more pluralistic as well as secularized, Jews, Christians and Muslims — whether in
Islamic or Western countries — no longer have any alternative but to
explore in common their various points of agreement." (p. 190).

At the end of the article Prof Talbi then sums up the situation as follows:

"... Islam needs the West and the West needs Islam, and all of us together,
with our vocations, or our universal pretensions, need the other cultures, all
the cultures, vigorous and very much alive..." (p. 193).

And clearly in the dialogue between Islam and the West a primary role,
in Prof Talbi's view, is allotted to the dialogue between Muslims and
Christians in particular.

More recently Prof Talbi has provided us with a more personal
account of some of his views. This may be found in his article
"Unavoidable dialogue in a pluralist world: a personal account" in
Encounters: Journal of Inter-cultural Perspectives, 1 (1995), pp. 56-69.
In this article, in a new journal, we have a broadly autobiographical
account of the development of the author's thinking. He tells of how he
was educated in the pluralistic world of a French school. Then, after
World War II, he went to France to study and found himself immersed
in a completely different society. One landlady was a particular influence:

"In her company, I attended for the first time in my life Dominical Mass
and, from this moment onwards, I discovered in Paris, in France and elsewhere, the beauty and majesty of the cathedrals which I had never before
visited in Tunisia." (p. 59).

He also discovered that

"... Western society cannot be reduced, as we used to think, to the twink-
ling and glittering facades of the public bars and dancing-halls. More than
ever before it appeared to me that the true 'followers of the Book'... are
really pious, seeking salvation, and striving sincerely in the way of God,
moved by values of charity and love of their neighbours. They pray. In
these conditions, how, without pain and questioning, to dedicate them to
Hell!" (p. 59).

Prof Talbi goes on to describe his fascination with the spirituality of
Louis Massignon, his return to France for doctoral studies, his marriage
to a German girl, and his interest in history:

"I found myself profoundly hurt by the way people of one faith, or different faiths, have always fought... each other in the name of God, for God
and/or guided by God." (p. 60).

It was on the basis of this kind of observation that the author then describes how he came to be committed to communication and to dialogue. He explains how close he felt himself to be to the general frame of thought of the Roman Catholic theologian Karl Rahner. And he concludes by saying that dialogue must not fail because there is no alternative to it. Dialogue is thus the solution for the future.

This more personal account of the development of an interest in dialogue in one contemporary Muslim writer is perhaps a very suitable way to end our review of contemporary Muslim writings concerning Christianity, which I hope has served to illustrate both the variety which exists and the extent to which change is evident in at least some writings. We turn now to look at the question of how and why these different thinkers have contributed, in different ways, to the growth of new, and usually more perceptive, Muslim understandings of Christianity.

Factors conducive to change

Firstly, as was the case for Muḥammad Kāmil Ḥusain and Syed Vahiduddin, our authors' biographies and life experiences are at least partly responsible for their changing views of Christianity. This is probably most obviously the case with Maḥmūd Ayoub, whose perhaps unique grasp of Christianity comes in part from his having been at times an insider in the Christian community: as a result of his blindness he was educated at a Mission School in South Lebanon which was run by American Southern Baptists. As a child he joined the Southern Baptist Church, but as he grew up he became increasingly dissatisfied with the way in which rather simple answers were given there to many questions, so he became involved with the Society of Friends (the Quakers), whose deeper, more mystical message, with its stress on "the inner light" clearly exercised a powerful appeal for him. Ayoub also felt the attraction of the mystery of worship as expressed in the Eastern Orthodox churches. The end result of this pilgrimage, however, was a return to his origins in the Shī'ī Muslim community, but as a result of this whole process Ayoub is surely a Shī'ī Muslim with an absolutely unique appreciation of Christianity, as illustrated in his paper entitled "A Muslim *appreciation* of Christian holiness" (my italics).

Just to take one other example from among the writers whom we have looked at, Prof Talbi, in his 1995 article on his personal account of his journey to the acceptance of dialogue in a pluralist world, shows clearly how important some of his experiences in France were for the development of not only his understanding of but also his attitude towards Christianity.

Secondly, the influence of particular teachers must also be recognised as being extremely significant. The fact that five of the ten contemporary authors whom we have looked at are originally from North Africa and thus operate in a Francophone intellectual milieu is important here, and the influence of the towering figure of Louis Massignon must therefore be recognised. Three of our authors, Profs Arkoun, Merad and Talbi, studied under Massignon and pay warm tribute to his influence, and since Profs Charfi and Ghrab then studied under Prof Talbi, the *silsila* (chain of transmission) continues. Another figure of considerable influence, especially for Prof Merad, was Charles de Foucauld, on whom Prof Merad wrote a short book *Charles de Foucauld au regard de l'islam* (Paris, Chalet, 1976). Given that one of the features in common between Massignon and de Foucauld was their recovery of faith, Christian faith, through contact with the faith of Muslims, it is interesting to see how their biographies through their later contacts with Muslim students in turn contributed to the development of changing Muslim perceptions of Christianity.

Something similar may also be seen with reference to our other contemporary thinkers, even if not so clearly focused on particular teachers. Nearly all of them studied at some stage of their careers in the West, either in other parts of Europe or in North America, and so the influence of a teacher such as Wilfred Cantwell Smith may be seen on, for example, Maḥmūd Ayoub, and the fact that for Crown Prince Hasan, while studying in England during the 1967 Middle East War, one of his tutors in Oxford was Jewish, is surely significant for explaining his positive attitude towards inter-faith dialogue.

Thirdly, the past forty years have also seen greatly increased opportunities for contact and serious discussion between Christian and Muslim scholars and the importance of this too cannot be underestimated in seeking to explain changing Muslim perceptions of Christianity. If we look, for example, at what, in my view, are the three most valuable products of different dialogues between Christians and Muslims, we will see how many of our authors were involved in them.

Firstly, Youakim Moubarac's *Verse et controverse: le chrétien en dialogue avec le monde 14: les musulmans, consultation islamo-chrétienne*, (Paris, Beauchesne, 1971) involved the sending of a questionnaire to seven Muslims and the editing of their responses by Fr. Moubarac. Four of the seven are among those whom we have discussed:

Muḥammad Kāmil Ḥusain from an earlier generation, and then Professors Arkoun, Askari and Nasr.

Secondly, the 1972 conference organised by the World Council of Churches and held in Broumana in the Lebanon, the report of which, edited by Stanley Samartha and John Taylor (Geneva, World Council of Churches, 1973), includes some of the most profound and original contributions to dialogue, and also reflects the real sense of encounter and engagement which characterised the meeting itself, included Professors Askari, Ayoub and Merad among its participants.

And thirdly, the Groupe de Recherches Islamo-Chrétien (GRIC), which has made a unique contribution to Christian-Muslim dialogue as a result of on-going participation over many years by the same members, helping to bring about continuity and progression, has included among its members Profs Arkoun, Charfi, Ghrab and Talbi. The results of the work of GRIC are most accessible in English in their report *The Challenge of the Scriptures* (Maryknoll, New York, Orbis, 1989), the introduction to which gives a useful account of the genesis and method of operation of the group, and there is a further article about the group by R. Caspar in *Islamochristiana*, 4(1978), pp. 175-186.

In connection with GRIC mention must also be made of the contribution of the Pontifical Institute of Arabic and Islamic Studies in Rome in facilitating interaction on an on-going basis between Christian and Muslim scholars. This may be seen in the fact that several of the important articles we have looked at were based on lectures which were originally given at the Institute; examples of this are Prof Merad's article on Christ in the Qur'ān (originally delivered in April 1968) and Prof Talbi's article on Islam and dialogue (originally delivered in November 1971). In his 1995 article outlining his own personal pilgrimage to dialogue Prof. Talbi explains how significant this invitation was for him, since it provided him with an opportunity to clarify his own thoughts in the city which had earlier destroyed Carthage, had in its turn been sacked (in 846) by the Aghlabids (from what is now Tunisia), and then more recently been the scene of Vatican II (p. 62). It is also from P.I.S.A.I. that there comes the journal *Islamochristiana*, and the importance of that may be seen in the number of times it has been referred to during the course of this paper.

The friendships which, as we have seen, were important for Muḥammad Kāmil Ḥusain and Syed Vahiduddin, have thus also enabled our contemporary Muslim thinkers to develop their thinking, and the importance of this in explaining changing perceptions of Christianity among Muslims, as indeed changing Christian perceptions of Islam, cannot be underestimated.

Conclusion

At the end of a survey such as this one obvious question springs to mind, namely how representative of Muslim opinion worldwide are the views and opinions which we have examined. The simple answer to this question may be "not very", not least since five of our ten contemporary writers (Profs Arkoun, Askari, Ayoub, Merad and Nasr) are currently working outside the Muslim world. But working in the West does not necessarily disqualify someone's claim to be making a legitimate or significant contribution to the development of Islamic thought. It could also be observed that of the five thinkers who are working inside the Muslim world, three are in one country — Tunisia — with the other two in Jordan and Malaysia. These countries may not be representative of the Muslim world as a whole. But all change has to begin somewhere, and from its beginnings, wherever and whenever they might be, it may or may not grow and gain wider acceptance. Given that the title of this paper, however, is "Christianity from the Muslim perspective: varieties and changes", I hope that it has succeeded in illustrating that at least in some parts of the world and in the minds of some Muslim thinkers, we may see both considerable variety and significant change in Muslim perceptions of Christianity.

BIBLIOGRAPHY

AKHTAR, S., *Be Careful with Muhammad: the Salman Rushdie Affair*, London, Bellew, 1989.
—, *The Light in the Enlightenment: Christianity and the Secular Heritage*, London, Grey Seal, 1990.
—, *A Faith for all Seasons: Islam and Western Modernity*, London, Bellew, 1990.
—, "Faust and the new idolaters: reflections on *shirk*" in *Islam and Christian-Muslim Relations*, 1 (1990), pp. 252-260.
—, *The Final Imperative: an Islamic Theology of Liberation*, London, Bellew, 1991.
—, "An Islamic model of revelation" in *Islam and Christian-Muslim Relations*, 2 (1991), pp. 95-105.
ARKOUN, M., "The notion of revelation: from ahl al-kitab to the societies of the book" in *Die Welt des Islams*, 28 (1988), pp. 62-89.
—, "New perspectives for a Jewish-Christian-Muslim dialogue" in *Journal of Ecumenical Studies*, 26 (1989), pp. 523-529, reprinted in L.E. Swidler (ed.)

Muslims in Dialogue: the Evolution of a Dialogue, Lewiston, New York, Edwin Mellen Press, 1992, pp. 345-352.

—, "Réflexions d'un musulman sur le 'nouveau catéchisme'" in *Islamochristiana*, 19 (1993), pp. 43-54.

—, "Is Islam threatened by Christianity?" in *Concilium*, 1994/3, pp. 48-57.

—, *Rethinking Islam: Common Questions, Uncommon Answers*, Boulder, Colorado, Westview, 1994.

ASKARI, H., *Inter-religion*, Aligarh, Printwell Publications, 1977.

—, "Within and beyond the experience of religious diversity" in J. Hick and H. Askari (eds.), *The Experience of Religious Diversity*, London, Gower, 1985, pp. 191-218.

—, *Spiritual Quest: an Inter-religious Dimension*, Leeds, Seven Mirrors, 1991.

AYOUB, M.M., "Islam and Christianity — a study of Muḥammad 'Abdūh's views of the two religions" in *Humaniora Islamica*, 2 (1974), pp. 121-137.

—, "Towards an Islamic Christology: an image of Jesus in early Shī'ī Muslim literature" in *The Muslim World*, 66 (1976), pp. 163-188.

—, *Redemptive Suffering in Islam*, The Hague, Mouton, 1978.

—, "Towards an Islamic Christology II: the death of Jesus, reality or delusion?" in *The Muslim World*, 70 (1980), pp. 91-121.

—, "Muslim views of Christianity: some modern examples" in *Islamochristiana*, 10 (1984), pp. 49-70.

—, "The word of God and the voices of humanity" in J. Hick and H. Askari (eds.), *The Experience of Religious Diversity*, London, Gower, 1985, pp. 53-65.

—, "A Muslim appreciation of Christian holiness" in *Islamochristiana*, 11 (1985), pp. 91-98.

—, "Martyrdom in Christianity and Islam" in *Newsletter of the Centre for the Study of Islam and Christian-Muslim Relations*, Birmingham, No. 14, November 1985, pp. 4-14, reprinted in R.T. Antoun and M.E. Hegland (eds.), *Religious Resurgence — Contemporary Cases in Islam, Christianity and Judaism*, New York, Syracuse U.P., 1987, pp. 67-77.

—, "Roots of Christian-Muslim conflict" in *The Muslim World*, 79 (1989), pp. 25-45.

—, "Islam and Christianity between tolerance and acceptance" in *Islam and Christian-Muslim Relations*, 2 (1991), pp. 171-181.

CASPAR, R., "Le groupe de recherches islamo-chrétien" in *Islamochristiana*, 4 (1978), pp. 175-186.

CHARFI, A., "L'islam et les religions non-musulmannes — quelques textes positifs" in *Islamochristiana*, 3 (1977), pp. 39-63.

—, "Christianity in the Qur'ān commentary of Ṭabarī" in *Islamochristiana*, 6 (1980), pp. 105-148.

—, *Al-fikr al-islāmī fī'l-radd 'alā'l-naṣārā ilā nihāyat al-qarn al-rābi'/al'āshir*, Algiers and Tunis, Maison Tunisienne de l'Édition, 1986.

—, "Pour une nouvelle approche du Christianisme par la pensée musulmane" in *Islamochristiana*, 13 (1987), pp. 61-77.

—, "La fonction historique de la polémique islamochrétienne à l'époque abbasside" in S.K. Samir and J.S. Nielsen (eds.), *Christian Arabic Apologetics during the Abbasid Period (750-1258)*, Leiden, Brill, 1994, pp. 44-56.

GHRAB, S., "Islam and Christianity: from opposition to dialogue" in *Islamo-christiana*, 13 (1987), pp. 99-111.

GODDARD, H.P., "Modern Pakistani and Indian Muslim perceptions of Christianity" in *Islam and Christian-Muslim Relations*, 5 (1994), pp. 165-188.

—, *Muslim Perceptions of Christianity*, London, Grey Seal, 1995.

GRIFFITHS, P.J., (ed.), *Christianity through non-Christian Eyes*, Maryknoll, New York, Orbis, 1990.

HASAN, Crown Prince, *Christianity in the Arab World*, Amman, Arabesque, 1994.

HERBERT, D., "Shabbir Akhtar on Muslims, Christians and British society" in *Islam and Christian-Muslim Relations*, 4 (1993), pp. 100-117.

ḤUSAIN, M.K., *Qarya ẓālima*, first published 1954, 4th printing, Cairo, Makta-bat al-nahḍa al-miṣriyya, 1974; English translation by Kenneth Cragg, *City of Wrong*, Amsterdam, Djambatan, 1959.

—, *Ṭā'ifat al-ismā'īliyya*, Cairo, Al-maktaba al-ta'rīkhiyya, 1959.

—, "Jarīma shan'ā'" in *Al-Hilāl*, March 1962, pp. 66-76; English translation, "Atrocity", in M. Manzalaoui (ed.), *Arabic Writing Today: Vol. I, The Short Story*, American Research Center in Egypt, 1968, pp. 54-75.

—, *Al-wādī al-muqaddas*, Cairo, Dār al-ma'ārif, 1968; English translation by Kenneth Cragg, *The Hallowed Valley*, American University in Cairo Press, 1977.

MERAD, A., "Le Christ selon le Coran" in *Revue de l'Occident musulman*, 5 (1968), pp. 79-94, translated into English in *Encounter*, No. 69, November 1970.

—, "Dialogue islamo-chrétien: pour la recherche d'un langage commun" in *Islamochristiana*, 1 (1975), pp. 1-10.

—, *Charles de Foucauld au regard de l'Islam*, Paris, Chalet, 1976.

MOUBARAC, Y., (ed.), *Verse et controverse: le chrétien en dialogue avec le monde, No. 14. Les musulmans, consultation islamo-chrétienne*, Paris, Beauchesne, 1971.

MUSLIM-CHRISTIAN RESEARCH GROUP, *The Challenge of the Scriptures: the Bible and the Qur'ān*, Maryknoll, New York, Orbis, 1989.

NASR, S.H., "Islam and the encounter of religions" in *Sufi Essays*, London, Allen and Unwin, 1972, pp. 123-151.

—, *Ideals and Realities of Islam*, 2nd ed., London, Allen and Unwin, 1975.

—, "Jesus through the eyes of Islam" in *Islamic Life and Thought*, London, Allen and Unwin, 1981, pp. 209-211.

—, "The Islamic view of Christianity" in *Concilium*, No. 183, February 1986, pp. 3-12.

—, "The prayer of the heart in Hesychasm and Sufism" in *Greek Orthodox Theological Review*, 31 (1986), pp. 195-203.

—, Response to Hans Küng's "Christianity and world religions: the dialogue with Islam as one model" in *The Muslim World*, 77 (1987), pp. 96-105.

ROUSSEAU, R.W. (ed.), *Christianity and Islam: the Struggling Dialogue*, Scranton, Pennsylvania, Ridge Row Press, 1985.

SAMARTHA, S.J., and Taylor, J., (eds.), *Christian-Muslim Dialogue: Papers from Broumana, 1972*, Geneva, World Council of Churches, 1973.

SIDDIQUI, A., *Christian-Muslim Dialogue in the Twentieth Century*, Houndmills, Basingstoke and London, Macmillan Press; New York, St. Martin's Press, 1997.

SWIDLER, L. (ed.), *Muslims in Dialogue: the Evolution of a Dialogue*, Lewiston, New York, Edwin Mellen Press, 1992.

TALBI, M., *Islam et dialogue*, Tunis, Maison Tunisienne de l'Édition, 1972, translated into English in *Encounter*, Nos. 11 and 12, February 1975, and reprinted in R.W. Rousseau (ed.), *Islam and Christianity: the Struggling Dialogue*, Scranton, Pennsylvania, Ridge Row Press, 1985, pp. 53-73.

—, "A Muslim's experience of prayer" in *Encounter*, No. 34, April 1977.

—, "A community of communities: the right to be different and the ways of harmony" in J. Hick and H. Askari (eds.), *The Experience of Religious Diversity*, London, Gower, 1985, pp. 66-90.

—, "Religious liberty: a Muslim perspective" in *Islamochristiana*, 11 (1985), pp. 99-113, reprinted in L.E. Swidler (ed.) *Muslims in Dialogue: the Evolution of a Dialogue*, Lewiston, New York, Edwin Mellen Press, 1992, pp. 465-482.

—, "Possibilities and conditions for a better understanding between Islam and the West" in *Journal of Ecumenical Studies*, 25 (1988), pp. 161-193, reprinted in L.E. Swidler (ed.) *Muslims in Dialogue: the Evolution of a Dialogue*, Lewiston, New York, Edwin Mellen Press, 1992, pp. 111-153.

—, "Unavoidable dialogue in a pluralist world: a personal account" in *Encounters*, 1 (1995), pp. 56-69.

VAHIDUDDIN, S., *The Islamic Experience in Contemporary Thought*, Vol. III of C.W. Troll (ed.), *Islam in India: Studies and Commentaries*, Delhi, Chanakya Publications, 1986.

—, "Qur'anic humanism" in *Islam and the Modern Age*, 18 (1987), pp. 55-72.

—, "Islam and diversity of religions" in *Islam and Christian-Muslim Relations*, 1 (1990), pp. 3-11.

VOGELAAR, H., "The Religious and Philosophical Thought of Dr. M. Kamel Hussein, an Egyptian Humanist", unpublished Ph.D. thesis, Columbia University, 1978.

WAARDENBURG, J., "Towards a periodization of earliest Islam according to its relations with other religions" in R. Peters (ed.), *Proceedings of the 9th Congress of the Union Européenne des Arabisants et Islamisants*, Brill, Leiden, 1981, pp. 304-326.

MUSULMANS ET JUDEO-CHRÉTIENS ENSEMBLE

(L'expérience de Bosnie-Herzégovine)

Adnan Silajdžić

AVANT-PROPOS

J'aimerais, avant de débuter cet exposé sur le thème annoncé, faire quelques remarques introductives. Bien qu'elle puisse nous sembler absurde, à nous habitants de Bosnie-Herzégovine, il semble, toutefois, que se réalise l'observation dont a fait part le célèbre historien Arnold Toynbee, juste avant sa mort (en 1977), affirmant qu'au 20e siècle le dialogue entre les religions aura un rôle décisif dans le destin du monde contemporain.

L'Occident, comprenez-le ici comme l'entité dans sa démarche métaphysique et religieuse, subit depuis ces quelques dernières décennies, de profonds changements[1].

Partant des isolationnismes culturels, des civilisations et surtout des religions, notre monde s'est progressivement engagé sur la voie d'une connaissance œcuménique et culturelle à une échelle planétaire. Comme conséquence des grands bouleversements mondiaux: — l'apparition de la pluralisation des cultures et des religions et le fait qu'il n'existe presque plus aucun endroit où vivent les représentants d'une seule et même tradition religieuse. Ainsi, depuis le temps où les gens commencèrent à rencontrer quotidiennement dans leurs villes, leurs usines, leurs universités, dans la rue, des personnes d'une autre tradition culturelle et religieuse, la question de leur propre identité devint incontournable. Oserons-nous ou non nous l'avouer, le monde contemporain est pluraliste. C'est aujourd'hui son *signum distinctivum,* et par conséquence son *signum temporis.* Le pluralisme religieux est donc un des signes caractéristiques des temps modernes dans lesquels la pensée théologique contemporaine existe[2].

---

[1] Voir René Guénon, *La Crise du monde moderne*, Paris, 1927; H. Küng, *Dieu existe-t-il*, trad. fr. Seuil, Paris, 1981.

[2] Voir S. H. Nasr, *Islam and the Plight of Modern Man*, Kuala Lumpur,1987; Hans Küng, *Le christianisme et les religions du monde: islam, hindouisme, bouddhisme*, Seuil, Paris, 1986.

C'est pour toutes ces raisons que j'ai accepté avec grand plaisir l'invitation des organisateurs à participer aux travaux de cette réunion. Du point de vue de notre histoire récente, le thème du Symposium comporte un intérêt majeur. Je crois profondément, pour ma part, que le dialogue entre les religions jouera un rôle décisif pour le destin du monde contemporain. Il dépend de nous, représentants des différentes traditions religieuses et théologiques de savoir si nous pourrons utiliser et profiter avec efficacité de cette réalité.

Comme vous le savez, la Bosnie est une communauté étatique multireligieuse, multinationale et multiculturelle. Comme telle, elle fut un modèle de tolérance religieuse dans la Yougoslavie d'hier. Ce phénomène, dans une Bosnie encore marquée par les souffrances de la guerre, est un élément de valeur intéressant, et même attractif. Dans ce contexte deux questions d'une exceptionnelle importance se posent à nous: les représentants des différentes traditions religieuses (musulmans, chrétiens, juifs et autres) par leur pratique, ont-ils contribué ou non à l'explosion de la guerre. Si oui, la question suivante s'impose: les communautés religieuses peuvent-elles par un dialogue approfondi et plus systématique influer pour une meilleure connaissance de leurs représentants mutuels? Deux questions auxquelles les habitants de Bosnie sont aujourd'hui confrontés. Elles sont stratiformes et primordiales. C'est pourquoi elles doivent être examinées en profondeur et avec le plus grand sérieux.

Avant de commencer l'examen du thème annoncé, il serait utile de donner un court aperçu sur le début et le développment des traditions religieuses qui s'expriment aujourd'hui sur le territoire de Bosnie-Herzégovine. Nous ne mentionerons ici, bien sûr, que les faits d'importance du point de vue d'un examen œcuménique des rapports interreligieux. L'aspect historique pur dépasse le cadre du thème donné. Ainsi, dans la discussion finale nous parlerons des perspectives du dialogue interreligieux, de ce qu'il nous faudra faire, afin que ce dialogue entre les représentants des différentes religions soit placé au plus haut niveau.

Je n'ai l'intention de faire une analyse poussée du problème posé. Mes intentions sont beaucoup plus modestes et je me contenterai ici de vous communiquer les informations qui me semblent, pour l'heure, être pour vous les plus intéressantes.

Quelques mots sur la littérature utilisée. En ce qui concerne l'aspect historique sur la question de la formation et du développement des communautés religieuses dans nos régions, j'avais à ma disposition une littérature volumineuse et conséquente. Mais pour ce qui est de l'aspect œcuménique, c'est-à-dire socio-anthropologique du dialogue interreligieux, je dois dire qu'il n'existe aucune œuvre d'importance dans ce domaine. Pour cette raison, dans ce contexte, je me contenterai de rester au niveau des observations et des impressions personnelles. Du besoin de recherche multidisciplinaire sur le phénomène spécifiquement bosniaque, je parlerai plus tard.

1. BREF SURVOL DE LA NAISSANCE ET DU DÉVELOPPEMENT DES COMMUNAUTÉS RELIGIEUSES EN BOSNIE

Le territoire de Bosnie-Herzégovine est spécifique par son mélange religieux, culturel et national-ethnique. Depuis longtemps, sur ce territoire vivent trois peuples, avec trois religions, liés aux trois modèles culturels: byzantin-orthodoxe, romain-catholique et oriental-islamique. A vrai dire, ce sont des peuples slaves, qui avec le temps ont divergé du fait de la foi et de l'influence culturelle dominante. Jusqu'au VIe siècle en Bosnie-Herzégovine ont vécu de nombreuses tribus (Illyriens, Celtes, Ostrogoths, Germains etc.). Au VIIe siècle, les tribus sud-slaves, qui selon leurs convictions religieuses étaient polythéistes, commencent à peupler intensivement ces régions. Plus tard, ils adopteront la religion chrétienne. Ce processus dura jusqu'au IXe siècle. L'année 1054 marque le conflit entre l'Eglise d'Occident et celle d'Orient, conflit qui aura de sérieuses conséquences dans les rapports interreligieux en Bosnie, qui passera à partir de cette date sous l'influence permanente, culturelle et religieuse de l'Orient et d'Occident. C'est ce nucléus qui déterminera en Bosnie le caractère multireligieux et multiculturel qui différencie la région de ses pays voisins.

Dans la période qui suit l'Eglise bosnienne autonome occupera une place importante dans la vie religieuse en Bosnie. Ce qui nous intéresse ici est de savoir quelle fut l'étendue de l'influence de l'Eglise bosnienne sur la vie religieuse, autrement dit sur l'espace d'intégration culturelle et politique bosnien[3].

---

[3] Pour ce qui est de l'origine et de la nature de l'Eglise de Bosnie, différents points de vue ont été exprimés. La thèse dominante étant celle de F. Racki, développée plus tard par Aleksandar Solovjev. L'Eglise de Bosnie est donc une église populaire, autonome, qui par sa doctrine, diffère du catholicisme et de l'orthodoxie. Nous appelons leurs représentants les bogomiles. C'est la théorie qui possède le plus grand nombre d'adhérents et sur laquelle les intellectuels bosniaques insistent aujourd'hui. Ils ont ainsi construit la thèse du «peuple des Bogomiles». L'historien suédois, Hans Furuhagenn explique l'actuelle brutalité des Serbes par le fait que «les musulmans sont des descendants des bogomiles».

Même avant l'arrivée des Ottomans, la Bosnie-Herzégovine était donc multiculturelle et multireligieuse et à travers les siècles des groupes religieux déterminés y ont dominé, appliquant les différentes lois religieuses en vigueur. Les rapports entre les religions étaient en principe déterminés par le développement historique, culturel, politique et national des peuples de Bosnie. Autrement dit, ils étaient avant tout conditionnés par les systèmes juridico-étatiques et socio-politiques dans lesquels les populations vivaient et agissaient.

Avec l'arrivée des Ottomans en 1463, la structure confessionnelle en Bosnie change. Un nombre important de ressortissants de l'Eglise de Bosnie, ainsi que certains de ceux qui avaient accepté le catholicisme, juste avant l'arrivée des Ottomans, acceptent l'islam et les conquêtes de la culture et de la civilisation islamiques. De l'expansion de l'islam dans ces régions et du statut des autres groupes religieux sous le gouvernement ottoman, je ne parlerai pas. Je soulignerai seulement que les études historiques effectuées mettent en relief le fait que cette période est placée sous le signe d'une grande tolérance religieuse[4].

Autrement dit, les peuples de Bosnie cultivaient de bons rapports entre voisins. Cette caractéristique, qui est devenue, avec l'arrivée des Ottomans (à la chute de l'état médiéval bosniaque) la spécificité principale de la réalité de Bosnie-Herzégovine, est encore aujourd'hui le lien interreligieux et interculturel entre les peuples de Bosnie-Herzégovine. Les auteurs les plus sérieux expliquent que le facteur fondamental réside dans la nature exceptionnellement tolérante de la doctrine islamique[5].

Comme dans l'état islamique théocratique, dont les souverains ottomans deviennent les califes à partir de l'année 1517, les nouveaux gouvernements respectent les instructions du Qur'an (Coran) et de la tradition religieuse:

Dans la foi, il n'y a pas de contrainte (S. 2,256).

En ceci, l'état ottoman reconnaissait toutes les religions monothéistes et garantissait la liberté de la confession, la protection juridique des biens sous réserve de loyauté. De nombreux exemples existent dans l'historiographie. Je ne mentionerai ici que le célèbre *ahdnama* (commandement) du sultan Mehmed II Fatih dans lequel la sécurité de leur confession ainsi que de leurs biens est garantie aux franciscains[6].

---

[4] «Extension de l'islam et de la culture islamique ... réunion scientifique», *Annexe de la philologie orientale*, nº 41, Sarajevo, 1991.
[5] J. Corm, *Communautes multiconfessionelles*, Sarajevo, 1977.
[6] Comp. M. Bogdanovič, *Chronique du couvent de Kreševo*, Sarajevo, 1981.

Au milieu du XVIᵉ siècle arrivent en Bosnie les juifs exilés d'Espagne, les séphardes, dont la langue parlée était l'espagnol. Ils se distinguent des ashkenases (juifs de l'Europe de l'Est) qui viendront plus tard. Ainsi, avant même la fin du XVIᵉ siècle, à Sarajevo existent les objets de culte des religions musulmane, orthodoxe, catholique et juive. C'est un exemple unique de cohabitation. Avec l'arrivée de la monarchie austro-hongroise en 1876, la situation change radicalement. Ce sont les employés de l'administration austro-hongroise qui feront sentir à la Bosnie les prises de position officielle de l'Eglise catholique vis-à-vis de l'islam et des musulmans. Nous le savons, la théologie chrétienne, comprenez en ce sens: catholique, orthodoxe, protestante, avant le IIᵉ Concile de Vatican, regardait les musulmans avec méfiance, pour ne pas dire avec mépris[7]. Telle position se reflète dans la mentalité des chrétiens de Bosnie, certaines personnes influentes, appartenant à la hiérarchie de l'Eglise, contribuaient à la promotion de cette position adoptée envers les non-chrétiens. Néanmoins, ces rivalités disparaissent rapidement devant les rapports traditionnellement bons, existant entre franciscains bosniaques, musulmans et autres, issus d'une cohabitation centenaire. A la différence des employés austro-hongrois, les catholiques locaux, travailleurs pastoraux de Bosnie (les franciscains) ont cultivé des relations amicales avec leurs voisins et l'on ne trouve dans les écrits aucune trace de conflit entre eux et les musulmans.

Cette «coloration» religieuse et culturelle est caractéristique du développement futur dans la région. Toutefois, il semble nécessaire de souligner certains faits. Dans «l'ancienne» Yougoslavie (Royaume des Serbes, des Croates et des Slovènes), principalement dirigée par les Serbes, il n'y a eu malheureusement que peu de compréhension pour les musulmans et l'on essayait par tous les moyens d'assimiler les populations musulmanes au corps national serbe, qui les considérait comme des «serbes de foi mahométane».

Chef de l'Etat croate indépendant, Ante Pavelič récupéra à son profit ce courant de pensée en faisant construire à Zagreb la grande mosquée, non parce que les musulmans l'intéressaient à cause de leur foi, mais pour les intégrer en tant que soldats, qu'il s'empressait de prêter au régime hitlérien pour la création de la tristement célèbre division Handžar.

---

[7] Voir N. Daniel, *Islam and the West, The Making of an Image*, Edinburgh Univ. Press 1960; Jean-Marie Gaudeul, *Encounters and Clashes: Islam and Christianity in History*, Rome, PISAI, 1985, 2 tomes.

2. LES RAPPORTS INTERRELIGIEUX EN BOSNIE PENDANT LE SOCIALISME

Avec la constitution de l'idéologie communiste se crée, après la Deuxième guerre mondiale, un contexte socio-politique et culturel spécifique. Le monde moderne traversait, alors, une crise de civilisation, culturelle et spirituelle, très sérieuse. C'est principalement l'athéisme scientifique qui formera la base de connaissance spécifique des populations. Sur le modèle de l'économie utilitariste, de l'hédonisme et de la morale humaniste sans Dieu, le monde devient profane et se déshonore presque. La résultante d'une telle profanation et d'une telle altération des rapports avec notre univers est le profit matériel et la crise des valeurs spirituelles. Cette «altération» est connue de Dieu et fut révélée par la Bible et le Coran.

Vis-à-vis de ce processus, les communautés religieuses ne surent malheureusement pas prendre position. Elles ne surent pas non plus s'incorporer aux processus évolutifs (et non mécaniques) du remodelage des valeurs. Autrement dit, les institutions religieuses n'ont pas su transposer fructueusement les messages saints dans un environnement transformé, en séparant, par example, ce qui est historique et transcendant de ce qui est amovible et issu de la civilisation moderne. A la place des institutions religieuses et sacrées, dynamiques et pastorales, se créent d'autres institutions, juridiques et fermées. Ceci fut le but du gouvernement communiste. Il était en effet plus facile et plus efficace de contrôler des institutions isolées et refermées sur elles-mêmes. Hauts dignitaires du régime et chefs religieux pouvaient se voir ensemble uniquement à l'occasion des réunions et des fêtes nationales. On peut, donc, parler pour cette période de l'existence de rapports interreligieux «institutionnels» s'exprimant dans le cadre et sous la forme idéologique du gouvernement. Ainsi à travers les unions de clergé on tenta de faire des communautés religieuses un instrument de réalisation du socialisme.

Le côté positif de ces unions fut que les imams et les prêtres vivaient en bonnes relations, faisant connaissance et échangeant leurs opinions plus que jamais auparavant. En dépit de cela, la crise de l'Eglise et de la religion s'approfondit et provoqua des répercussions négatives dans l'ensemble du système des rapports sociaux. Il faut parler, dans ce contexte, de la grande responsabilité des communautés religieuses et, plus précisément, de leurs représentants hiérarchiques.

Ajoutons que la création de préjugés par rapport aux traditions personnelles des autres peuples provoquèrent la réticence systématique de nombreuses générations. De la fréquentation artificielle, parfois forcée, naquit avec le temps une certaine confiance entre les gens, malheureusement fondée, non sur une communication religieuse, mais dépersonnalisée, non spirituelle mais basée sur l'intérêt personnel, ce contre quoi luttent toutes les religions.

L'univers fragile, spirituel et émotif des jeunes gens dans ce contexte eut pour résultat une accumulation d'énergie négative qui, pour ce qui est des ressortissants du corps national serbe, se traduira sous forme d'une incroyable brutalité. En bref, on peut dire que l'incompréhension des esprits de ce temps et l'insuffisance d'apports spirituels et religieux ont contribué à une mauvaise qualité des relations interreligieuses. C'est dans ce contexte que se sont créés les rapports mutuels et que les communautés religieuses ont agi. Politiquement instrumentalisés par le pouvoir communiste, tous les représentants des traditions religieuses se sont sentis menacés dans ce nouveau contexte, qui détermine et définit des contacts institutionnels entre les hiérarchies religieuses et les sentiments œcuméniques des populations.

Le dialogue interreligieux devint politique, considéré comme un fait de culture, par lequel le public local et international fut manipulé. C'est par un renouveau islamique au sein même du monde arabo-islamique, en correlation avec le concile Vatican II, qu'un nouvel esprit pourra alors éclairer les communautés religieuses de Bosnie-Herzégovine. Musulmans et chrétiens, tournés vers le monde, pourront alors redéfinir leur relation avec les uns et les autres, jusqu'à ce que les effets se fassent sentir sur le sol même de Bosnie. Profondément ancrée dans son traditionalisme, l'Eglise orthodoxe maintiendra ses positions, à l'égard des musulmans et des autres traditions liturgiques enracinées dans l'histoire.

Le dialogue a commencé et les effets ont été ressentis dans les assemblées, lors de visites à l'occasion des cérémonies[8]. Il ne fut jamais célébré de messe d'ouverture (*primitiae*) en Bosnie, à laquelle ne participèrent quelques imams, alors que pour la construction des mosquées et des églises, les représentants de tous les groupes religieux participaient. En conséquence de quoi, la théologie commença à se développer d'une manière qui aurait pu paraître, auparavant, comme inimaginable. Une pléiade de théologiens exceptionnels, larges d'esprit et de culture théologique, fera son apparition. Par leur enseignement, ils surmontent les anciens différends théologiques, promouvant une rencontre décisive entre musulmans et chrétiens.

---

[8] Voir Fra Leonard Ore, «Konjic a voté pour la bonté, «paix et bien», *Périodique de la province des franciscains herzégoviniens*, No. 6/1971 p. 251-252.

Ils découvrent les bienfaits du dialogue sous tous ses aspects. Partant de la simple parole du dialogue, ils désignent non pas seulement l'éloquence, mais aussi l'écoute de l'autre, l'aveu, la compréhension du prochain dans ses différences. Ainsi le théologien musulman, Husein D'ozo, célèbre en ce temps et le théologien chrétien, de l'époque conciliaire et proconciliaire, Šagi Bunič, informèrent leurs croyants du fait que le dialogue est une conquête de la civilisation contemporaine (qui n'est pas faite que de l'humanisme européen) mais qui est un principe divin où se trouvent les fondements du monde[9].

Dans le cosmos, tout est signe de dialogue, ont ainsi souligné les deux hommes. Notre obligation est de respecter ce principe, mais aussi de l'anoblir. La qualité de la vie entre tous en dépend. Là se trouve la plus grande responsabilité de l'homme. Le résultat de ces avancées progressistes fut que dans les facultés de Sarajevo et de Zagreb le christianisme et l'islam ne seront plus étudiés dans le cadre de l'histoire des religions, mais dans des séminaires spéciaux. Ce ne fut qu'un essai pionnier. Malgré tout, ils auront marqué par leur forte influence l'œcuménisme en Bosnie. Qu'avons-nous fait? Qu'avons-nous manqué, telles sont les questions qui devraient être traitées.

La création d'institutions scientifiques pour la recherche d'un dialogue de tolérance interreligieuse, malgré l'intérêt évident, n'a pas eu lieu. Il y a eu des essais de recherche par les sociologues marxistes, inspirés de certains aspects de la phénoménologie religieuse, mais excepté cela, il est significatif que hormis quelques études, on ne traitait pas les théologiens, qui sont les représentants de sociologies religieuses[10].

3. OBLIGATION ET PERSPECTIVE DU DIALOGUE INTERRELIGIEUX

1991 sera l'année de la dissolution du système communiste sur le territoire de l'ex-Yougoslavie. Les processus démocratiques qui s'ouvrent en cette période influeront sur le climat religieux et culturel de la Bosnie-Herzégovine. Malheureusement, quand la Bosnie est reconnue inter-

[9] Com. Husein D'ozo, *Les rapports de la communauté islamique avec les autres communautés religieuses de la Yougoslavie*, Binoza, Zagreb, 1970, pg. 135; Tomislav Šagi-Bunič, *Mais il n'y a pas d'autre chemin,* Zagreb, 1969, p. 377.

[10] Par exemple, Esad Čimić, *La société socialiste et la religion,* Svjetlost, Sarajevo 1969; F. Franič, «Dialogue comme voie vers la paix, Chemins de dialogue», *Eglise au monde*, Split, 1973; Čedomir Draškovič, *Orthodoxie et œcuménisme*, «Bonoza», Zagreb, 1970.

nationelement, la guerre éclate le 6 avril 1992, alors que s'étaient déjà exprimés de nouveaux courants au sein de certaines communautés religieuses. L'Eglise serbe orthodoxe[11], pour sa part, entra au service de la politique expansionniste de ses dirigeants et il existe de nombreuses attestations de ses incitations au génocide et à la destruction de la culture religieuse non orthodoxe dans l'espace de la Bosnie. Bien sûr, l'histoire jugera. C'est dans ce contexte que les questions suivantes s'imposent: les croyants et les représentants de toutes les communautés religieuses sont-ils capables, ont-ils suffisamment de force et d'intelligence pour s'incorporer aux mouvements œcuméniques internationaux? Quelles sont les motivations et l'objet d'un dialogue entre les individus des différentes traditions religieuses? Quelles sont les perspectives d'un tel dialogue et que peut-on faire en ce sens?

En tant que théologien musulman, j'aimerais exprimer ici quelques idées sur ce que les musulmans devraient entreprendre dans le sens d'un approfondissement du dialogue avec les non-musulmans. Chaque musulman croyant doit savoir que le dialogue avec les représentants du Livre (juifs et chrétiens) n'est pas conditionné par les problèmes de la société contemporaine, séculaire et pluralement structurée, dont la provocation serait l'homme moderne[12]. La recherche d'un tel dialogue est le fruit même de la nature de l'islam dans l'ordre fondamental, délivré aux musulmans par la révélation de Dieu. Dans le Coran, il est écrit:

> «O, disciples du Livre, venez à nous, vous réunir autour d'une parole qui nous est commune: de n'adorer personne que Le Dieu, sans considération pour les dieux» (S. 3,64).

Selon l'avis de presque tous les commentateurs et interprètes du Coran, le texte cité ne s'adresse pas aux juifs et aux chrétiens comme à des représentants d'une religion, ni comme à des adeptes d'un système de pensées philosophico-théologiques, mais au contraire, comme à des possesseurs d'un unique message de Dieu, qui est la source transcendante, dans laquelle reposent les bases de l'histoire de la révélation de la parole de Dieu. Révélation qui appelle juifs et chrétiens à la réunion autour d'un

---

[11] Voir Jean Damascene, *Pègè gnoseôs* (De Haeresibus), *MIGNE*, 101, (PG 94, 764A-773A; Marius Baar, *Das Abendland am Scheideweg*, Frankfurt, 1980. A. T. Khoury, *Les théologiens byzantins et l'islam*, Paris-Louvain, Nauwelaerts, 1960; nouvelle édition, *Polémique byzantine contre l'islam*, Leiden, Brill 1972.

[12] Voir M. Arkoun, *Ouvertures sur l'islam*, Jacques Grancher, Paris, 1989; Mohammad Abd Allah Draz, *Initiation au Coran*, Presses Universitaires de France, Paris, 1951; H. Djaït, *L'Europe et l'islam*, Edition du Seuil, Paris, 1978; Sadek Sellam, *L'islam et les musulmans en France*, Tougui, Paris, 1987; Michel Lelong, *L'islam et l'Occident*, Albin Michel, Paris, 1982.

Dieu avant chaque parole de Dieu, avant chaque connaissance de Dieu, et avant chaque pensée de Dieu. Donc, avant toute théologie, avant toute théodicée et toute philosophie. Le porteur d'un tel message est l'envoyé de l'islam, qui, au temps où le Coran était publié, ne regardait pas les juifs et les chrétiens comme des personnes derrière lesquelles se trouve Nicée-Chalcédoine, *ecclesia* (église) ou le temple de Jérusalem, dans lequel les tablettes sont entreposées, mais des individus chez lesquels arrivaient les envoyés[13].

Tel dialogue doit être engagé avec les personnes et non pas avec les systèmes de pensées. Il se crée avec des êtres vivants, riches de leur histoire, mais conditionnés par leur passé, leur intellect et leur tempérament, en un mot, avec des individus ayant réalisé une expérience humaine et religieuse déterminée.

Le dialogue entre les système théologiques ou les institutions liturgiques n'a de sens que s'il contribue aux rencontres entre les personnes, en combattant les préjugés et en supprimant les obstacles. L'important est donc la rencontre de l'homme avec l'homme. Nous ne devons pas regarder «l'autre» comme un object d'investigation: il est plus facile de comprendre des systèmes socio-culturels que d'approcher les personnes qui en vivent et s'expriment dans la diversité de leur être.

D'autre part, il est important de souligner la commune descendance d'Abraham et les éléments communs de sa foi, détails sur lesquels les représentants de la philosophie perennis insistent[14]. Il faut insister sur ce qui permet d'éviter les conflits dans le monde.

Donc, le Coran place le dialogue au niveau des obligations strictes. Ce principe, les musulmans de Bosnie doivent le suivre et l'appliquer à la lettre, car il s'agit du dialogue des uns et des autres avec Dieu. Il ne peut s'exprimer que sur un plan horizontal, mais doit exister également dans une approche verticale, dans la fidélité à Dieu et en symbiose avec Lui. Ce dialogue doit également s'exprimer au niveau des réalités concrètes et existentielles de l'homme de Bosnie-Herzégovine, préoccupé par les problèmes quotidiens de son existence et de la recherche dynamique de solutions.

---

[13] Voir Muhammad S. Abdullah, *Christentum und Islam. Möglichkeit in der Ökumene*, «Moslems und Christen-Partner?», Köln, 1976; Ahmad Abdel-Wahab, *Dialogue transtextuel entre le christianisme et l'islam*, Centre Abaad, Paris, 1987.

[14] R. Guénon, *Aperçus sur l'ésotérisme islamique et le taoisme*, Gallimard, Paris, 1973; Frithjof Schuon, *Islam and The Perenial Philosophy*, World of Islam Festival Publishing Company Ltd, 1976; Idem, *The Transcendent Unity of religions*, Revised Edition (Harper and Row, 1975.)

Le dialogue interreligieux d'aujourd'hui doit dépasser les problèmes d'hier, ceux qui tourmentaient nos ancêtres, pour tenir compte de la problématique à laquelle musulmans, catholiques, juifs et orthodoxes d'aujourd'hui sont confrontés. Il doit tenir compte de l'individu ici et maintenant. Pour un dialogue complet, nous devons inclure la volonté de vivre avec les autres, d'être psychologiquement avec eux, tout en restant fidèle à ses propres traditions culturelles et spirituelles. Il s'agit de comprendre et connaître maintenant «l'autre» plus profondément. Comprendre sa langue, sa culture, son passé et sa situation présente, ses désirs et ses espoirs. Ceci est une condition fondamentale pour le dialogue possible entre les religions. Par les croisades et les conquêtes, les musulmans de Bosnie connaissent et acceptent les chrétiens de longue date. Tant que les chrétiens ont perçu les musulmans comme des guerriers extrémistes et cruels, désirant à n'importe quel prix imposer l'islam, la confrontation de deux n'a pu donner que des résultats négatifs[15].

Sans chercher à minimiser le choc violent des cultures, c'est en dépassant ces anciennes réalités que cette exclusivité de la confrontation entre chrétiens et musulmans, problème d'importance qui n'a jamais bien sûr favorisé le dialogue, doit être surmonté. S'efforcer d'accepter l'autre tel qu'il est, connaître son histoire, sa culture, ses sentiments et son système de réflexion. Ces actions ne doivent pas être réalisées froidement et sèchement, par un théologien ou un sociologue, cloîtré dans son cabinet, mais doivent être l'action d'un ami qui essaie de découvrir dans l'autre ce qui est le meilleur, ce qui a le plus de valeur.

Aucun dialogue véritable n'est possible sans un minimum d'acceptation et de sympathie envers les autres. Tous en Bosnie se doivent d'en être conscients et doivent pour cela se débarrasser des préjugés qui ont conduit aux erreurs du passé. L'islam appartient-il aux religions du salut? La Bible est-elle authentique ou pas, sont maintenant des questions marginales. Pour un dialogue contemporain ce qu'il est important de savoir, c'est quelles sont les religions qui tiennent compte du destin des peuples vivant sur le territoire de Bosnie-Herzégovine et quelle est la mesure du destin individuel de l'homme de cette région.

Le fait est que les représentants de ces religions vivent ensemble. Cela dirige notre attention sur les réalités plus importantes et plus vitales de tous les jours. Pourquoi ne pas introduire une éducation multi-religieuse pour les jeunes? En connaissant mieux la culture musulmane, les valeurs

---

[15] Voir N. Daniel, *op. cit.*; H. Küng, *Le christianisme et les religions du monde*....pag. 10-30.; M. Arkoun, *op. cit.*, pag. 116.

religieuses et spirituelles de l'autre, on sera en droit d'attendre de meilleurs résultats du dialogue. Il faut aussi compter avec les différents interlocuteurs qui peuvent s'appeler libéraux, conservateurs, fanatiques, radicaux etc. C'est ensemble et sans généraliser que nous devons définir le tout, afin d'en tirer les conclusions adéquates.

Aujourd'hui, les musulmans de Bosnie subissent un terrifiant génocide. Derrière ce génocide qui est aussi un urbicide, se trouvent malheuresement les détenteurs de la foi orthodoxe. Ce fait nouveau place les représentants de l'islam dans un rapport radicalement différent avec les représentants de la religion du Livre. Un dialogue est-il possible et sous quelles conditions? Deux conditions préalables doivent être nécessairement remplies, que l'Eglise orthodoxe mette un terme au génocide que subissent les populations musulmanes et les autres confessions. Deuxièmement, que ceux qui viennent au dialogue comprennent que son objet est la parole universelle de Dieu (*kalimatin sawain*) et comme nous l'avons déjà noté, l'union avec Lui. Le Coran invite tous les non-musulmans, mais aussi l'homme en tant que détenteur de la foi et créature parfaite de Dieu. Chrétiens et juifs doivent savoir que l'islam invite à l'union autour d'Un seul Dieu. Avant même toute lettre, avant tout discours et avant ce qui ici est plus important, toute histoire nationale, surtout si elle est chargée jusqu'à l'extrême de préjugés.

Tant que la pensée œcuménique ne s'élaborera pas sur ces prémices, je pense personnellement que le dialogue entre les musulmans de Bosnie et les représentants du Livre n'aura aucun sens et n'est pas même possible.

Enfin, j'aimerais dire quelques mots sur le dialogue institutionnel. Un tel dialogue aujourd'hui est d'une importance exceptionnelle[16]. Dans de nombreux pays d'Afrique, dont certains sont musulmans, les œcuménistes ont depuis longtemps déjà, compris la valeur du dialogue interreligieux. De nombreuses institutions ont été crées, dont le but est d'étendre et d'entretenir ce dialogue. Nous sommes, malheuresement, en Bosnie très en retard sur ce phénomène. Il n'y a, chez nous, aucune institution traîtant du dialogue interreligieux, malgré l'intérêt qui existe. Je pense, pour ma part, que si Dieu nous accorde de vivre dans une Bosnie constitutionnelle et démocratique, la confrontation par le dialogue entre chrétiens, musulmans et juifs jouera un rôle décisif. Notre tragédie est peut-être le résultat d'un très long silence ainsi que de la non-existence d'une telle dynamique de confrontation.

---

[16] Voir Emilio Galindo Aguilar, «The Second International Muslim-Christian Congress of Cordoba» (March 21-27, 1977), dans *ISCH* 3 (1977). 480-483; M. Borrmans, «La deuxième rencontre islamo-chrétienne de Tunis (30 avril - mai 1979)», dans *ISCH* 5 (1979) 221-242); A.D.I.C., *Dialogue islamo-Chrétien*, Editions Tougui, 1992.

Il n'est plus admissible que nous nous réfugions derrière nos multiples symboles religieux, alors que ce sont eux qui ont façonné notre environnement pluriculturel et multiconfessionnel. Sans ruse ni dissimulation, nous devons maintenant nous engager sur les voies du dialogue et du progrès, car le temps passe inexorablement.

Nulle part au monde, excepté chez nous en Bosnie, on ne rencontre les signes de toutes les grandes religions mondiales dans un espace aussi réduit. Mais pour les musulmans, après les horreurs qu'ils viennent de vivre, ceci ne signifie presque rien. Ce n'est plus, pour eux, qu'un fait culturel utilisé, par lequel en tous cas, il faudra qu'ils retrouvent leur dignité, tant que l'on comptera dans cette région plus d'une confession.

De tout cela, tous, les musulmans, les chrétiens et les juifs, en sont responsables.

BIBLIOGRAPHIE

ABU-KURRA, *Opuscula,* Migne, PG 97.

AGUILAR E.G., «The Second International Muslim- Christian Congress of Cordoba» (March 21-27, 1977, dans *ISCH (Islamochristiana)* 3 (1977). 480-483.

AHMAD Abdel-Wahab, *Dialogue transtextuel entre le christianisme et l'islam,* Centre Abaad, Paris, 1987.

A.D.I.C., *Dialogue islamo-Chretien,* Editions Tougui, Paris, 1992.

AKVINSKI T., *Summa contra Gentiles,* Paris, 1874.

ARKOUN M.,*Ouvertures sur l'islam,* Jacques Grancher, Paris, 1989.

AYOUB M., «Muslim views of Christianity: some modern examples», *ISCH,* 10 (1984).

BAAR M., *Das Abendland am Scheideweg,* Frankfurt, 1980.

BERGER P., *La religion dans la conscience moderne,* Paris, 1972.

M. BORRMANS, «La deuxième rencontre islamo-chrétienne de Tunis (30 avril - mai 1979), dans *ISCH* 5 (1979) 221-242).

CASPAR R., «Vatican II, Textes et Commentaires», le volume: «Les relations de l'Eglise avec les religions non-chrétiennes», Paris, Cerf, *Unam Sanctam* 61, 1966.

DAMASCENE J., *Pègè gnoseôs* (De Haeresibus), *MIGNE,* 101, (PG 94, 764A-773A).

DANIEL N., *Islam and the West, The Making of an Image,* Edinburgh Univ. Press, 1960.

DRAZ M., *Initiation au Coran,* Presses Universitaires de France, Paris, 1951.

DUCELLIER A., *Le miroir de l'islam. Musulmans et chrétiens d'Orient au Moyen Age,* Paris, 1971.

DJAIT H., *L'Europe et l'islam,* Editions du Seuil, Paris, 1978.

ETIENNE B., *L'islamisme radical,* Hachette, Paris, 1987.

FAZLUR Rahman, *Islam and Modernity: Transformation of an intellectual tradition,* Chicago et Londres, 1982.

GARDET L., *Regards chrétiens sur l'islam*, Desclée de Brouwer, Paris, 1986.

GAUDEUL J.M., *Encounters and Clashes: Islam and Christianity in History*, Rome, PISAI, 1985, 2 tomes

GUENON R., *La Crise du monde moderne*, Paris, 1927; *Aperçus sur l'ésotérisme islamique et le taoisme*, Gallimard, Paris, 1973.

JOMIER J., *Le Commentaire Coranique du Manar*, Paris, 1954 (Analyse toutes les idées des réformateurs: M. Abduh et R. Rida).

KHOURY A. T., *Les théologiens byzantins et l'islam*, Paris-Louvain, Nauwelaerts, 1960; nouvelle édition *Polémique byzantine contre l'islam*, Leiden, Brill 1927.

KUNG H., *Dieu existe-t-il*, trad. fr. Paris, Seuil, 1981.; *Le christianisme et les religions du monde: islam, hindouisme, bouddhisme*, Seuil, Paris, 1986.

LELONG M., *L'islam et l'Occident*, Albin Michel, Paris, 1982.

NASR S.H., *Islam and the Plight of Modern Man*, Kuala Lumpur, 1987.

SCELLES-MILLE J., *Pierres d'attente entre le christianisme et l'islam*, G.P. Maisonneuve et Larose, Paris, 1960.

SCHUON F., *Islam and the Perennial Philosophy*, World of Islam Festival Publishing Company Ltd, 1976; *The Transcendent Unity of Religions*, Revised Edition, Harper and Row, New York, 1975.

SELLAM S., *L'islam et les musulmans en France*, Tougui, Paris, 1987.

SMITH W.C., *On understanding Islam*, Mouton, Den Haag, 1981; *L'islam dans le monde moderne*, trad. fr., Payot, Paris 1962.

TALBI M., *Islam et Dialogue*, Tunis, MTE, 1972.

THILS, *Propos et problèmes de la théologie des religions non-chrétiennes*, Casterman, Paris, 1966.

THE AGE OF GLOBAL DIALOGUE

Leonard SWIDLER[1]

1. A Radically New Age

Those scholars who earlier in the twentieth century with a great show of scholarship and historical/sociological analysis predicted the impending demise of Western Civilization were "dead wrong." After World War I, in 1922, Oswald Spengler wrote his widely acclaimed book, *The Decline of the West*[2]. After the beginning of World War II Pitirim A. Sorokin published in 1941 his likewise popular book, *The Crisis of Our Age*[3]. Given the massive, world-wide scale of the unprecedented destruction and horror of the world's first global war, 1914-18, and the even vastly greater of the second global conflict, 1939-45, the pessimistic predictions of these scholars and the great following they found are not unununderstandable.

In fact, however, those vast world conflagrations were manifestations of the dark side of the unique breakthrough in the history of humankind in the modern development of Christendom-become-Western Civilization, now becoming Global Civilization. Never before had there been world wars; likewise, never before had there been world political organizations (League of Nations, United Nations). Never before did humanity possess the real possibility of destroying all human life — whether through nuclear or ecological catastrophe. These unique negative realities/potentialities were possible, however, only because of the correspondingly unique accomplishments of Christendom/Western/ Global Civilization — the like of which the world has never before seen. On the negative side, from now on it will always be true that humankind could self-destruct. Still, there are solid empirical grounds for reasonable hope that the inherent, infinity-directed life force of humankind will nevertheless prevail over the parallel death force.

---

[1] Leonard SWIDLER is Professor of Catholic Thought and Interreligious Dialogue at Temple University, and Editor of the *Journal of Ecumenical Studies*.

[2] Oswald SPENGLER, *Der Untergang des Abendlandes* (Munich: Beck, 1922-23), 2 vols.

[3] Pitirim A. SOROKIN, *The Crisis of Our Age* (New York: Dutton, 1941).

The prophets of doom were correct, however, in their understanding that humanity is entering into a radically new age. Earlier in this century the nay-sayers usually spoke of the doom of only Western Civilization (e.g., Spengler, Sorokin), but after the advent of nuclear power and the Cold War, the new generation of pessimists — as said, not without warrant: *corruptio optimae pessima* — warned of *global* disaster. This emerging awareness of global disaster is a clear, albeit negative, sign that something profoundly, radically new is entering onto the stage of human history.

There have, of course, also recently been a number of more positive signs that we humans are entering a radically new age. In the 1960s there was much talk of "The Age of Aquarius," and there still is today the continuing fad of "New Age" consciousness. Some may be put off from the idea of an emerging radically new age because they perceive such talk to be simply that of fringe groups. I would argue, however, that the presence of "the crazies" around the edge of any idea or movement, far from being a sign of the invalidity of that idea or movement, is on the contrary a confirmation precisely of its validity, at least in its core concern. I would further argue that if people are involved with a movement which does not eventually develop its "crazies," its extremists, the movement is not touching the core of humankind's concerns — they should get out of the movement, they are wasting their time!

Moreover, there have likewise recently been a number of very serious scholarly analyses pointing to the emergence of a radically new age in human history. I will deal in some detail with two of them below. The first is the concept of the "Paradigm-Shift," particularly as expounded by Hans Küng[4]. The second is the notion of the "Second Axial Period," as articulated by Ewert Cousins[5]. Then, including these two, but setting them in a still larger context, I shall lay out my own analysis, which I see as the movement of humankind out of a multi-millennia long "Age of Monologue" into the newly inbreaking "Age of Dialogue," indeed, an inbreaking "Age of Global Dialogue."

Of course there is a great deal of continuity in human life throughout the shift from one major "Paradigm" to another, from one "Period" to

---

[4] See among others, Hans Küng, *Theologie im Aufbruch* (Munich: Piper Verlag, 1987), esp. pp. 153 ff.

[5] See especially Ewert COUSINS, "Judaism-Christianity-Islam: Facing Modernity Together," *Journal of Ecumenical Studies*, 30:3-4 (Summer-Fall, 1993), pp. 417-425.

another, from one "Age" to another. Nevertheless, even more striking than this continuity is the ensuing break, albeit largely on a different level than the continuity. This relationship of continuity and break in human history is analogous to the transition of water from solid to fluid to gas with the increase in temperature. With water there is throughout on the chemical level the continuity of H^2O. However, for those who have to deal with the water, it makes a fantastic difference whether the H^2O is ice, water, or steam! In the case of the major changes in humankind, the physical base remains the same, but on the level of consciousness the change is massive. And here too it makes a fantastic difference whether we are dealing with humans whose consciousness is formed within one paradigm or within another, whose consciousness is Pre-Axial, Axial-I or Axial-II, whose consciousness is Monologic or Dialogic.

2. *A Major Paradigm Shift*

Thomas Kuhn revolutionized our understanding of the development of scientific thinking with his notion of paradigm shifts. He painstakingly showed that fundamental "paradigms" or "exemplary models" are the large thought frames within which we place and interpret all observed data and that scientific advancement inevitably brings about eventual paradigm shifts — from geocentricism to heliocentrism, for example, or from Newtonian to Einsteinian physics — which are always vigorously resisted at first, as was the thought of Galileo, but finally prevail[6]. This insight, however, is not only valid for the development of thought in the natural sciences, but is also applicable to all major disciplines of human thought, including religious thought — religion being understood as "an explanation of the ultimate meaning of life, and how to live accordingly."

A major paradigm shift in systematic religious reflection, i.e., in "theology," then, means a major change "in the very idea of what it is to do theology[7]". Let me give an example from my own Christian tradition: The major Christian theological revolution that occurred at the first ecumenical council (Nicaea, 325 A.D.) did not so much resolve the battle

---

[6] Thomas KUHN, *The Structure of Scientific Revolutions* (Chicago: University of Chicago Press, 2nd ed., 1970).

[7] Quentin QUESNELL, "On Not Negotiating the Self in the Structure of Theological Revolutions," typescript at Jan. 3-11, 1984 conference in Honolulu on "Paradigm Shifts in Buddhism and Christianity: Cultural Systems and the Self," p. 2.

over whether the Son and Father were of "the same substance," *homoousion*, important as that was, but rather that, "by defining 'homoousion,' it tacitly admitted that here were issues in theology which could not be solved simply on the basis of recourse to the language of the Scriptures[8]". In the next several centuries a flood of new answers poured forth to questions being posed in categories unused by Jesus and his first, Jewish, followers in this case — in Greek philosophical categories of thought.

As the paradigm within which the data of what Jesus thought, taught and wrought and how his Jewish followers responded was perceived and understood shifted from the Semitic, concrete biblical thought world to a Hellenistic, largely abstract philosophical one, the questions asked, and the terms in which they were asked, shifted accordingly, and of course so did the answers. As always, when a new major paradigm shift occurs, old answers are no longer helpful, for they respond to questions no longer posed, in thought categories no longer used, within a conceptual framework which no longer prevails. It is not that the old answers are now declared wrong; it is simply that they no longer apply. Aristotle's answers in physics and chemistry in terms of the four elements of air, fire, water and earth, for example, simply do not speak to the questions posed by modern chemists and physicists. Tenth-century Christian theologians answering that Mary remained a virgin while giving birth to Jesus (i.e., her hymen was not broken) were answering a question that no modern critical-thinking Christian theologian would pose, for it presupposed a thought-world which placed a high value on unbroken hymens. That thought world is gone. Hence, the old answer is im-pertinent.

3. *The Modern Major Paradigm-shift*

Since the eighteenth century Enlightenment, Christendom-now-become-Western Civilization has been undergoing a major paradigm shift, especially in how we humans understand our process of understanding and what meaning and status we attribute to "truth," to our statements about reality — in other words, our epistemology. This new epistemological paradigm is increasingly determining how we perceive, conceive, think about, and subsequently decide and act on things.

---

[8] Ibid., p. 3.

It is difficult to overestimate the importance of the role in religion, in the "ultimate understanding of reality and how to live accordingly," played by the conceptual paradigm or model one has of reality. The paradigm or model within which we perceive reality not only profoundly affects our theoretical understanding of reality, but also has immense practical consequences. For example, in Western medicine the body is usually conceived of as a highly nuanced, living machine, and therefore if one part wears out, the obvious thing to do is to replace the worn part — hence, organ transplants originated in Western, but not in Oriental, medicine.

However, in Oriental, Chinese, medicine, the body is conceived of as a finely balanced harmony: "pressure" exerted on one part of the body is assumed to have an opposite effect in some other part of the body — hence, acupuncture originated in Oriental, but not in Western, medicine[9]. Our conceptual paradigms have concrete consequences.

Furthermore, obviously some particular paradigms or models for perceiving reality will fit the data better than others, and they will then be preferred — e.g., the shift from the geocentric to the heliocentric model in astronomy. But sometimes differing models will *each* in their own ways "fit" the data more or less adequately, as in the example of Western and Oriental medicines. The differing models are then viewed as complementary. Clearly it would be foolish to limit one's perception of reality to only one of the complementary paradigms or models.

Perhaps at times a more comprehensive model, a mega-model, can be conceived to subsume two or more complementary models, but surely it will never be possible to perceive reality except through paradigms or models; hence *meta*-model thinking is not possible, except in the more limited sense of meta-*mono*-model thinking, that is, by perceiving reality through multiple, differing models which cannot be subsumed under one mega-model, but must stand in creative, polar tension in relationship to each other. Such might be called multi-model thinking. This pattern in fact has been characteristic of physics for decades as it uses both particle and wave descriptions of subatomic matter.

Let me turn now to the post-Enlightenment epistemological Paradigm Shift. Whereas our Western notion of truth was largely absolute, static, and monologic or exclusive up to the past century, it has since become deabsolutized, dynamic and dialogic — in a word, it has become "rela-

---

[9] I am grateful for this exemplary comparison to Henry Rosemont, whom I met when he was the Fulbright Professor of Philosophy at Fudan University, Shanghai, 1982-84.

tional[10]". This "new" view of truth came about in at least six different, but closely related, ways. In brief they are:

1. Historicism: Truth is deabsolutized by the perception that reality is always described in terms of the circumstances of the time in which it is expressed.

2. Intentionality: Seeking the truth with the intention of acting accordingly deabsolutizes the statement.

3. Sociology of knowledge: Truth is deabsolutized in terms of geography, culture, and social standing.

4. Limits of language: Truth as the meaning of something and especially as talk about the transcendent is deabsolutized by the nature of human language.

5. Hermeneutics: All truth, all knowledge, is seen as interpreted truth, knowledge, and hence is deabsolutized by the observer who is always also interpreter.

6. Dialogue: The knower engages reality in a dialogue in a language the knower provides, thereby deabsolutizing all statements about reality.

Before the nineteenth century in Europe *truth, that is, a statement about reality*, was conceived in quite an absolute, static, exclusivistic either-or manner. If something was true at one time, it was always true; not only empirical facts but also the meaning of things or the oughtness that was said to flow from them were thought of in this way. For example, if it was true for the Pauline writer to say in the first century that women should keep silence in the church, then it was always true that women should keep silence in the church; or if it was true for Pope Boniface VIII to state in 1302, "we declare, state, and define that it is absolutely necessary for the salvation of all human beings that they sub-

---

[10] Already two millennia and more ago some Hindu and Buddhist thinkers held a non-absolutistic epistemology, but that fact had no significant impact on the West; because of the cultural eclipse of those civilizations in the modern period and the dominance of the Western scientific worldview, these ancient nonabsolutistic epistemologies have until now played no significant role in the emerging global society — though in the context of dialogue, they should in the future.

Since the middle of the nineteenth century Eastern thought has become increasingly better known in the West, and proportionately influential. This knowledge and influence appears to be increasing geometrically in recent decades. It is even beginning to move into the hardest of our so-called hard sciences, nuclear physics, as evidenced by the popular book of the theoretical physicist Fritjof Capra, *The Tao of Physics* (Boulder, CO: Shambhala, 2nd ed., 1983).

mit to the Roman Pontiff[11]", then it was always true that they need do so. At bottom, the notion of truth was based exclusively on the Aristotelian principle of contradiction: a thing could not be true and not true in the same way at the same time. Truth was defined by way of exclusion; A was A because it could be shown not to be not-A. Truth was thus understood to be absolute, static, exclusivistically either-or. This is a *classicist* or *absolutist* view of truth.

1. Historicism: In the nineteenth century many scholars came to perceive all statements about the truth of the meaning of something as partially the products of their historical circumstances. Those concrete circumstances helped determine the fact that the statement under study was even called forth, that it was couched in particular intellectual categories (for example, in abstract Platonic or concrete legal language), in particular literary forms (for example, mythic or metaphysical language), and in particular psychological settings (such as a polemic response to a specific attack). These scholars argued that only if the truth statements were placed in their historical situation, in their historical *Sitz im Leben*, could they be properly understood. The understanding of the text could be found only in *con*text. To express that same original meaning in a later *Sitz im Leben* one would require a proportionately different statement. Thus, all statements about the meaning of things were now seen to be deabsolutized in terms of time.

This is a *historical* view of truth. Clearly at its heart is a notion of *relationality*: Any statement about the truth of the meaning of something has to be understood in relationship to its historical context.

2. Intentionality: Later thinkers like Max Scheler added a corollary to this historicizing of knowledge; it concerned not the past but the future. Such scholars also saw truth as having an element of intentionality at its base, as being oriented ultimately toward action, praxis. They argued that we perceive certain things as questions to be answered and set goals to pursue specific knowledge because we wish to do something about those matters; we intend to live according to the truth and meaning that we hope to discern in the answers to the questions we pose, in the knowledge we decide to seek. The truth of the meaning of things was thus seen as deabsolutized by the action-oriented intentionality of the thinker-speaker.

---

[11] Boniface VIII, "Unam sanctam," in J. Neuener and J. Depuis, eds., *The Teaching of the Catholic Church* (Dublin: Mercier Press, 1972), no. 875, p. 211.

This is an *intentional* or *praxis* view of truth, and it too is basically *relational*: A statement has to be understood in relationship to the action-oriented intention of the speaker.

3. The sociology of knowledge: Just as statements of truth about the meaning of things were seen by some thinkers to be historically deabsolutized in time, so too, starting in this century with scholars like Karl Mannheim, such statements began to be seen as deabsolutized by such things as the culture, class and gender of the thinker-speaker, regardless of time. All reality was said to be perceived from the perspective of the perceiver's own world view. Any statement of the truth of the meaning of something was seen to be perspectival, "standpoint-bound," *standort-gebunden*, as Karl Mannheim put it, and thus deabsolutized.

This is a *perspectival* view of truth and is likewise *relational*: All statements are fundamentally related to the standpoint of the speaker.

4. The limitations of language: Following Ludwig Wittgenstein and others, many thinkers have come to see that any statement about the truth of things can be at most only a partial description of the reality it is trying to describe. Although reality can be seen from an almost limitless number of perspectives, human language can express things from only one, or perhaps a very few, perspectives at once. If this is now seen to be true of what we call "scientific truths," it is much more true of statements about the truth of the meaning of things. The very fact of dealing with the truth of the "meaning" of something indicates that the knower is essentially involved and hence reflects the perspectival character of all such statements. A statement may be true, of course — it may accurately describe the extramental reality it refers to — but it will always be cast in particular categories, language, concerns, etc., of a particular "standpoint," and in that sense will be limited, deabsolutized.

This also is a *perspectival* view of truth, and therefore also *relational*.

This limited and limiting, as well as liberating, quality of language is especially clear in talk of the transcendent. The transcendent is by definition that which "goes beyond" our experience. Any statements about the transcendent must thus be deabsolutized and limited far beyond the perspectival character seen in ordinary statements.

5. Hermeneutics: Hans-Georg Gadamer and Paul Ricœur recently led the way in developing the science of hermeneutics, which, by arguing that all knowledge of a text is at the same time an *interpretation* of the text, fur-

ther deabsolutizes claims about the "true" meaning of the text. But this basic insight goes beyond knowledge of texts and applies to all knowledge.

Some of the key notions here can be compressed in the following mantra (a mantra is a seven-syllable phrase which encapsulates an insight): "Subject, object, two is one." The whole of hermeneutics is here *in nuce*: All knowledge is interpreted knowledge; the perceiver is part of the perceived; the subject is part of the object. When the object of study is some aspect of humanity the obvious fact that the observer is also the observed "deobjectivizes," deabsolutizes, the resultant knowledge, truth. But the same thing is also fundamentally true of all knowledge, of all truth, even of the natural sciences, for the various aspects of nature are observed only through the categories we ourselves provide, within the horizons we establish, under the paradigms we utilize, in response to the questions we raise, and in relationship to the connections we make — a further deabsolutizing of truth, even of the "hard" sciences.

"Subject, object, two is one." Knowledge comes from the subject perceiving the object, but since the subject is also part of its object, as described above the two are in that sense one. In knowing also the object in some form is taken up into the subject, and thus again the two are one. And yet, there is also a radical twoness there, for it is the very *process* of the two *becoming* one — or the two being perceived as one, or, even better, the becoming aware that the two, which are very really two, are also in fact *on another level* very really one — that we call knowing.

This is an *interpretative* view of truth. It is clear that *relationality* pervades this hermeneutical, interpretative, view of truth. (It is interesting to note that one dimension of this interpretative understanding of truth can already be found in St. Thomas Aquinas, who states that "things known are in the knower according to the mode of the knower — *cognita sunt in cognoscente secundum modum cognoscentis*[12]".)

The sixth category, a dialogical understanding of truth, will be discussed below.

In sum, our understanding of truth and reality has been undergoing a radical shift. This new paradigm which is being born understands all statements about reality, especially about the meaning of things, to be historical, intentional, perspectival, partial, interpretative and dialogic. What is common to all these qualities is the notion of *relationality*, that is, that all expressions or understandings of reality are in some fundamental way related to the speaker or knower.

---

[12] Thomas AQUINAS, *Summa Theologiae*, II-II, Q. 1, a. 2.

4. *The Copernican Turn in the Catholic Church*

As a Catholic theologian let me lift up for brief examination my own religious community. The Catholic Church offers a clear example of the post-Enlightenment Paradigm Shift on a global communal level. A major paradigm shift has also occurred in the Catholic Church in this century. The 1960s were a momentous turning-point decade for the entire world: 1) American Catholics broke out of their ghetto in the election of President Kennedy; 2) the American civil rights movement began a transformation of the Western psyche; 3) the anti-war, environmentalist, anti-Establishment and related movements in the West brought the transformation to a fever pitch; 4) through Vatican Council II (1962-65) the Catholic Church leapt into modernity, and edged even beyond.

The Copernican turn that occurred in the Catholic Church at Vatican II took place in five major ways:

a) The turn toward freedom

The image Catholicism projected at the end of the 1950s was of a giant monolith, a community of hundreds of millions who held obedience in both action and thought as the highest virtue. If the pope said, "have babies," Catholics had babies; if he said, "don't associate with Protestants and Jews," Catholics avoided them like the plague; if he said, "believe in papal infallibility, in Marian dogmas," they believed. For a hundred years (but really not much more than that!) Catholics were treated like children in the Church, acted like children, and thought of themselves as children.

With the Second Vatican Council, however, this very unfree image, and reality, was utterly transformed. Suddenly it seemed humanity, including Catholics, became aware of their "coming of age," hence, their freedom and responsibility. This was clearly expressed in many places, but perhaps nowhere more clearly than in the "Declaration on Religious Liberty."

b) The turn toward the historical/dynamic

For centuries the thinking of official Catholicism was dominated by a static understanding of reality; it resisted not only the democratic and human rights movements of the nineteenth and twentieth centuries, but also the growing historical, dynamic way of understanding the world, including religious thought.

That changed dramatically with Vatican II where the historical, dynamic view of reality and doctrine was officially fully embraced (unfortunately the present leadership largely resists that radical turn)[13].

c) The turn toward inner reform

Since the sixteenth century, inside the Catholic Church even the word "reform" was forbidden, to say nothing of the reality (there were periods of notable exception[14], but they were largely obliterated — even from Catholic church history textbooks!). At the beginning of the twentieth century Pope Pius X, leapfrogging back to his predecessor, Pope Pius XI (pronounced in Italian, "Pio No-no"), launched the heresy-hunting Inquisition of Anti-Modernism, crushing all creative thought in Catholicism for decades. In the middle of the twentieth century leading theologians were again censured and silenced (e.g., Jean Danielou, Henri de Lubac, Pierre Teilhard de Chardin, John Courtney Murray, Karl Rahner).

But Pope Saint John XXIII (so canonized by the traditional method of popular acclamation by the Association for the Rights of Catholics in the Church — ARCC) burst those binding chains and called the Second Vatican Council. He spoke about "throwing open the windows of the Vatican" to let in fresh thought, about *Aggiornamento*, about bringing the Church "up to date."

Indeed, the Vatican II documents even used that neuralgic word "reformation": "Christ summons the Church, as she goes her pilgrim way, to that continual reformation of which she always has need"; "All [Catholics] are led to...wherever necessary, undertake with vigor the task of renewal and reform," and insisted that All Catholics' "primary duty is to make an honest and careful appraisal of whatever needs to be renewed and achieved in the Catholic household itself" (Decree on Ecumenism).

d) The turn toward this world

Until very recently the term "salvation" was understood exclusively to mean going to heaven after death; its root meaning from *salus* of a

---

[13] See, e.g., Leonard SWIDLER and Hans KÜNG, eds., *The Church in Anguish: Has the Vatican Betrayed Vatican II?* (San Francisco: Harper & Row, 1987); Bernard Häring, *My Witness For the Church*, Translation and Introduction by Leonard Swidler (Mahwah, NJ: Paulist Press, 1992).

[14] See, e.g., Leonard SWIDLER, *Freedom in the Church*, (Dayton: Pflaum Press, 1969); Leonard SWIDLER, *Aufklärung Catholicism 1780-1850*, (Missoula, MT: Scholars Press, 1978); Leonard and Arlene Swidler, *Bishops and People*, (Philadelphia: Westminster Press, 1970).

"full, healthy life" was largely lost in Christianity after the third century[15]. Marx was not far from the mark when he claimed that Christianity (and religion in general) was mainly concerned about "pie in the sky bye and bye." But that focus shifted radically with Vatican II, especially as reflected in the document "The Church in the Modern World," which in effect, though without the name, launched Liberation Theology.

e) The turn toward dialogue

For centuries, especially since the sixteenth century, the Catholic Church has been largely trapped in a kind of solipsism, talking only to itself, and shaking its finger at the rest of the world. When, e.g., a committee of Protestant churchmen shortly after World War I visited Pope Benedict XV to invite the Catholic Church to join in launching the Ecumenical Movement to work for Church reunion, he told them that he was happy they were finally concerned about Church unity, but that he already had the solution to the problem of Christian division: "Come home to mama!" The forbidding of Catholic participation in dialogue was subsequently constantly repeated (e.g., 1928 *Mortalium animos*, 1948 "Monitum," 1949 "Instructio," 1954 barring of Catholics at the Evanston, IL World Council of Churches World Assembly).

Again, Saint John XXIII and Vatican II changed all that navel-staring radically. Ecumenism was now not only not forbidden, but was said to "pertain to the whole Church, faithful and clergy alike. It extends to everyone" (Decree on Ecumenism). Pope Paul VI issued his first encyclical (*Ecclesiam suam*, 1964), specifically on dialogue:

> Dialogue is demanded nowadays....It is demanded by the dynamic course of action which is changing the face of modern society. It is demanded by the pluralism of society and by the maturity man has reached in this day and age. Be he religious or not, his secular education has enabled him to think and speak and conduct a dialogue with dignity.

This turn toward dialogue naturally was directed toward the first obvious dialogue partners for Catholics: fellow Christians, Protestants and Orthodox. But this turn from an inward gazing outward had its own inner dynamic: why stop at talking with Protestants and Orthodox; why not continue on to dialogue with Jews, and then Muslims, Hindus, Buddhists, etc., and even non-believers? And so it is now happening in an explosion of interreligious/interideological dialogue of exponentially

---

[15] For a discussion of "salvation" and other key terms about the ultimate goal of life see, Leonard SWIDLER, *The Meaning of Life? Some Answers at the Edge of the Third Millennium*, (Mahwah, NJ: Paulist, 1992).

increasing magnitude. One need only look at the flood of books now appearing in the field.

Moreover, this dimension of the Copernican turn will be at least as radical in its creative transformation of Catholic, Christian, self-understanding as the other three, and hence will profoundly affect all aspects of Christian life. For example, since in this new Age of Dialogue we Christians understand that our Jewish or Muslim neighbors can be "saved" without becoming Christian, our relationship to them ceases being one of "convert-making," and becomes one of dialogue and cooperation.

5. The Second Axial Period[16]

It was Karl Jaspers, the German philosopher, who some forty-five years ago pointed out the significance of this phenomenon in his book *The Origin and Goal of History*[17]. He called this period from 800-200 B.C.E. the Axial Period because "it gave birth to everything which, since then, man has been able to be." It is here in this period "that we meet with the most deepcut dividing line in history. Man, as we know him today, came into being. For short, we may style this the 'Axial Period.'"[18] Although the leaders who effected this change were philosophers and religious teachers, the change was so radical that it affected all aspects of culture, for it transformed consciousness itself. It was within the horizons of this form of consciousness that the great civilizations of Asia, the Middle East, and Europe developed. Although within these horizons many developments occurred through the subsequent centuries, the horizons themselves did not change. It was this form of consciousness which spread to other regions through migration and explorations, thus becoming the dominant, though not exclusive, form of consciousness in the world. To this day, whether we have been born and raised in the culture of China, India, Europe, or the Americas, we bear the structure of consciousness that was shaped in this Axial Period.

[16] I am in this section especially indebted to Ewert Cousins' essay "Judaism-Christianity-Islam: Facing Modernity Together," *Journal of Ecumenical Studies*, 30:3-4 (Summer-Fall, 1993), pp. 417-425.

[17] Karl JASPERS, *Vom Ursprung und Ziel der Geschichte* (Zurich: Artemis, 1949), pp. 19-43.

[18] Ibid., p. 19; trans. Michael Bullock, *The Origin and Goal of History* (New Haven: Yale University Press, 1953), p. 1. For the ongoing academic discussion of Jaspers' position on the Axial Period, see *Wisdom, Revelation, and Doubt: Perspectives on the First Millennium B.C., Daedalus* (Spring, 1975); and *The Origins and Diversity of Axial Age Civilizations*, ed. S.N. Eisenstadt (New York: State University of New York Press, 1989).

What is this structure of consciousness and how does it differ from pre-Axial consciousness? Prior to the Axial Period the dominant form of consciousness was cosmic, collective, tribal, mythic, and ritualistic. This is the characteristic form of consciousness of primal peoples. It is true that between these traditional cultures and the Axial Period there emerged great empires in Egypt, China, and Mesopotamia, but they did not yet produce the full consciousness of the Axial Period.

The consciousness of the tribal cultures was intimately related to the cosmos and to the fertility cycles of nature. Thus there was established a rich and creative harmony between primal peoples and the world of nature, a harmony which was explored, expressed, and celebrated in myth and ritual. Just as they felt themselves part of nature, so they experienced themselves as part of the tribe. It was precisely the web of interrelationships within the tribe that sustained them psychologically, energizing all aspects of their lives. To be separated from the tribe threatened them with death, not only physical but psychological as well. However, their relation to the collectivity often did not extend beyond their own tribe, for they often looked upon other tribes as hostile. Yet within their tribe they felt organically related to their group as a whole, to the life cycles of birth and death and to nature and the cosmos.

The Axial Period ushered in a radically new form of consciousness. Whereas primal consciousness was tribal, Axial consciousness was individual. "Know thyself" became the watchword of Greece; the Upanishads identified the *atman*, the transcendent center of the self. The Buddha charted the way of individual enlightenment; the Jewish prophets awakened individual moral responsibility. This sense of individual identity, as distinct from the tribe and from nature, is the most characteristic mark of Axial consciousness. From this flow other characteristics: consciousness which is self-reflective, analytic, and which can be applied to nature in the form of scientific theories, to society in the form of social critique, to knowledge in the form of philosophy, to religion in the form of mapping an individual spiritual journey. This self-reflective, analytic, critical consciousness stood in sharp contrast to primal mythic and ritualistic consciousness. When self-reflective *logos* emerged in the Axial Period, it tended to oppose the traditional *mythos*. Of course, mythic and ritualistic forms of consciousness survive in the post-Axial Period even to this day, but they are often submerged, surfacing chiefly in dreams, literature, and art.

Following the lead of Ewert Cousins, if we shift our gaze from the first millennium B.C.E. to the eve of the twenty-first century, we can discern another transformation of consciousness, which is so profound and far-reaching that he calls it the Second Axial Period[19]. Like the first it is happening simultaneously around the earth, and like the first it will shape the horizon of consciousness for future centuries. Not surprisingly, too, it will have great significance for world religions, which were constituted in the First Axial Period. However, the new form of consciousness is different from that of the First Axial Period. Then it was individual consciousness, now it is global consciousness.

In order to understand better the forces at work in the Second Axial Period, Cousins draws from the thought of the paleontologist Pierre Teilhard de Chardin[20]. In the light of his research in evolution, he charted the development of consciousness from its roots in the geosphere and biosphere and into the future. In a process which he calls "planetization," he observed that a shift in the forces of evolution had occurred over the past hundred years. This shift is from divergence to convergence. When human beings first appeared on this planet, they clustered together in family and tribal units, forming their own group identity and separating themselves from other tribes. In this way humans diverged, creating separate nations and a rich variety of cultures. However, the spherical shape of the earth prevented unlimited divergence. With the increase in population and the rapid development of communication, groups could no longer remain apart. After dominating the process for millennia, the forces of divergence have been superseded by those of convergence. This shift to convergence is drawing the various cultures into a single planetized community. Although we have been conditioned by thousands of years of divergence, we now have no other course open to us but to cooperate creatively with the forces of convergence as these are drawing us toward global consciousness[21].

According to Teilhard this new global consciousness will not level all differences among peoples; rather it will generate what he calls creative unions in which diversity is not erased but intensified. His understanding of creative unions is based on his general theory of evolution and the

[19] For a more comprehensive treatment of Cousins' concept of the Second Axial Period, see his book *Christ of the 21st Century* (Rockport, MA: Element, 1992).

[20] Pierre TEILHARD DE CHARDIN, *Le Phénomène humain* (Paris: Editions du Seuil, 1955); see also *L'Activation de l'énergie* (Paris, Editions du Seuil, 1962) and *L'Energie humaine* (Paris: Editions du Seuil, 1962). For a more detailed study of Teilhard's thought in relation to the second Axial Period, see Ewert Cousins' paper "Teilhard de Chardin and the Religious Phenomenon," delivered in Paris at the International Symposium on the Occasion of the Centenary of the Birth of Teilhard de Chardin, organized by UNESCO, September 16-18, 1981, UNESCO Document Code: SS.82/WS/36.

[21] TEILHARD, *Le Phénomène humain*, pp. 268-269.

dynamic which he observes throughout the universe. From the geosphere to the biosphere to the realm of consciousness, a single process is at work, which he articulates as the law of "complexity-consciousness" and "union differentiates." "In any domain," he says, "whether it be the cells of a body, the members of a society or the elements of a spiritual synthesis — *union differentiates*[22]". From subatomic particles to global consciousness, individual elements unite in what Teilhard calls center to center unions. By touching each other at the creative core of their being, they release new energy which leads to more complex units. Greater complexity leads to greater interiority which, in turn, leads to more creative unions. Throughout the process, the individual elements do not lose their identity, but rather deepen and fulfill it through union. "Following the confluent orbits of their center," he says, "the grains of consciousness do not tend to lose their outlines and blend, but, on the contrary, to accentuate the depth and incommunicability of their *egos*. The more 'other' they become in conjunction, the more they find themselves as 'self.'"[23] At this point of history, because of the shift from divergence to convergence, the forces of planetization are bringing about an unprecedented complexification of consciousness through the convergence of cultures and religions.

In the light of Teilhard's thought, then, we can better understand the meeting of religions on the eve of the twenty-first century. The world religions are the product of the First Axial Period and the forces of divergence. Although in the first millennium B.C.E., there was a common transformation of consciousness, it occurred in diverse geographical regions within already differentiated cultures. In each case the religion was shaped by this differentiation in its origin, and developed along differentiated lines. This produced a remarkable richness of spiritual wisdom, of spiritual energies and of religious-cultural forms to express, preserve, and transmit this heritage. However, now that the forces of divergence have shifted to convergence, the religions must meet each other in center to center unions, discovering what is most authentic in each other, thereby releasing creative energy toward a more complexified form of religious consciousness.

Such a creative encounter has been called the "dialogic dialogue" to distinguish it from the dialectic dialogue in which one tries to refute the claims of the other[24]. This dialogic dialogue has three phases:

[22] Ibid., p. 292; trans. Bernard Wall, *The Phenomenon of Man* (New York: Harper and Row, 1965), p. 262.

[23] Ibid.

[24] On the concept of dialogic dialogue, see Raimundo Panikkar, *Myth, Faith and Hermeneutics* (New York: Paulist Press, 1979), pp. 241-245; see also his *The Intrareligious Dialogue* (New York: Paulist Press, 1978).

(1) The partners meet each other in an atmosphere of mutual understanding, ready to alter misconceptions about each other and eager to appreciate the values of the other.

(2) The partners are mutually enriched, by passing over into the consciousness of the other so that each can experience the other's values from within the other's perspective. This can be enormously enriching, for often the partners discover in another tradition values which are submerged or only inchoate in their own. It is important at this point to respect the autonomy of the other tradition: in Teilhard's terms, to achieve union in which differences are valued as a basis of creativity.

(3) If such a creative union is achieved, then the religions will have moved into the complexified form of consciousness that will be characteristic of the twenty-first century. This will be complexified global consciousness, not a mere universal, undifferentiated, abstract consciousness. It will be global through the global convergence of cultures and religions and complexified by the dynamics of dialogic dialogue.

This global consciousness, complexified through the meeting of cultures and religions, is only one characteristic of the Second Axial Period. The consciousness of this period is global in another sense, namely, in rediscovering its roots in the earth. At the very moment when the various cultures and religions are meeting each other and creating a new global community, our life on the planet is being threatened. The very tools which we have used to bring about this convergence — industrialization and technology — are undercutting the biological support system that sustains life on our planet. The future of consciousness, even life on the earth, is shrouded in a cloud of uncertainty.

Cousins is not suggesting a romantic attempt to live in the past, rather that the evolution of consciousness proceeds by way of recapitulation. Having developed self-reflective, analytic, critical consciousness in the First Axial Period, we must now, while retaining these values, reappropriate and integrate into that consciousness the collective and cosmic dimensions of the pre-Axial consciousness. We must recapture the unity of tribal consciousness by seeing humanity as a single tribe. And we must see this single tribe related organically to the total cosmos.

This means that the consciousness of the twenty-first century will be global from two perspectives:

(1) from a horizontal perspective, cultures and religions must meet each other on the surface of the globe, entering into creative encounters that will produce a complexified collective consciousness;

(2) from a vertical perspective, they must plunge their roots deep into the earth in order to provide a stable and secure base for future development. This new global consciousness must be organically ecological, supported by structures that will insure justice and peace. The voices of the oppressed must be heard and heeded: the poor, women, racial and ethnic minorities. These groups, along with the earth itself, can be looked upon as the prophets and teachers of the Second Axial Period. This emerging twofold global consciousness is not only a creative possibility to enhance the twenty-first century; it is an absolute necessity if we are to survive.

6. *The Age of Global Dialogue*

Ewert Cousins has basically affirmed everything Hans Küng has described as the newly emerging contemporary paradigm-shift, but he sees the present shift as much more profound than simply another in a series of major paradigm-shifts of human history. He sees the current transformation as a shift of the magnitude of the First Axial Period which will similarly reshape human consciousness. I too want to basically affirm what Küng sees as the emerging contemporary Major Paradigm-Shift, as well as with Cousins that this shift is so profound as to match in magnitude the transformation of human consciousness of the Axial Period, so that it should be referred to as a Second Axial Period.

More than that, however, I am persuaded that what humankind is entering into now is not just the latest in a long series of major paradigm-shifts, as Hans Küng has so carefully and clearly analyzed. I am also persuaded that it is even more than the massive move into the consciousness transforming Second Axial Period, as Ewert Cousins has so thoroughly demonstrated. Beyond these two radical shifts, though of course including both of them, humankind is emerging out of the "from-the-beginning-till-now" millennia-long "Age of Monologue" into the newly dawning "Age of Dialogue."

The turn toward dialogue is, in my judgment, *the most fundamental, the most radical and utterly transformative* of the key elements of the newly emerging paradigm, which Hans Küng has so penetratingly outlined, and which Ewert Cousins also perceptively discerns as one of the central constituents of the Second Axial Age. However, that shift from monologue to dialogue constitutes such a radical reversal in human consciousness, is so utterly new in the history of humankind *from the beginning*, that it must be designated as literally "revolutionary," that is, it turns everything absolutely around.

Up until almost the present just about *all* were convinced that they alone had the absolute truth. Because all were certain that they had the truth — otherwise they wouldn't have held that position — therefore others who thought differently necessarily held falsehood. But with the growing understanding that all perceptions of and statements about reality were — even if true — necessarily limited (the opposite of "absolute," that is, literally "un-limited"), the permission, and even the necessity, for dialogue with those who thought differently from us became increasingly apparent.

Thus dialogue — which is a conversation with those who think differently, the *primary* purpose of which is *for me* to learn from the other — is *a whole new way of thinking* in human history.

At the heart of this new dialogic way of thinking is the basic insight that I learn not by being merely passively open or receptive to, but by being in dialogue with, extramental reality. I not only "hear" or receive reality, but I also — and, I think, first of all — "speak" to reality. I ask it questions, I stimulate it to speak back to me, to answer my questions. In the process I give reality the specific categories and language in which to respond to me. The "answers" that I receive back from reality will always be in the language, the thought categories, of the questions I put to it. It can "speak" to me, can really communicate with my mind, only in a language and categories that I understand.

When the speaking, the responding, grow less and less understandable to me, if the answers I receive are sometimes confused and unsatisfying, then I probably need to learn to speak a more appropriate language when I put questions to reality. If, for example, I ask the question, "How far is yellow?" of course I will receive an non-sense answer. Or if I ask questions about living things in mechanical categories, I will receive confusing and unsatisfying answers. Thus, I will receive confusing and unsatisfying answers to questions about human sexuality if I use categories that are solely physical-biological; witness the absurdity of the answer that birth control is forbidden by the natural law — the question falsely assumes that the nature of humanity is merely physical-biological. This dialogic view of truth, like the five other shifts in modern epistemology described above, is *relational*, as its very name, *dia-logos*, indicates.

With the new and irreversible understanding of the meaning of truth resulting from all the above-outlined epistemological advances, culminating in the insight of a dialogic view of truth, the modern critical thinker has undergone a radical Copernican turn. Recall that just as the vigorously resisted shift in astronomy from geocentrism to heliocentrism revolutionized that science, the paradigm or model shift in the understanding of truth statements has revolutionized all the humanities, including theology-ideology. The macro-paradigm or macro-model with which critical thinkers operate today (or the "horizon" within which they operate, to use Bernard Lonergan's term) is, as noted, characterized by historical, social, linguistic, hermeneutical, praxis and dialogic — *relational* — consciousness. This paradigm or model shift is far advanced among thinkers and doers; but as in the case of Copernicus, and even more dramatically of Galileo, there of course are still many resisters in positions of great institutional power.

At the same time, with the deabsolutized view of the truth of the meaning of things we come face to face with the specter of relativism, the opposite pole of absolutism. Unlike *relationality*, a neutral term which merely denotes the quality of being in relationship, *relativism*, like so many "isms," is a basically negative term. If it can no longer be claimed that any statement of the truth of the meaning of things is absolute, totally objective, because the claim does not square with our experience of reality, it is equally impossible to claim that every statement of the truth of the meaning of things is completely relative, totally subjective, for that also does not square with our experience of reality, and of course it would logically lead to an atomizing isolation which would stop all discourse, all statements to others.

Our perception, and hence description, of reality is like our view of an object in the center of a circle of viewers. My view and description of the object, or reality, may well be true, but it will not include what someone on the other side of the circle perceives and describes, which also may well be true. So, neither of our perceptions and descriptions of reality can be total, complete — "absolute" in that sense — or "objective" in the sense of not in any way being dependent on a "subject" or viewer. At the same time, however, it is also obvious that there is an "objective," doubtless "true" aspect to each perception and description, even though each is relational to the perceiver-"subject."

At the same time that the always partial, perspectival, deabsolutized view of all truth statements is recognized, the common human basis for perceptions/descriptions of reality and values must also be kept in mind. All human beings experience certain things in common. We all experience our bodies, pain, pleasure, hunger, satiation. Our cognitive faculties perceive such structures in reality as variation and symmetries in pitch, color and form. All humans experience affection and dislike. Here, and in other commonalities, we find the bases for building a universal, fundamental epistemology, aesthetics, value system. Although it will be vital to distinguish carefully between those human experiences/perceptions which come from nature and those which come from nurture, it will at times, however, be difficult to discern precisely where the distinction lies. In fact, all of our "natural" experiences are more or less shaped by our "nurturing" because all of our experience and knowledge are interpreted through the lens of our "nurturing" structures.

But if we can no longer hold to an absolutist view of the truth of the meaning of things, we must take certain steps so as not to be logically forced into the silence of total relativism. First, besides striving to be as accurate and fair as possible in gathering and assessing information and submitting it to the critiques of our peers and other thinkers and scholars, we need also to dredge out, state clearly, and analyze our own presuppositions — a constant, ongoing task. Even in this of course we will be operating from a particular "standpoint."

Therefore, we need, secondly, to complement our constantly critiqued statements with statements from different "standpoints." That is, we need to engage in dialogue with those who have differing cultural, philosophical, social, religious viewpoints so as to strive toward an ever fuller perception of the truth of the meaning of things. If we do not engage in such dialogue we will not only be trapped within the perspective of our own "standpoint," but we will now also be aware of our lack. We will no longer with integrity be able to remain deliberately turned in on ourselves. Our search for the truth of the meaning of things makes it a necessity for us as human beings to engage in dialogue. Knowingly to refuse dialogue today would be an act of fundamental human irresponsibility — in Judeo-Christian-Muslim terms, a sin.

7. Conclusion

To sum up and reiterate: In the latter part of the twentieth century humankind is undergoing a Macro-Paradigm-Shift (Hans Küng). More than that, at this time humankind is moving into a transformative shift in consciousness of the magnitude of the Axial Period (800-200 B.C.E.) so that we must speak of the emerging of the Second Axial Period (Ewert Cousins). Even more profound, however, now at the edge of the Third

Millennium humankind is slipping out of the shadowy Age of Monologue, where it has been since its beginning, into the dawn of the Age of
Dialogue (Leonard Swidler). Into this new Age of Dialogue Küng's
Macro-Paradigm-Shift and Cousins' Second Axial Period are sublated
(*aufgehoben*, in Hegel's terminology), that is, taken up and transformed.
Moreover, as Ewert Cousins has already detailed, humankind's consciousness is becoming increasingly global. Hence, our dialogue partners necessarily must also be increasingly global. In this new Age of
Dialogue dialogue on a global basis is now not only a possibility, it is a
necessity. As I noted in a title of a recent book — humankind is faced
with ultimately with two choices: Dialogue or Death[25]!

----

[25] Leonard SWIDLER ET ALII, *Death or Dialogue* (Philadelphia: Trinity Press International, 1990).

SELECTED BIBLIOGRAPHY

Jacques WAARDENBURG

The following bibliography is confined to certain representative books about new Christian and Muslim views of each other's religions and new forms of dialogue and cooperation between them. For further publications on the subject, see the references included in the contributions to this volume, especially pp. 73-77 for Christian (mostly Catholic) authors, and pp. 252-255 for Muslim authors. Most of the following books also contain bibliographies.

1. New Christian perceptions of Islam

BORRMANS, Maurice, *Guidelines for Dialogue beween Christians and Muslims.* (Pontifical Council for Interreligious Dialogue). Translated by R. Marston Speight. New York and Mahwah, N.J.: Paulist Press, 1990.

CASPAR, Robert (and a Group of Christians living in Tunisia), *Trying to answer questions.* (Studi arabo-islamici del PISAI, No 3). Rome: PISAI (Pontificio Istituto di Studi Arabi e d'Islamistica), 1990.

CRAGG, Kenneth, *Muhammad and the Christian. A question of response.* London: Darton, Longman and Todd & Maryknoll, NY: Orbis Books, 1984.

—, *Jesus and the Muslim. An exploration.* London: Allen & Unwin, 1985.

—, *Returning to Mount Hira'. Islam in contemporary terms.* London: Bellew, 1994.

HADDAD, Yvonne Yazbeck and HADDAD, Wadi Z. (Eds.), *Christian-Muslim Encounters.* Gainesville etc.: Univ. Press of Florida, 1995.

HAINES, B.L. and COOLEY, F.L. (Eds.), *Christians and Muslims Together. An exploratian by Presbyterians.* Philadelphia, 1987.

HOCK, Klaus, *Der Islam im Spiegel westlicher Theologie.* (Kölner Veröffentlichungen zur Religionsgeschichte, 8). Köln-Wien: Böhlau, 1986.

LELONG, Michel, *L'Eglise nous parle de l'Islam. Du Concile à Jean-Paul II.* Paris: Chalet, 1984.

LEUZE, Reinhard, *Christentum und Islam.* Tübingen, 1994.

MOUBARAC, Youakim, *Recherches sur la pensée chrétienne et l'islam dans les temps modernes et à l'époque contemporaine.* (Publications de l'Université Libanaise, Section des Etudes Historiques, 22). Beyrouth, 1977.

—, *L'Islam et le dialogue islamo-chrétien* (Pentalogie islamo-chrétienne, 3). Beyrouth: Ed. Cénacle Libanais, 1973.

RAJASHEKAR, J. Paul and WILSON, H.S. (Eds.), *Islam in Asia. Perspectives for encounter.* Report of a consultation sponsored by the Lutheran World Federation and the World Alliance of Reformed Churches, Bangkok, June 11-5, 1991. Geneva, 1992.

WATT, W. Montgomery, *Islam and Christianity Today. A contribution to dialogue*. London: Routledge and Kegan Paul, 1983.

—, *Christian-Muslim Encounter. Perceptions and misperceptions*. London: Routledge and Kegan Paul, 1991.

ZEBIRI, Kate, *Muslims and Christians Face to Face*. Oxford and Rockport, MA: Oneworld, 1997.

ZIRKER, Hans, *Christentum und Islam. Theologische Verwandtschaft und Konkurrenz*. Düsseldorf: Patmos, 1989, 2nd ed. 1992.

—, *Islam. Theologische und gesellschaftliche Herausforderungen*. Düsseldorf: Patmos, 1993.

2. New Muslim Perceptions of Christianity

ANEES, M.A., Abedin, S.A., and Sardar, Z., *Christian-Muslim Relations: Yesterday, today, tomorrow*. London: Grey Seal, 1991.

ASKARI, Hasan, *Spiritual Quest. An inter-religious dimension*. Leeds: Seven Mirrors, 1991.

FARUQI, Ismail R. al-, *Christian Ethics*. Montreal: McGill Univ. Press, 1967.

GODDARD, Hugh, *Muslim Perceptions of Christianity*. (CSIC Studies on Islam and Christianity). London: Grey Seal, 1996.

HASSAN bin Talal, Crown Prince al-, *Christianity in the Arab World*. Amman: Royal Institute for Inter-Faith Studies, 1994.

KIMBALL, Charles Anthony, *Striving Together in the Way of God. Muslim participation in Christian-Muslim dialogue*. Ph.D. Dissertation, Harvard Divinity School, 1987.

NAZIR Ali, M., *Frontiers in Muslim-Christian Encounter*. Oxford: Regnum Books, 1987.

SIDDIQUI, Ataullah, *Christian-Muslim Dialogue in the Twentieth Century*. Houndsmill and London: Macmillan & New York: St. Martin's Press, 1997.

SWIDLER, Leonard (Ed.), *Muslims in Dialogue. The evolution of a dialogue*. New York, etc.: Edwin Mellen Press, 1992.

TALBI, Mohamed, *Islam et dialogue*. Tunis: Maison Tunisienne de l'Edition, 1972.

WAARDENBURG, Jacques (Ed.), *Muslim Perceptions of Other Religions throughout History*. New York: Oxford Univ. Press, 1999.

ZEBIRI, Kate, *Muslims and Christians Face to Face*. Oxford and Rockport, MA: Oneworld, 1997.

3. New forms of Dialogue and Cooperation

A. Religious subjects

BROWN, Stuart, *Meeting in Faith. Twenty years of Christian-Muslim conversations sponsored by the World Council of Churches*. Geneva: WCC Publications, 1989.

Christians Meeting Muslims. World Council of Churches Papers on Ten Years of Christian-Muslim Dialogue. Geneva: World Council of Churches. 1977.

CRISLAM, *La foi en marche. Les problèmes de fond du dialogue islamo-chrétien. Premier congrès international à distance.* (Collection "Studi arabo-islamici del PISAI", No 4). Rome: PISAI, 1990.

Déclarations communes islamo-chrétiennes 1954-1995c. / 1373-1415h. Textes originaux et traductions françaises. Dir. Augustin Dupré la Tour s.j. et Hisham Nashabé. Présentation par Juliette Nasri Haddad. Beyrouth: Dar el-Machreq, 1997.

MUSLIM-CHRISTIAN RESEARCH GROUP (GRIC), *The Challenge of the Scriptures. The Bible and the Qur'ân.* New York, 1989.

ROUSSEAU S.J., RICHARD W. (Ed.), *Christianity and Islam. The struggling dialogue.* Montrose, PA: Ridge Row Press, 1985.

B. Social and Cultural Subjects

BSTEH, Andreas (Ed.), *Peace for Humanity. Principles, problems and perspectives of the future as seen by Muslims and Christians.* New Delhi: Vikas, 1996 (Conference Vienna 1993).

GROUPE DE RECHERCHES ISLAMO-CHRETIEN (GRIC), *Foi et justice. Un défi pour le christianisme et pour l'islam.* Paris: Centurion, 1993.

—, *Pluralisme et laïcité. Chrétiens et musulmans proposent.* Paris: Bayard/Centurion, 1996.

LEVRAT, Jacques, *Une expérience de dialogue. Les Centres d'étude chrétiens en monde musulman.* Altenberge: Christlich-Islamisches Schrifttum, 1987.

MITRI, Tarek (Ed.), *Religion, Law and Society. A Christian-Muslim discussion.* Geneva: World Council of Churches and Kampen: Kok Pharos, 1995.

—, *Religion and Human Rights. A Christian-Muslim discussion.* Geneva: World Council of Churches, Office on Inter-Religious Relations, 1996.

WAARDENBURG, Jacques, *Islam et Occident face à face. Regards de l'histoire des religions.* Genève: Labor et Fides, 1998.

INDEXES

The following three Indexes are meant to facilitate consultation of the book.

The first Index, of *Personal Names*, comprises only those names which figure in the text of the book.

The second Index, of *Terms*, offers a wide variety of terms used throughout the book. The terms printed in *italics* refer to French language texts.

The third Index, of *Arabic Terms*, contains key terms in Arabic which occur in several chapters.

Although different authors have used different systems of transliteration, the transliteration of Arabic names and terms in the Indexes has been unified according to a simplified English transliteration system, except for those proper names which have a standard form in English or French.

1. INDEX OF PERSONAL NAMES

2. INDEX OF TERMS

Christian mission and Islamic *da'wa* 95
Christian mission and Western imperialism 214
Christian-Muslim encounter theological challenge to Christian faith 95
Christian-Muslim Relations in Africa, project for 87
Christian reading of Islam (H. Sanson) 65-67
Christian self-examination 22
Christian study of the Qur'an 47-48
Christian universalism (Y. Moubarac) 46, 71
Christianisme vu par Fadlallāh 161-186 (spécialement 170-178)
Christianisme vu par Huwaydī 186-207
Christians in a Muslim society 12
Christians' views of Muhammad 33
Christianity and Islam as interwoven movements 60
Christianity and Islam, difference between (S.H. Nasr) 244-245
Christianity and Islam in secular and plural society 63
Christianity and Judaism, fundamentalist analyses of 121
Christianity, "Evangelical principle" of 62
Christianity from the Muslim perspective 213-252
Christianity, history of (according to S. Qutb) 123
Christianity in global perspective 8
Christianity, intolerance of 146
Christology, Christian and Islamic 61
Christology, earliest Judeo-Christian 73
Christology, Islamic 236-237
Christology, Muhammad's 60
Churches' program of dialogue 8
Civil rights movement 280
Civil society 139n., 155, 156
Cluny Collection 81
Concile de Vatican I 111
Concile de Vatican II 111, 112
Condition féminine 109
Conference of European Churches (CEC) 88
Congrès islamo-orthodoxes 103

Contextes d'après-guerre 108
Conversion mission 94
Coran et Histoire 105
Council of Nicaea (325 A.D.) 273
Courant fondamentaliste musulman et orthodoxe 99
Crise relationnelle 187
Croyants, attitudes individuelles 114
Crusade against Islam 86
Crusade against the Muslim world, international 131
"Crusadism" 127, 128, 136, 137
Cultures, choc des 267

D

Da'wa et dialogue 193-194
Decalogue 28
Democracy 147, 156
Democratic interpretation of Islam according to al-Turābī 150
Despotism 148
"Dialogic dialogue" 286-287
Dialogic view of truth 289
Dialogue and mission. See also: mission and dialogue 4, 85
Dialogue as a primary, not a secondary task 63
Dialogue, deux approches du 159
Dialogue de personnes, pas de systèmes 266
Dialogue des dialoguants avec Dieu 266
Dialogue entre les religions, selon A. Toynbee 257-258
Dialogue et Da'wa 193-194
Dialogue et mission 169
Dialogue institutionnel 268
Dialogue interreligieux devenu politique 263
Dialogue interreligieux, aspect socio-anthropologique 259
Dialogue islamo-chrétien selon Fadlallāh 163-170
Dialogue islamo-chrétien selon Kishk 187n.
Dialogue: méthode islamique selon Fadlallāh 164-165

3. INDEX OF ARABIC TERMS

THE AUTHORS

Astérios Argyriou was born in Greece in 1935. He studied at the University of Saloniki and he continued with graduate studies at the University of Strasbourg. Here he obtained a doctorate in Science of Religion (Faculty of Theology) and defended a *thèse de doctorat d'Etat* in the Faculty of Arts. He has been teaching at this university since 1962, except for the years 1970-74 when he taught at the University of Algiers.

He published his French *thèse d'Etat, Les exégèses grecques de l'Apocalypse à l'époque turque (1453-1821)*, in Saloniki in 1982. Among his other books are *Macaire Makrès et la polémique contre l'Islam* (Vatican City, 1986), *Oeuvres complètes de Macaire Makrès* (Saloniki, 1996), *Spirituels néo-grecs (XVe-XXe siècles)* (Namur, 1967). He published *Coran et Histoire* (Athens, 1983), of which a Greek edition also appeared (Athens, 1992).

Dr. Argyriou is at present Professor of Modern Greek Literature and Chairman of the Department of Modern Greek Studies at the *Université des Sciences Humaines* in Strasbourg. His interests concentrate on Greek Byzantine and post-Byzantine literature related to Islam, Muslim-Christian dialogue, and the history of modern Greek thought.

Jean-Claude Basset was born in Switzerland in 1950. He studied theology at the University of Lausanne where he obtained a *licence* in 1972, and at the University of Strasbourg where he obtained a *doctorat de 3ème cycle* in 1976. He continued his graduate theological studies at the United Theological College of Bangalore, India, and at the Harvard Divinity School, U.S.A., where he obtained the degree of Master in Theology (Study of Religion) in 1984. He obtained his doctorate in Theology at the University of Lausanne in 1993, with a thesis entitled *Dialogue des croyants, chance ou déchéance de la foi?*

His publications include *Le dialogue interreligieux. Chance ou déchéance de la foi.* (Paris, 1996), *Fêtes sans frontières. Calendrier interreligieux 96/97 & 97/98* (Lausanne, 1996 & 1997), and (edited) *Quand nos voisins sont musulmans. Analyses et perspectives chrétiennes* (Lausanne, 1993).

Dr. Basset is at present a Reformed pastor in charge of the Protestant Study Centre of the Reformed Church of Geneva. He also teaches at the Faculty of Theology of the University of Lausanne, giving special attention to Islam and Christian-Muslim dialogue. He is the secretary of the Islam in Europe Committee on which the Roman Catholic, Orthodox and Protestant Churches in Europe are represented.

Abdelmajid Charfi was born in Tunisia. He studied at the University of Tunis and in France, and obtained his *doctorat d'Etat* at the University of Tunis with a study entitled *Islamic Thought in Refuting Christianity, Up to the End of the 4th/10th Century* (published in Arabic, Tunis and Algiers, 1986).

Besides his thesis he has edited two 12th century manuscripts, one on the Inimitability of the Qur'ân and the other a Muslim polemical text against Christianity. He has also published *Islam and Modernity* (*Al-islâm wa'l-hadâtha*, Tunis, 1990, 2nd edition 1991) and a collection of essays, also in Arabic (*Labinât*, Tunis, 1994). He is General Editor of a book series published in Tunis, *Ma'âlim al-hadâtha*, of which some twelve titles have appeared until now.

Dr. Charfi is Professor of the History of Islamic Thought at the Faculty of Arts of the Manouba, at the University of Tunis I. Besides the development of Islamic thought he is interested in relationships between Islam and Christianity/Europe and in the history of religions.

Hugh P. Goddard was born in England. He studied Oriental Studies (Islamic History) at the University of Oxford (1972-75) and pursued graduate studies in the Department of Theology at the University of Birmingham (1977-81). There he obtained his Ph.D. degree in 1984, with a dissertation entitled *Christianity as Portrayed by Egyptian Muslim Authors since 1950. An Examination in the Light of Earlier Muslim Views*.

His publications include *Christians and Muslims. From Double Standards to Mutual Understanding* (London, 1995) and *Muslim Perceptions of Christianity* (London, 1996).

Dr. Goddard is at present Senior Lecturer in the Department of Theology of the University of Nottingham, U.K. His special interest is in the field of Christian-Muslim relations, in general and also nationally and locally, both on the level of theology and on that of praxis. He has undertaken several research trips in order to familiarize himself with situations in which Muslims and Christians are living side by side.

Waheed Hassab Alla was born in Egypt in 1952. He studied Theology at the Faculty of Coptic Orthodox Theology in Cairo where he obtained the *licence* in 1975. He continued his studies in Switzerland where he did graduate studies in the Faculty of Theology at the University of Fribourg, also taking a number of other courses. He obtained his doctorate here in 1984 with a thesis entitled *Le baptême des enfants dans la tradition de l'Eglise Copte d'Alexandrie*.

His thesis appeared as a book under the same title (Fribourg, 1985). He has also published various articles, amongst them "Discours pour la fête de la Croix attribué à Saint Cyrille d'Alexandrie" (*Oriens Christianus*, Vol. 75 (1991), pp. 166-197).

Dr. Hassab Alla has held various teaching assignments in Fribourg and was Assistant in the Faculty of Theology at the University of Lausanne in 1995. He lives at present in Lausanne.

Ahmad S. Moussalli was born in Lebanon, where he obtained his primary and secondary education. From 1976 to 1980 he studied at the College of Languages of Al-Azhar University in Cairo where he obtained his B.A. degree. In 1980 he moved to the U.S.A. where he obtained his M.A. degree at St John's College, Santa Fe, New Mexico, in 1981. He pursued graduate studies at the University of Maryland where he obtained his Ph.D. in Government and Politics in 1985. Since 1987 he has been teaching at the American University of Beirut, with occasional teaching assignments in the U.S.A.

Apart from a number of articles he has published several books on Islamic fundamentalism such as *Radical Islamic Fundamentalism. The Ideological and*

Political Discourse of Sayyid Qutb (Beirut: A.U.B., 1992 and 1995), and in Arabic *World Order and Islamic Fundamentalism* (Beirut, 1992), *Islamic Fundamentalism. A Study in Sayyid Qutb's Ideological and Political Discourse* (Beirut, 1993), *A Theoretical Reading in Islamic Fundamentalism Discourse* (Beirut, 1993).

Dr. Moussalli is at present Associate Professor of Islamic Political Thought and Western Political Theories at the American University of Beirut. His interests encompass Islamic political history and political theory, and philosophy of contemporary Islamic social movements.

Adnan Silajdžič was born in Visoko (Bosnia) in 1958. He had his secondary education in Sarajevo and subsequently studied at the Faculty of Islamic Sciences of the University of Sarajevo from 1977 until 1981. He pursued postgraduate studies at the Catholic Theological College in Zagreb from 1985 until 1988. In 1990-91 he studied history of religions at the Catholic Institute in Paris. He obtained his doctorate in Sarajevo in 1997 with a thesis on the philosophical and theological work of Al-Ash'arî.

He published *Forty Hadiths with Commentary* (1993) and *Muslims between Tradition and Modernism* (1994) in Serbo-Croatian.

He is at present teaching Religion at the Faculty of Islamic Sciences in Sarajevo.

Leonard Swidler was born in the U.S.A. in 1929. Graduating in philosophy and theology in 1954, he went on to study history at Marquette University and the University of Wisconsin. Here he obtained his Ph.D. in History in 1961, after studying history and theology for two years in Germany, at the Universities of Tübingen and Munich (1957-59). From 1960 until 1966 he taught history at Duquesne University and he started teaching at Temple University in the Religion Department in 1966. He has held numerous guest professorships at universities in the U.S.A., Germany, Austria, China and Japan. He is the Editor and co-founder with Arlene Swidler of the *Journal of Ecumenical Studies*, since 1964.

Aside from many articles, Professor Swidler authored and edited some fifty books of which may be mentioned in particular *After the Absolute. The Dialogical Future of Religious Reflection* (Minneapolis, 1990), *Death or Dialogue. From the Age of Monologue to the Age of Dialogue* (Philadelphia, 1990), *Attitudes of Religions and Ideologies towards the Outsider: the Other* (New York, 1990), *Muslims in Dialogue. The Evolution of a Dialogue* (New York, 1992), *Theoria — Praxis. How Jews, Christians, Muslims and Others can Together Move from Theory to Practice* (Kampen, 1997).

Professor Swidler may be considered one of the main proponents of Christian-Muslim and Christian-Jewish dialogue, and of dialogue as a fundamental life orientation. He is at present Professor of Catholic Thought and Interreligious Dialogue at Temple University, Philadelphia, Pennsylvania.

Christian W. Troll was born in Germany in 1937. He studied Philosophy and Theology at the Universities of Bonn and Tübingen (1957-61) and Arabic and Islam at the Université St Joseph in Beirut (1961-63). In 1963 he entered the

Societas Iesu in Germany. From 1966 to 1976 he studied in London, mainly at the School of Oriental and African Studies, where he obtained his Ph.D. degree in 1976. From 1976 until 1985 he was Professor of Islamic Studies at the Vidya-jyoti Institute of Religious Studies in Delhi. From 1988 until 1993 he was Senior Lecturer at the Centre for the Study of Islam and Christian Muslim Relations in Birmingham, and since 1976 he has been lecturing at a number of institutions in Europe and Asia.

Among his books may be mentioned *Sayyid Ahmad Khan. A Reinterpretation of Muslim Theology* (Delhi, 1978 and Karachi, 1979). He has edited four books in the series *Islam in India: Studies and Commentaries* (Delhi, 1982-89).

Dr. Troll is at present Professor of Islamic Institutions at the Pontifical Oriental Institute in Rome and a regular Guest Professor at the Faculty of Theology of Ankara University. Since 1990 he has been a member of the Commission for Religious Relations with Muslims, which is part of the Pontifical Council for Interreligious Dialogue of the Vatican.

Jacques Waardenburg was born in the Netherlands in 1930. He studied Theology and Phenomenology with History of Religions at the University of Amsterdam (1949-54). Subsequently he studied Arabic and Islam in Amsterdam, Leiden and Paris and obtained his doctorate at the University of Amsterdam with a dissertation on some Western scholars of Islam in 1961. He spent two years in the Near East and a year at the Institute of Islamic Studies of McGill University, Montreal (1962-63). His regular teaching appointments were for Arabic and Islamic History at the University of California at Los Angeles (1964-68), for Islam and Phenomenology of Religion at the University of Utrecht (1968-87), and for Science of Religion (*Science des religions*) at the University of Lausanne (1987-95).

Apart from his dissertation *L'islam dans le miroir de l'Occident* (The Hague and Paris, 1961, 3rd ed. 1970), his books include *Les universités dans le monde arabe actuel* (1966), *Classical Approaches in the Study of Religion* (1973/4), *Reflections on the Study of Religion* (1978), *Islamisch-christliche Beziehungen: geschichtliche Streifzüge* (1992), *Islam et Occident face à face. Regards de l'histoire des religions* (1998), *Islam et sciences des religions* (1998). He edited *Muslim Perceptions of Other Religions throughout History* (1998).

He retired from the University of Lausanne in 1995 and lives at present in Lausanne. His main interests are the scholarly study of Muslim-Christian relations in the past and at present, and questions of method in studying Islam and religion in general.

TABLE DES MATIÈRES

*

*

*